India in the 21st Century

Foreign Policy Perspectives in a Complex World

Edited by

Aneek Chatterjee

ATLANTIC

PUBLISHERS & DISTRIBUTORS (P) LTD

Published by

ATLANTIC

PUBLISHERS & DISTRIBUTORS (P) LTD

7/22, Ansari Road, Darya Ganj, New Delhi-110002
Phones : +91-11-40775252, 40775214, 23273880, 23275880
Fax: +91-11-23285873
Web: www.atlanticbooks.com
E-mail: orders@atlanticbooks.com

Printed & bound in India by Atlantic Print Services

Dedicated to

Our Students

Acknowledgements

This volume has many architects. All contributors to this volume, through their insightful articles, have helped immensely in the final production of the book. The Editor wishes to sincerely thank Jayita Mukhopadhyay, Oindrila Roy, Siuli Mukherjee, Sohini Nayak, Gouri Sankar Nag, Prosenjit Pal, Souradeep Sen, and Udayan Das, faculty members in different colleges and universities, for their noteworthy contributions to the volume. The management and staff members of Atlantic Publishers & Distributors (P) Ltd., New Delhi, have worked tirelessly towards a decent production of this volume. The Editor extends his profound thanks to all management and staff members of the organization. He also wishes to thank Professor Raj Kumar Kothari for his gracious support. As always, two women back home, Sarbani and Prerna Chatterjee provided backstage assistance. The Editor extends his heartfelt thanks to them for such invaluable help. Our students have always motivated us, through their questions and deliberations, to shape and reshape our thoughts. With love, this volume is dedicated to all of them.

Preface

In the third decade of the twenty first century, Indian foreign policy faces challenges incomprehensible before. The rise of China signals the presence of a giant in the vicinity, who has been following a policy of engaged antagonism with India in recent times. With China's irresistible wish to spread its influence in India's neighbourhood, known geographically as South Asia, India is facing the danger of encirclement. Frequent intrusion of Chinese forces into Indian territory has been matters of immense concern for India. At the same time, India–China trade relations are growing to new heights. In 2021, bilateral trade volume reached a staggering USD 125.66 billion, although there existed a trade deficit for India, like in previous years. India has also been raising its concern over this recent trade deficits, alongside Chinese security build-up around the borders. Therefore, two rising nations in South Asia and in the world, China and India, are in a dilemma about how to perceive each other—a fierce competitor or a forceful adversary. This challenge makes India rethink about possible bilateral or multilateral engagements in global politics, in the event of India unable to counter the giant in China singularly. India must augment its global presence in the 21st century, as far as bilateral and multilateral engagements and economic diplomacy are concerned. A big power aspirant like India must tone up its foreign policy accordingly. The toning and shaping up of Indian foreign policy are much necessary now and in the foreseeable future.

How India will look up to Russia, for instance, falls within this new toning up of policies. Russia currently nurtures a strengthened relationship with China. Can India get Russia along in its plans of countering the asymmetry of power calculations in Asia in general and South Asia in particular? Russia has been largely carrying the legacy of former Soviet Union, with whom India enjoyed a strong relationship. After the Cold War, India has been successful in developing a meaningful and strategic partnership with the Russian Federation. But, a big question is—Can India count on Russia if it wants to offset the asymmetry of power balance in our region? As far as India is concerned, the same question is relevant in its relations with the United States (US), which is also concerned about the rise of China in international politics. Can India and the US see each other as potential allies? What about Japan, another leading power of Asia? Will Japan come along to counter regional power imbalance? Future holds the key and may be challenging, as well as exciting for India's foreign policy.

Leaving aside political calculations, India must also shape up its economic diplomacy. As argued in different chapters of this volume, India's trade and commercial engagements with different countries and multilateral forums need huge boost. India must reach out, commercially, to all the regions of the world, from Asia to Africa to the two Americas, as well as to Australia and New Zealand. India's trade and commercial relations with Central Asia, South-East Asia, Africa, West Asia, and Latin American nations are insufficient. With Australia, New Zealand, and South Asian neighbours, India's economic diplomacy needs to be strengthened. With multilateral forums like the UNO, European Union, ASEAN, and African Union, India must nurture closer economic and political relations. Therefore, in different chapters of this volume, India's engagements—economic, political, and security—have been highlighted and analysed thoroughly.

To fulfil its foreign policy ambitions, India must have strong foreign policy establishments, with adequate personnel to man its missions and offices throughout the globe and at home. India does not have robust foreign policy establishments with sufficient personnel to back up its foreign policy goals—an area the editor of this volume, has been focusing for long. A country with big power ambitions must have strong foreign policy mechanisms—institutions and personnel included—to realise its potentials. This aspect has been given importance and analysed in detail in the present volume, with a separate chapter dedicated to this issue. This volume also goes deep into the debate as to whether India needs to develop a strategic culture in its foreign policy. Further, India's current positions vis-à-vis the Global South, New International Economic Order (NIEO), Non Aligned Movement, QUAD, AUKUS, Afghanistan, West Asia, and Israel have been taken up for in-depth analyses in this volume. Hence, this volume contains, within its covers, extensive deliberations on many diverse and important areas related to Indian foreign policy today. However, the opinions expressed in each article of the volume belong exclusively to the author of the article, and do not, in any way, reflect the views of the editor and the publisher of the volume.

This volume may prove to be useful for students, researchers, scholars, and others interested in Indian foreign policy, now and in the future. This treatise has endeavoured to predict the unfolding of India's foreign policy in the future and also, India's position in the global power matrix till 2050—not a frequent area of study in foreign policy discourses. As such, this volume may also be helpful for policy planning and implementation. This volume is a combined effort. All contributors to this volume, through their thought provoking articles, have enriched its pages. The editor, however, humbly accepts onus for any limitation in the volume. All contributors to this volume and its editor will be happy and consider their efforts successful, if this volume proves beneficial for the students, researchers, and general readers.

Aneek Chatterjee

Contents

Notes on Contributors

Aneek Chatterjee is a senior academic and analyst on international politics. He has authored and edited 15 books and published nearly 100 articles and book chapters in reputed journals and edited volumes. He is currently teaching at the Post Graduate Department of Political Science, Hooghly Mohsin College, West Bengal. Earlier he served as Professor and Head of Political Science at Presidency University (erstwhile Presidency College), Kolkata. Dr. Chatterjee has been a Fulbright Visiting Professor at the University of Virginia, U.S.A., and a recipient of the prestigious ICCR Chair for teaching in reputed foreign universities. He has delivered more than 150 professional lectures in 16 countries. He currently sits in the Editorial Boards of three reputed international academic journals.

Gouri Sankar Nag is Professor and Head of Political Science at Sidho-Kanho-Birsha University, West Bengal. He has 21 years of teaching experience including seven years at the PG level. He has authored and edited seven books and published more than 70 articles in journals of national repute. Around 26 editorial articles written by him on different contemporary aspects of Indian foreign policy has been published in the leading Bengali daily *Bartaman Patrika* from August 2016 to June 2020. He has delivered lectures at a number of institutes and centres and in national webinars on various aspects of Indian foreign policy. Dr. Nag is coordinator of 'Atish Dipankar Srigyan

Centre for South Asian Studies' at Sidho-Kanho-Birsha University.

Jayita Mukhopadhyay is currently an Associate Professor at the Department of Political Science, Women's Christian College, Kolkata, and specialises in International Relations and Indian Politics. She has published her works in reputed national and international journals. Her authored book entitled *ASEAN's Role in Conflict Management: Potentialities and Pitfalls* (Levant Books, Kolkata, 2010) has been well received by the academia. Dr. Mukhopadhyay has also co-edited two books entitled *Ambedkar's Idea of Social Justice and Indian Polity* (Levant Books, Kolkata, 2018) and *Climate Change in South Asia: Unravelling the Conundrum* (Routledge, 2021). She has also contributed articles to these two co-edited volumes.

Oindrila Roy is an Associate Professor of International Relations/ Political Science at Cottey College, Nevada, Missouri (USA). She has received her Ph.D. in Political Science from Kent State University, USA, in 2014. Her research expertise is in the analysis of the domestic sources of US foreign policy, with a focus on the religious sources of foreign policy and public opinion in the United States. Oindrila's peer-reviewed publications have appeared in multiple academic journals, including *Foreign Policy Analysis*, *Congress & the Presidency*, and *Politics, Religion, and Ideology*.

Prosenjit Pal is currently an Associate Professor and Head of Political Science at Diamond Harbour Women's University. Earlier, he was a faculty of Political Science at Burdwan University, West Bengal. He has been teaching International Relations and Indian Politics for over 16 years at the university level. He has presented papers in seminars and conferences at national and international levels and published 32 research articles and 22 book chapters. He has been guiding Doctoral and M.Phil. students at DHWU and BU. He has also visited Japan for his research work on an invitation from the Government of Japan in 2008. Dr. Pal has authored three books entitled *Contemporary Essays in International Relations; India in South Asia: Challenges and Opportunities;* and *Changing Dimensions of International Criminal Law*.

Siuli Mukherjee is an Assistant Professor of Political Science at Shri Shikshayatan College, Kolkata. She did her Graduate, Post-graduate, and Doctoral studies from the Department of International Relations, Jadavpur University. She was a Research Fellow at the Asiatic Society on SAARC Studies. She has presented papers in different national and international levels seminars and conferences. Dr. Mukherjee's important publications include "Secularism in the Light of Pandit Jawaharlal Nehru: an Enquiry" in the edited volume entitled *On Secularism* (2019); "Engaging with South Asia: Foreign Policy of Narendra Modi" in the book entitled *Modi's Foreign Policy: Innovations and Challenges* (2018); "Tribal Development in Orissa: an Appraisal" in the journal entitled *Journal of Humanities and Social Sciences* (2015); "Political Socialisation: Nature, Types and Agencies" in the book entitled *Political Sociology* (2015), and others.

Sohini Nayak is working as a Junior Fellow at the Observer Research Foundation. She is also pursuing her Ph.D. from the Department of International Relations, Jadavpur University. Her areas of interest include Nepal-India bilateral relations and regional multilateral institutions in South Asia and the Bay of Bengal. Some of her important publications are "India and Nepal's Kalapani Border Dispute: An Explainer", Issue Brief No. 356, ORF, April 2020; "Maritime Opportunities Await the India-Japan-France Trilateral," Special Report No. 133, ORF, March 2021; "The Role of BIMSTEC in Revitalizing India's Northeast," Special Report No. 150, June 2021, ORF; Sohini Nayak and Mihir Bhonsale, "Exploring Energy Cooperation within BIMSTEC: Leveraging the Potential Beyond Asymmetries," in Sreeradha Datta (ed.), *BIMSTEC: The Journey and the Way Ahead*.

Souradeep Sen is an Assistant Professor of Political Science at North Bengal University, India. He was a topper in B.A. Political Science (Hons.) in Presidency College, Kolkata and also a gold Medalist for securing the top position at the M.A. in Political Science from Presidency University, Kolkata. He completed his Ph.D. in International Relations from Jadavpur University. He has published research papers, book chapters, and book reviews in reputed journals of Sage, the Council for Political Studies, Kolkata ("Socialist Perspective"), and Vivekananda International Foundation ("National Security") among others, as well as in edited volumes, on Strategic Studies, International Relations Theory, Foreign Policy, and Political Philosophy.

Udayan Das is presently an Assistant Professor at the Department of Political Science, St. Xavier's College, Kolkata. He is pursuing his Ph.D. at the Department of International Relations, Jadavpur University. He was awarded the James Roach Fellowship in International Relations by the Centre for International Programmes, Osmania University, Hyderabad. Previously, he has taught at Scottish Church College, Kolkata, and Amity University, Kolkata. His research interests and publications cover themes in India's foreign policy, maritime affairs, and political and strategic matters pertaining to the subcontinent.

1

Introduction: Locating India in a Complex World Order

Aneek Chatterjee

Many raging questions surround the formulation and application of Indian Foreign Policy today, in the third decade of the new century. At the outset, a listing of these questions would not be superfluous; because such a list could help in a succinct analysis of the focuses of Indian Foreign Policy (IFP) today. The possible list would include questions like the following ones: (i) What are the important perspectives of IFP today?, (ii) Has India gone for multi-alignment, in place of non-alignment?, (iii) Should India pursue its economic diplomacy more vigorously, like the United States (US) or China?, (iv) Is IFP too much obsessed today with China, much like its earlier obsession with Pakistan, leaving aside other important areas IFP should have put more emphasis on?, (v) Can India effectively counter-balance China in the near future?, (vi) What is the future of QUAD of which India is a member; and how India will deal with the new Taliban Government in Afghanistan?, (vii) How does India perceive its security threats?, (viii) Has any strategic culture developed in IFP?, and (ix) What the future holds for India, from the viewpoints of foreign policy? These questions are related to other issues like India's nuclear policy; pragmatism or idealism in IFP; India's foreign policy mechanism or institutions concerned with the formulation and implementation of foreign policy; India's power ambitions; and changes in IFP. Therefore, a look into the questions listed above, will help to understand the nature and goals of IFP today.

Important Perspectives of IFP Today

To begin with the question about important perspectives of IFP today; one would be inclined to point towards a multi-faceted direction. There are many areas of importance in IFP today: neighbourhood; major powers; security issues including maritime security; economic diplomacy; and also, hitherto neglected areas in IFP like Africa, Latin America, European Union; and the more hyped, but not vigorous 'Look East'/'Act East' policies. A former Indian diplomat, in a recent write-up, provided an overview of broad conceptual themes of IFP today: "neighbourhood first; balancing the continental and the maritime; balancing regional and extra regional powers; consolidating a favourable external environment for domestic economic growth and safeguarding national security. This cocktail of priorities is not substantively new in themselves but each of its themes constantly acquires new characteristics".[1] This is a comprehensive portrayal of priority areas of IFP today, but like many other narratives of IFP, it has also not included the importance of IFP establishments/mechanisms as back up forces to the nation's foreign policy. What are the important institutions for the formulation and application of IFP today? Do these institutions have adequate manpower to handle India's expanded foreign policy priorities? What are the determining factors behind the formulation of IFP? These are important questions many narratives of IFP normally skip. However, this volume has a full chapter (Chapter 2), written by Prosenjit Pal, dedicated to these issues. In this chapter, the author analysed in detail the basic determinants of IFP and the institutions which play crucial roles in the making and implementation of foreign policy. Other chapters of this volume have taken up for analysis all the priority areas, as noted earlier, of IFP today.

Multi-alignment seems to be the new favourite of IFP today, although it was not totally absent in the nation's foreign policy earlier. Multi-alignment refers to India's engagements with regional and extra-regional powers and bilateral and multilateral initiatives for such engagements. India's presence in global, multilateral forums is an integral part of this process of multi-alignment. This volume has committed itself seriously to focus on this multi-alignment of IFP. Chapter 4 has an in-depth analysis on India's engagements in South and South East Asia. This chapter, authored by Siuli Mukherjee, has elaborate discussions on SAARC (South Asian Association for Regional Cooperation), SAFTA (South Asian Free Trade Area), and ASEAN (Association of South East Asian Nations). Challenges to regional cooperation in South Asia like border disputes, illegal migration, water disputes, ethnic conflicts, etc. have been analysed thoroughly in this chapter. The author provided a major subsection in this chapter to focus on India's Look East and Act East policies. Therefore, South Asia, India's immediate neighbourhood; and South East Asia, country's expanded neighbourhood have been analysed in this volume with utmost care, as priority areas of IFP. Does emphasis on multi-alignment refer to India's apathy towards non-alignment? As evident from the analysis presented in Chapter 3 of this volume, non-alignment has not lost its way in IFP. Oindrila Roy, who authored this chapter on Non Aligned Movement (NAM), believes that NAM could be a useful platform for multi-lateral cooperation in a world showing multi-polar tendencies, with the rise of China, Russia, India, EU, and others. She analysed the current role of NAM to conclude that it could be an important forum for the nations of the Global South including India.

Global South, UNO, EU and West Asia

The Global South consists of regional and extra-regional nations of Africa, Asia and Latin America; India should put more emphasis on in its foreign policy in the new century. Any discourse on IFP must devote more pages to India's relations with the Global South today. Keeping in mind this perspective, the present volume has dedicated a complete chapter to India's engagements with the Global South (Chapter 5). Authored by Souradeep Sen, this chapter traced elaborately, India's relations with Africa and Latin America. Sen trudged along history to arrive to the present, in his analysis on India's relations with Africa and Latin America,—not frequently discussed areas in discourses on IFP. India's role in the demand for leadership in the New International Economic Order (NIEO) and World Trade Organization (WTO) comprised a unique area of study undertaken by Souradeep Sen in Chapter 5 of this volume. Jayita Mukhopadhyay termed the U.S. and China as the 'leading powers' of the world today, while analysing India's relations with these nations, in Chapter 6. While India's engagements with both nations have been close after the end of the Cold War; China has become, of late, a challenging area to IFP. With both countries trying to see themselves in leadership roles in Asian politics, and in a broader way, global politics; India and China have turned into fierce competitors. This is evident from their recent border skirmishes in the Ladakh region, in the high altitudes of the Himalayas. Both nations are in the quest for military and economic supremacy over the other. Although China is ahead of India at this point of time, can India counter balance China in the future? Jayita Mukhopadhyay has taken up the issue in Chapter 6 of this volume. In another chapter, Mukhopadhyay does an extensive study of India's relations with two 'important powers' of the world today, Japan and Russia. Japan is a technological giant, while Russia is a top military power in the world, trying also for economic revival, at this point of time. Therefore, India's engagements with these nations are crucial. In Chapter 7 of this volume, Jayita Mukhopadhyay goes deep to explore India's relations with these two important nations.

India was a founding member of the United Nations Organization (UNO). Since its inception, India has been working closely with this world body in different areas, like peace-keeping and peace-making operations; socio-economic activities; financial issues; refugee problems and other human rights and human security issues. After the end of the Cold War, with new political equations emerging in a new world order; India had been vociferous for a permanent seat in the UN Security Council (UNSC), along with few other nations. There have been supports and oppositions to India's demands, coming from different corners of the globe. With some of the current P-5 members of the UNSC involved in this debate (about inclusion of new permanent members), proposed reforms of the UNO would not be easy.[2] Does India have a chance to sit at the UNSC as a permanent member? In Chapter 9 of this volume, Souradeep Sen explores these issues along with India's role at this organization of global governance. Another inter-governmental organization that has acquired enormous prominence in international relations today is the European Union (EU). As a successful and important economic bloc, the EU could offer huge trade and business opportunities to India. Have we harnessed these potentials to satisfactory levels, both from Indian and EU points of view? India has a strategic partnership with the EU, and the EU remains a top trading partner of India in recent years. But have we realized the full potential of this strategic partnership? As two authors recently observed, "India and the EU have many common interests, but transforming them into coordinated policies has been rather elusive. One should not, therefore, overrate the instrument of strategic partnerships because they were never meant to promise more than they could deliver".[3] India deals directly with EU member states when it comes to trade and investment; but Brexit has created some hindrances for India in this matter. In Chapter 8 of this volume, Udayan Das analyses these issues while exploring the changing dynamics of India-EU relations. The EU often complaints about dealing with a small staff at the Indian Ministry of External Affairs (MEA); which it views as an impediment to progress in economic relations with India.[4] This view again reinforces the argument put forward earlier in this article that the organizational structure of foreign policy mechanisms in India (like the MEA) should have a prominent place in the discourses on IFP.

West Asia always proved to be a challenging area for IFP. Growing unrest in Iraq, Iran, and Syria, and major powers' involvement, covertly or overtly, in these crises; continued hostility between Palestine and Israel; the presence of a large Indian diaspora in the region and their welfare; oil imports, etc. have made West Asia very important and sensitive an area for India's foreign policy managers. According to an estimate provided by the Government of India, 8.5 million Indian migrants lived in different countries of West Asia in 2018, with United Arab Emirates (UAE) and Saudi Arabia having the largest numbers of Indian diaspora.[5] Region wise, West Asia hosts the largest number of Indian diaspora in the world. As far as petroleum imports by India are concerned, in December 2020, among all countries, Iraq, Saudi Arabia, and UAE remained top three crude oil suppliers to India respectively.[6] Nearly 70 per cent of India's energy needs are supplied by countries of the region. These basic statistical data reveal the importance of West Asia to India. With the growth of Indian economy in the last three decades, India's non-oil economic relations with countries of the region have also improved. Israel and India have established close defence and security relations after the end of the Cold War. Israel-India relations also point to the radical departure Indian policy makers have made, for the region. Today, India's West Asia policy is part of a broader liberal outlook to reach to different nations and regions, hitherto overlooked by IFP. Israel, much like India's 'Look East' policy, fitted in this broader spectrum. But India's growing relations with Israel were definitely not achieved at the cost of losing the trust of Arab nations in the region. India maintains very cordial relations with all members of the Gulf Cooperation Council (GCC), as well as with most other nations of West Asia.[7] Like West Asia, Afghanistan also remained a foreign policy challenge for India, mostly due to its strategic importance and volatile political conditions. From the Indian point of view, Afghanistan is a gateway for both Central Asia and West Asia. Therefore, an unstable Afghanistan and extra-regional power's involvement in the politics of the nation, may not be always convenient for India. Further, Pakistan's geographical proximity to Afghanistan, and Pakistan's wish to influence the ruling elites of Afghanistan, are also matters of foreign policy challenges for India. All these issues,—India's current relations with West Asia, Israel, and Afghanistan,—have been taken up for thorough analysis by Gouri Sankar Nag in Chapter 10 of this volume. In this chapter, Gouri Sankar Nag has put special emphasis on India's policy priorities in these areas, in a rapidly changing political scenario. As noted above, growing relations with Israel and India's non-oil diplomacy in West Asia are certainly new trends in IFP. Keeping these points in mind, a whole chapter in this book has been devoted to these developments.

QUAD, AUKUS and the Return of the Talibans

The Quadrilateral Security Dialogue, a new group of four democratic nations comprising Australia, India, Japan, and the U.S., has generated considerable interest in international politics. Popularly known as the QUAD, this group came into existence in the year 2004 for maritime cooperation in the wake of massive tsunamis in the Indian Ocean region. But today, this group works on many other areas of cooperation like economic, security, health, and environmental issues. Although QUAD is still not a formal alliance, and the framework is somewhat loose; some observers view this grouping as an effort to counterbalance China's presence in the Indo-pacific region. Will QUAD emerge as a formidable alliance to counter China or will it remain as a mere friendship group? In Chapter 11 of this volume, Sohini Nayak has analysed the prospects and problems of QUAD. Along with QUAD, Sohini Nayak has also taken up for analysis AUKUS, a trilateral security partnership among Australia, the United Kingdom and the United States, formed on September 15, 2021. Under this security partnership, the UK and the US will help Australia acquire nuclear submarines to strengthen its security. Although a very new security pact among the three nations, AUKUS is also viewed as a force to counter China in international politics. In Chapter 11, the prospects of AUKUS and its impact on global politics have been thoroughly dissected.

The return of the Talibans in Afghanistan in September 2021 has raised many questions, not only for the security of the regions of South, West, and Central Asia, but also about the future stakes of big powers like the US, Russia, and China. Has the image of the US as a savior of democracy received a jolt with the return of the Talibans? Is American power and supremacy on the wane? What roles will Russia and China play in future Afghanistan? How will they view the new Taliban Government in Afghanistan? What will be India's stance vis-à-vis the Taliban Government, in the short run and also, in the long run? These are some of the questions students and scholars of International Relations ask and desire to know the likely answers. Therefore, whole sections in Chapter 10 and Chapter 11 have been devoted to discussion of these issues. There is little doubt that the return of the Talibans has posed a challenge to Indian foreign policy. The mandarins of Indian foreign policy must rise up to this serious challenge.

A Strategic Culture for IFP

A strategic culture for IFP has been deliberated upon by many authors in recent times. While some view that India needs to develop a strong strategic culture as a backup force for its foreign policy, others believe that it has been in existence in India since independence. This debate will be located shortly here; but before highlighting on this debate, one should have some basic ideas about strategic culture. Although no separate chapter has been devoted in this volume to strategic culture in IFP, this space has been used to focus on the importance of strategic culture in our foreign policy. Strategic culture (SC) refers to a nation's attitudes, values, symbols, traditions, practices and ways of adapting to the environment for solving problems with respect to the threat or use of force. In simple words, SC refers to a nation's attitude towards threat or use of force. Such attitude should not be bereft of a nation's traditions, values, and cultural aspects. SC involves mainly three areas related to the threat or use of force: (1) security outside national borders or external security; (2) security of the national borders; and (3) security within the country, or internal security. Indian beliefs, attitudes, and ways of dealing with these security issues refer to a strategic culture in India. Foreign policy is more concerned with first two types of security, although the third is important for achieving goals of national interest. SC refers to warfare strategy, and also, security issues during peace time. The most pertinent question, as far as the existence of SC in Indian foreign policy is concerned is: do we have a warfare strategy or any strategy to meet security concerns during peace time? Do we need a grand strategy in Indian foreign policy to deal with these security issues? As noted above, SC encompasses traditions and cultural history of a nation. Now if one looks at Indian traditional documents, (s)he would find important treatises of warfare in ancient India like Kautilya's *Arthashastra*, two epics *Mahabharta* and *Ramayana*, etc. *Arthashastra* talked about covert war, open war and silent war; how to engage in war; and what to do in case one is a target of covert or silent war. Although the actual author and time of *Arthashastra* is debated, there is no doubt that the treatise comprises an important document of diplomacy and warfare in ancient India. In epics like *Mahabharata* and *Ramayana*, references to strategies of warfare could also be traced. Therefore, ancient India provided us with valuables sources to look at in our search for a SC in India. But are these treatises adequate as policy documents of warfare strategies for modern India? Well, there are divergent views again. Some scholars hold the view that as a treatise on statecraft, diplomacy and warfare, *Arthashastra* is significantly relevant in modern India.[8] There are others, however, who value *Arthashastra* as a theoretical gem, but unable to guide modern Indian foreign policy much.[9] Without delving deep into this debate on *Arthashastra*, which is not the point of reference here, it may be noted that documents on diplomacy and warfare were available in ancient India.

According to a noted historian, medieval India was not able to continue the rich legacy of warfare documents from ancient India; as this period actually lacked warfare strategies. He believed that interstate relations and war were the weakest aspects of Indian polity during the medieval period. There were large kingdoms, enormous armies, individual heroes, but no alliances or strategies to thwart the aggressor or for empire building. As a consequence, these kingdoms could not withstand foreign aggressors like the Turks.[10] Moving from pre-colonial period to the post-colonial era (because during the colonial period, India was not sovereign to decide its own course, the reigning question persisted: could we develop a SC in India? As already noted, there are contradictory views about the development of a SC in IFP in modern India (since independence). While some refer to the development of SC during the premiership of Nehru and its continuity by subsequent governments, others think that India lacked a coherent SC during the Nehru period. One author found three streams of strategic thought in independent India: Nehruvian, Neo-liberal, and Hyperrealist.[11] Likewise an Indian diplomat believes that independent India had always possessed some kind of SC.[12] On the contrary, a former Lieutenant General of Indian army lamented the lack of a strategic culture in India after independence.[13] One foreign scholar saw the continuity of Nehruvian strategic thought in subsequent governments, up to the premiership of Narendra Modi; while another, drawing mainly from ancient Indian epics, referred to fatalistic and moral characteristics of Indian SC, which according to him, lacked realism and activism.[14]

Viewed in terms of warfare strategies, Indian SC did not develop during the Nehru period, believes this author. Nehru developed an autonomous course for Indian foreign policy, away from influences of the superpowers. But he had no military strategy, not even any inkling of it. This was evident when China attacked India in 1962. Nehru failed to presume this attack, and as a consequence, India faced a humiliating defeat. So it is improper to assume that Nehru developed some kind of SC. He was an architect of Indian foreign policy, minus any security strategy. His daughter, Indira deviated from his policies, although unofficially, and tested India's first nuclear device in 1974. During her tenure, India inflicted a quick and resounding defeat on Pakistan in the 1971 war, and established itself as a regional power. But no grand strategy on security or SC could be visible during her tenures as Prime Minister (PM). Narasimha Rao was credited with India's economic reforms in an era of globalization; but a SC was still invisible. It was during Vajpayee's last tenure as PM that India had a 'Nuclear Doctrine', the first of its kind since independence. After the 1998 nuclear tests, India boldly claimed that nuclear options were necessary for India to safeguard its security, a departure from a rather ambiguous 'test for peaceful purposes' as proclaimed by India after the 1974 test. Therefore, this author would argue that while a security consciousness developed in India during the Indira Gandhi period and sustained thereafter, a SC actually started developing from the later part of the A.B. Vajpayee tenure as PM.

From a pragmatic point of view, a SC is still in the process of developing in India. Whether we adopt a grand strategy or not, like China or the U.S., an inquisitive mind would tend to ask whether we have strategies for wars, or border security strategy when sudden attacks like in the Galwan area of the Ladakh valley happened in the year 2020. Are we ready for prolonged covert wars, happening in the border areas in the west, north, north-west and north-east? As this author argued elsewhere, open wars may not happen in the near future due to economic factors, but covert wars will continue along India's vast borders.[15] Do we have one grand or different strategies to deal with such undeclared wars? The answer has to be provided in the negative at this point of time. While Indian military is well-equipped in terms of man power and weaponry, our foreign policy establishments need to be strengthened further. India also needs to have well-articulated strategies for war, open or covert; border security policies; and internal security policies. India has major power ambitions. A strong SC must be developed in the near future to guide us fulfill such ambitions.

Conclusion: The Future

Any discourse on IFP must try to locate India's position in the global power matrix, now and in the future. There is no denying the fact that India wishes to play a prominent role in global politics; and wants to achieve a big power tag. But is India on the road to a big power? What the future holds for India? Chapter 12 of this volume explores India's tasks at hand to be on the road to a big power. These tasks include measures to be taken in both domestic and foreign policy segments. India has become the third largest economy in the world after China and the U.S. in terms of Purchasing Power Parity (PPP). But is that enough? With several constraining factors in the social and economic sectors, India also faces many roadblocks. This chapter tried to prescribe ways to overcome these roadblocks in the socio-economic segments. It also pointed out the course Indian foreign policy needs to follow to achieve a big power tag. Among many recommendations for IFP, an important one for strengthening the IFP mechanisms refers to the recruitment of additional personnel in foreign policy establishments. A vigorous economic diplomacy and more global engagements by India in bilateral and multilateral diplomacies comprise other foreign policy recommendations for India. India must strengthen its presence in the whole of Africa, Latin America, Central Asia and East Europe, in areas of trade, security and political engagements. In IFP, these areas are either overlooked (Africa, Latin America) or less prioritized (Central Asia, East Europe). China has made deep inroads in these areas, in terms of trade and business and resultant political influence. IFP has been slow to arrive in these areas. Chapter 12 titled "Vision of a New World Order and India's Role in It" also tried to position India in the global power race now,—in the third decade of the 21st century; and in the foreseeable future. Such projections are not frequently found in current studies on IFP. These projections endeavoured to answer about India's proper place in the global power matrix, now and in the coming decades.

There are many challenges for IFP in the current world order where globalization as well as post-globalization factors remains present side by side. If the global economic network created by both state and non-state actors refers to the process of globalization; other factors like climate change, international terrorism, spread of pandemics, civil wars, problems of refugee, and internally displaced persons, etc., point towards gaps in the process of globalization, and the need for more concerted efforts by all stakeholders in international society, in the 'post-globalization' world order. For instance, Covid 19 pandemic and the resultant economic setback have already proved to be more detrimental than the 'Great Depression' of the 1930s. The process of globalization was hit hard by the pandemic. International politics and economics will certainly undergo many changes in the post-pandemic world. As one expert observed, "it is hard to deny that the post-corona world will be very different. Comparatively at least, we will see more de-globalization, regionalization, de-coupling, self-reliance and shorter supply chains".[16] India will have to adjust its foreign policy and economic diplomacy in a deft manner in the post-pandemic world order. Both policy planning and effective executions of policy, i.e. theoretical and applied sides of IFP must be adequately strengthened by India to find its avowed position in world politics. India will have to find its right place in a multi-aligned world, where the U.S. and China will vie for leadership role. India must also find suitable ways to reach its goals in this complex international order. In different chapters of this volume such roads have been identified. In short, India will need to strengthen its multi-alignment, economic diplomacy, military and foreign policy establishments and preparations to be on the race for a big power status in a convoluted, difficult world order.

Endnotes

1. T.C.A. Raghavan (2019), "Some conceptual underpinnings of Indian Foreign Policy Today", Media Center, Ministry of External Affairs, Govt. of India; on line source: https://www.mea.gov.in/articles-in-indian-media.htm?dtl/32013/Some_conceptual_underpinnings_of_Indian_Foreign_Policy_Today. Accessed on 25 May 2021.
2. See in this connection, Spencer Zifcak (2009), *United Nations Reform: Heading North or South?*, New York: Routledge.
3. Rajendra Jain and Gulshan Sachdeva (2019), "India-EU Strategic Partnership: A New Roadmap", in *Asia Europe Journal*; on line source; https://www.researchgate.net/publication/334114034_India-EU_strategic_partnership_a_new_roadmap. Accessed on 25 May 2021.
4. *Ibid.*
5. Ministry of External Affairs, Govt. of India (2019), "Population of Overseas Indians"; on line source: http://mea.gov.in/images/attach/NRIs-and-PIOs_1.pdf. Accessed on 26 May 2021.
6. *The Economic Times* (2021), "India's oil imports at near 3 year high in December", 19 January; on line source: https://economictimes.indiatimes.com/news/economy/foreign-trade/indias-oil-imports-at-near-3-year-high-in december/articleshow/80348206.cms?utm_source=contentofinterest&utm_medium=text&utm_campaign=cppst. Accessed on 26 May 2021.
7. See in this connection, Ranjit Gupta (2017), "India's Relations with West Asia: A New Era Dawns", Middle East Institute; on line source: http://www.mei.edu/publications/indias-relations-west-asia-new-era-dawns. Accessed on 26 May 2021.
8. See in this connection, Subrata K. Mitra and Michael Liebig (2017), *Kautilya's Arthashastra: An Intellectual Portrait: The Classical Roots of Modern Politics in India*, New Delhi: Rupa; Also, L.N. Rangarajan (1992), *Kautilya: The Arthashastra*, New Delhi: Penguin Books.

9. See in this connection, Krzysztof Iwanek (2020), "India Does Not Follow *Arthashastra* in Its Foreign Policy", *The Diplomat*; on line source: https://thediplomat.com/2020/11/india-does-not-follow-arthashastra-in-its-foreign-policy/. Accessed on 27 May 2021.
10. A.L. Basham (1991), *The Wonder That was India*, New Delhi: Rupa, p. 137.
11. Kanti Bajpai (2001), "Through a Looking Glass: Strategic Prisms and the Pakistan Problem", *India International Centre Quarterly*, 28 (2).
12. MEA, Govt. of India (2013), "Address by National Security Advisor Shiv Shankar Menon on Strategic Culture and IR Studies in India at the 3rd International Studies Convention held at JNU Convention Centre, New Delhi", Media Center; on line source: https://www.mea.gov.in/Speeches-Statements.htm?dtl/22632/Address+by+National+Security+Advisor+Shiv+Shankar+Menon+on+Strategic+Culture+and+IR+St. Accessed on 27 May 2021.
13. Lt. Gen. S.C. Sardeshpande (2016), "Our Strategic Culture", *Indian Defence Review*; on line source: http://www.indiandefencereview.com/news/our-strategic-culture/. Accessed on 28 May 2021.
14. See in this connection, Ian Hall (2016), "The Persistence of Nehruvianism in India's Strategic Culture", The National Bureau of Asian Research; on line source: https://www.nbr.org/publication/the-persistence-of-nehruvianism-in-indias-strategic-culture/. Accessed on 28 May 2021. Also, George K. Tanham (1992), "Indian Strategic Thought: An Interpretive Essay", RAND Corporation; on line source: https://www.rand.org/pubs/reports/R4207.html. Accessed on 28 May 2021.
15. Aneek Chatterjee (2020), "India needs to develop a strong strategic culture", *South Asia Monitor*, August 12.
16. S. Jaishankar (2020), *The India Way: Strategies for an Uncertain World*, Noida: HarperCollins, p. 204.

2

Indian Foreign Policy: Determinants and Institutions

Prosenjit Pal

SECTION 1: DETERMINANTS OF FOREIGN POLICY

Introduction

Simply stated, foreign policy of a state is the reflection of the way a country perceives its relations with other states in the international system, in tune with its national interests and objectives (socio-economic and political) and attempts to interact with its co-actors in the system. A nation's foreign policy flows from several sources, from the international system to its domestic political imperatives to the cultural factors that underline its society to the personal characteristics and perceptions of individual decision-makers. Like most of the nations, India's foreign policy is no exception. But as a nation's weight in the global balance of power rises, it becomes imperative to pay greater attention to the systemic constrains. India, in the Indo-centric South Asian Region may be conceptualized as a pre-eminent yet reluctant power, strong in the capability quotient but lacking the endeavor to stamp assertively its dominance in the region; and its foreign policy also seems to reflect such a lack of an attitude identifiable with an emerging power in the contemporary world order. In the interplay between the theoretical aspects of Idealism and Realism in the realm of Indian foreign policy, pragmatism and hard-core realism has often been arrested by an adherence to inherent idealistic culture of peace, non-violence, open diplomacy and adherence to moral norms, and reluctance to project hard power in astute military sense of term.

According to one expert, India will face two major internal constraints in its quest for a major power status. "First, India will have to recognize the need to exploit the extant structure of international system to its advantage more effectively. Structural constraints are the most formidable ones a state encounters in its drive towards the status of a major power. Yet, Indian foreign policy continues to be reactive to the strategic environment rather than attempting to shape the strategic realities. While such an ad hoc response to the structural imperatives carried little costs when India seems poised to play a significant role in global politics. Second, India must come to grips with its discomfort with the very notion of power and in particular its wariness of the use of 'hard-power'".[1] He further observes that all along the course of history, "all the major powers have been required to employ the military instrument skillfully. India's reluctance to accept a more sophisticated understanding of power, in general, and military power, in particular, will continue to undermine Indian foreign and as well as security policy".[2]

It is relevant in this context to discuss the basic determinants of India's foreign policy. Foreign policy is never uniquely determined by any single factor or a set of factors, but is a result of the interplay of a large number of factors that affect the formulation of policy in different ways and under different circumstances.[3] A few of these factors are relatively constant and are perceived by makers of foreign policy as given, and hence they may be regarded as the basic determinants. But the variable factors are the institutional factors and the personality traits of the decision-makers, which are nonetheless important in the decision-making process.

Basic Determinants of Indian Foreign Policy

The importance of the basic determinants of Foreign Policy may also vary according to time and circumstances and hence, generally, decision-makers need to be aware of the same while attempting to formulate a rational foreign policy. The same is applicable for Indian Foreign Policy as well.

National Interest

The national interest of a country may be regarded as an end of foreign policy—the values which the country tries to uphold, preserve, and protect under all circumstances. Foreign policy of India, like other countries, reflects the core interests of the nation. Both short-term and long-term interests of India, including the preservation of national unity, territorial integrity, external and internal security, goals of national development, ensuring India's distinct place in the global order, maintenance of tranquillity and cordiality with other states, are basically inherent in India's foreign policy architecture which has evolved since Nehruvian times till date. From Non-alignment as the cornerstone of Indian foreign policy, India has transcended to the level of multi-alignment, under the present NDA-led Government. But the core values centering around India's national interests have remained fundamentally unaltered.

Geographical Factors

Geopolitical considerations assume prominence in the process of foreign policy formulation and India is no exception. India's geopolitical positioning in the South Asian region has imparted a uniqueness in her character as a state. South Asia is an Indo-centric region. India's geographical pre-eminence is the source of her strength as well as a factor conditioning her relations with her neighbours as well as its closest rival in Asia-China. India's strategic location at the centre of the great Asian arc stretching from Aden to Tokyo and on the Indian Ocean has conditioned her position as a 'pivot' in Asia, in spite of her relative geographical insularity. The same strategic location imparts on India a central position in Asian and global politics. All the major air and sea routes of the world pass through India. India and the Indian Ocean are an indispensable link in world trade and commerce. India is a major connecting link among the countries of West Asia, East Asia, and the Far East.[4]

In such a situation, any big incident in the whole of Asia affects India. The Himalayas are like sentinels of India which play an important role in determining relations with other Himalayan countries such as Nepal, Bhutan, Myanmar. But the desire of China to maintain its dominance in the region continuously since 1962 has a clear impact on India's foreign policy. India shares a 4000-km long border with China and the border dispute between the two countries is still unresolved with occasional flare-ups, the latest being in the Galwan Valley in the Ladakh region in 2020. India shares borders with Pakistan, Nepal, Bhutan, and Bangladesh and her relations with her smaller neighbours have witnessed more volatility than cordiality. India's geographical preponderance has naturally created a hegemonic imaging of her in the minds of her neighbours who continue to perceive her in that way.

Apart from Bangladesh, India's neighbourhood relations need more strength at this point of time. The Kashmir dispute between India and Pakistan, apart from cross-border terrorism and other issues have perennially conditioned India's Pakistan policy. India's China policy has been of an ad hoc nature, her response often lacking in the required amount of aggression (in the realist sense of the term); India lacks the pre-emptive instinct in countering threat of the rising dragon. But the same is only a part of the shortcomings in the broader context of mainstream Indian foreign policy. Yet India is unable to tame the Dragon from interfering in its neighbourhood, meddling in the Indian Ocean, wooing her Himalayan neighbours, inching into parts of her territory, keeping the border dispute in an unresolved status and stepping up volatility quotient.

However, India has a natural edge in the Indian Ocean. India's dominance over the Indian Ocean is necessary to become an important power of the Indian-Pacific region. At present, the Indian Ocean region is an important route of trade and communication for the whole world. Hence, it also plays an important role in determining the foreign policy of India. In the IOR region US-China-India trilateral power rivalry continues with Chinese forays in the region increasing leaps and bounds with the inception of China's ambitious Belt And Road Initiative (BRI) and her policy of strategic encirclement of India known as the *String of Pearls* strategy.[5]

Population

India is currently the second most populous country in the world. Demographically, India has one of the youngest populations in the world. India is also becoming a consumption-oriented country. In such a situation, it will fulfil the need of a big market for all the producing nations, which is going to be a key factor of Indian foreign policy. But with such a large population, problems like hunger, poverty may affect India's foreign policy. Many times there has been a dispute in the World Trade Organization between India and America about the government's intervention in agricultural subsidies.

Economic Development

Economic sovereignty is of utmost importance in determining foreign policy. India opened up its economy in 1991. Indian economy gained strength after liberalisation. India's economic growth has attracted many countries. Today, India is an important energy consumer, with countries like Turkmenistan, Iran, Russia having economic alliances with India. But still the negative trade balance with China remains India's main concern.

Culture

History and culture are important variables in the formulation of India's foreign policy. Kautilya's theory of a powerful kingdom and peace ideals of Buddha and Gandhi show the path of India. For long, religious tolerance has been nurtured in Indian society, where different religious communities coexited. India has been opposing imperialism, colonialism, building of armaments and racial discrimination. These views are embedded in Indian culture and get reflected in Indian foreign policy also.

SECTION 2: INSTITUTIONS OF FOREIGN POLICY MAKING

MEA (Ministry of External Affairs)

MEA is the most important organization in India's foreign relations. MEA acts like the foreign policy secretariat in India, which receives numerous policy inputs from various sources, and analyzes and channelizes the different options to the political leadership, i.e. the Cabinet headed by the PM. Other sources, as pointed out by a former Indian Ambassador, are "relevant ministries, departments, and agencies in India, from think tanks and research centres like the IDSA and IWCA, from trade and industry associations like CII, FICCI, and ASSOCHAM, from academic institutions, and from individual subject specialists. After processing and analysis, the MEA's views and options approved by the External Affairs Minister (EAM) are forwarded to the Cabinet/Cabinet Committee for consideration."[6] The Policy Planning and Research Division of MEA acts as the coordinating agency in the whole process.

In the MEA specialized divisions have been set up for tasks like Counter Terrorism, Cyber Diplomacy, E-Governance, etc. One area on which the MEA has put extra focus in recent times has been economic diplomacy, with emphasis on foreign investment and technology promotion. Now an Economic Diplomacy Division (EDD) is fully operational within the MEA. The EDD also looks after Multilateral Economic Relations (MER) and specialized centres for India's economic ties with regional organizations like the ASEAN, BIMSTEC and other regional and subregional organizations. A Development Partnership Administration (DPA) was also created to promote India's role in development assistance to many countries of the third world. The Disarmament & International Security Affairs (D&ISA) Division has been functioning for more than three decades "dealing with nuclear proliferation, disarmament and related issues, including India's bid for membership of the Nuclear Suppliers Group (NSG) and related bodies. Functional divisions like Administration, Establishment, Finance and Legal and Treaties, provide the tools and environment needed by Indian diplomats at home and abroad to discharge their functions effectively."[7] The External Publicity Division of MEA, receives foreign policy inputs from various sources including the media, both domestic and international. The MEA works in tandem with the Ministry of Home Affairs (MHA) as far as passport, visa and consular services are concerned.

Subrahmanyam Jaishankar, who retired as foreign secretary, could be credited with building a bridge between the external affairs ministry and the Prime Minister's Office and helping shape a more robust foreign policy. During his tenure as foreign secretary, which included a one-year extension, Jaishankar, who was later inducted into the Modi cabinet as External Affairs Minister, provided more muscle to the external affairs ministry's policy, planning, and research division that was created to help decision-makers in the future.

Cabinet and Cabinet Committees

The Indian Cabinet, headed by the Prime Minister, is the top decision-making body in almost all affairs, domestic and international. Naturally, the cabinet has an important voice when it comes to the making and implementation of Indian foreign policy. Cabinet Ministers, especially Minister of External Affairs, Minister of Home Affairs, Minister of Defence and Minister of Finance aid and advise the Prime Minister of India on external issues. The Prime Minister may also take the assistance of any other minister in the cabinet closer to him/her on foreign policy issues. Today the scope of foreign policy issues has widened a lot and includes external security; economic matters like foreign trade and commerce and investment; terrorism including cyber terrorism; development assistance programs et al. As a consequence, the cabinet plays a crucial role in India's foreign policy domain.

An important function of the "relevant cabinet committee", as one former Indian diplomat observed, "is to examine the various activities of the ministry and to give policy directives to the respective departments. Though none of the current cabinet committees (like the CC on Security or CC on Economic Affairs) deal exclusively with foreign affairs, the issues dealt by such CCs, directly impact India's foreign policy and practices."[8] Therefore Cabinet Committees (CCs) make important mechanisms of Indian foreign policy now a days.

Prime Minister's Office (PMO)

In India, the PMO has assumed enormous significance over the years. Although institutions like the legislature and bureaucracy play some roles in the making of foreign policy in India, but it is largely the Prime Minister and his office (PMO) that make foreign policy in the country. This trend is nothing new in India. Since the days of Jawaharlal Nehru, the Prime Minister and his office, which was known earlier as the Prime Minister's Secretariat (PMS), played significant role in India's foreign policy. Following Nehru, all Indian Prime Ministers, irrespective of party and ideology, played a pivotal role in Indian foreign policy. As a natural outcome, the PMO became a very powerful body in the making and execution of Indian foreign policy. "The PMO consisting of senior level bureaucrats provides secretarial assistance and advice to the PM and functions as the centre of policy making in India. It coordinates various central agencies like the Cabinet, Cabinet Committees, Council of Ministers and other stakeholders to sort out interdepartmental hurdles in domestic and foreign policy execution."[9]

The organizational structure of the current PMO comprises "the Principal Secretary to PM, the National Security Advisor (NSA), an Additional PS to PM, Secretary to PM, two Additional Secretaries, five Joint Secretaries and several other officers at the levels of Director, Deputy Secretary and Under Secretary."[10] All important issues on foreign policy and security need the approval of the Indian Prime Minister before execution. Nowadays, the NSA plays a crucial and impacting role in the process of advice channelized to the PM. "Successful foreign policy formulation and execution depends on the degree of coordination between the PMO and MEA. PM's approval is crucial in appointment of Indian Ambassadors and High Commissioners abroad, though the formal letter of appointment is issued by the President in his capacity as Head of State. In other words, on all major foreign policy issues, the buck stops at the door of the Prime Minister."[11] As a consequence, important foreign policy phraseology like the Gujral Doctrine, Modi Doctrine, Neighbourhood First, to name a few, practically emanate from the directions provided by the PMO on suggestions from the MEA or other advisory bodies.

National Security Council (NSC)

In recent years, the NSC has assumed a significant position in matters related to India's security and foreign policies. This apex body of the Government of India is a three-tier organization comprising the Strategic Planning Group, the

National Security Advisory Board and the Joint Intelligence Committee. NSC advices the Government on matters pertaining to India's National Security, Foreign Policy and Defence. "Although the final decisions rest with the PM and the Cabinet, in recent years, the National Security Council has emerged as an important stakeholder in the shaping of India's foreign and security policies. Chaired by the PM, the NSC consists of the Ministers of External Affairs, Defence, Home and Finance, the NSA (National Security Advisor) and the Deputy Chairman of Niti Ayog (successor to Planning Commission). The NSA is the Secretary to the National Security Council."[12]

Among the three tiers of the NSC, the Strategic Planning Group (SPG) is the highest decision-making body. The SPG is mainly assigned with tasks of formulating and executing India's strategic policies. Headed by the Cabinet Secretary, the SPG is also responsible for making strategies for India's defence forces. "Its members include secretaries of all important ministries and departments like Home, Defence, External Affairs, Defence Production, Revenue, Atomic Energy, Space, the heads of R&AW and IB, the Chiefs of the Army, Navy and Air Force, Chairman CBDT, RBI Governor, Scientific Advisor to RM and Chairman JIC. This Group meets periodically and continuously observes national and international security environment and takes necessary steps to neutralize possible threats."[13]

At the next tier of NSC comes the National Security Advisory Board (NSAB). The NSAB which has members from outside the government, advises the Indian Government on matters related to national security and development. "It does long term analysis and provides perspectives on issues of national security. Its membership includes eminent professionals, academics, scientists, administrative experts and retired bureaucrats."[14] Currently, the NSAB consists of four members.

The Joint Intelligence Committee (JIC) makes the third tier of NSC. JIC receives intelligence reports from the IB (Intelligence Bureau), R&AW (Research & Analysis Wing), and the Directorates of Military, Naval and Air and Naval Intelligence, respectively. "It is the highest intelligence assessment organization, tasked with inter-agency coordination, collection and analysis of intelligence data."[15] Normally an Additional Secretary from the Cabinet Secretariat acts as the chairperson of the JIC. The JIC has representatives from Ministry of External Affairs, Ministry of Defence, Ministry of Home Affairs, IB, R&AW, in addition to top personnel from military, air and naval intelligence. "It sometimes directs the relevant intelligence agencies to conduct certain intelligence gathering tasks, based on the input or demand from the Government. The JIC is an important and effective advisory body to the PM and Cabinet in decision making on matters related to foreign affairs and defence."[16]

Ministry of Defence and Ministry of Commerce & Industry

These two ministries of the Government of India play important parts in India's strategic and economic relations with foreign nations. Ministry of Defence's views are usually sought by the PMO and the Cabinet on matters relating to India's defense policy and national security. The Defence Minister of India is a member of the Cabinet Committee on Security and of the National Security Council. "The Secretary, Department of Defence, Secretary (Defence Production) and the three service chiefs (Army, Navy and Air Force) are members of the Strategic Planning Group. In recent years, a joint secretary level officer from MEA is seconded to the MoD to handle Planning and International Cooperation tasks of the Ministry."[17]

In an era when economic diplomacy has become crucial for every nation, India does not wish to lag behind. The Department of Commerce (DoC) together with the MEA and the Ministry of Finance plays a significant role in India's economic diplomacy. "On trade issues at the WTO, bilateral and multilateral FTAs, etc, policy is largely initiated and formalised at the DoC. Investment and taxation issues are coordinated by the MoF in consultation with MoC, MEA, CBDT, Customs, etc."[18]

Parliament

India is the largest democracy in the world. Like other democratic nations, the Indian Parliament also enjoys many powers as far as the country's foreign policy is concerned, because theoretically, peoples' representatives have control over the executive branch of the government in a democracy. The two houses of the Indian Parliament namely, the Rajya Sabha (upper house) and the Lok Sabha (lower house) have powers to legislate on foreign affairs. Such powers include making and amending any law for the successful implementation of bilateral and multilateral treaties, agreements and conventions. As in other democracies, the Indian government remains accountable to the parliament which is empowered by the constitution of India to seek information and clarification from the government on foreign policy issues. Further, the parliament, through budgetary control and amendment in the proposed law, may force the government to act as per the wish of the Legislature. However, if the ruling party enjoys a majority in the parliament such control by the Legislature may not be possible. But in the case of a minority government or coalition government, parliament can exert control over the executive. The Indian parliament has "a Standing Committee on External Affairs and a Standing Committee on Defence, which grill the officials on issues pertaining to foreign relations and external security. Parliament may also constitute ad hoc committees to look into specific issues. Debates on various issues related to foreign policy in the Parliament, often has a bearing on the final decision-making process related to several key aspects of foreign policy."[19] The Indo-U.S. Nuclear Deal of 2005 was one example in recent times when the government had to go for some alterations in the final draft, known as the 'Indo-U.S. Nuclear Agreement', due to intense debates and criticisms in the Indian parliament.

SECTION 3: CONTINUITY AND CHANGE IN INDIA'S FOREIGN POLICY

During the last three decades since India's economic liberalization, Indian foreign policy has been rapidly evolving. As India has risen economically and militarily in recent years, its political clout in international affairs has also seen a commensurate increase. From the peripheries of international affairs, India is now at the center of global politics. It is viewed as a balancer in the Asia-Pacific, a democracy that can be an ally of the West in countering China, although India has many policy differences with the West; on issues like climate change, international trade and nuclear non-proliferation. Indian foreign policy, which was largely driven by a sense of idealism since its independence, had two goals: retention of complete autonomy in the wake of 'bloc politics' pursued by the two superpowers during the Cold War period; and finding a rightful place for India in international politics. India had other foreign policy objectives as well, like providing support to decolonization and disarmament; strong moral and material help for the United Nations and peaceful co-existence in a world threatened by nuclear arsenals. However, it was strongly believed that the two primary goals (noted above) would strengthen India's position as a major actor in global politics. The fundamental instrument chosen by Jawaharlal Nehru to pursue the basic goals of India's foreign policy, was non-alignment which was meant to perform the essential functions of ensuring the autonomy of India's foreign policy as well as give it a significant voice in international relations as the heir to a great civilisational heritage.[20]

A review of India's foreign policy over the past two decades reveals the extent to which Indian foreign policy mandarins have been successful in dovetailing the elements of continuity and change.[21] There is a general consensus that any analysis of India's foreign policy in the 21st century must take into account the dramatic transformation of the world following the end of the Cold War and its consequent ramifications for India's foreign policy, whose contours and character have acquired dimensions hardly imaginable even in the late 1980s.

India's main concern during the Cold War period, was about getting drawn into the superpower rivalry. As a consequence, India opted for a non-aligned foreign policy that preserved India's decision-making autonomy in international politics. Behind the policy of Non-alignment, there was a calculation that aimed at protecting vital Indian interests, given India's limited economic and military abilities. Pakistan's security strategy was India's most immediate threat and India's obsession with Pakistan was not all that surprising. But beyond Pakistan, there was little vision. For instance, Indian policy makers misread China and paid dearly in the 1962 war against China. The Chinese puzzle could not be solved by India, and it severely impacted Nehru's international and domestic image.

The 1962 war with China and the 1965 war with Pakistan revealed India's inadequate military preparations. Therefore, Prime Minister Indira Gandhi put emphasis on India's military preparedness. In the 1971 war against Pakistan, India could show its military might and after the war India could also establish itself as a regional military power. But poor economic growth proved to be a hindrance for India in the road to major power. This scenario continued till the early 1990s. India went for economic liberalization in the year 1991. The Cold War also came to an end in the same year and the world was witnessing paradigmatic shifts. Many priority areas of Indian foreign policy had to be reviewed in the light of changed circumstances. The shape of global politics changed and Indian foreign policy required new visions and a fresh national security strategy. A rapidly shifting geo-strategic landscape confronted India as it made its way up in the inter-state hierarchy. At the beginning of the new millennium, India was on the threshold of achieving the status of a major global power, exemplified not only by its growing economic and military might and also the attraction of its political and cultural values.[22] However, in the changed circumstances in the world material might and political influence are means and not ends to pursue interests and foreign policy objectives. According to policy makers in New Delhi the desire to attain great power status is primarily for 'defensive' reasons. It is meant to be a protection against external domination or intimidation.[23]

Keeping this context in mind five major challenges in the arena of India's foreign policy in the 21st century can be identified. These are:

- *Discomfort with Power*: India's lack of an "instinct for power".[24]
- *Inability to Use Force Effectively*: India's lack of an instinct for power is most palpable in military realm where, unlike other major global powers throughout history, India has failed to master the certain deployment

and use of its military instruments in support of its national objectives.[25]

- *Marginalization of Military*: Indian military was viewed with suspicion by the political elites immediately after independence in 1947, as the last supporters of the British Raj. Accordingly, Indian civil political elites isolated the military from policy and influence. However, this schism faded away soon and the military became a very trusted institution.
- *Strategic Culture Deficit*: There is a perceptible strategic culture deficit in India. As one expert observes: "A state can promulgate law and pursue strategy once it has not only achieved a legitimate monopoly on violence but also when it is free of the coercive violence of other states".[26] As noted in chapter one of this volume also, a strategic culture is still in the process of making in India.
- *Lack of Institutionalization*: India also suffers from a major lack of institutionalization as far as foreign policy-making in the country is concerned. India needs adequate foreign policy mechanisms, in terms of institutions and personnel, to reach its avowed position in international politics and economic diplomacy.

The Modi factor: Since coming to office in May 2014, the Narendra Modi government has been successful in gradually pushing back India's foreign policy legacy of non-alignment. Prime Minister Modi went ahead engaging confidently with all major global powers without inhibitions. The foreign policies of nations do not alter radically only with changes in governments, but with the backing of the masses. With a huge and decisive mandate, Modi got the opportunity to bring about a realignment of Indian foreign policy priorities and goals. Out of Modi's several new foreign policy initiatives, the 'Neighbourhood First' policy has been much debated about in political as well as in academic circles.[27]

The five pillars of Modi's foreign policy are: *Samman* (respect for every nation's sovereignty); *Samvaad* (greater engagement with all countries); *Suraksha* (security); *Samriddhi* (shared prosperity); *Sanskriti* and *Sabhyata* (civilisational philosophy and republican and democratic ethos, reach of cultural values).

To tap the dynamics of Indian foreign policy under Modi's prime ministership, numerous scholars have studied the different dimensions of the Indian foreign policy. However, their opinion is divided. Some have talked about the substantial change and described him as a rescuer of Indian foreign policy, while others do not see any major shift. Rajesh Basrur has found that 'foreign policy under Modi picks up from where his predecessors left off and is characterized by essential continuity'[28] Ian Hall virtually concurs with this view and argues that despite bringing a proactive turn in Indian foreign policy, 'Modi has not made major modifications to the aims and methods of Indian foreign policy'[29]. In contrast, another group represented by C. Raja Mohan sees the changes as 'so seminal as to mark the beginning of the "Third Republic" in Indian foreign policy.[30] Kanti Bajpai (2015) has found a 'new zeal' and rebooting of Indian foreign policy under the new regime.[31] However, there are some weaknesses in our neighbourhood policies especially the execution aspects and the same is more perceptible in India's China policy. Elements of continuity is more visible rather than real and effective changes in India's foreign policy at this point of time.

One can argue that the designing, grandeur, and planning of the restructuring of foreign policy under the present government may be astute but proper execution of the same is still found wanting. Real and effective change in Indian strategic culture, thought and planning needs to be ushered in. The hardwire and software of Indian foreign policy making needs to be overhauled and attuned to the hard core realities of the strategic environment confronting India, during the Covid-dominated global order and even in the futuristic post-Covid order, the prospective nature of which has already sparked of debates in strategic and academic circles. India's China policy is only a part of the broader architecture of Indian foreign policy making apparatus,—the inherent 'virus' of lack of pre-emptive strategic culture, reactiveness, lack of proper planning, academia-elite gap in planning and implementation. Therefore, an adept foreign policy apparatus, is an urgent necessity for India in the post-Covid global order and even beyond.

Endnotes

1. Harsh V. Pant (2009), 'A Rising India's Search for a Foreign Policy', *Orbis*, 53 (2).
2. *Ibid.*
3. Jayantanuja Bandyopadhyay (2003), *The Making of India's Foreign Policy*, New Delhi: Allied Publishers, 3rd Edition.
4. *Ibid.*
5. String Of Pearls: In 2004, U.S. defense contractor Booz Allen Hamilton (BAH) coined the term "String of Pearls" in a report (Energy Futures in Asia), submitted to the Office of Net Assessment at the U.S. Department of Defense to describe China's strategy in the waters stretching south of the Eurasian continent.
6. MEA, Govt. of India (2018), "Distinguished Lectures: Making of Indian Foreign Policy", delivered by Amb (Retd.) Debnath Shaw, NEHU, Sept. 13; on line source: https://www.mea.gov.in/distinguished-lectures-detail.htm? 764; retrieved: 20 Nov, 2021.
7. *Ibid.*
8. *Ibid.*
9. *Ibid.*
10. *Ibid.*
11. *Ibid.*
12. *Ibid.*
13. *Ibid.*
14. *Ibid.*
15. *Ibid.*
16. *Ibid.*
17. *Ibid.*
18. *Ibid.*
19. *Ibid.*
20. See Purusottam Bhattacharya (2014), "Quest for Major Power Status: An Overview of the Challenges Facing India's Foreign Policy in the 21st Century", *JAIR: Journal of International Relations*, 1(1), January-June.

21. Aneek Chatterjee (2010), "Does India have a Foreign Policy? A Review of Six Decades of Indian Foreign Policy", *Socialist Perspective*, 37(3-4), December 2009-March 2010.
22. *Ibid.*
23. Harsh V. Pant (2009), "A Rising India's Search for a Foreign Policy", *Orbis*, 53 (2).
24. Aneek Chatterjee (2010), "Does India have a Foreign Policy? A review of Six Decades of Indian Foreign Policy", *Socialist Perspective*, 37(3-4), December 2009-March 2010.
25. *Ibid.*
26. Harsh V. Pant (2009), "A Rising India's Search for a Foreign Policy", *Orbis*, published by Elsevier Limited on behalf of Foreign Policy Research Institute.
27. Vikash Chandra (2017), "Modi Government and Changing Patterns in Indian Foreign Policy", *Jadavpur Journal of International Relations*, 21(2).
28. *Ibid.*
29. *Ibid.*
30. C. Raja Mohan (2015), *Modi's World-Expanding India's Sphere of Influence*, Noida: HarperCollins.
31. Kanti Bajpai (2015), 'Continuity-But With Zeal', *Seminar*, 668(2), April.

3

India's Contribution to the Non-Aligned Movement

Oindrila Roy

Introduction

The Non-Aligned Movement (NAM) was formally established in 1961 to help developing countries preserve their autonomous identity in the face of intense pressure from the United States and the former Soviet Union to absorb the newly independent nations into their respective blocs. The Movement provided the former colonies with a platform for raising their collective voices to hasten decolonization, promote peace, and advocate for economic development. The Movement, which started with 20 odd members, currently stands strong with the support of 120 member states and 27 observers. In the subsequent paragraphs, I describe the historical background, structure, and different stages in the evolution of the Movement. Finally, a critical assessment of the Movement shows that despite the end of the Cold War, the NAM remains relevant for providing developing countries with a collective forum for addressing their unique challenges and negotiating the power politics of the current unipolar international system with clear multipolar tendencies.

Historical Background and Current Structure

The end of World War II ushered in a new era in world politics. On the one hand, the international distribution of power underwent a massive transformation with the emergence of a bi-polar world order, which quickly devolved into the Cold

War between the ideologically divergent superpowers, with the United States championing a liberal economic order and the former Soviet Union committed to the worldwide expansion of Communism. Concurrently, due to the devastation caused during World War II, the economic health of the Western colonial powers was significantly depleted, which, in turn, hastened the process of decolonization. These historical events provide the backdrop for understanding the evolution of the NAM. The NAM brought together former colonies to assert their independence from the bloc politics of the superpowers and to provide a collective platform for amplifying their autonomous posture on global politics.[1]

The major factors contributing to the emergence of the NAM may be broadly categorized into four categories including the bloc politics of the Cold War and the threat of nuclear weapons,[2] the pursuit of economic development in the newly independent states of the global South and their demand for rapid decolonization across the world,[3] and the assertion of nationalism in the former colonies.[4] In the following paragraphs, I provide a more detailed account of the role played by each of the above factors in shaping the evolution of the NAM.

As the Cold War gained momentum, the world was rapidly getting divided into two rival blocs with some states siding with the West, and others with the Communist bloc. The newly independent states of the developing world were reluctant to be a part of either since they perceived such ties as direct threats to their autonomy in international relations.[5] Simultaneously, they could not ignore that any altercation between the superpowers would lead to far-reaching consequences that would not spare the security and stability of their own nations. The nuclear arms race between the United States and the former Soviet Union in the 1950s aggravated this fear,[6] and the former colonies quickly discerned they could not afford to stay passive. Moreover, they realized they could collectively create a more forceful impact as opposed to raising individual voices on the threat of nuclear weapons. Thus, leaders of the NAM representing Yugoslavia, India, Egypt, and Indonesia took upon themselves the role of creating a collective platform for asserting their autonomy in global politics and promoting world peace.

In this context, it is worthwhile to note that non-alignment as conceptualized by the NAM did not imply passive neutrality commensurate with isolationism. To the contrary, the idea of non-alignment propagated by the leaders of the NAM signified a form of positive neutrality, which "was based on moral persuasion for achieving peace and acting as mediators and brokers of peace, when need be."[7] Here, it is equally relevant to acknowledge that member countries of the NAM represented an eclectic group of states, which hardly held identical views on the nature of non-alignment and Cold War politics.[8] For instance, although some countries were less critical of the Communist bloc because it did not have a history of colonizing, others like Pakistan, Sri Lanka (formerly known as Ceylon), and Thailand leaned more toward the West. Regardless of this difference, all parties to the NAM agreed to the need for a non-aligned force to promote peace in a world ravaged by superpower rivalry.

According to Graham,[9] the second major factor triggering the development of the NAM was "the creation of international political leverage to hasten the decolonization process."[10] As experience with colonial exploitation was a common factor binding the diverse member states, active resistance to colonialism played a vital role in the development of the NAM. Hence, decolonizing African societies which continued to exist under the control of European powers long after the end of World War II became a top priority for the movement.[11]

In addition to general policy stances on anti-colonialism and anti-racism, the NAM was outspoken against the apartheid regime in South Africa.[12] Furthermore, the movement also remained deeply committed to furthering the economic development of its member countries. In the 1970s, this emphasis on economic development crystallized into a demand for the New International Economic Order (NIEO), which would structure global economic institutions in favor of developing countries.

Finally, the NAM was used as a vehicle by leaders to forge a sense of national unity among the people of their newly independent states.[13] This sense of unity was channelized toward bolstering the legitimacy for the newly established regimes in their home countries. The movement's commitment to positive neutrality convinced the domestic audience about the sovereign identities of their countries in the international arena and the importance of equal relations across nation-states. Furthermore, the ideals of the movement made it clear that the newly independent countries were not merely politically independent, but free from 'non-indigenous' influences in the conduct of their external affairs.

The seeds of the NAM were sown at the Bandung Conference of 1955. The conference was organized under the initiative of India, Pakistan, Sri Lanka (Ceylon), Indonesia, and Myanmar (Burma), and was attended by 29 Asian and African countries.[14] At this conference, Indian Prime Minister Jawaharlal Nehru, Yugoslavian President Josip Tito, and Egyptian President Gamal Abdel Nasser conceptualized the nature and purpose of the NAM. According to Arnold,[15] there were three immediate reasons for the conference: first, the organizing countries were disgruntled about the West's insufficient interest in engaging them in a dialogue about the former's policies in Asia, especially as witnessed during the Korean War. Second, they were equally concerned about the deteriorating relationship between the United States and China, and were keen on stabilizing the relationship between the two countries, and that between China and themselves. Finally, given the conference's organic stance against colonialism, it was deeply critical of France's involvement in North Africa, and the Netherlands' policies toward New Guinea.

Given this background, the conference—as a precursor to the NAM—revolved around three key themes: the acceleration of economic development in the newly independent countries of the developing world; the stabilization of international conflicts; and the assertion of the Panchsheel principles; or the five tenets on international cooperation and peaceful coexistence. The above themes formed the crux of the ten principles adopted at the conference, which later guided the evolution of the NAM.[16] These foundational ideas, which became popular as the "Ten Principles of Bandung," upheld respect for human rights, the United Nations Charter, "the sovereignty and territorial integrity" of all nation-states, the equal treatment of all races and nation-states, the right to individual and collective self-defense for all states, complete freedom from external interference in the internal matters of nation-states, and the peaceful resolution of all international disputes.[17]

Six years after the historic Bandung Conference, the first NAM conference was held in Belgrade in 1961. 25 countries attended the conference, representing a quarter of the United Nations' membership.[18] Presidents Nasser (Egypt) and Tito (former Yugoslavia) sponsored the Summit with support from Prime Minister Nehru (India) and Presidents Nkrumah (Ghana), Sukarno (Indonesia), and Keita (Mali). Earlier in 1961, the main criteria for non-alignment were defined at a preparatory meeting in Cairo. According to these criteria,[19] a non-aligned country must pursue "an independent policy of coexistence" vis-á-vis other nations, consistently support "national independence," refrain from being a part of multilateral alliances and bi-lateral agreements developed in the context of Cold War rivalry with either of the superpowers, and deny access to bases, if such a demand was made in the context of Cold War politics.

According to LeoGrande,[20] the key themes of the Belgrade Summit included international peace, decolonization, and hastening economic development for the newly independent countries. Although the NAM members considered both superpowers equally guilty for contributing to the ongoing international tensions, they were definitely more condemning of the West for the after-effects of colonialism and insufficient economic progress in the developing world. Both China and the former Soviet Union welcomed the newly founded movement. Due to the limited capabilities of the developing countries, the United States had largely ignored the NAM in the 1950s; however, its position changed in the 1960s as the US became less hostile to the movement.

Almost 60 years after the official founding of the NAM at the Belgrade Summit, the current membership of the movement includes 120 countries and 27 observers.[21] Even after a prolonged period of existence across six decades, the movement still operates without a formal structure;[22] it does not have a charter, a permanent secretariat, or a standing website. The loosely defined organizational structure only refers to three institutions: the office of the Chair, the Joint Coordination Committee (for coordinating with the G77), and the Coordinating Bureau in New York. The position of the Chair along with a temporary secretariat is rotated every three years across the member states. Likewise, summit meetings are held at an interval of three years, and major decisions are reached through consensus, with the interpretation of the latter principle being both capacious and variable.

Stages in the Development of NAM

For analytical purposes, the stages in the development of the NAM may be broadly divided into two main phases: the NAM during the Cold War and that after the Cold War. In the following paragraphs, I will focus on the main themes of the NAM during each decade of the Cold War since its first summit in Belgrade in 1961. Thereafter, the discussion of the post-Cold War era will be divided into the pre-9/11 and the post-9/11 periods. The latter section will emphasize the continuing relevance of the NAM after the end of superpower rivalry.

After Belgrade, the second summit of the NAM was held in Cairo in 1964. Egypt, Ceylon, and the former Yugoslavia organized the summit and 47 member-states attended it.[23] The summit resulted in the creation of the Program for International Peace and Cooperation and the Political and Economic Committee. According to Arnold,[24] the main themes of the conference included nuclear non-proliferation, global economic inequality, a call for defeating imperialism and neocolonialism, China's admission to the United Nations, and garnering support for the newly established Organization of African Unity (OAU). In LeoGrande's[25] opinion, this summit was not substantively distinct to the previous one; however, it witnessed the growing divide between the radical and the moderate members. The division manifested itself in the radicals' (e.g., Egypt and Ghana) demand for treating colonialism and economic development with equal importance, whereas moderates like India and Ceylon preferred to engage with the impacts of the Cold War.

The 1970s turned out to be an eventful decade for the NAM with growing membership and four summit meetings in Lusaka (1970), Algiers (1973), Colombo (1976), and Havana (1979). Also, with the 'thawing of the Cold War' between 1969 and 1979,[26] economic development became its top priority.[27] Hence, the summits primarily focused on the issues of decolonization in Africa, the perils of neo-colonialism, the Israel-Palestine conflict, and economic development.

The Algiers Summit (1973) was critical due to its advocacy for the NIEO, which contributed to serious discussions on the topic at the UN General Assembly. This period also coincided with Fidel Castro's rise to prominence within the movement.[28] The moderate members of the NAM resented Castro's close ties with the former Soviet Union, and his "radical thesis"[29] of embracing the Soviet bloc as a natural ally to the NAM. Regardless of the reservations, the following summit for NAM was held in Havana in 1979. The location of the summit piqued the United States' interest due to its radical implications for the future of the movement; however, the final draft of the summit was anticlimactic, as it did not directly indicate the possibility of a natural alliance between the NAM and the Soviet bloc.[30]

In the last decade of the Cold War, three NAM summits were held in New Delhi (1983), Harare (1986), and Belgrade (1989). By the 1980s, the NAM clearly emerged as a solid platform for voicing the grievances of the developing world against the global North.[31] For example, at the New Delhi Summit, the member states worked on disarmament and economic and technological cooperation. Likewise, in Belgrade, the movement declared commitment to economic progress as its central focus, and drew attention to other related issues like international debt and the status of the global environment. By the end of the 1980s, the membership of the movement included hundreds of states, and as the superpowers made positive strides toward containing their conflict, the NAM sensed the need for reassessing its role and relevance in world affairs.[32]

The end of the Cold War created a new set of challenges for the NAM. While the collapse of the Soviet Union brought an end to the bipolar world order, the NAM was significantly weakened from within due to the disintegration of Yugoslavia, the conflict between members Iraq and Kuwait, Argentina's departure from the movement, and multiple members gravitating toward the United States for both economic and military assistance.[33] Following these changes, the NAM remained sluggish for a while before it could reassess its new role in a unipolar world order.

In the 1990s, the movement continued with its customary summits at an interval of three years in Jakarta (1992), Cartagena (1995), and Durban (1998). The Jakarta Summit, held immediately after the end of the Cold War, called for a serious reassessment of the Movement's priorities, especially in light of the changing geopolitical realities, and the growing inequalities between the global North and South. Therefore, the major themes of the Cartagena Summit revolved around economic globalization, trade relations including unfair trade restrictions imposed by the United States, combatting terrorism, and support for human rights and democracy. By the time of the Durban Summit, due to its expansive membership, operating through broad agreements over general policies instead of specific decisions became an accepted reality for the NAM.

The international political climate underwent a dramatic change after the terrorist attacks of September 11. The unilateral foreign policy decisions of the Bush administration coupled with the War on Terror and the subsequent regime-changing efforts in three member countries created new challenges as well as opportunities for the NAM to reassert its influence in world politics.[34] In the first decade of the 21st century, NAM summits were held in Kuala Lumpur (2003), Havana (2006), and Egypt (2009). The main issues addressed in these summits include nuclear disarmament and international security,[35] reforming the UN, especially the composition of the Security Council, and closer coordination with the G7.[36] The last three NAM summits were held in Tehran (2012), Margarita (2016), and Baku (2019). In these summits, similar issues including dangers of unilateral moves from the West, disarmament, economic marginalization of developing countries due to globalization, UN reform, and unfair practices in the progress of information and technology in the global South were discussed.[37]

Assessment of the Movement and the Way Forward

Any discussion of the NAM is incomplete without an assessment of its accomplishments over the last sixty years. From the time of its inception, the main goals of the movement focused on creating an independent platform for developing countries to voice their positions without getting dragged into superpower rivalry, promoting international peace, hastening decolonization and the end of apartheid, and pursuing economic development for the global South. With the end of colonization, apartheid, and the bloc politics of the Cold War era, the main challenges before the NAM have largely dwelled on issues of economic development, disarmament, and the reform of the UN system—especially in the membership structure of the Security Council—to promote an equitable representation of developing countries in the highest multilateral forum for global governance. In the subsequent paragraphs, I focus on a critical assessment of the NAM's achievement in the aforementioned areas and its contemporary relevance.

Maintaining international peace and security through nuclear disarmament has always been a priority for the NAM. However, its achievements in this issue area have drawn significant criticism, particularly due to the contradictions between the NAM's positions and the national interests of its member states. For example, while commenting on the Movement's performance between 1961 and 1973, Luthi[38] noted,

> Even some of the main leaders of the NAM could not resist the allure of nuclear weapons and their promise to confer upon the aspiring nuclear state increased international (or, at least, regional) political influence. With India's refusal to sign the Non-Proliferation Treaty in 1968, the Non-Aligned Movement had surrendered its unity in opposing nuclear armament.

Likewise, contradictions within the movement became apparent in 2005 with the change in the United States' nuclear trade policy with India, which was aggravated further when the

United Kingdom, the United States, Russia, and France lobbied to relax nuclear trade policies for India at the Nuclear Suppliers Group (NSG).[39] Although this development was welcomed by some NAM members including Brazil and South Africa, it was condemned by Iran and other Arab countries, which viewed this as a precursor to similar allowances for Israel.

In addition to disarmament, fostering economic development for the global South has been one of the original goals of the NAM. The Movement's signature campaign for the NIEO in the 1970s sought to radically change the structure of international trade by creating policies in favor of developing nations.[40] The demand for NIEO gained significant attention at the UN General Assembly and led to the adoption of the Declaration Programme of Action on the Establishment of the New International Economic Order. Despite such developments, the plan for establishing NIEO failed to gain momentum[41] and was quickly replaced by Structural Adjustment Programs (SAPs) entrenched in neo-liberal policy prescriptions.[42] Similarly, NAM's efforts to reform the UN and the membership structure of the Security Council—both permanent and nonpermanent—met with little success.[43]

The NAM's inability to successfully meet many of its goals has invited a plethora of criticisms, especially from commentators in the West. Focusing on the Movement's trajectory in the 1960s and 70s, Luthi[44] discounted the Movement as too eclectic for maturing into a robust and unified force in global affairs. Furthermore, he believed internal contradictions within the members of the Movement were amplified by external developments like the Arab-Israeli conflict, which made the NAM "as much a participant in the Cold War in the period from 1961 to 1973 as it was a victim."[45]

While discussing the role of the NAM in the post-Cold War era, many have chastised it as redundant[46] in the absence of bipolar rivalry. Others[47] have critiqued the movement for its double standards (e.g. condemning Israel for human rights violations, while remaining silent about the heinous track record of the Sudanese Government in Darfur) and the inability to realize that the success of multilateral interventions require resilient political structures within states, which is non-existent in most developing countries representing the NAM.

Notwithstanding such harsh criticisms, there are several compelling reasons for developing countries to sustain the movement while adapting it to the changing needs of the current era. Although the original threat of Cold War bloc politics is no longer relevant, developing countries continue to face common challenges like poverty, neocolonialism, environmental decay, civil wars, and terrorism.[48] The members of the Movement can use the NAM as a collective platform for addressing their unique challenges by countering Western dominance at multilateral forums where laws on global governance are shaped.[49] Moreover, with the decline in the United States' influence, and the rise of China and Russia to prominence, the current international system has clearly developed multipolar tendencies; this trend has the potential to revive a new pattern of bloc politics, and resurrect the need for creating an independent arena for articulating the position of the global South.[50]

Endnotes

1. Lorenz M. Luthi (2016), "The Non-aligned Movement and the Cold War, 1961-73", *Journal of Cold War Studies*, 18(4).
2. *Ibid.*
3. S.I. Keethaponcalan (2016), "Reshaping the Non-Aligned Movement: Challenges and Vision", *Journal of the Global South*, 3(4).
4. Kristin S. Tassin (2006), "'Lift Up Your Head My Brother': Nationalism and the Genesis of the Non-Aligned Movement," *Third World Quarterly*, 23(1).
5. Guy Arnold (2006), *Historical Dictionary of the Non-Aligned Movement and Third World*, Maryland. The Scarecrow Press, Inc., pp. 208-12.
6. Lorenz M. Luthi (2016), *op. cit.*
7. William M. LeoGrande (1980), "Evolution of the Nonaligned Movement," *Problems of Communism*, 29(1).
8. Guy Arnold (2006), *op. cit.*
9. John A. Graham (1980), *The Non-Aligned Movement after the Havana Summit*, New York, Trustees of Columbia, University in the City of New York, pp. 155-60.

10. *Ibid.*, p. 153.
11. S.I. Keethaponcalan (2016), *op. cit.*
12. *Ibid.*
13. Kristin S. Tassin (2006), "'Lift Up Your Head My Brother': Nationalism and the Genesis of the Non-Aligned Movement," *Third World Quarterly*, 23(1).
14. Guy Arnold (2006), *op. cit.*
15. *Ibid.*
16. Ministry of External Affairs (MEA), Govt. of India (2012), "History and Evolution of Non-Aligned Movement", New Delhi: 22 August; on line source: https://mea.gov.in/in-focus-article.htm?20349/History+and+Evolution+of+NonAligned+Movement, Accessed on July 25, 2020.
17. William Potter and Gaukhar Mukhatzhanova (2012), *Nuclear Politics and the Non-Aligned Movement: Principles vs Pragmatism*, London, The International Institute of Strategic Studies, pp. 18-19.
18. Guy Arnold (2006), *op. cit.*
19. *Ibid.*, pp. 213-14.
20. LeoGrande (1980), *op. cit.*
21. Azarbaijani Chairmanship to the Non-Aligned Movement 2019-2022 (n.d.); on line source: https://www.namazerbaijan.org/pdf/Members-and-observers.pdf. Accessed on July 25, 2020.
22. William Potter and Gaukhar Mukhatzhanova (2012), *op. cit.*
23. Guy Arnold (2006), *op. cit.*
24. *Ibid.*
25. LeoGrande (1980), *op. cit.*
26. The US Department of State (n.d.), "Détente and Arms Control, 1969-1979"; on line source: https://history.state.gov/milestones/1969-1976/detente. Accessed on July 27, 2020.
27. LeoGrande (1980), *op. cit.*
28. *Ibid.*
29. Guy Arnold (2006), *op. cit.*
30. LeoGrande (1980), *op. cit.*
31. Guy Arnold (2006), *op. cit.*
32. *Ibid.*
33. William Potter and Gaukhar Mukhatzhanova (2012), *op. cit.*
34. *Ibid.*

35. The Nuclear Threat Initiative (2018), "Non-Aligned Movement (NAM)", Washington D.C.: May 31; On line source. Accessed on July 27, 2020.
36. Guy Arnold (2006), *op. cit.*
37. Azarbaijani Chairmanship to the Non-Aligned Movement 2019-2022 (n.d.), "Documents"; on line source: https://www.namazerbaijan.org/documents. Accessed on July 25, 2020.
38. Lorenz M. Luthi (2016), "The Non-aligned Movement and the Cold War, 1961-73", *Journal of Cold War Studies*, 18(4), p. 127.
39. William Potter and Gaukhar Mukhatzhanova (2012), *op. cit.*
40. H.W. Singer (1978), "The New International Economic Order: An Overview", *The Journal of Modern African Studies*, 16(4), December.
41. Guy Arnold (2006), *op. cit.*
42. Dani Rodrik (2008), *One Economics, Many Recipes: Globalization, Institutions, and Economic Growth*, Princeton, NJ: Princeton University Press.
43. Hennie Strydom (2007), "The Non-Aligned Movement and the Reform of International Relations", *Max Plank Year Book of United Nations Law*, 11(1).
44. Lorenz M. Luthi (2016), *op. cit.*
45. *Ibid.*, p. 147.
46. Antoinette Handley (1998), *Non-Aligned against What? South Africa and the Future of the Non-Aligned Movement.* Johannesburg: The South African Institute of International Affairs
47. Hennie Strydom (2007), *op. cit.*
48. S.I. Keethaponcalan (2016), *op. cit.*
49. Daniel W. Drezner (2007), "The New World Order", *Foreign Affairs*, 86(2).
50. S.I. Keethaponcalan (2016), *op. cit.*

4

India's Engagements in South and South East Asia

Siuli Mukherjee

The post-Cold War scenario had opened up a new horizon for the countries of the world. India, a major player in South Asia had to redefine her national interest in the changed milieu and also reassess her strength in negotiating with other powers. There were contradictions and divergence of opinions which had cast their shadows over the regional milieu. But India engaged herself in searching for a greater atmosphere of peace and prosperity of the region. India took the advantage of the changed ecological environment. She also revised her old linkages with the South East Asian region. Against this backdrop, this chapter is segmented into four sections. The first section will focus on the evolution of the Regional Organization in South Asia named SAARC (South Asian Association for Regional Cooperation) and find its future prospects. The second part will highlight the South Asian Free Trade Area or SAFTA. The third section deals with an analysis of the different challenges faced by South Asia as a region. The last part will uphold India's engagement in South East Asia through her policies of 'Look East' and 'Act East'.

I. SAARC—EVOLUTION AND FUTURE PROSPECT

The formation of regional organizations across the world reflects the identical aspirations of the nation-states in geographical proximity to search for greater prospects and seek solutions of their common challenges. The world had already experienced the birth and growth of regional organizations like Organization of American States, European Union, Caribbean Community, ASEAN and others. In South Asia, the regional organization called SAARC was created on December 8, 1985, with an ambition to promote collective self-reliance, to upgrade the welfare of the people of South Asia, to accelerate economic growth etc. The initiative was taken by the President of Bangladesh, Ziaur Rahman who expressed his idea of forming a regional organization in South Asia in the Commonwealth and Non-Aligned Summit held in Lusaka and Havana respectively in the year 1979. The final proposal for establishing a regional organization in South Asia was placed by him on May 2, 1980. The aim of the organization was to accelerate the process of economic and social development of the member-states of that organization which would have a spill over effect on the South Asia as a region. The first summit meeting of SAARC was held in Dhaka from December 7-8, 1985. Since its inception SAARC comprised of seven South Asian countries, namely India, Bangladesh, Bhutan, Maldives, Nepal, Pakistan, and Sri Lanka. Afghanistan joined SAARC as the eighth member in 2007. The Secretariat of SAARC is based in Kathmandu, Nepal. It was decided that SAARC would work with certain clear objectives and adhere to certain principles. This commitment was laid in the SAARC Charter. The objectives, principles, and general provisions, as mentioned in the SAARC Charter, are as follows:

(a) to promote the welfare of the people of South Asia and to improve their quality of life;

(b) to accelerate economic growth, social progress, and cultural development in the region and to provide all individuals the opportunity to live in dignity and to realise their full potentials;

(c) to promote and strengthen collective self-reliance among the countries of South Asia;

(d) to contribute to mutual trust, understanding and appreciation of one another's problems;

(e) to promote active collaboration and mutual assistance in the economic, social, cultural, technical, and scientific fields;

(f) to strengthen cooperation with other developing countries;

(g) to strengthen cooperation among themselves in international forums on matters of common interests; and

(h) to cooperate with international and regional organisations with similar aims and purposes.[1]

However, it was decided that in achieving the aforesaid objectives, the member countries of SAARC should respect the principles of sovereign equality, territorial integrity, political independence, non-interference in the internal affairs of other states. The bilateral and contentious issues should be excluded from its deliberation. The decisions at all levels in SAARC should be taken on the basis of unanimity. The following table highlights the SAARC Summits held so far. A brief insight on the significant steps taken in these Summit would help us in understanding the growth and maturity of this regional organization.

Table 4.1: SAARC Summits (1985-2016)

SAARC SUMMITS	YEAR	HOST COUNTRY
First SAARC Summit	Dec. 7-8, 1985	Bangladesh
Second SAARC Summit	Nov. 17-18, 1986	India
Third SAARC Summit	Nov. 2-4, 1987	Nepal
Fourth SAARC Summit	Dec. 29-31, 1988	Pakistan
Fifth SAARC Summit	Nov. 21-23, 1990	Maldives
Sixth SAARC Summit	Dec. 21, 1991	Sri Lanka
Seventh SAARC Summit	April 10-11, 1993	Bangladesh
Eighth SAARC Summit	May 2-4, 1995	India
Nineth SAARC Summit	May 12-14, 1997	Maldives
Tenth SAARC Summit	July 29-31, 1998	Sri Lanka
Eleventh SAARC Summit	Jan. 4-6, 2002	Nepal
Twelfth SAARC Summit	Jan. 4-6, 2004	Pakistan

SAARC SUMMITS	YEAR	HOST COUNTRY
Thirteenth SAARC Summit	Nov. 12-13, 2005	Bangladesh
Fourteenth SAARC Summit	April 3-4, 2007	India
Fifteenth SAARC Summit	Aug. 1-3, 2008	Sri Lanka
Sixteenth SAARC Summit	April 28-29, 2010	Bhutan
Seventeenth SAARC Summit	Nov. 10-11, 2011	Maldives
Eighteenth SAARC Summit	Nov. 26-27, 2014	Nepal
Nineteenth SAARC Summit	Nov. 15-16, 2016	Pakistan

In the respective Summits, SAARC members have pledged to take positive steps for the development of the region. In the First SAARC Summit held in Dhaka, Bangladesh in 1985, the Heads of the State or Government pledged to make an optimum utilization of the natural and human resources available in their country so that it can bring an overall development of the region. The goal was to bring pace in the process of economic and social development for improving the lives of the people. The Heads of the State emphasised on promoting people-to-people contact for greater cohesiveness and solidarity. Ensuring peace and security were the twin objectives of the establishment of regional organization called SAARC.

The Heads of the State or Government agreed in the Second SAARC Summit held in Bangalore, India in 1986 in joining hands for the prevention and elimination of terrorism from South Asia. For attaining this objective, SAARC highlighted the importance of the Resolution 2625 passed by United Nations. This resolution would refrain the member states from organizing, instigating, assisting or participating in acts of civil strife or terrorist acts in another State. The Heads of the State affirmed to this principle and vowed to cooperate with each other for eliminating the menace of terrorism and drug trafficking from South Asia. Moreover, the Summit emphasised on the issue of development of women along with other items in the agenda.

The Third SAARC Summit was hosted at Kathmandu, Nepal in 1987 in which the Heads of the State or Government expressed their deep concern on the slowing of world economy which had an adverse impact on South Asia. The condition of the small and landlocked developing countries of South Asia had also turned dismal. The Summit observed that the developing countries need to participate in the international trading and economic system so that they can reconcile themselves with the macro economy of the world. The North-South Dialogue needs to be initiated so that the voices and demands of the Southern countries may be formally placed. The Member countries expressed their satisfaction on the launching of SAARC Audio Visual Exchange programme. They also hoped that the SAARC Documentation Centre and the SAARC Youth Volunteer Programme would be implemented at the earliest.

The Fourth SAARC Summit was held in Islamabad, Pakistan in December 1988. The Heads of State or Government focussed on certain key issues in the Islamabad Declaration. In order to improve the quality of life of the people of the region a regional plan called "SAARC 2000" was framed to provide for basic needs such as shelter, education, and literacy to over one billion population of the region. The member-states decided to identify these areas in their national plans. The Heads of the State or Government expressed their satisfaction over the development of South Asian Food Security Reserve. An expert group was appointed to conduct a study on the greenhouse effect and its impact on the region. The group also studied natural disaster and the protection of environment. The Islamabad Declaration called for a war against narcotics and ratified the SAARC Convention on Suppression of Terrorism. The leaders emphasized on promoting people to people contact and special SAARC travel document to freely visit any country under SAARC without any visa restriction. The Members of SAARC also declared to reorient their foreign policies in order to induce positive bilateralism.

The Fifth SAARC Summit held at Male, Maldives in 1990 emphasised on the development of women and thus reiterated the agenda of the Second SAARC Summit. The Member States gave a collective call to observe 1990 as the "SAARC Year of the Girl Child" and declared the years 1991-2000 AD to be observed as the "SAARC Decade of the Girl Child". The Head of the State or Government expressed their serious concern over the increase of international arms trade and terrorist activities but conveyed their satisfaction on the initiative taken by SAARC in combating drug trafficking and drug abuse. They appealed to the International Community to mobilize finances and to assist with new technologies in coping with the challenge of climatic changes and rising sea-levels. The Summit also observed the year 1992 as the "SAARC Year of Environment".

The Sixth SAARC Summit held in Colombo, Sri Lanka in 1991 also encouraged the member-states to discuss on the priorities of their respective national economies. The Heads of the State or Government concluded that there was a need to secure less restriction on trade and increase more opportunities for trade of products. They felt that multilateral financial institutions might help in debt relief and grant concessions while dealing with the developing and underdeveloped countries of South Asia. At the same time, encouragement should be made for technological and resource transfer. The Sixth Summit expressed satisfaction on the increased people to people contact among the countries of South Asia. They welcomed greater consultation and synergic relations between business organisations, professional bodies, scholars, academicians, cultural councils, and the media in South Asia. The Summit recommended Standing Committees to formulate guidelines for making this instrumental.

In the Seventh SAARC Summit held in Dhaka in 1993, the Heads of the State or Government emphasised on the role of youths in the development of regional organisation. The youth of South Asia were passing through multifaceted problems which needed attention at the policy-making level. In this context, Maldives offered to host a Ministerial Conference on Youth in South Asia in the year 1994. It was decided to designate the year 1994 as the "SAARC Year of the Youth". The Heads of the State or Government emphasized that for research cooperation the call of the hour was through networking arrangements in the field of bio-technology, genetic engineering and energy modelling techniques. The Heads of the State or Government expressed their appreciation for the responsibility taken by India to host the First South Asian Festival of SAARC countries in the year 1992. The festival would promote people-to-people contact in South Asia through celebration of their rich heritage and culture.

In the Eighth SAARC Summit held in New Delhi, India in 1995, the Heads of the State or Government expressed their satisfaction on the completion and achievements of the First Decade of SAARC, although a lot was still left to be attained. The Summit year 1995 to be observed as the "SAARC Year of Poverty Eradication". The Summit decided to observe the year 1996 as the "SAARC Year of Literacy" as illiteracy was the root cause of poverty, backwardness, and social injustice. The Eighth Summit expressed its concern over the upsurge of terrorism in South Asia. The Summit aimed at creating a South Asian Development Fund for the infrastructural development of the region. The leaders also welcomed the establishment of the SAARC Documentation Centre (SDC) and the SAARC Meteorological Research Centre (SMRC) in New Delhi and Dhaka respectively.

In the Ninth SAARC Summit held in Male in 1997, the Heads of the State or Government expressed their satisfactions over the implementation of the Agreement on SAARC Preferential Trading Arrangement (SAPTA) on December 7, 1995. The Summit even targeted to achieve a free trade area by the year 2001 so that the developing and underdeveloped countries gain from the economic discourse equitably. The Summit focused on the status of children in South Asia and declared the launching of SAARC Decade of Rights of Child from the year 2001 to 2010. A Convention on Regional Arrangement on the Promotion of Child Welfare in South Asia was to be enacted. The Heads of the State or Government emphasized an urgent need to legislate for implementing SAARC Regional Conventions on Suppression of Terrorism and on Narcotic Drugs and Psychotropic Substances. The Heads of the State or Government reiterated the UN Declaration on Measures to Eliminate International Terrorism enacted in the year 1996 and appealed the member-states to implement that in their respective countries. They welcomed the establishment of the SAARC Terrorist Offences Monitoring Desk (STOMD) and the SAARC Drug Offences Monitoring Desk

(SDOMD) in Colombo to which they would provide relevant information on a regular interval. In the Tenth SAARC Summit held in Colombo in 1998, the Heads of the State or Government showed their concerns for the developing as well as the less developing countries of South Asia regarding their independence to the policies of new multilateral investment agreement. The need for greater connectivity between the South Asian countries was also sought after. It was decided that professional bodies, artists, creative personalities, media, pilgrims and others should be encouraged to travel across the borders of South Asia for greater interactions between countries. The development of human resources in South Asia was targeted this time.

In the Eleventh SAARC Summit held in Kathmandu in 2002, the Heads of the State or Government welcomed the signing of the SAARC Convention on Preventing and Combating the Trafficking in Women and Children for Prostitution. The member-states condemned the trafficking in women and children for commercial sexual exploitation and considered such trafficking as a criminal offence of serious nature. They also welcomed the signing of the SAARC Convention on Regional Arrangements for the Promotion of Child Welfare in South Asia. It was decided in the meeting that SAARC Awards would be given to individuals and organizations that would make positive and outstanding contributions in the field of peace, development, and regional cooperation. In the Twelfth Summit held in Islamabad in 2004, the Heads of the State or Government expressed their satisfaction on the signing of the Framework Agreement on SAFTA. This was a positive step for broadening of economic cooperation. The members expected that the Free Trade Area in South Asia should benefit both developing and least developed countries of the region. Apart from trade and commerce, this economic intercourse would promote South Asia as a tourism destination. The twenty years of the establishment of SAARC was made commemorative by designating the year 2005 as "South Asia Tourism Year". All the member-states of SAARC were to be connected by air-link and each country should take the responsibility for organizing special events. An initiative would be taken for encouraging women to turn up as entrepreneurs and contribute to the socio-economic development of the region. The SAARC Autonomous Advocacy Group of Prominent Women Personalities (SAWAG) was decided to be formed.

In the Thirteenth SAARC Summit held in Dhaka, in 2005, the Heads of the State or Government affirmed their faith in the people of South Asia as the real source of power and thus hoped to make the regional organization more responsive as well as effective. The Summit hoped for the development of a vibrant civil society that would take the regional organization in a forward direction. The member-states should encourage people-to-people contact and make them proud of their South Asian solidarity. The Heads of the State expressed their concern over issues like poverty, illiteracy, malnourishment, under-development and declared the decade of 2006-15 as the SAARC Decade of Poverty Alleviation. It was expected that SAFTA, established in January 1, 2006, would bring economic development in the region. Moreover, the Heads of the State or Government welcomed the Joint Statement of the First SAARC Energy Ministers meeting held at Islamabad in the year 2005 for establishing the SAARC Energy Centre in Islamabad. The development of hydel power, renewable as well as alternative energy resources and conservation of energy in the region were made a priority. A South Asian Energy Dialogue process was to be initiated so that officials, experts, academics, environmentalists, and NGOs could exchange views for cooperation in energy sector.

In the Fourteenth SAARC Summit held in New Delhi in 2007, Islamic Republic of Afghanistan joined SAARC as a new member-state. All the Heads of the State or Government welcomed the new member and accorded it a respectable position in the SAARC fraternity. The Summit focussed on improving connectivity which is the lifeline for greater integration in South Asia. Intra- and inter-regional connectivity between countries would help to promote economic development and greater people-to-people contact. The Summit decided for a SAARC Car Rally as a symbol of connectivity between SAARC Nations. The

Heads of the State or Government also showed their concern for the increasing energy needs of the SAARC countries.

In the Fifteenth SAARC Summit held in Colombo in 2008, the Heads of the State or Government again emphasised on the energy need of the countries of South Asia. The escalation of oil prices had a great economic impact on the countries. So the conventional as well as renewable alternative energy resources which include indigenous hydro power, solar, wind and bio-energy were needed to be replenished. The Heads of the State or Government also emphasised on an effective regional telecommunication for promoting greater connectivity not only in the region but with other parts of the world. The people centric partnership in South Asia was also encouraged for greater peace and prosperity.

The Sixteenth Summit of SAARC held in Thimphu, Bhutan in 2010, marked the Silver Jubilee of SAARC in which the Heads of the State or Government developed a 'Vision Statement' projecting the future of the organization. They agreed to create a 'South Asian Forum' for encouraging debate and the exchange of ideas. The leaders emphasised on the role of public diplomacy for attaining this end. They endorsed the year 2010-20 as the "Decade of Intra-regional Connectivity in SAARC." They realized that the private sectors, media personnel, think-tanks, civil society, youths, and students had important roles to play in it. The Summit finalized two agreements on motor vehicles and railways. The leaders noted the proposal from India for preparing a roadmap for developing a SAARC Market for Electricity (SAME) on a regional basis. Moreover, the Summit emphasised on the conservation of aquatic ecosystem and trans-boundary bio-diversity zones. The automated network of weather stations, water management, transfer of eco-friendly ecology, regular, and systematic sharing of scientific data were identified as the goal of SAARC members.

The Seventeenth SAARC Summit held in Male in 2011 condemned the threat of terrorism in all its forms, organized transnational crimes like illegal trafficking in narcotic drugs and psychotropic substances, trafficking in persons as well as small arms and increased incidents of maritime piracy in the region. The Summit pledged to give a tough fight against these evils in South Asia. The Summit also welcomed moves like the signing of the SAARC Agreement on Rapid Response to Natural Disasters, the SAARC Seed Bank Agreement, the SAARC Agreement on Multilateral Arrangement on Recognition of Conformity Assessment, and the SAARC Agreement on Implementation of Regional Standards. The rights of women were declared to be inalienable and integral. The gender-based violence and discriminatory practices against the women were considered as the violation of human rights. The role of Media was also highlighted in the Seventeenth SAARC Summit. In the Eighteenth Summit of SAARC held in Kathmandu in 2014, the Heads of the State or Government expressed their strong determination to collaborate in the field of trade, investment, finance, energy, security, infrastructure, connectivity, and culture in South Asia. These goals were aimed to be attained in a result-oriented and time-bound manner. The leaders renewed their commitment to achieve South Asian Economic Union (SAEU) in a phased and planned manner by creating a Free Trade Area, a Customs Union, a Common Market, and a Common Economic and Monetary Union. The Heads of the State or Government expressed their satisfaction over the significant progress made in preparing the roadmap for the SAARC Motor Vehicles Agreement and SAARC Regional Railways. A greater network of building and upgrading roads, railways, waterways infrastructures, energy grids, communication and air links were necessary for forging greater connectivity. The Summit advocated the effective implementation of SAARC Agreement on Rapid Response to Natural Disasters, SAARC Convention on Cooperation on Environment and Climate Change. In addition to these, the Summit declared the year 2016 as the SAARC Year of Cultural Heritage and agreed to develop a cultural trail linking major Buddhist historical sites in the region. This would make South Asia as a tourist destination and invite more tourists across the world. The leaders further agreed to facilitate access of persons visiting prominent and holy sites of Islam, Hinduism, Christianity and all other major religions in South Asia. The Summit also emphasized on the skillful use of the talents of youths in countries of South Asia and enacts national policies regarding that. The leaders welcomed the declaration of the United Nations General Assembly to commemorate July 15 as the World Youth Skills Day. It is important to mention that, out of the 18 Summits that SAARC had...organised, only five were held on previously announced dates and venues, Five other summits could only be convened after reshuffling their venues and eight after changing their scheduled or expected dates. The Summits were deferred for different time periods, ranging from six weeks to over two years, on one pretext or another.[2]

The Nineteenth SAARC Summit was supposed to be held at Pakistan from November 15 to 16, 2016. However, because of the Uri Terror Attack that took place in India in 2016, India, Afghanistan, Bhutan, Bangladesh, Sri Lanka and Maldives did not attend SAARC Summit. Pakistan declared to postpone the Summit Meet but new dates were never announced. However, Prime Minister of Pakistan Nawaz Sharif in his address to the 19th SAARC Summit held in Pakistan's capital city on Nov. 15 -16, said that the objective of this summit was to address the security issues in South Asia.

The formation of the South Asian Association for Regional Cooperation (SAARC) in December 1985 was definitely a milestone achieved in the region of South Asia. However, the slow progress and mediocre achievements in the past thirty-five years have often raised questions about the vitality and achievements of the organisation. SAARC is a product of a unique interplay of mutually incompatible sources of security orientation, development thrust, and external inducements.[3] SAARC as a regional body had experienced diverse problems like migration, terrorism, ethnic-conflict, inter-state water dispute, border disputes, security issues, and others. There had been a lack of trust among the member states which delayed the implementation of decisions. The compulsory exclusion of contentious issues in bilateral relation acts as an impediment to achieve cooperation at the multilateral level. The Summits had been postponed several times on one pretext or other. Moreover, the big size of India and the geo-political position of India in the region have created some kind of insecurity in the minds of other countries of South Asia. They feel India's dominance would prevail in every SAARC decision and that all other smaller member states would have to make compromise on taking unbiased and firm decisions on any issue raised. The smaller countries of South Asia often seek the assistance of the major powers of the world instead of depending on the regional organization for redressing their problems. Moreover, lack of political will at the leadership level, unnecessary formalities, red-tapism and bureaucratic hurdles at the secretariat level have also constrained SAARC to prosper. It has made satisfactory progress in the field of economic growth and peace in South Asia but it is often argued that SAARC has worked as a half-hearted organization. It has not served to the best of its capability. The minimal endowments of a regional organization supposed to tackle such issues, need to involve politics in the form of discussion, bargaining, and agreement procedures. In other words, this implies dissent, in some form or another, and absence of structured channels to overcome it and yield common policies.[4]

Although the organization has been unable to achieve its objects in many fields, there are areas of prospects for SAARC. Firstly, it is true that SAARC had been unable to solve all the problems confronted by the nations of South Asia. SAARC is merely a talking shop for some scholars, providing nothing more than a lip service to the various issues of peace and development in the region. While to some others, SAARC may not be a panacea to the region's problems, but its existence has certainly provided an opportunity for the policy makers, administrators, and experts to meet and hold informal dialogues on important regional issues.[5] The holding of Summits however gives a space to its members to bring their problems to the common table. The journey of SAARC has completed thirty-five years which speaks of its vitality. It provides a platform to the policy makers, administrators, and experts to meet at intervals and hold informal dialogues on important bilateral and regional issues. The period when bilateral relations improved, has coincided with the rise of new issues of concern while some of the old concerns have assumed more lethal character.

Thus, while concerns, which dominated in the past are being addressed, effective mechanisms have yet to be devised to address the new issues.[6] The Heads of the State identify the area of cooperation and commit themselves for the attainment of the same. There are number of Regional Centres, Working Groups, Specialized Agencies under SAARC which discuss the feasibility and modalities of cooperation among the member-states.

Secondly, South Asia, as a region is characterized by poverty and underdevelopment. All the Summits of SAARC held so far had vowed to strive for economic growth and prosperity of the nations at large. SAARC as a regional organization needed to ensure economic cooperation among members in full swing and make the best use of the available opportunities. The signing of SAPTA (South Asian Preferential Trade Agreement) and later SAFTA (South Asian Free Trade Area) were definitely two definite moves towards economic integration in the region but not much has been achieved in intra-regional trade. SAARC may strive for greater cooperation in the field of trade, investment, finance, and infrastructural development in a result-oriented and time-bound manner. The South Asia Development Fund (SADF) has been created to serve as an umbrella financial institution for all SAARC projects and programme and comprises three windows—the social window, infrastructure window, and economic window.[7]

Thirdly, SAARC in its different Summits have time and again given high priority to the area of Energy Cooperation. The countries of South Asia are endowed with different forms of energy resources. For instance, countries like Bangladesh, India, and Pakistan are the hub of natural gas and coal resources in the region. Bhutan and Nepal, on the other hand, have great hydropower potential in generating electricity. In 2000, a Technical Committee on Energy Sector was created with the recommendation of SAARC. As per the recommendation of the Dhaka Declaration in 2004, SAARC has established its own energy centre (SEC) in Islamabad in the year 2006 along with other institutional mechanisms for energy cooperation like South Asia Sub-regional Economic Cooperation (SASEC) and Bangladesh-India-Myanmar-Sri Lanka-Thailand-Economic

Co-operation (BIMSTEC). However, the regional energy trade arrangement and energy produced are not sufficient to meet the commercial demand of the countries of South Asia. Consequently, South Asia has to depend heavily on imports from Central and West Asia. The meeting of Energy Ministers held in Colombo in the year 2009 resulted in the formation of expert groups for focussing on various sectors of energy like oil and gas, electricity, renewable energy, technology, and knowledge sharing. In this area, SAARC has a constructive role to play. In the process of transfer and procurement of energy through a more dynamic intra- and inter-regional trade, a greater benefit can be accrued by all countries of South Asia. The demand of energy supply in the regional market would bring a greater cooperation among the member-states. SAARC as a regional organization can play an instrumental role in developing energy trade infrastructure with a legal as well as regulatory framework to facilitate it. The energy security of the region can be enhanced through diversifying the sources and forms of energy resources. In the Eighteenth SAARC Summit held in November 26-27, 2014, the SAARC Framework Agreement on Energy Cooperation (Electricity) was signed. This was a welcome step to create a regional power market for meeting the energy need of the region.

Fourthly, in the task of improving connectivity and infrastructural development SAARC has much to offer. In the Fourteenth Summit held in New Delhi in April 2007, the Heads of the State emphasised on the importance of connectivity as an urgent necessity. The development of physical infrastructure might result in increase of intra-regional trade. The increasing regional investment would promote people-to-people contact. The Asian Development Bank, World Bank also funded various projects to strengthen intra SAARC linkages. The SAARC visa exemption scheme was launched in 1992 after the Fourth Summit held at Islamabad in December 1988. This emphasised the importance of having people-to-people contact among the member countries and decided that certain categories of people should be entitled to a special travel document that would exempt them from visas within the region. SAARC designated the year 2010-20 as the 'Decade for Intra-regional Connectivity in South Asia'. However, for the implementation of transit trade and success of SAFTA, agreements relating motor vehicles, railways and inland water transport, and shipping are yet to be translated into reality. This would give SAARC a greater prospect.

Fifthly, terrorism is a menace in the world and South Asia is no exception to this. SAARC has identified this menace and attached high importance to this in almost all the Summits held so far. The prevention and suppression of terrorism and terrorist acts have been given high priority. The members of SAARC have become a signatory to the SAARC Regional Convention on Suppression of Terrorism in 1987. Different conventions and directives had also been passed from time to time for combating cybercrimes, drug and human trafficking, and other transnational crimes. However, despite adopting and formulating a number of strategies at both bilateral as well as multilateral levels, SAARC has not been able to evolve a common and comprehensive approach to counterterrorism in South Asia. For instance, Pakistan has been the hotbed in nurturing terrorist groups like Lashkar-e-Taiba (LeT), Hizbul Mujahideen, Jaish-e-Mohammad and exporting it to neighbouring countries like India for destabilizing her from within. The series of terrorist attacks in India bears the testimony to the fact. The tension between two great powers of South Asia, India and Pakistan have caused great damage to SAARC, often threatening its existence. The Nineteenth SAARC Summit was boycotted by India on the pretext of this reason. Afghanistan, the new member to SAARC has also been an extended corridor of Pakistan which gives the space to the militants and terrorist to find refuge. Bangladesh had also been held responsible for the growth of terrorist organizations like Harkat-ul-Jihad-al-Islami (HUJI-B) and Jama'atul-Mujahideen Bangladesh (JMB) which throw significant challenges to the North Eastern region of India. The definition of 'terrorism' has been drastically changed after the September 11, 2001 attack. SAARC has to play a more decisive role in arresting terrorism in South Asia and take concrete actions to combat it. All the countries of South Asia had been affected with terrorism and hence for securing the country's own well-being the SAARC members should coordinate their actions, improve monitoring, share intelligence information and create a common database. SAARC should prepare a security mechanism for arresting terrorism. They should learn from the experience of other organizations like Organization for Security and Cooperation in Europe (OSCE) and Association of Southeast Asian Nations (ASEAN) and mitigate terrorist challenges. SAARC needs to reflect a zero tolerance policy towards terrorism, avoid blame game among the member countries for harbouring terrorism. SAARC should rather prepare a multi-prolonged strategy for defeating the same.

Sixthly, in the area of environmental change, climate change, and controlling natural disasters, SAARC has a greater responsibility to shoulder. All the Summits held since 1987, the Heads of the State or Government of the member-states of SAARC have emphasized on the need of greater regional cooperation to address the challenges posed by climate changes and natural disasters. Moreover, there was an urgent need to preserve, protect, and manage the fragile eco-systems of the region. The environmental problems are transnational in character which necessitates collective action involving national, regional, and international institutions. The member-states need to cooperate with each other for reducing risk in disaster management. An emphasis has to be given to the field of research, dissemination of education, strategic learning and training system. The member-states should develop the expertise and exchange information for the realization of higher goal. The climate change has resulted in the proliferation of climate refugees and high incidence of poverty in South Asia. The problem is that countries of SAARC adhere to different policies regarding environmental protection which are framed mostly from the national perspective and not from the regional one. Some countries often tend to adhere to their own policies by ignoring the dictates of SAARC. It took nearly two decades to approve the "SAARC Convention on Cooperation on Environment". The Summits held after 2008 focussed more on the vulnerability of the region to climate changes. Many South Asian countries have not revised and updated their national environmental policies despite many new measures taken by SAARC. The proximity of South Asian states had also complicated the situation by allowing the climate change migrants to move easily to neighbouring countries, thus complicating relations among them. Another dimension has been added by the COVID-19 crisis which has united the SAARC countries to adopt international travel bans, to enforce strict lockdowns, to announce special economic packages, to set up a joint fund and to ban all religious gatherings. Throughout South Asia, the countries have responded proactively to the daunting challenge with India taking the lead by pledging USD 10 million toward a COVID-19 emergency fund. It was an initiative led by Prime Minister Narendra Modi in bringing the SAARC leaders together through a video-conference in the month of December 2021 amid rising coronavirus cases in the populous region. PM Modi's move revived India's proximity with SAARC which was absent in the last three years for security reasons affecting the region from terror networks based in Pakistan.[8]

Lastly, SAARC started its journey in 1985 with seven members which was expanded with the addition of Afghanistan in 2007. Right now, SAARC has eight member-states, of which five are listed as the world's least developed countries by the United Nations. SAARC cannot meet the basic needs of regional development itself in the capital, technology, resources, markets, education, and other related elements, so it welcomes outside countries, especially the stronger countries, to invest in financial intermediation, resource integration, technology transfer, market development, and educational support. In recent sessions of the SAARC summit, the leaders reached a consensus to cooperate with countries outside the region in the hope that all observers would give cooperation in trade, counter-terrorism, society, and economy.[9] The organization can be made more vibrant as well as strong with the broadening of membership and granting the observer status. Countries which have been granted Observer Status are Australia, China, European Union, Iran, Japan, Mauritius, Myanmar, South Korea, and the United States. Russia and Turkey had showed their interest in becoming an

Observer in the SAARC platform. Myanmar had also expressed its interest in upgrading its status from an observer to a full member of the SAARC. The Observer Nations can participate in the Meetings but are not allowed to engage in discussions and vote on issues. However, dialogue partners can have much deeper economic and strategic engagement with member countries. The ten-member ASEAN has assigned dialogue partner status to countries such as India, China, and Japan with whom it later signed free-trade agreements.[10] Hence, by extending observer status to different powers, SAARC may consolidate its own position and become more relevant. It is important to mention that South Asia comprises some of the less developing countries of the world. In spite of that SAARC had been instrumental in reducing poverty, providing educational opportunity, health protection, food security, bringing social welfare, improving trade, establishing development-related fund and food bank, people-to-people contact, establishing South Asian University in 2010 and took many other constructive steps. The SAARC Social Charter which was initiated in 2003-04 embodied the set of expectations and aspirations for the South Asian countries. The Charter not only highlighted cooperation at the governmental level but also at the paradigm of civil society in South Asia. Track I is the official channel of inter-governmental decision-making. Tracks II and III represent civil society: Track II, the 'top-down' approach, of 'shadow diplomacy' involving retired policy makers and other individuals who have ready access and relationships with, members of Track I. This to bridge the divide between the government intelligentsia.[11] Track III Dialogues are essential in the contemporary times where the intellectuals, non-governmental organizations, activists, cultural forum can play a meaningful role. There is a need to continue with the best practices and address the grey areas to make SAARC a more effective and efficient regional grouping. It is hoped that regional cooperation will remove the "long winter of mistrust, coldness and suspicion." The region now looks forward to a "new spring giving birth as it were to a new era of enlightened self-interest based on a common desire to replace conflict with cooperation, to substitute discord with harmony, and finally, move from horizon of contacts in the region in a spirit of reciprocity, give and take, live and let live.[12]

II. SAFTA

In the Twelfth SAARC Summit held on January 6, 2004 in Islamabad, Pakistan, the SAARC countries reached a decision for the creation of a free trade zone named South Asian Free Trade Area or 'SAFTA'. The agreement of SAFTA came into force on July 6, 2006. The initiative was taken to boost up the region economically by virtue of free trade and greater economic intercourse with each other. The experience of other regional organizations in different parts of the world like Southern Common Market (MERCOSUR), Bay of Bengal Initiative for Multi Sectoral Technical and Economic Cooperation (BIMSTEC), Association of South-East Asian Nations (ASEAN), Southern African Customs Union (SAC) and others also acted as stimuli. The idea of liberalizing trade among SAARC countries was first mooted by Sri Lanka at the Sixth Summit of SAARC held in Colombo in December 1991. This resulted in the signing of trade arrangement South Asian Preferential Trading Agreement (SAPTA) in April 1993. The goal of SAPTA was to create a Preferential Trading Area among seven member-states of SAARC, viz. Bangladesh, Bhutan, India, Maldives, Nepal, Pakistan, and Sri Lanka. However, SAPTA had its own limitations, which resulted in the pitching of another trade arrangement named SAFTA. The sorry state of economic intercourse in South Asia gave an urgent call for an arrangement like this. The regional trade in South Asia is dismally low at 4 percent as compared with the regional trade of the European Union at 67 percent, the North American Free Trade Agreement (NAFTA) at 62 percent, the Association of Southeast Asian Nations (ASEAN) at 26%, the Common Market for Eastern and Southern Africa at 22%, Gulf Cooperation Council at 8%, Latin America and Caribbean at 22%. Regional trade among the seven SAARC countries in 2002 was US$5 billion out of which India's share was 76 percent (US$3.8 billion) and Pakistan's share was 8 percent (US$0.4 billion). The regional trade among the remaining five countries is limited to around 16 percent (US$0.8 billion) of the total regional trade.[13] Hence, the SAARC members were encouraged to boost up trade in the South Asian region in order to rectify the disequilibrium. It is true that intra-regional trade in South Asia has languished owing to a combination of politics and protectionism.[14] Hence, in order to turn the region to an economic hotspot, the objectives of SAFTA were set as follows:

- to promote mutual trade, economic cooperation, and competition amongst members of SAARC.
- Members should show reciprocity to each other for furthering trade benefit, concession, and mutuality of advantage.
- Remove barriers in trade and initiate reforms.
- Special arrangement to be curved for less developing countries in terms of extended timeslots and concessions for bringing them at par with developed countries.

With these set of objectives, SAFTA started its journey. Article 4 of the Agreement mentioned of Trade Liberalization Programme, Rules of Origin, Institutional Arrangement, Consultations, Dispute Settlement Procedures and Safeguard Measures for the effective implementation of the objectives mentioned above. The SAFTA Agreement designed its plan in two-fold phases to be followed in step by step manner. In the first phase, India, Sri Lanka, and Pakistan were to reduce their custom duty to 20 percent from January 2008 while countries like Bangladesh, Bhutan, Nepal, and Maldives to reduce their tariff to 30 percent. In the second phase, all the countries were to reduce their custom duties from 0 to 5 percent. SAFTA was expected to be effective for non-LDC member countries of SAARC by 2013 and for the LDCs, the target was 2016. The signing of the Agreement on SAFTA raised much hope and aspiration amongst the SAARC members however some bottlenecks appeared with the passage of time.

Firstly, SAFTA was characterised by some of the features which limited its prospect. The existence of Negative List, restricted rules of origin and limited product coverage created obstacles for SAFTA to flourish. The members of SAARC have retained a long Negative List of items which are not devoid of concessions. Although it seems that countries are engaged in liberalizing trade but the value of imports subjected to Negative List does not conform to it. This restricts the smooth flow of goods and hinders the process of trade liberalization. Almost 53 per cent of the total import trade between SAFTA members has been subject to the negative lists of the member countries. Among the large member countries, India and Sri Lanka have restricted up to 38 per cent and 52 per cent respectively of their total imports by value from the SAFTA members under the sensitive list category. The existence of a Negative List has significantly limited the scope of the SAFTA regime.[15] The Specific Duties imposed by countries also throw a challenge to the spirit of integration of trade in South Asia. For instance, India imposes specific duties on textile fabrics and readymade garments which challenge other countries to have a market access to India. Moreover, as per the SAFTA Agreement, there is no formal responsibility of the member states to reduce their items in the 'sensitive list'. Member-countries adopt a variety of criteria to prepare their sensitive lists. A negative list in a preferential or free trade agreement is often justified on the grounds that it would provide protection to vulnerable sectors such as nascent industries (infant industry argument), small-scale producers (socio-economic arguments) or agricultural producers (food security concerns). However, often, sensitive lists are prepared consulting the stakeholders. This results in the inclusion of the powerful domestic lobbies seeking government protections. Sensitive lists, particularly in the case of India, have come to be dominated largely by such sectors.[16] However, the situation is changing with the passage of time.

Table 4.2: SAFTA: Items of Sensitive List

Serial No.	Name of Countries	Number of Items in Sensitive List- PHASE I Pre 2014	Number of Items in Sensitive List- PHASE II Post 2014
1	Afghanistan	1072	858
2	Bangladesh	1233 (LDCs) 1241 (NLDCs)	987 (LDCs) 993 (NLDCs)
3	Bhutan	150	156

Serial No.	Name of Countries	Number of Items in Sensitive List- PHASE I Pre 2014	Number of Items in Sensitive List- PHASE II Post 2014
4	India	480 (LDCs) 868 (NLDCs)	25(LDCs) 614(NLDCs)
5	Maldives	681	154
6	Nepal	1257 (LDCs) 1295 (NLDCs)	998 (LDCs) 1036 (NLDCs)
7	Pakistan	1169	936
8	Sri Lanka	1042	837 (LDCs) 963 (LDCs)

Source: Compiled from the Report of Department of Commerce, Govt. of Sri Lanka.

On line source: http://www.doc.gov.lk/index.php?option=com_content&view=article&id=32&Itemid=157&lang=en. Accessed on 10 July 2020.

The above-mentioned data justifies that items reserved in the Sensitive List are less in number in post-2014 period in comparison to pre-2014. Moreover, in a move to boost trade within South Asia, India, Bhutan, Pakistan, and Maldives have proposed to drastically reduce the sensitive list, that defines products which will not be eligible for lower import tariffs, in the South Asian Free Trade Area (SAFTA) to 100 items by 2020. While Sri Lanka is yet to respond to the proposal, Bangladesh has said that the timeline may be a little ambitious for the LDCs.[17] However, it is an unavoidable fact that if the South Asian countries do not reduce the Negative List, the free flow of goods can never be realized.

Secondly, the lack of political will had been a major drawback for a full scale implementation of SAFTA. Countries were found to be suspicious of each other. The bitter chemistry in bilateral relations got reflected in the multilateral forum and decision-making. For instance, the conflicting relationship between India and Pakistan resulted in the latter's refusal to implement provisions of SAFTA while trading with India. Moreover, Pakistan had expressed its apathy in allowing Afghanistan to transit its products through Pakistan to the markets of India and Bangladesh. Such obstacles and restrictions have given rise to smuggling and unofficial trade especially amongst the countries with porous borders. This reduced trades amongst SAARC countries, compared to trades within other regional blocs. World Bank in a report titled "A Glass Half Full: The Promise of Regional Trade in South Asia", estimates India's potential trade in goods with South Asia at $62 billion against its actual trade of $19 billion, which is a mere 3% of its global trade and about $43 billion below its potential.[18] It is therefore necessary to rise above the bilateral interest and delve for greater trading opportunities amongst the members of SAARC. The gains of bilateral relationship in the form of 'Free Trade Agreements' often win over multilateral arrangement. In the backdrop of such bilateral agreements, Sri Lanka, Nepal, and Bhutan have limited interest in the SAFTA process. These countries have obtained far more favourable treatment for their key markets in South Asia through the bilateral process, which will be fully implemented well ahead of SAFTA.[19]

Thirdly, Article 1 of the Agreement defines Para-Tariffs as "border charges and fees, other than 'tariffs', on foreign trade transactions of a tariff-like effect which are levied solely on imports, but not those indirect taxes and charges, which are levied in the same manner on domestic products. Import charges corresponding to specific services rendered are not considered as para-tariff measures."[20] SAFTA could not address the issue of tariff and para-tariff that the member states were suffering from. The countries of SAARC have to pay for both para-tariff as well as custom duties. This has turned the trade balance dismal. Moreover, the different rules and regulations imposed by the Certified Bodies and Standard Enforcement Agencies have also complicated the situation and prevented the region to become economically vibrant.

Fourthly, poor connectivity and infrastructural bottlenecks of South Asia hindered the development of the region into an economic hotspot. All the countries of South Asia are not well connected to each other through roads, railways or waterways. Hence, the logistic cost increases multifold. There are problems of rail connectivities. The air connections between the regional centres of SAARC are also not quite good. The entries for trade through ports are also limited. The SAARC members often specify the port through which they aim to import their products. Apart from this, issues relating to custom operation excesses, informal payments, lack of warehouse securities, banking facilities, etc. also have thrown challenges to the players of trade at different point of time. Formalism and red-tapism affect the spontaneity of free trade between countries. When the goods reach another country, too much time is wasted for getting custom clearance and verification certificate. This costs a huge loss for the trading country. This also results for the trading country to divert into informal trades and its cascading effect is obvious loss at government levels. In order to address this issue, the Twelfth SAARC Summit held in Islamabad in 2004 highlighted the impediments for free trade among the SAARC countries. SAARC aims to improve connectivity amongst its members in terms of road, railway, air, and water linkages for boosting up of trade in the region. However, more practical steps are needed to be taken to translate the decisions to reality. An effective implantation of SAFTA would determine the success of SAARC to a considerable extent.

Fifthly, Article 18 of the Agreement lays down that 'Rules of Origin' shall be negotiated by the Contracting States and incorporated in this Agreement as an integral part. However, there are some problems associated with it. There is a need of adequate monitoring and efficient regulatory mechanism for this negotiation. Rules should be simplified and harmonized for the member countries of SAARC. The issues of licensing, registration, financing, custom clearance procedure, fair competition should be promoted adequately for the greater movement of goods in South Asia.

Theoretically, SAFTA had pinned high hopes for economic integration in South Asia so as to stimulate the region as a whole. However, the process of integration had been slow because of the various complexities mentioned above. It is an unavoidable fact that there is an asymmetry in the economic status of the eight members of SAARC. Although, SAFTA had given "protection to those countries having balance of payment problem; however it is silent on how to improve the export basket of the least developed countries."[21] It is difficult to bring the LDCs and

BOX 4.1: SAARC and SAFTA

- In South Asia, the regional organization called SAARC was formed on December 8, 1985, mainly by the initiatives of the President of Bangladesh, Ziaur Rahman.
- SAARC has eight members, namely India, Bangladesh, Bhutan, Maldives, Nepal, Pakistan Sri Lanka, and Afghanistan.
- The Secretariat of SAARC is based in Kathmandu, Nepal.
- SAARC functions by following certain objectives and principles codified in the SAARC Charter.
- Bilateral and contentious issues are excluded from deliberation in SAARC Summit.
- Since its formation in 1985, SAARC has convened Nineteen Summit, although the last one was boycotted by India, Afghanistan, Bhutan, Bangladesh, Sri Lanka, and Maldives.
- SAARC has completed thirty-six years of existence but there are various trans-national issues like terrorism, environment, water, migration, traditional and non-traditional threats to security which throws a challenge to the success of this organization.
- In the Twelfth SAARC Summit held in 2004 in Islamabad, Pakistan, the SAARC countries reached out an agreement for the creation of a free trade zone named South Asian Free Trade Area or SAFTA.
- The agreement of SAFTA came into force on July 6, 2006.
- SAFTA was preceded by another trade agreement South Asian Preferential Trading Agreement (SAPTA) signed in April 1993.

non-LDCs together because of their diversity of interests. There were inadequacies in the SAFTA Agreement too. However, as originally designed, SAFTA was a shallow agreement.[22] Initially, it only focused on the liberalization of goods and not on services. In 2012, however, the SAARC Agreement on Trade in Service (SATIS) was implemented for expanding intra-regional investments and trade liberalization in the services sector. The five LDCs in the region, viz. Afghanistan, Bangladesh, Bhutan, Maldives, and Nepal, are accorded with special and differential treatment depending on their developmental needs. India as a developed country in the region can play a more active role by lowering tariffs and promote unilateral liberalisation with other stakeholders of SAARC. India had imposed various tariff barriers, included many tradable items in the sensitive list and imposed specific duties on some goods. This made both the LDCs and the Non LDCs a little uncomfortable. India needs to change its trade policy and play the role of a strategic leader to pave the way for greater economic integration in South Asia.

III. CHALLENGES TO REGIONAL COOPERATION

(a) River Water Disputes

Disputes over water are central to South Asia. The four major rivers of the region are Indus, Ganges, Brahmaputra and Meghna. They flow across the countries of Pakistan, India, Nepal, Bhutan and Bangladesh. All these countries are dependent on the water resources and hence are concerned about their entitlement to the same. The upper riparian countries enjoy a greater strategic benefit in terms of the access and allocation of water resources than the lower ones. Water is precious and hence it has the ability to strain the relationship between neighbouring countries through which the river flows. India and Pakistan had a strained relationship over the distribution of water of river Indus, India and Bangladesh over the Ganga Brahmaputra water, India and Nepal over the Kosi and Mahakali river. In most Asian transboundary rivers, agreements have been difficult to negotiate between the appropriate co-basin countries because of many interrelated factors, among which are historical rivalries, political mistrust, asymmetric power relationships, increasing nationalism, short term requirements of national political parties as compared to long-term national interests, growth of religious extremist groups, negotiations exclusively on water issues which invariably reduce water allocation to a zero-sum game.[23] In this section, efforts will be made to illuminate the river water disputes in South Asia with a focus on India.

Firstly, relationship between India and Bangladesh has been dampened by river water dispute. River Padma of Bangladesh is a distributary of River Ganges. Padma joins with Jamuna river and in further downstream it is fed by the second largest distributary of Brahmaputra and is known as River Meghna. The major water of the Ganga, Brahmaputra, and Meghna river flow through the northern region of India as well as Bangladesh.

Hence, the water distribution as well as management is a great part of it. The Ganges (or Ganga) water dispute presents a textbook example of a conflict where two states have locked horns by calculating their interest in what they perceive as a zero-sum situation.[24] In 1961, India proposed a plan to build the Farakka Barrage which was to be constructed seventeen kilometres upstream from the border of Bangladesh. The Barrage would help to divert water from the Ganges to the Bhagirathi-Hooghly river system and reduce the silt deposition in the Calcutta Port. India started construction of the barrage in 1962. A 75-foot-high and 7000-foot-long barrage was completed in 1970 at a cost of U.S. $208 million. The 26.5-mile-long feeder canal into the Bhagirathi River, however, took another four years to complete.[25] In 1972, Indo-Bangladesh Joint Rivers Commission was instituted. Bangladesh soon realised that during the lean period, there would not be enough water in the Ganges after being diverted by the barrage. This would have severe impact on water availability in Bangladesh. In addition this would result in degradation of surface water and groundwater, threat to fisheries and increased salinity in the reduced water supplies. In 1977, the Ganges Water Agreement was negotiated between the two countries which regulated the water distribution between India and Bangladesh for five years. A comprehensive bilateral treaty was signed by Indian Prime Minister H.D. Deve Gowda and Bangladeshi Prime Minister Sheikh Hasina Wajid on December 12, 1996 in New Delhi. The treaty established a 30-year water-sharing arrangement between India and Bangladesh. The treaty permits both the countries to co-operate for harnessing the water resources and also to the construct barrages and irrigation projects. The treaty tried to find a long-term solution to the hiccups in the Indo-Bangladeshi relations. The Ganges Water Treaty had a limited ability to meet the needs of both India and Bangladesh as millions of people depend on the Ganges and its tributaries for their food and water security. However, political factions in Bangladesh allege that India is guilty in drawing excess water by depriving Bangladesh in an unjust manner. India, on the other hand, rejected this claim. Another, thorn in the India and Bangladesh relation had been the sharing of water of Teesta river. Teesta is the fourth largest among the 54 trans-boundary rivers between India and Bangladesh. The Teesta River flows through Sikkim, West Bengal in India and Rangpur in Bangladesh. It is a perennial river which is characterized by extreme variability in its flows throughout the year. Bangladesh as a lower riparian state is dependent on India as Teesta is her lifeline. The lives of millions of people in Bangladesh depend on this river for agriculture, irrigation, and fishing. India had constructed dams which, according to Bangladesh, had reduced the flow of water to Bangladesh especially in lean months. Again during monsoon the release of excess water causes flood in Bangladesh. Against this backdrop, Bangladesh demanded a fair agreement with India so that her survival and security are ensured in lean as well as monsoon time. Negotiations on the Teesta River had been going on and the agreement was expected to be signed in 2011 between India's Prime Minister, Manmohan Singh and Prime Minister of Bangladesh Sheikh Hasina. However, as the item of distribution of water resource comes under the State list, the deal could not be translated into reality. The Government of West Bengal refused to ink the agreement fearing a loss of higher volume of water. Another source of dissention which irked India and Bangladesh developed in the year 2002 when India tried to initiate 'River Linking Project' in which the giant rivers of Ganga and Brahmaputra would be connected to the Kaveri and Mahanadi rivers in the south. These would ultimately join their flow to the Beas River in western India. India aimed to connect the Ken river in Madhya Pradesh to the Betwa river in Uttar Pradesh. However, the project got suspended because of the decision of the UPA Government which came to power in 2004. Bangladesh on the other hand expressed deep concern in such unilateral decision making of India. Such linkages would drastically reduce the flow of water to lower riparian Bangladesh and affect the food security of millions. The environmental experts also criticised it from the viewpoint of ecology and hydrological feasibility.[26] The linking of rivers may be instrumental in judicious transfer of water from the area of surplus to the area of deficit in India. But for

Bangladesh this would be an extremely compromising situation. Thus, the disputes over agreement of Farraka Barrage, Teesta River, and the River Linking Project between the two countries had nurtured a conviction in Bangladesh that her interest has been compromised to India in relation to the control and management of water resources.

Secondly, India and Nepal had a row over sharing of river waters. Nepal has four major river basins consisting of River Mahakali, Karnali, Gandaki, and Kosi. The rivers of Ganges basin in India originates from Nepal and flows through Uttarakhand, Uttar Pradesh, North Bihar, and West Bengal. These rivers are pivotal for the source of hydel-power and irrigation projects for both India and Nepal. However, the relationship between India and Nepal got tarnished by the long-drawn dispute over river Mahakali, Kosi, and Gandaki. River Kosi originates in the Tibetan Himalaya and then flows through Nepal and India. The river is hailed as the 'Sorrow of Bihar' because of the massive damage it causes to life and property by the devastating flood. In order to address this loss, the Kosi Agreement was signed between India and Nepal in 1954. A barrage was constructed at Bhimnagar in 1962 for controlling the floods caused by Kosi river and for providing irrigation facilities to both the countries. India has always considered that this agreement was beneficial to Nepal as the latter had little to invest. On the other hand, Nepal had nurtured the feeling that she had not been given her due share and the balance was favourable to India. The Treaty had given extraterritorial rights to India for an indefinite period without seeking an adequate compensation. A similar story is with River Gandaki which has the history of damaging crops, property and human lives in both sides in times of flood. India and Nepal entered into an agreement for the Gandaki Irrigation and Power Project in December 1959. The agreement, however, came into force with certain amendments in 1964. In 1968-69, the Gandaki barrage was constructed over the Gandaki river in order to provide irrigation facilities to Nepal and India. Similarly, in the Kosi Agreement, Nepal had no financial involvement in the construction of the Gandaki Project but her rights were ensured in the provisions of the Agreement. The amendments made in the treaty gave Nepal the riparian rights in distinct terms. She would continue to exercise the rights of withdrawing water for irrigation and other purposes. Both Nepal and India agreed to construct one powerhouse to generate electricity with an installed capacity of 15 MW. The powerhouse was constructed and handed over to Nepal in the year 1981. The most noteworthy understanding between India and Nepal is reflected in the Mahakali Treaty which was signed between Prime Minister of Nepal Sher Bahadur Deuba and Prime Minister of India P.V. Narasimha Rao on February 12, 1996, in New Delhi. The parties concerned shared their commitment for the integrated development of the Mahakali River, Sarada Barrage, Tanakpur Barrage, and Pancheshwar Project. The Pancheshwar Project under the treaty was expected to produce 6,000 MW of hydropower with the investment cost of US$4 billion for the eight years up to 2002. The treaty would be operational for a term of seventy-five years. In the Mahakali Treaty, Nepal, and India agreed for Power Stations of equal capacity on each side of the river Mahakali and the energy so generated would be shared by the two countries. The Pancheshwar Multipurpose Project was to be constructed on a stretch of river and both the countries would have equal stake over the water. The countries would bear the cost of the project on the basis of the benefit accrued from it. The Mahakali Treaty was a diplomatic success as no sides would be able to harness the water resource without the consent of each other. However, there is a feeling in certain quarters in Nepal that there are unequal benefits in the water-sharing deal with India especially with the Kosi and Gandaki Agreement. Even in the signing of Mahakali Agreement, it is said that Nepal could have asked for greater compensation from the lower riparian state, i.e. India. It is argued that India has taken a larger portion of water from these rivers for irrigating greater tracts of land and violated the provisions in the Mahakali Treaty. The Nepalese view India as a dominant power who tries to impose unfair terms on the neighbouring countries. On the other hand, India blames Nepal for creating irritants in bilateral relationship. However, India had tried to mitigate the river water disputes with Nepal by giving adequate compensation to the latter. The Mahakali Agreement was more progressive and liberal over the past engagements. No water deal in Nepal has received as much public support as the Mahakali Treaty, because India addressed all the genuine demands of the Nepalese people. It could be argued that no other country has achieved a better deal in hydropower development on a river serving as a common boundary between two countries as Nepal has achieved. It was for this reason that the treaty was supported by more than two-thirds of the members of the Nepalese Parliament in 1996.[27]

Thirdly, India and Pakistan has nurtured a blame game over the water of river Indus, since the aftermath of Partition. India claimed her greater stake over the river water which flows through the Indian Punjab first and then enters Pakistan. Pakistan however refused to accept the terms of India regarding the distribution of water of river Indus considering it as her lifeline. The dispute ended with the signing of Indus Water Agreement between Indian Prime Minister Jawaharlal Nehru and Pakistan President Ayub Khan in Karachi on September 19, 1960. The Indus Waters Treaty is one of the most liberal water distribution agreements between the two countries where the waters of the River Sutlej, Beas, and Ravi were allocated to India for exclusive use. On the other hand, the waters of the western rivers Indus, Jhelum, and Chenab were allocated to Pakistan by honouring India's right of specified domestic, non-consumptive agricultural use and generation of hydroelectricity from the river projects. However, Pakistan had a reason for her concern as her lifelines Indus, Chenab, and Jhelum flows through the country through India. The instrumental role played by World Bank in the signing of Indus Water Treaty was praiseworthy as it brought a watershed in the Indo-Pak bilateral relationship over decades of dissention. The Indus Waters Treaty represents the only agreement between India and Pakistan that has not been disrupted by wars or periods of high tension. Cooperation that builds on this treaty could not only present opportunities for better water management between those two countries, but also serve as a model for water-sharing arrangements between India, Bangladesh, and Nepal.[28] The dispute between India and Pakistan over the Tulbul Project since 1987 was of great significance. The Tulbul Project was constructed on the mouth of Wulur Lake in Jammu & Kashmir. The Lake is one of the largest fresh water in Asia, fed by the Jhelum river. Pakistan alleged that India had violated the Indus Water Treaty by signing this agreement as a minimum depth of water should be maintained. India was forced to stop working on the Project on that year. Eight rounds of secretary-level talks have been held since work was suspended on the project, followed by five more meetings in 1998, 2004, 2005, 2006, and 2007 under Composite Dialogue between the two countries. In the last meeting in August 2007, it was decided that technical-level talks would form part of the officials' dialogue. The Tulbul navigation project is located just below the exit of the Wular Lake, a natural lake. India envisages controlled release of water from the lake during the lean-season months of October to February to facilitate year-round navigation for commercial trade, employment, and tourism. New Delhi maintains that the regulating structure is permitted under the Indus Waters Treaty of 1960 for the non-consumptive use of navigation. Moreover, it holds that the project is beneficial for Pakistan for lean-season water supplies and also for the Mangala dam in the PoK region. Pakistan, however, contests it as a "storage project" and charges India with violation of the provisions under the Treaty.29 The rivalry between the two countries was reflected on the start of the Baglihar Hydroelectric Power Project built on the River Chenab in the Ramban district of the Jammu & Kashmir. The construction of the Baglihar Dam, a $1 billion project commenced in 1999. Pakistan however claimed that this Project contradicted the Indus Water Treaty entered between the two countries in 1960. India was given the right over Chenab with a clause to maintain a minimum flow and reservoir capacity in the river. This initiated 'Hydropolitics' between Pakistan and India. Effort was made to mitigate this problem by holding dialogues. Several rounds of talks between the two from 1999-2004 failed. Pakistan accused World Bank playing a major role in signing of Indus Water Agreement, of bias. However, the dispute was ultimately resolved on June 1, 2010 and the project got completed in the year 2016. India and Pakistan had a row over water resources manifested from time to time due to the water crisis, increased demand, and political rivalry. The Kishanganga Hydroelectric Plant in Jammu & Kashmir was one for diverting water from river Kishanganga to a power plant in river Jhelum river. It is a project of $864 million with installing capacity of 330 MW. The project began in 2007. But Pakistan made a controversial claim that India was overusing and diverting water for this Project. However, the Hague's Permanent Court of Arbitration rejected the grounds of objection raised by Pakistan and assigned India with the right to proceed with the Project in 2013. India was asked by the Commission to ensure a minimum of 9 cumecs of water in the riverbed as minimum at all times. This fulfils the basic criterion of customary international law. Nevertheless, the hydropolitics and the conflict over water resources between upper and lower riparian countries have become pressing from time to time. This becomes apparent during times of political crisis. Union Minister Nitin Gadkari stated that the government has been working on project to divert water from three rivers flowing into Pakistan from India in order to improve availability of water in the Yamuna. He believed that both the countries hold the right to use water flowing in three rivers each under the Indus Waters Treaty signed in 1960. But India has not utilised river waters as permitted to use under the agreement, Gadkari said, "The construction of dam has started at Shahpur-Kandi on Ravi river. Moreover, UJH project will store our share of water for use in J&K and the balance water will flow from 2nd Ravi-BEAS Link to provide water to other basin states." Gadkari's comment has come at a time when India has mounted pressure on Pakistan in the wake of a terror attack in Jammu and Kashmir's Pulwama last week. At least 40 Central Reserve Police Force (CRPF) jawans were killed in the attack, for which Pakistan-based terror outfit Jaish-e-Mohammed claimed responsibility.[30]

The period from 2005 to 2015 was declared as the decade of water cooperation by the UN. Co-riparian states were requested to take measures to initiate transboundary water collaboration, shared water, and shared responsibilities. This was to promote a common use of resources for development and not for conflicts and wars.[31] However, despite the commonality of interest, water resource development has suffered from technical issues, economic problems, lack of political will and ambiguity of decisions. Lack of specificity in water agreements have also cast a shadow in settling river water disputes between the upper and lower riparian regions. There is a prevalent doctrine that future wars will be fought over water and not over oil because water is the basic requirement for sustaining human life.[32] Hence, it is the time for the South Asian countries to delve into this issue and search for amicable solution for enhancing the prospect of the region.

(b) Illegal Cross Border Migration

Illegal Cross Border Migration denotes the unlawful movement of people from one territory to other by crossing the boundary line for either voluntary or non-voluntary purpose. The term 'Migrants' is broader in scope as it includes the refugees as well as asylum seekers. Migrants have a far-reaching effect on the country of origin as well as the destination. Illegal Cross border migration remains a burning issue for tensions among countries. The countries of South Asia have a history of illegal migration across borders. India shares an open border with Bangladesh, Nepal and Bhutan. India's border with Pakistan is closed and well demarcated. India has maritime boundaries with the island countries of Sri Lanka and Maldives. Broadly, there are two major causes of Migration; the Push factor and the Pull factor. The pull factors include reasons of better living, security, job opportunities which tempt natives to cross the border even illegally and enter another country. The push factors are events like civil war, political upheavals, threats regarding security, etc. which forces the citizens of one country to penetrate and take refuge in other neighbouring country.

Firstly, India and Bangladesh have a long history of cross border migration considering the porous and longest border between the two countries. India has a 4,156-km border with Bangladesh which runs across the states of Assam, Meghalaya, Tripura, and West Bengal. All efforts to curb the movement of people and goods, have failed. Out of a combination of despair and political pressure, the government of India has built barbed wire fencing on parts of both Assam and West Bengal sides of the border.[33] The porous border helps the illegal migrants to enter and work as cheap labours. They often forge their identity cards and enrol themselves as voters of India. There is a great deal of ethnic resemblance between people of both side of the border in terms of language, culture and physical features. This gives the migrant greater advantage to penetrate into the Indian soil. Bangladesh is also environmentally one of the most vulnerable countries which suffer because of its spatial location,and density of population. Climate change occurs due to natural disasters like flood, cyclone, drought, rising sea level, coastal inundation, low elevation, etc. which may induce people to migrate to neighbouring country by crossing national borders. The climate refugees from Bangladesh add to the burden of India. The influx of migrants multiplies with the passage of time and disturbs the demographic composition of that region. The influx of such a large number of illegal Bangladeshi immigrants, particularly in the border state of Tripura, Assam, West Bengal, Mizoram, and Meghalaya, has proved to be a huge challenge for India with serious implications for its resources and national security. India has expressed concern over the illegal entry of migrants on different political and diplomatic levels. They pose a challenge to the security of the country, especially in the sensitive North-Eastern region. They have emerged as a potential competitor with the natives in regard to land, water, services, and jobs. India's efforts to check the immigration through strict border surveillance over barbed-wire fence failed to produce the desired results. This illegal migration has changed the demographic shape of many border states, which has resulted in separatist movements.[34] There is no exact figure of the illegal migrants entering and settling in India over decades. In the absence of any authentic figure number of immigrants from Bangladesh estimates are hayward. One such estimate notes: "The migration from East Pakistan/Bangladesh to India has resulted in the creation of a sub-nation, the size of Australia, within India. This population of between 12 and 17 million has moved illegally, without proper visas, passports or documents and it has settled in northeast India".[35] The Indian Parliament enacted the Illegal Migrants (Determination by Tribunal) Act in 1983 for addressing the problem, but the measure had failed to make any impact. In 2004, the Congress-led UPA Government and in 2014 the BJP Government had declared of taking strong measures against the migrants entering India unlawfully. Bangladesh has never acknowledged the entry and infiltration of a large number of illegal Bangladeshi immigrants in India. She has not taken any effective measures to control the flow of nationals to India. However, the continuous influx of illegal migrants from Bangladesh results in the rise of identity politics in the Indian states. The situation has turned dismal with the growth of insurgency and terrorism. Since the time of Partition of India in 1947 and the subsequent communal riots, massive migration of Hindus (erstwhile East Bengal) to India has taken place. India had generously extended refuge to the lakhs of migrants which had ultimately opened the pandora's box of innumerable complexities. The Chakma Refugees from Bangladesh had already thrown a tremendous challenge to India's security for decades. Coupled with that, the continuous influx of illegal immigrants has compounded the problem. Every government in India had criticized Bangladesh for not taking adequate measures to check the entry of illegal migrants to India. But the problem remains unresolved.

Secondly, India and Nepal has also open and porous border of 1900 km which runs through the areas of the Indian States of Uttar Pradesh, Bihar, West Bengal and Sikkim. People have an unrestricted entry to the other's territory for diverse purposes given the advantage of the open border. In fact, it is said that there are houses situated on the border where one door opens towards Nepal and the other towards India. Such close interaction between people of the two countries has created ideological and political linkages....[36] However, the open border has added to the problem of illegal migrants as we have seen in the case of Bangladesh. India has a long historical tie with Nepal. In 1950, both countries signed the Treaty of Peace and Friendship which granted the right to the citizens of both countries to travel and work in each other's territory. The flow of migrants was substantially greater from Nepal to India than from India to Nepal. Gurkhas serving in the Indian army and then retiring and settling in Nepal drew their life time pensions from India. Nepalis also found employment as watchmen in Calcutta, in the tea plantations of Darjeeling and Assam, and as milk herders in Assam.[37] The socio-economic need propels them to migrate and settle in India. They have developed an inclination to work in India as unskilled labours either seasonally or permanently. Better employment opportunities and higher wages in India are the driving force for tempting migrants from Nepal. The flow of remittance improves their family condition. They can avail better education, health facility and standard of living by staying in India. The flow of remittances also helps to improve the condition of the domestic economy and make significant contribution to the national economy. However, illegal migration to India has remained constant and created a pressure on the Indian states like West Bengal, Sikkim, Uttarakhand, etc. They also migrate and settle in the Terai region in India where they have geographical proximity and other opportunities of employment. This however results in a clash between the stakeholders as they consider the migrants from Nepal responsible for snatching away their resources. The migration done unlawfully from hills to the plains creates ripples in the social, economic, ecological and political paradigm and disturbs the equilibrium. There are twenty-two points through which movement of goods takes place between India and Nepal. However, there are no agreement relating to the movement of people and the fixing of routes for the same. In the treaties that govern the regulation of Indo-Nepal border, no procedure for regulating the border has been codified. There is a need for strengthening monitoring and surveillance at terminals and borders to develop a common mechanism for checking the misuse of the open borders.

Thirdly, the bilateral relation between India and Sri Lanka is also strained by the illegal entry of the Sri Lankan migrants by crossing the maritime boundary. The maritime border between the two countries is of 400 kilometres with Bay of Bengal in the North, Palk Bay in the Centre and Gulf of Mannar in the

South. This proximity has increased the flow of migrants over the last decades. Irregular migration is considered illegal, and in Sri Lanka at least, is punishable by fines or imprisonment.[38] There were push and pull factors for the flow of migrants from Sri Lanka to India. The prolonged Civil War, fear of persecution, human rights violation had forced many to enter India illegally in search of refuge. The Sri Lankan Tamil Refugees had mostly settled in the Indian State of Tamil Nadu because of the identical culture and idioms. Many others had also entered the Indian soil as economic migrant. The maritime boundary is often crossed by the fishermen who aim to settle in parts of India without any permit and license. The insurgents and criminals often smuggle narcotics and weapons by waterway. The Indian Government has imposed restrictions on this entry after the assassination of former Prime Minister of India Rajiv Gandhi and the official ban on the LTTE in India. The migrants who have entered the country illegally stayed here in camps for decades. They were not conferred with citizenship. The Indian Citizenship Act 2003 has categorically defined that all non-citizens who entered the country without a visa are illegal migrants who are not exceptions for refugees or asylum-seekers. The crux of the problem is that India is not a signatory to the 1951 Refugee Convention or the 1967 Protocol. India does not have any defined law on National Refugee as well. India ascribes to the Foreigners Act, 1946, which simply defines a foreigner as "a person who is not a citizen of India." It does not distinguish between refugees and illegal immigrants and consider them as special category. However, India has taken drive in completing the process of National Register of Citizens for arresting the problem of illegal migrants.

(c) Ethnic Conflict and Insurgencies

South Asia is the largest hub of multi-ethnic identities of culture, language, and religion that are distributed among the states and transcend and influence the socio-political life of the diversified people. The multi-ethnic states comprise diversities without strong internal cohesion and unity. Consequently, the ethnic conflicts occur among the entities to dominate each other in the form of separatist movements and insurgent activities going against the state, weakening its strength, unity and integrity.[39] In this section, the rise of ethnicity and insurgency will be discussed in three segment of South Asia.

Firstly, India had been sensitive to the ethnic conflict and insurgency problem in her body politic especially in the North Eastern India and Kashmir region. The seven sister states of North-Eastern India comprise Arunachal Pradesh, Assam, Manipur, Meghalaya, Mizoram, Nagaland, and Tripura. The strategic location of this area is significant because of its proximity to neighbouring countries like Bangladesh, Myanmar, Nepal, Bhutan, and China. The North-Eastern (NE) region is connected to India through the 'Chicken Neck' Corridor. The NE region of India had experienced the functioning of insurgent groups who had nurtured separatist tendencies. The main arguments behind these secessionist movements are that the unification of NE with India was illegal, and people of NE are neglected, deprived and humiliated time and again by the political elite from the Indian mainland during last five decades after independence.[40] Hence, the vulnerability of the region has made India to delve into the pressing issues on a serious note. The Nagas of Nagaland launched the first major insurgency in North East India to ventilate their grievances after India attained independence. In Assam, the insurgent group United Liberation Front of Asom (ULFA) had been waging a struggle since 1979. The Bodos in Assam had been instrumental in carving out a space called Bodoland under the leadership of the National Democratic Front of Bodoland since 1988. The insurgents of Kamtapur Liberation Organization were craving for different states for the Koch-Rajbongshi tribe. Likewise other insurgents groups like Rabha National Security Force, Karbi National Volunteers, Tiwa National Revolutionary Force and others also involved in low intensity conflicts. The ethnic groups often get involved in squabbles and power struggles amongst each other. In Manipur also, the insurgent groups are proactive especially the United National Liberation Front (UNLF) which occupies a predominance in the Meitei. Tripura experienced constant immigration from Bangladesh which had disturbed her equilibrium from different aspects. The grievances of the original inhabitants got ventilated with underground activities of wings like Tripura Tribals' Youth League, Tripura National Volunteers Groups, National Liberation Front of Tripura (NLFT), All Tripura Tiger Front (ATTF) and the Tripura Resurrection Army (TRA). They have harped on the issue of migration and alienation of original dwellers. Myron Weiner has shown how accelerating mobility in the context of scarce resources in a poly-ethnic society can lead to mobilization along ethnic lines and result in inter-ethnic tensions. Faced with such increased demands and other ethnic tensions, states can resort to coercive strategies, which are, inevitably, short-term palliatives.[41] However, governments of our country had taken initiatives from time to time to address ethnic conflicts and insurgency issues in the North Eastern region. Negotiations, cease-fire, peace agreements had been crafted from time to time. For instance, Indian governments had entered into peace agreements with the Nagas in the form of Naga Accord in 1947, 1960, and 1975. The Assam Accord of 1985 addressed the issue of illegal immigration to Assam. The demand for Bodoland was negotiated in the signing of Memorandum of Settlement among the Government of India, State Government of Assam and the Bodo Liberation Tigers in the year 2003. The Autonomous Bodoland Territorial District was formed to fulfil their aspirations. In 1986, the Mizo insurgency was resolved with the carving out of Mizoram with statehood. The Mizo Accord was signed between the Government of India, the Chief Secretary of Mizoram and the Mizo National Front as the latter renounced secessionist activity and joined mainstream politics. In Tripura, the issue of immigration was addressed by the Memorandum of Understanding reached among the Government of India, Government of Tripura and the Tripura National Volunteers in 1988. It is important to mention that the ethnographic mosaic of the North-Eastern India had been affected by the influx of the Chakma Refugees from Bangladesh since 1961. The completion of the Kaptai reservoir in the Chittagong Hill Tract had internally displaced the Buddhist Chakmas who pushed through the borders of India as 'environmental refugees'. While the Chakmas suffered from statelessness, they exerted a tremendous pressure on the resources available to the people of North-East, especially of Arunachal Pradesh, Mizoram, and Tripura. The ethnic groups of North Eastern India are possessive of their distinct history and exclusive features. They are against clubbing up with people of different ethno-cultural origin. It is an unavoidable fact that the North Eastern region of India had been subjected to indifference and underdevelopment for decades. The waves of immigrants from Bangladesh, unemployment, poverty, lack of education, and health facilities had pushed them to the wall. Alienation of land and resources were major causes of conflict. Developmental projects without adequate rehabilitation to the displaced indigenous people became the source of new conflict. These reasons collectively provided a fertile ground to the rise of insurgency and consequent threat to the internal security of the country. Many of the measures taken by the Government of India had been piecemeal which provided temporary relief to the problem. However, the embracing of policies like 'Look East' demands for an urgent need to address the insurgency problem and ensure peace in the North Eastern region for greater development.

Another challenge from which India has suffered for a long period of time had been the Kashmir insurgency or Kashmir Intifada. The historical rivalry between India and Pakistan had been reflected by claims and counter-claims over Kashmir. The rise of ethnic nationalism, fuelling of anti-Indian sentiment had brewed the rise of insurgency since 1989. The Kashmiri Muslims were asserting their identity for 'Kashmiriyat' against the 'occupying Indian forces' over their territory. The insurgent leaders of Jammu and Kashmir Liberation Front (JKLF) who were struggling with the secessionist struggle were countered by the Indian side. The decline of JKLF in 1995 resulted in the rise of other radical Islamic groups in Kashmir like Hizbul Mujahideen (HM), Lashkar-e-Taiba (LeT), Jaish-e-Mohammed (JeM), and Harkat ul-Ansar (HuA), Hezbollah, and Ikhwanul Muslimin who were fighting for Jihad. They are connected to the global terrorist organizations. The Inter-Services Intelligence of Pakistan has been instrumental in supplying sophisticated weapons and training the Mujahideens to continue the insurgency in Jammu and Kashmir. Pakistan had exported cross border terrorism to destabilize India from within and the latter had undertaken various operations to quash the insurgents. The lives of many innocent civilians have been sacrificed in cross-fire. However, neither war nor diplomacy has succeeded in resolving the Kashmir dispute to the mutual satisfaction of the contending states; fighting continues in the form of minor skirmishes and artillery exchanges at the Line of Control (LOC)....[42]

Secondly, the question of Tamil minorities in Sri Lanka had posed a challenge to the country. This tension had a spill-over effect in neighbouring country like India. The minority people of Tamil ethnic origin based in North and North-East of Sri Lanka had experienced a sense of alienation and powerlessness ever since the time of country's independence in the year 1948. The people of Sinhala-Buddhist majority had occupied the centre stage and imposed terms on the Tamil minorities. There were historical rivalries between the two on lines of ethnic racial identity and claim over natural resources. Sinhala nationalism had resulted in the counter growth of Tamil nationalism. The demands of the latter were left unheard and this humiliation over decades forced the Tamil minorities to stand for their own. The root causes of the Tamil ethnic insurgency can be traced to socio-economic reasons, identity politics, cultural discrimination and failure of state reform. Initially, the Tamil minority in Sri Lanka wanted to curve out an autonomous region under the federal arrangement. But when the demand for autonomy failed, demand for statehood became the sole objective. They placed their demand of a separate state for the Tamil nationality and their right to self-determination. The militant outfit Liberation Tigers of Tamil Eelam (LTTE) had continued their war against the state machinery in Sri Lanka for fulfilling their demand of separate homeland. A vicious circle thus commenced, with Tamil demands for separation, punctuated by the terrorism of the Tigers, prompting retaliatory Sinhalese attacks on Tamils who happened to be at hand and vulnerable. The riots, in turn, presumably heightened alienation among the Tamil population and probably increased support for the cause of separation.

The state machinery was unable to control and mitigate the discontent among the two groups. This resulted in escalating violence as the country became a theatre of ethnic rivalry.[43] Sri Lanka, which is strategically located in the Indian Ocean region became a reason of concern for India. India sharing long maritime boundary with Sri Lanka was anxious because the peace and security of the region was getting compromised. Moreover, the violence perpetrated by LTTE was a source of tension for India with regard to the peace of natural harbours of Trincomalee and Palk Strait. The ethnic riot of 1983 took a toll and the situation turned grave. India involved herself in 1987 for resolving this issue in Sri Lanka because of the immigration of Tamil refugees from Sri Lanka and involvement of extra-regional actors in the politics of the region. The Indian Tamils were anxious for their blood relations in Sri Lanka who were 22 miles away across the Palk Strait. This motivated India to send Indian Peace Keeping Force to Sri Lanka which culminated in the Indo-Sri Lankan Accord in 1987. However, the assassination of Rajiv Gandhi by a LTTE militant turned the entire situation topsy-turvy. The Indian Government banned LTTE in the country and took a hard-line posture for repatriating the Tamil refugees to their country of origin. The Indian Peace Keeping Force which operated in Sri Lanka from 1987 to 1990 was called back under domestic pressure. After two decades of fighting in Sri Lanka, a ceasefire was declared in December 2001 and an agreement was signed with international mediation in 2002. However, violence returned in 2005, but ultimately ended with the acceptance of defeat by the LTTE on May 17, 2009. During the course of conflict India supported the move of the Sri Lankan Government to fight against the insurgent forces.

Thirdly, Nepal, a small country in the map of South Asia reflects a great mosaic of ethnicity. Several indigenous groups like Madhesis, Tharus, Magar, Dalits, Limbuwans, Chhetris, Newar, Gurung, Kiranti and others are there who have been nurturing feelings of deprivation for ages. Historically, Nepal was ruled under a monarchical system that received a great jolt with the Jano Andolan which took place in 1990. The ethnic groups of Nepal participated in the Movement for 'Democracy' and placed their demands based on ethnicity. A new constitution was enacted after the movement which defined Nepal as "a multi-ethnic, multilingual, democratic, independent, indivisible, sovereign, Hindu and Constitutional Monarchical Kingdom". The end of the Panchayat System and the acknowledgement of the multi-ethnicity in the Constitution of 1990 gave a sigh of relief to the ethnic groups in Nepal but their demands became more forceful with the passage of time. The Janajatis expressed their discontent against the Brahmins very sharply who had an overwhelming presence of domination in every aspect of the life. Politics, the judiciary, the universities, and the civil services were all dominated by bahuns. According to one estimate, bahuns and chetris together just 31 per cent of the population had two-thirds of the jobs, whereas hill janajatis (i.e. excluding newars and tharus), with 22 per cent of the population had just 7 per cent of the jobs, and madhesis, with 31 per cent of the population had only 11 per cent of the jobs. Dalits with nearly 9 per cent of the population had just 0.3 per cent of the jobs.[44] Hence, to organize the different ethnic groups, a new national organisation called the Nepal Janajati Adivasi Mahasangh or Nepal Association of Indigenous Nationalities or NEFIN, was formed in 1990. Against this backdrop, there was a growth of the Communist Party of Nepal or CPN (Maoist) in Nepal who launched the People's War on February 12, 1996, and took the thread of protests of the ethnic groups. The Jana Andolan II of 2006 sealed the fate of Monarchy in Nepal with the assertion of ethnic groups for political power and representation. The Madhesis, Janajatis, Tamang became the forerunner of this struggle. In the Terai region, conflict broke out between the Madheshis and Parbatiyas (Hill dwellers). The Tharus in Madhesh refused to be part of the Madhesh province and wanted their own province in order to promote their distinct cultural, linguistic, and religious identity. They were scared to join the Madhesh groups, especially after the people of hill origin were driven away by the locals en masse during the Madheshi agitation in 2007. The Madheshis insisted on a large federal province, which would reinforce ethnic divisions.[45] The demand of the Madhesis was 'One Madhesh, One Pradesh' which kept on ringing in the valleys of Kathmandu. The Maoist gave a priority for creating ethnic autonomy with a regional devolution of power and ending all ethnic suppression. They prepared their forty-point programme and took recourse to insurgency to achieve this objective. The lives of thousands of people including civilians, police personnel, and insurgents were claimed because of the Peoples' war. Since then, terror had swept over Nepal and the violent conflict engulfed different parts of the country. A gross human rights violation took place because of this insurgency. Although they did not achieve all the objectives, but the 'Peoples' War' gave them certain legitimacy in domestic politics. The Maoist joined the Comprehensive Peace Agreement in 2006 and became a part of the peace process. The Constituent Assembly election held on April 10, 2008, marked a major watershed in the history of Nepal as well as for the Maoist. They renounced the use of violence and emerged as a constitutional political group. The party led the government thrice under Pushpa Kamal Dahal and Baburam Bhattarai. It had been a unique achievement that had enabled the CPN(M), to shift from militarised politics towards a strategy of "peaceful revolution"; to work through a democratic constitutional politics to transform the socio-political structure of the Himalayan kingdom.[46] The domestic convulsion in Nepal due to ethnic assertion and the rise of insurgency amidst other problem were a cause of concern to India because of its proximity to Terai region. From Nepal, Maoists reportedly often escaped into India when pursued by Nepalese security agencies during the period of Maoist insurgency in Nepal. The districts of East and West Champaran and Sirohi of Bihar were particularly frequented by the Maoists, mostly to seek medical aid and shelter. This trend of Maoist rebels escaping into India has presumably stopped since they had agreed to become a part of the government in Nepal.[47]

It is to be remembered that India shares a symbiotic relationship with Nepal because of the long historical and cultural linkages. Moreover, the assertion of CPI(M) in Nepal had an impact on the growth of Naxalites in India. In the tribal belt of West Bengal, Bihar, Jharkhand, Chhattisgarh, and Orissa where there was acute poverty and pockets of discontent against the government, a resurgence of Naxalite movement became evident. Interestingly enough, the Communist Party of India (Marxist)—the CPI(M)—which is up in arms against the homebred Maoists in India, has been acting for quite some time, on a low key, as an intermediator between the Nepalese parliamentary opposition and the underground Maoists of Nepal. The latter also, while keeping active links with the Naxalites in India, kept its doors open for discussions with the CPI(M).[48] However, Nepal is presently governed by the Constitution promulgated in 2015 which defined Nepal as an "independent, indivisible, sovereign, secular, inclusive, democratic, federal democratic republican state." The Maoist insurgency which was a pressing issue at one point of time had been resolved with the making of the society and politics in Nepal an inclusive one. In the three cases discussed above, it is quite pertinent that as an Indo-centric region, serious ethnic or racial upheavals in any country that is a part of South Asia are bound to have a spill-over effect in India.[49] India's regional clout, combined with its geopolitical position as the center of a hub-and-spokes regional system, reinforces this expectation.[50]

(d) Border Disputes

India and Pakistan share borders stretching 3,323 km and the dispute revolving around the borders is of enormous significance in the geo-politics of South Asia. In the Kashmir region, borders extend to the Line of Control which demarcates India-administered Kashmir and Pakistan-administered Kashmir. The border dispute centering Kashmir had existed since the Partition of India in 1947. It is India's assertion that Kashmir acceded to the Republic of India the minute Maharaja Hari Singh signed the Instrument of Accession. Pakistan asserted that Maharaja Hari Singh exercised influence in only small pockets of the state, enjoying little or no support from the local population.[51] Both India and Pakistan claimed Kashmir as their own which ultimately escalated into three wars between them in the year 1947-48, 1965, and 1999 respectively. While India has a control over Jammu, the Kashmir valley, Ladakh and

Siachen glacier, Pakistan on the other hand has a control over some parts of Kashmir and Gilgit-Baltistan. China too has her stakes over Aksai Chin region, Trans-Karakoram Tract and a part of Demchok. After the Indo-Pakistani war of 1947, United Nations mediated a ceasefire line known as Line of Control. The Shimla Agreement however formally institutionalized the Line of Control between the two. The Kargil conflict took the enemity of border dispute to a new height. Different militant groups like Lashkar-e-Taiba, Hizbul Mujahideen had also become active and were claiming lives and properties of the innocent civilians residing in Kashmir. Insurgency began to proliferate in Indian-administered Kashmir in the late 1980s. The Indian Army also retaliated to these threatening challenges in its own way. No matter what steps had been taken by the two countries at the political level, skirmishes, proxy wars between India and Pakistan had occurred from time to time. India had accused Pakistan for sponsoring terrorist groups to export terrorism to India. The terrorists conducted attack on the Parliament of India on 13 December 2001, the Mumbai attack in 2008, the attack on Pathankot Air Force Station and Indian Army Brigade Headquarter in Uri in 2016, attack on the Commando Training Centre at Lethpora in 2017, and in Pulwama in 2019. India retaliated by surgical strike against militant launch pads, dropped bombs into Balakot, Pakistan which killed a large number of terrorists of a Jaish-e-Mohammed. However against the backdrop of such attacks and counter attacks, India under Prime Minister Modi took a decisive step which drastically changed the status of Kashmir. The Government of India repealed the special status accorded to Jammu & Kashmir under Article 370 of the Indian Constitution. The Parliament of India passed the Jammu and Kashmir Reorganisation Act which took away the autonomy and dissolved the state and reorganised it into two union territories—Jammu & Kashmir in the West and Ladakh in the east since October 31, 2019. The state therefore has no longer the autonomy of her own constitution, a separate flag and legislation in matters of her own governance. However, unless and until the aspirations of the three ethnically distinct regions of the state (Jammu, Kashmir, and Ladakh) are reconciled, the tensions would complicate matters.[52] Other border issues which took the Indo-Pakistan bilateral relation to a challenging point was that of Siachen and Sir Creek.

Siachen Glacier, first discovered in 1907, is the world's longest glacier outside the polar regions, measuring 47 miles in length and three miles in width with an elongation of about 16,000 feet. The glacier emanates near the Indra Koli Pass on the Pakistan-China border, 37 aerial miles south-east of K-2, the second highest mountain peak in the world. It then runs along the Saltoro Range in a south-eastern direction until its snout turns into the Nubra River near Dzingrulma, in Indian-held Kashmir near Ladakh.[53] The geographical location speaks of the strategic positioning and significance of Siachen. India and Pakistan entered into a military conflict over the dispute of 1000 square miles of the territory in Siachen Glacier, Kashmir on April 13, 1984. Indian troops reached the glacier twelve days earlier than Pakistan could send her army. The conflict over Siachen Glacier was a part of the bitter and unresolved conflict over Kashmir between Pakistan and India. India launched 'Operation Meghdoot' under Colonel Narendra 'Bull' Kumar by airlifting a battalion of fully acclimatized soldiers from the Kumaon Regiment and Ladakh Scouts to the glaciers.

India successfully captured 70 km of Siachen Glacier including Saltoro Ridge, Sia La, Bilafond La and Gyong La. The Saltoro Ridge of the Siachin glacier serves as a divide that prevents direct linking of PoK with China, stopping them to develop geographical military linkages in the area. Siachen also serves as a watchtower for India to keep a deep watch on Gilgit and Baltistan regions of Pakistan. If Pakistan gets the location advantage in Siachen, it would become a big threat to India.[54] The conflict with Pakistan continued till April 13, 1984. More than 2000 people died in this mountain warfare and inhospitable terrain. On return, the soldiers looked like zombies having lost a fifth of their body weight. Some would have been afflicted by frostbite or pulmonary or cerebral edema.[55] India however maintained her position in the Siachen glacier after the victory. Stephen Cohen, a specialist on South Asia said the conflict between India and Pakistan over Siachen is like "A struggle of two bald men over a comb". He dismissed the Siachen as "not militarily important". This would perhaps be comforting if the two combatants did not both have nuclear weapons.[56] As a reaction to the launch of the Siachen war, Pakistan pitched conflict in Kargil and proxy war in Kashmir. However, some others suggested that India launched the Siachen operation to shore up the army's prestige, which had never been fully restored after the 1962 India-China war.[57]

It is important to mention 'Sir Creek', centring which the India-Pakistan rivalry boiled to a new height. 'Sir Creek' is a tidal estuary on river Indus located in the India-Pakistan border which flows into the Arabian Sea. The demarcation of Sir Creek and the boundary between India-Pakistan had been defined by the Tribunal Award of 1968. However, there were controversies between the two countries over greater claims over this marshy border which is the area of greater strategic significance. Sir Creek is located in the west of the Great Rann of Kutch area of India. In its course, Sir Creek shifts from Indian territory and enters Pakistan. It again re-enters India which causes difficulty in patrolling. As it is marshy, there are no physical barrier and demarcation by fencing. The Indian military Border Security Force (BSF) and Indian Coast Guard patrols Sir Creek as the area is sensitive from the viewpoint of security. Moreover, the area is geographically resourceful and economically viable. It is rich in gas and oil below the sea bed. Hence, both India and Pakistan were eager to settle on this boundary as the determination of the maritime boundaries would help in the fixation of the Exclusive Economic Zones and Continental Shelves. There were rounds of discussion regarding the claim over Sir Creek. But all of them failed to resolve the dispute. In 2008, both the sides agreed to resolve the issue by delimitation and demarcation. But again a dissention arose between the two. While Pakistan wanted to refer the territorial dispute for international arbitration, India considered the provisions of Shimla Agreement to be followed by the two. Later on both sides had resolved to settle this dispute in a speedy manner, given their obligations under the UN Convention on the Law of the Sea (UNCLOS). Any delay in the delineation of the maritime boundary could lead to the continental shelf of both countries coming under the purview of the International Seabed Authority.[58]

Secondly, India and Bangladesh share 4156 km long international border which is the fifth longest in the world. It demarcates the Indian states of Assam, Tripura, Mizoram, Meghalaya, and West Bengal on one side and the Bangladeshi division of Mymensingh, Khulna, Rajshahi, Chittagong, Rangpur, and Sylhet on the other side of the border. The border between India and Bangladesh crosses over plains, river, jungles, and hills. The border especially the riverine one is difficult to be patrolled. The pieces of land or 'Char' get submerged during flood while they act as posts in normal times. Hence, the border management offer a great deal of challenges to both the sides. On May 16, 1974, Prime Minister of India, Indira Gandhi and Bangladeshi counterpart Sheikh Mujibur Rehman signed the Indo-Bangladesh Agreement which dealt with the exchange of enclaves in the border. Under this agreement, India and Bangladesh were to handover the Tin Bigha Corridor and South Berubari to each other so that an access can be ensured to the Dahagram, Angarpota and other adjacent enclaves to South Berubari. Bangladesh was prompt to hand over South Berubari to India but India was unable to transfer the Tin Bigha Corridor to Bangladesh as per Agreement because of political and constitutional reasons. In 2011, an Additional Protocol for the Land Boundary Agreement was signed between Prime Minister of India Manmohan Singh and Sheikh Hasina of Bangladesh. The 2011 Protocol aimed to address the issue of adverse possession of land whereby India will receive 2,777.038 acres of land from Bangladesh and in turn transfer 2,267.682 acres of land to Bangladesh. It also made an accord with the State Governments of Assam, Meghalaya, Tripura, and West Bengal but unfortunately could not be implemented due to adverse political circumstances. In 2015, the historic Land Boundary Agreement was signed between Prime Minister Narendra Modi and Sheikh Hasina by which India took the initiative to transfer 111 enclaves which cover around 17,160.63 acres to Bangladesh. On the other hand, India received 51 enclaves which cover 7,110.02 acres which were in Bangladesh. The exchange of enclaves and land parcels were implemented in phases. The residents were given with the opportunity to choose their citizenship during the transfer of enclaves. The 119th Constitution Amendment Bill, 2013 was passed in both Lok Sabha as well as Rajya Sabha. President Pranab Mukherjee gave his assent to the Act on May 28, 2015. Although it was argued that in land swapping India gave up the claim of about 10,000 acres of land to Bangladesh, but this was done to make the Border Management effective and enforceable. The 2015, Land Boundary Agreement could address the long-drawn complexities of un-demarcated border (which passes through Tripura, Assam, and West Bengal) and the issue of enclaves. It is important to mention that the border between India and Bangladesh has informal trading points like Fakiragram, Mankachar in Assam, Lichubari and Dawki in Meghalaya, Kailashahar, Agartala, Sonamora, Bilonia in Tripura and Petrapole, Bagdha, Mejdia, Lalgola, Kaliagang and Hilli in West Bengal. However, these are the points in border areas which are used for smuggling of goods and other illegal activities. There are numerous cattle corridors which are used for transporting of cattle to and from India. Moreover, the enclaves have also acted as the hotspot of different criminal activities like drug peddling, trafficking and others. The problem of cross border infiltration and insurgency had thrown a challenge to the security of India. Bangladesh has become the hotbed of terrorist activities of groups like Harkat-ul Jihad al-Islami Bangladesh (HuJI-B) which has strong links with the Pakistan-based terrorist organization Lashkar-e-Taiba, Bangladesh's Jamaat-e-Islami (BJeI), Jagrata Muslim Janata Bangladesh (JMJB), etc. They conduct training camps in the soil of Bangladesh and export terrorism to neighbouring countries including India. The terrorist groups are equipped with sophisticated arms which often lead to cross firing between the insurgents and Border Security Force. It has been suspected that Pakistan's ISI has been coordinating anti-India activities along with outfits like the United Liberation Front of Assam, the National Socialist Council of Nagaland, the National Liberation Front of Tripura, and the All Tripura Tiger Force. Bangladesh is also viewed as a safe haven by *jihadis*, who use its friendly government and infra-structure to regroup for training purposes.[59]

Thirdly, two South Asian neighbours India and Nepal share 1751 km of open and porous border. People from both the sides are allowed to enter each other's territory with the right to residence, employment, and acquisition of property. The unrestricted flow over the years has fostered close economic interdependence and greater people to people contact. The Terai region brings the two countries so close that many Madheshi are of Indian origin and are inherently linked with the people across the frontiers. Every family in Tarai shares a *roti-beti* relationship (involving matrimonial alliances) with families across the border in Indian states of Bihar and Uttar Pradesh.[60] On the other hand, the crossing of border by the insurgents and criminals challenges the bilateral relationship. The criminals who are often convicted of smuggling, kidnapping, extortion, running syndicates, escape to the other country through the open border. Trafficking, both human and drug is a major cause of concern in the Indo-Nepal border. Women and child trafficking is an extremely heinous crime which takes place in hundreds every year. Many criminal groups which operate in Uttar Pradesh and Bihar also take sanctuary in Nepal for the sake of survival. The relationship between the two countries is governed by the Treaty of Peace and Friendship which was signed in 1950. A demand for a revision of the treaty had surfaced over time as some of the clauses of the treaty had become obsolete. But not much has been done to repeal or amend the clauses to keep pace with specific needs of the changing time. It is an undeniable fact that the bilateral relation of India with Nepal had both highs and lows. The buffer kingdom had a tradition of playing the China card for acquiring leverage from the Indian side. India on the other hand had also imposed blockade in the border which resulted in the scarcity of essential goods in the latter. The geographical reality of being a landlocked country is disadvantageous for Nepal as it is hugely dependent on India for transit. In other words, geography helps India to be decisive. New Delhi in the past had used this advantage to pursue its strategic agenda. During the Chinese sale of arms to

Nepal (1989), India had closed '13 of 15 transit points on its border with Nepal', precisely to pressurize it into obedience.[61] In 2015, another blockade in Nepal border began which severely affected the Nepali economy. Nepal blamed India for imposing an undeclared blockade and severing the supply of essential commodities, perishable items and earthquake relief material. India however denied all allegations put forward by Nepal and claimed that commodities could not reach Nepal because of the protests by Madheshis in border. However, after the blockade and the settling of impasse, India under Prime Minister Modi had made many conscious efforts to improve relationship with Nepal. In 2014, with Indian Prime Minister Narendra Modi's reinvigorated regional diplomacy, representatives from the Indian and Nepali survey offices sat down in Kathmandu, Nepal to work out border disputes. The topic of the border with India is a hot-button issue in Nepal; many feel that the current border does not protect Nepali sovereignty.[62] There had been a growth of anti-India feelings in the minds of the people of Nepal which got boiled up due to such blockade impasse. If anger could melt ice, Mount Everest would be standing bare and brown today—so angry are the people of Nepal with India. The four-month-old blockade of its border with India has pushed the erstwhile Himalayan kingdom face tremendous hardships.[63] Another recent controversy regarding the India and Nepal border had been the claims of both the countries on about 300 square kilometers (115 square miles) of mountainous land incorporating Lipulekh, Limpiyadhura, and Kalapani areas. The strategic Lipulekh pass holds a very significant position as it connects the Indian State of Uttarakhand with the Tibet region of China. In May 2020, Indian Defence Minister, Rajnath Singh inaugurated 80-km road from Dharchula to Lipulekh pass. This move had been protested by Nepal. In retaliation Nepal established her own claim over Lipulekh Pass on paper. By printing her new map Nepal claimed Lipulekh, Limpiyadhura, and Kalapani areas as integral to Nepal. India opposed this declaration as this claim of Nepal was not based on any historical or territorial evidence. This move from Nepal came after New Delhi published its new map of the border region in November 2019 in which the Indian-administered Kashmir has been divided into Jammu & Kashmir and Ladakh. The same map also portrayed that the disputed 'Kalapani' region in the Greater Himalayas was within the Indian jurisdiction. This move of India had fanned antagonism in Nepal as a result of which she immediately registered her objection and claimed that the Kalapani region is an unsettled territory of the Darchula district in the Sudurpashchim province of Nepal. India however was obstinate on her point that Kalapani was India's part. This brought a tremendous disagreement over border areas between the two countries. Nepal is strategically sandwiched between India and China. Nepal at different point of time had played the China card against India. The new political map of India was seen as a disregard to the sovereignty of Nepal. It is important to mention that the Kalapani region is strategically significant. It serves as a tri-junction between India, Nepal, and China. Hence, the dissention between India and Nepal is of much strategic importance as the interest of China is also involved in this. Nepal as a landlocked country had a long dependence on India. However, Nepal had been trying to come out of the shadow of India and move closer to China for aid, investment and loan. China also considers Nepal an indispensable part of the Belt and Road Initiative (BRI) and finds it judicious to invest in Nepal so that her drift from India could be institutionalied.

IV. FROM LOOK EAST TO ACT EAST

The collapse of Soviet Union resulted in a radical change in the world as well as in the realm of Indian foreign policy. This strategic shift in the Indian foreign policy domain was enacted during the Prime Ministership of P.V. Narsimha Rao (1991-96) when India accepted the free trade regime and embraced the 'Look East Policy'. It was aimed at engagement with South East Asian countries, viz. Indonesia, Philippines, Malaysia, Brunei, Singapore, Cambodia, Laos, Myanmar, Thailand, and Vietnam. The then Finance Minister Manmohan Singh, was the chief architect of the Look East Policy. However, the policy was thereafter continued by the successive Prime Ministers Atal Bihari Vajpayee (1998-2004) and Manmohan Singh (2004-14) himself. Under Prime Minister Narendra Modi (2014-), the Look East Policy got rechristened as 'Act East Policy'. Under the aegis of different Prime Ministers, the Look East Policy could be divided into three phases.

- Phase I—Look East Policy from 1991
- Phase II—Link East Policy from 2000
- Phase III—Act East Policy from 2014 and continuing.

The relationship between India with South East Asian countries dated for a long period of time as the former had a great cultural influence on the latter. Buddhism, a religion predominantly followed in the South East Asian countries had its origin from India. The 'Asian' identity was a reflection of the common linkage between the two. This was reiterated by the freedom fighters during the struggle of Indian independence. Pandit Jawaharlal Nehru was an apostle of Asianism. India's first Prime Minister, Jawaharlal Nehru organized and celebrated

BOX 4.2: Challenges and Responses in South Asia

- India has river water disputes with Bangladesh, Nepal and Pakistan.
- Some disputes have been resolved by agreements like Indus Water Treaty (1960), Kosi (1954), Gandaki Agreement (1964) and Mahakali Treaty (1996). While agreement of water sharing of River Teesta (Bangladesh) could not be achieved.
- India shares porous borders with Bangladesh and Nepal which result in migrants entering illegally. The maritime boundary with Sri Lanka is also crossed by migrants unlawfully for taking refuge in India.
- India faces major ethnic challenges and insurgency from her North-Eastern region and Kashmir. Sri Lanka and Nepal are the two countries whose ethnic problems and insurgency have a spill over effect on India.
- The India-Pakistan Border stretching up to 3,323 km; India and Bangladesh up to 4156 km; India and Nepal up to 1751 km had been a source of security concern to India.
- The Kashmir issue, Siachen and Sir Creek had resulted in deteriorating the bilateral relationship of India and Pakistan.
- The role of extra-regional powers could not be underestimated in aggravating complexities related to border.

"Southeast Asia Day" at Lucknow on October 24, 1945, and expressed solidarity with Indonesia.[64] But with the passage of time the linkages between India with the South East Asian countries had suffered a decline. The relationship however experienced an upsurge by the introduction of the Look East Policy by India. The driving factor was to integrate India's economy with the world economy by collaborating it with South East Asian countries regional grouping. However, the objective of attaining a multi-layered relationship between India and the different countries of South East Asia were also there. This section will focus on the motivations for India to embrace the Look East Policy.

To begin with, Southeast Asia is a hub of natural resources with high economic potentials. During the decades of the 1970s and 1980s, the Asian newly industrializing economies (NIEs) of Hong Kong, Singapore, South Korea, and Taiwan had achieved phenomenal growth. By the second half of the 1980, however, their growth rates began to decline with the rise of the four largest ASEAN (Association of South East Asian Nations) economies of Indonesia, Malaysia, the Philippines, and Thailand. The South East Asian countries, especially the ASEAN Four was successful in transforming the region to an economically vibrant one by shifting their focus from export of commodities to that of manufacturing and services. Countries like Myanmar, Thailand, and Vietnam was blessed to be the 'Rice Bowl of Asia'. Their export of rice to other countries also ranked high. Another factor that brought India closer to the South East Asian countries was the need of alternative energy resources. The Gulf War and the Iraqi invasion of Kuwait had resulted in a massive oil shock in the world. As South East Asia especially Myanmar and Indonesia are the hub of petroleum and gas, so India could be a beneficiary of the same by cultivating ties with these countries. The abundance of natural resources, increasing intra and inter regional trade motivated India to enter the orbit of South East Asia.

Secondly, one of the cardinal issues for India to frame her Look East Policy was to check China's increasing influence in the South East Asian region. China had a strong foothold in

South East Asia by virtue of its economic might and assertive leadership. The countries of South East Asia and the members of ASEAN did not look upon China through the lens of threat and insecurity as China refused to devalue its currency during the Asian financial crisis (1997) in order to help stabilize the Asian currency market. The East Asian economic crisis of 1997-99 undermined ASEAN's international image and revealed the weaknesses of ASEAN's organizational model.[65] Such a benevolent attitude of China had earned her credibility to the countries of ASEAN. India was therefore keen in engaging herself to check China's assertiveness by launching the Look East Policy. The installation of Chinese monitoring centre in the Coco Island which was close to Andaman and Nicobar Islands was also a cause of security concern for India.

Thirdly, for three and a half centuries Europe and America had dominated the world. Almost the whole of Asia was a colony of Europe. Now in the 21st century, Asia and the Pacific rim are likely to be the West's true peer in the wealth, in technology and in skilled human resources.[66] India is a greater player in the South Asian region. However, South Asia as a region did not give much opportunity to India for trade and investment. SAARC as a regional organization started its journey in 1985 but political bickering and lack of transparency challenged the organization to perform in full swing. The economic underdevelopment of the region compelled India to come closer to South East Asian countries. Moreover, the disappointment emanating from India's Look West Policy reinforced her faith in optimizing her South Eastern neighbours.

Fourthly, India's geography and strategic positioning is another determinant for India's Look East Policy. The geography of North Eastern India which comprises eight sister states, viz. Arunachal Pradesh, Assam, Manipur, Meghalaya, Mizoram, Nagaland, Sikkim, and Tripura holds a very strategic location. It is the gateway to the South East Asian countries. This region shares a long international border of 5182 km across Bhutan, Nepal, China, Bangladesh, and Myanmar. The North East region comprises eight percent of India's total land area and three percent of the population of the country. The socio-economic development of the region in terms of its economy, infrastructure, connectivity, and stability is highly sensitive to India because of the region's geographical positioning and proximity to neighbouring countries. Past attempts to integrate the north east with the Indian mainstream, economically at least, have yielded no tangible results. Therefore, the focus has now shifted to trans-national and sub-regional cooperation between India and Southeast Asian countries, as the only way to bail out the region from its state of underdevelopment and political crisis.[67] By constructing different means of communication in the form of air, rail, and road, the geographical distance between North East and South East Asia could be bridged.

Against this background, India embarked on her Look East Policy. In 1992, India became the Sectoral Dialogue Partner of ASEAN for Tourism, Commerce, Investment, Science, and Technology and consequently attained the status of Full Dialogue Partner at the Fifth ASEAN Summit held in Bangkok on December 14-15, 1995. In 1996, India achieved the membership of ASEAN Regional Forum which offered India to play a more meaningful role with the South East Asian countries. The relationship between India and ASEAN countries suffered a minor setback after India conducted Pokhran II Nuclear Test in May 1998. While countries like Malaysia and Thailand showed their initial displeasure over the Indian nuclear tests; other countries of ASEAN continued to have steady relationship with India. On November 5, 2002, India- ASEAN Summit was held in Phnom Penh. Given a dynamic surge of ASEAN-India cooperation, they agreed to further promote people-to-people interaction not only through dialogue at the level of policymakers but also through exchange programmes of youth, media personnel, academics, business people, government officials, and artists. Interaction among these groups of people would help promote better understanding and lasting friendship which will be important in forging greater cooperation between ASEAN and India. They also agreed to support the development of ASEAN-India relations.[68] In the Second ASEAN-India Summit held in 2003, the ASEAN-India Framework Agreement on Comprehensive Economic Cooperation was signed by the leaders of ASEAN and India for the establishment of ASEAN-India Regional Trade and Investment Area for free trade in goods, services, and investment. Elaborating on the so-called second phase of the Look East policy, Yashwant Sinha, India's former External Affairs Minister, noted in 2003: India's 'Look East' policy has now entered phase two. Phase one was focused primarily on ASEAN countries and on trade and investment linkages. Phase two is characterised by an expanded definition of 'East' extending from Australia to China and East Asia with ASEAN as its core. Phase two marks a shift from exclusively economic issues to economic and security.[69] However, in November 2005 India and ten ASEAN members signed a partnership pact for encouraging trade, investment, tourism, culture, sports, and people-to-people contacts. They vowed to arrest international terrorism and other trans-national crimes to make the region safe from such malaises. In 2005, India participated at the East Asia Summit (EAS) for the first time, comprising 16 countries, which included the 10 members of the Association of Southeast Asian Nations (ASEAN), Japan, China, Republic of Korea, Australia, and New Zealand. Initially, India was considered as one of the Founding Members but reservation was shown by China and Malaysia. In June 2005, India signed a Comprehensive Economic Cooperation Agreement (CECA) with Singapore for a free trade area. The ASEAN-India Free Trade Area (AIFTA) which was signed amongst the ten member states of the ASEAN and India at Bali in 2003 came into effect on 1 January 2010. At the 10th ASEAN-India Summit held in New Delhi on December 20, 2012, India and ASEAN concluded negotiations for FTAs in services and investments. With the impressive achievement of India with regard to her Look East Policy, US Secretary of State Hillary Clinton commented: "We encourage India not just to look East, but to engage East and act East. And its leadership in South and Central Asia is critically important."[70]

India's Look East Policy (LEP) promoted her engagement with neighbours of South-East and Asia-Pacific for nearly two and a half decades. The policy was rechristened as the 'Act East Policy' (AEP) in 2014 under the leadership of Prime Minister Narendra Modi. The NDA Government adopted the

Act East Policy which was finally launched at the East Asia Summit in Myanmar in November 2014. Foreign policy of a country is a mixture of 'symbolism and substance' in the case of India-ASEAN relations, India appears to have grown from rhetoric to reality with its shift from LEP to AEP.[71] The policy sought to extend India's relationship with countries of ASEAN and expanded the country's engagement from Korea in the North to Australia and New Zealand in the South, and from neighbouring Bangladesh to Fiji and Pacific Island countries in the Far East. While the Look East Policy engaged the South East Asian countries, the Act East Policy focussed on South East Asia along with the countries of East Asia. "India's Act East policy is an important part of our Indo-Pacific vision. ASEAN is and always will be the heart of our Act East policy," Modi told a gathering that included the top leadership of the grouping.[72] The Act East Policy aimed at intensifying economic, strategic, and diplomatic relations with the countries and mainly rested on three pillars, viz. connectivity, commerce and culture.

Connectivity

Connectivity is a lifeline of any relationship. The connectivity-related projects which started under the Look East Policy continued under the Act East Policy. However, some of the major thrust areas of connectivity are as follows:

First, The Kaladan Multi-modal transit transport project deserves a special mention. The Kaladan Multimodal Transit Transport Project focuses on the development of land, river, and sea routes. These routes aimed to connect Kolkata port in India with Sittwe port in Myanmar by sea. It would also link Sittwe to Paletwa in Myanmar by the Kaladan river and Paletwa to be connected by road to the state of Mizoram in North Eastern India. The Kaladan project intends to connect Kolkata and Sittwe by bridging a distance of 539 km. It is a big project for which a fund of US$ 484 million has been invested. The deadline of this project was 2014, but various issues and challenges have stretched it to 2019-20.[73] The Kaladan multi-modal project intended to accelerate the economic intercourse between Northeast India, Myanmar and beyond for making the region vibrant. Moreover, the Trans-Asian Highway, the India-Myanmar rail linkages, the gas and oil pipeline project between Myanmar, India, and Bangladesh, and International Optical Fibre Network between North-East India and Southeast Asia, etc. are also extremely positive steps to increase connectivity in the region. In addition to these, the ASEAN Highway has also been developed which can be accessed from Assam through Dimapur, Kohima, Imphal to reach the border town of Moreh which is located just next to Myanmar. India undertook the construction of two sections of the trilateral highway in Myanmar, aimed at building 120.74 km Kalewa-Yagyi road section and constructing 69 bridges along with the approach road on the 149.70 km Tamu-Kyigone-Kalewa (TKK) road section....[74] The Asian Highway I which is of seventy-one km stretch has connected Thailand, Laos, Vietnam Cambodia, Malaysia, and Indonesia. This is a very significant linkage for giving a new status to North East region.

Secondly, the development of North East had been given high priority for improving connectivity under Act East Policy. For this end, Narendra Modi had enlarged his vision from South East Asian countries to that of Asia Pacific. In August 2017, India and Japan committed themselves to establish the Japan-India Coordination Forum (JICF) for development of North-Eastern Region, and give priority to development areas like improving connectivity by constructing highways and waterways, roads, and developing electric infrastructure. Prime Ministers Narendra Modi and Prime Minister of Japan Shinzo Abe, in their first summit meeting in 2014, emphasised the importance of the North Eastern Region. At the next summit held in 2015, Abe expressed his intention to provide Japan's official development assistance (ODA) loans for connectivity projects in the North Eastern Region. In May 2016, Modi announced a proposal to develop an Asia-Africa Growth Corridor (AAGC) with the aid of Japan. It proposed for creating a "free and open Indo-Pacific region" by constructing sea corridors that will connect India and other countries of South and Southeast Asia. India and Japan also signed an agreement in 2017 to establish the India-Japan Act East Forum which was conceived of as a

BOX 4.3: Look East and Act East Policies

- India's Look East Policy was initiated in 1991 during the Prime Ministership of P.V. Narsimha Rao and Finance Minister Manmohan Singh.
- India established her relations with the ASEAN countries namely, Indonesia, Philippines, Malaysia, Brunei, Singapore, Cambodia, Laos, Myanmar, Thailand, and Vietnam.
- In 1992, India became the Sectoral Dialogue Partner of ASEAN and later, Full Dialogue Partner in 1995.
- In 2003, the ASEAN-India Framework Agreement on Comprehensive Economic Cooperation was signed by the leaders of ASEAN and India for free trade in goods, services, and investment.
- Look East Policy was modified to 'Act East Policy' in 2014 under the premiership of Narendra Modi.
- The Policy included South East Asia and Asia Pacific countries under its ambit.

platform for bilateral cooperation. The forum will focus on connectivity projects and promote people-to-people contacts through tourism and culture. Japan had supported India's connectivity initiatives taken in Bangladesh, Myanmar, and other neighbouring countries. Both India and Japan had tried to resist Chinese Belt and Road initiative. Thus, India's Act East policy and Japan's 'Open and free Indo-Pacific strategy' had a good blending to be implemented in the Indo-Pacific region.

Thirdly, the Act East Policy aims to connect India's northeast with Thailand. Northeast is being developed as a gateway to south-east Asia. The India-Myanmar-Thailand Trilateral Highway, which will span more than 1,300 km will connect Moreh in Manipur in India to Mae Sot in Thailand via Myanmar. As part of a drive to enhance connectivity with Myanmar, the Moreh-Tamu land route joining Moreh in India with Tamu in Myanmar became operational in 2018.[75] "This initiative will immensely strengthen India's Act East Policy and Thailand's Act West Policy," Modi said in his address at the 'Sawasdee PM Modi' event in Bangkok on day one of his visit for ASEAN, EAS, and RCEP Summits... "Once the India-Myanmar-Thailand trilateral highway is opened, there will be seamless connectivity between both our countries. I am glad that all of you will have a chance to be part of this story," he said.[76]

Fourthly, digital connectivity is another objective of India's Act East Policy. In November 2015 at the India-ASEAN Summit, Prime Minister Modi announced his objective to boost physical and digital connectivity between India and the ASEAN nations. During the Republic Day celebrations in New Delhi, Modi offered to set up digital villages in Cambodia, Laos, Myanmar, and Vietnam by utilising India's $1 billion line of credit to ASEAN for 'connectivity, culture, and commerce'. Among other things, India hopes to work towards an India-ASEAN Single Aviation Market and would like to facilitate more business and leisure tourists by having more direct flights connecting its Tier II and Tier III cities.[77] On the eve of his visit to Laos to attend ASEAN and East Asia Summits, Prime Minister Narendra Modi said India wishes to enhance physical and digital connectivity with the South East Asian nations and leverage the modern interconnected world for the mutual benefit.[78]

Fifthly, India has also taken steps for developing and finalising projects on ports for enhancing connectivity. The countries which have collaborated with India are Bangladesh, Sri Lanka, Myanmar and others. India is interested in collaborating with Bangladesh for developing the Payra port which is located in Bangladesh. New Delhi has expressed interest in developing the neighbour's newest sea port Payra. It's a big move by India and an expression of the trajectory of strategic ties between the two countries.[79] Moreover, during his visit to Sri Lanka, Prime Minister Modi finalised several projects including the Trincomalee port project. India will help develop both Colombo and Trincomalee ports in Sri Lanka. The development potentially extends India's outreach in the Indian Ocean, where China is pursuing an expansionist policy. India is also helping build road and rail projects in Sri Lanka.[80] India and Myanmar are also involved in development of port as a part of sea-river-land Kaladan Multi-Modal Transit Transport Project. The port facilities at Sittwe and the Paletwa inland water transport terminal have been set up with the help of India.

The joint statement issued during Prime Minister Modi's visit to Myanmar indicated that the two countries would create a MoU on appointing a port operator that may include both sides to be responsible for the operation and maintenance of the ports.

In early 2016, the commencement of coastal shipping service between India and Bangladesh marked another milestone in connecting the BIMSTEC sub-region. This bilateral coastal shipping agreement is significant because it not only allows India better access to its North-eastern region but also gives Bangladesh access to Nepal and Bhutan through India. This puts in place a sub-regional multimodal connectivity among these countries. During the Fourth BIMSTEC Summit held in Kathmandu, Nepal on 30-31 August 2018, the leaders of the BIMSTEC member-states reiterated their resolve to establish seamless multi-modal transportation linkages and smooth, synchronized, and simplified transit facilities through the development, expansion, and modernization of highways, railways, waterways, sea routes, airways in the region. It was directed to speed up efforts to conclude the BIMSTEC Coastal Shipping Agreement and the BIMSTEC Motor Vehicle Agreement as early as possible taking into account the special circumstances and needs of the member-states. Transport and communication is one of the 14 sectors of cooperation since the inception of BIMSTEC in 1997. This sector is led by India.[81]

Culture

Prime Minister Narendra Modi had very strategically used the 'Culture' mechanism for extending the Act East Policy. He had used the Soft Power status for promoting cultures across region. We may recall Joseph Nye in order to understand the content and implication of Soft Power. According to Joseph Nye, the person who coined the term, 'soft power' is the ability to influence others to get the results one wants through 'attraction' rather than 'coercion' or 'payment'.[82] If a country has the potential to exercise her soft power then she can afford to pursue her own objectives without much harder resistance from others. One author, in his article "India's Soft Power Diplomacy Under the Modi Administration: Buddhism,

Diaspora and Yoga" has referred to Buddhism, Diaspora and Yoga as parts of Modi's Cultural Diplomacy.[83] We can take an insight into three of these elements.

India had been the birthplace of Buddhism and it was a common linkage between India and South East Asian countries especially Cambodia, Thailand, Indonesia. The tie of Buddhism, which was acknowledged by the Look East Policy, got a greater expression under the Act East Policy. Buddha's message of peace, equality, non-violence had a tremendous relevance in today's life. In fact, there had been a chord of similarity between Buddhism and Hinduism. Prime Minister Modi had brilliantly embraced the philosophy of Buddhism in crafting the 'Act East Policy'. During his official trips to China, Japan, and Vietnam he had visited the Buddhist temples and shrines. In 2014, ancient seat of learning, the Nalanda University was restored under the aegis of Modi administration, although the work had started during the tenure of Prime Minister Manmohan Singh. The initiative for restoring this ancient seat of learning came from different corners of the world including Thailand, Singapore, South Korea, Japan, China and others who had also funded the project in different proportion. During his trip to Vietnam in 2016, Modi announced special scholarships for Vietnamese students who would engage in pursuing advanced Buddhist studies at Indian Centres of Learning. An initiative was taken on May 4, 2015 when the International Buddha Poornima Diwas was celebrated by paying homage to Lord Buddha. Prime Minister Modi graced this occasion along with other invited Buddhist monks. They paid their tributes to the philosophies and teachings of Gautama Buddha. Prime Minister Modi wanted to project India as an integral part of Buddhist Asia and used his Cultural Diplomacy for this purpose.

Secondly, Prime Minister Narendra Modi has appealed the Diaspora in a sustained manner and cultivated their sentiment to connect them to their motherland India. They are considered to be an integral part of our country. The practice of staying connected with the diaspora helps in getting partners and even investors for development. For this end, the "Pravasi Bharatiya Divas" or Non-Resident Indian Day is celebrated for commemorating the success of the Indian diaspora and to recognize their contributions to India's growth and development. This practice is in motion as a part of India Government's programme for some time. Prime Minister Narendra Modi had used his charisma and leadership style in pooling diaspora members to contribute in their own ways. The Modi Government had also decided to give a single identity card to all the Indian Diaspora to make it easier for them to remain in touch with their homeland and secure lifelong Indian visas if they wanted to become Indian citizens. The Modi Government had allowed visitors from 43 nations, who shared cultural linkages with India, to get visa upon arrival in India.[84] This initiative was a soft power mechanism of not only earning investment and remittances but to nurture a strong lobby of Indians stationed in foreign land. Thus, steps had been taken by Narendra Modi to improve closer ties with other countries by boosting culture, economy and people-to-people contact.

Thirdly, another element of the Soft Power Strategy has been the use of Yoga. Yoga forms an integral part of Indian tradition and culture. It aims for the spiritual and emotional well-being of individuals. The West has realized that Yoga, an Indian practice acts a reliever of the emotional stress and physical hazards of contemporary life. It brings a balance between mind and body and helps to attain wellness. The United Nations has also acknowledged the importance of this practice and adopted the International Yoga Day to be celebrated on June 21 every year. Prime Minister Modi tried to reach the people of South East and East Asia by promoting this Indian practice.

Commerce

India's trade and commerce received a boost in recent times. Indian Prime Minister Modi went on record saying that when his government took over in 2014, India's GDP was about US$ 2 trillion. But in just five years, it was increased to nearly US$ 3 trillion. He also referred to his government's plans to make India a US$ 5 trillion economy.[85] Under the leadership of Prime Minister Modi, the economic interactions between India and the South Eastern countries including Asia

Pacific had reached a new height. India had meaningfully entered into trade and investment with countries of South East Asia especially Singapore. On the other hand, ASEAN countries also invested in India for construction of roads, ports, ships, etc. India's trade pattern with Japan and South Korea was also noteworthy. By emphasising the long bilateral ties with Japan, Prime Minister Modi appealed for investment in the manufacturing sector. In September 2014, in his first interaction with Prime Minister Narendra Modi, Japan's Prime Minister Shinzo Abe had promised US$ 35 billion in corporate investments and financing for infrastructure development in India. Prime Minister Modi had assured special mechanisms to fast-track approvals for Japanese investors. Japan's Prime Minister Abe had also set a target of doubling the number of Japanese companies operating in India in five years.[86] Moreover, some flagship initiatives taken by Indo-Japan collaboration had been crafted for smart cities, Delhi-Mumbai Industrial Corridor and Shinkansen bullet train between Mumbai and Ahmedabad. Japan agreed to extend US$ 33.5 billion public and private investments in India for supporting projects in various sectors including infrastructure, connectivity, transport, smart cities, energy and skill development. Prime Minister Modi decided to set up a number of Japanese industrial townships and electronic parks in India. The Prime Minister of Japan on the other hand agreed to support 'Make-in India', 'Digital India', and 'Skill India' programmes. Both the countries had sincerely tried to make the journey smooth. During 2014-19, the quality and quantity of Japan's official development assistance (ODA) witnessed remarkable strides and India has been the biggest recipient of Japan's aid for several years now. Though Japan's private investment has also increased during these years, it has not lived up to its potential.

The relationship between India and South Korea had also flourished under the Act East Policy. In 2011, bilateral trade amount was US$ 20.5 billion but it dropped radically thereafter. However, after 2014, trade recovered to US$ 21.5 billion. India and South Korea had set a target to increase bilateral trade to US$ 50 billion by 2030 from US$ 20 billion in 2017-18 and to speedily conclude negotiations to upgrade the bilateral Comprehensive Economic Partnership Agreement (CEPA). While India's exports to South Korea increased meagerly from US$ 3.72 billion in 2010-11 (the year the CEPA was implemented) to US$ 4.46 billion in 2017-18, its imports from South Korea jumped from US$ 10.47 billion in 2010-11 to US$ 16.36 billion in 2017-18. The Indian Prime Minister praised the companies operating in India and said that they had made large-scale investments in India, participated in the 'Make in India' programme and also generated jobs. The South Korean President said that it was the right time to take bilateral relationship to the next level.[87] Korea's presence in the automobile sector had become prominent. South Korean FDI to India had steadily increased in recent years, reaching US$ 5.71 billion by the end of 2018. Actually, South Korean economy is heavily export dependent. To keep the export engine that drives its economy running, South Korea is now targeting economies with the greatest growth potential and India (and its huge consumer market) is projected as a strong trade partner.[88]

India's relation with Australia had also improved under the Act East Policy. Former Prime Minister of Australia Tony Abbott visited India from 4-5 September 2014 and signed a number of agreements including Civil Nuclear Cooperation, Sports, Water resources and Enhancement of Skills, etc. Prime Minister of India Narendra Modi also visited Australia for G20 Leaders' Summit at Brisbane in November 2014, followed by an official visit from 16-18 November 2014. The India-Australia economic relationship has grown significantly in recent years. The Seventh India-Australia Economic Policy Dialogue was held in Canberra during July 16-18, 2017 in which a Comprehensive Economic Cooperation Agreement (CECA) was discussed. The "natural partnership" between India and Australia witnessed a steady growth in 2019 on several fronts, especially in the defence sector primarily due to a common concern about China's increasing military presence in the Indo-Pacific.[89] India's bilateral trade with the ASEAN economies had also increased. India's exports item to ASEAN economies was also high and diversified. From the level of US$ 142 billion which was the export amount in 2018, it was expected to be doubled by 2025. Some of the measures taken for boosting India-ASEAN trade were enhancing cooperation to exporters, increase services trade, continuous review of the ASEAN-India trade in goods and agreement, simplifying the customs procedures, promote greater private sector engagement and support greater financial inclusion towards improving access to financial services. Going ahead, there had been huge trade and investment opportunities for enhancing India-ASEAN cooperation in sectors such as infrastructure and Fintech, culture and tourism, IT/ITES and e-commerce, education and skill development, healthcare and pharmaceuticals and agriculture and food processing, among others.[90] Prime Minister Modi had enlarged India's vision by including countries like Fiji and Mongolia under the domain of Act East Policy. PM Modi visited Fiji in Nov. 2014. It was the first visit by an Indian Prime Minister to Fiji in 33 years. The strengthening of economic ties was the motivating factor behind this visit.

Conclusion

India's engagement in South and South East Asia has evolved over a period of time. The economic and political development of the country has given her a strong foothold in the South Asian region. Nevertheless, it faces volatile and bitter challenges from the region on issues like river water dispute, illegal migration, ethnic conflict, insurgency, and border disputes. SAARC as a regional body has tried to address the problems but the organization suffers from multiple myopia. The organization was created with strictly non-political and multilateral vision but politics and bilateral problems have continued to overshadow its image and existence. Article 3 of the SAARC Charter says that the Heads of States should meet at least once a year while the actual picture depicts high irregularity of SAARC Summits. SAARC as an organization needs to accept its institutional deficit and try to function in accordance with the prevailing realities. A new understanding of the region, politics, and economy would help to revitalize the organization and its economic initiative like SAFTA. The Government of India, from time to time, had taken positive steps to improve ties with the countries of South Asia as well as South East Asia. The Gujral Doctrine and the subsequent 'Neighbourhood First Policy' had been designed to boost up the relationship with our neighbours. India as a major power in South Asia very enthusiastically prioritized relations with South Asian neighbours and extended concessions for bringing them closer. Likewise, by embracing the Look East and the subsequent Act East Policy, the Government of India had extended its orbit of engagement from South East Asia to Asia Pacific. The strategic and economic imperatives had made the countries of the region to complement each other. If the present trend continues, then India would very successfully evolve as a greater strategic player in its engagement with South and South-East Asia respectively.

Endnotes

1. SAARC Secretariat, "SAARC Charter"; on line source: http://www.saarc-sec.org/SAARC-Charter/5/. Accessed on 22 April 2020.
2. Manzoor Ahmad (2017), "SAARC Summits1985-2016: The Cancellation Phenomenon", *IPRI Journal*, XVII(1), Winter, p. 90.
3. S.D. Muni (1987), "South Asian Association for Regional Cooperation: Evolution and Prospects", *Internationales Asian Forum*, 18(3-4), p. 238.
4. Francesco Obino (2009), "SAARC: The Political Challenge for South Asia and Beyond", *Economic and Political Weekly*, 44(9), p. 119.
5. Kishore C. Dash (1996), "The Political Economy of Regional Cooperation in South Asia", *Pacific Affairs*, 69(2), p. 185.
6. Padmaja Murthy (2000), "India and its Neighbours: The 1990s and Beyond", *Strategic Analysis*, XXIV(8), p. 1419.
7. Smruti S. Pattanaik (2006), "Making Sense of Regional Cooperation: SAARC at Twenty", *Strategic Analysis*, 30(1), p. 153.
8. *The Hindu* (2020), "Coronavirus | SAARC countries unite to combat COVID-19 infections", April 21; on line source: https://www.thehindu.com/news/international/coronavirus-saarc-countries-unite-to-combat-covid-19-infections/article31397086.ece. Accessed on 15 May 2020.
9. Ma Jiali (2012), "SAARC: Achievements and Challenges", *Policy Perspectives*, 9(1), p. 163.

10. Ashit Ranjan Mishra and Elizabeth Roche (2015), "Saarc to review Observer Status only after five years", *Livemint*; on line source: https://www.livemint.com/Politics/japiR4cqvcSW9HgIbxUuxO/Saarc-to-review-observer-status-only-after-five-years.html. Accessed on 11 April 2020.
11. Saman Kelegama (2015), "Changing Face: The Trials and Fortunes of Regional Cooperation Under Saarc", *India International Centre Quarterly*, 41(3-4), p. 43.
12. Meena Rao, S. Subba Rao (2011), "SAARC: Regional Co-operation Through Track-III Diplomacy", *The Indian Journal of Political Science*, 71(4), p. 1268.
13. Priyanka Kher (2012), "Political Economy of Regional Integration in South Asia", Regional Value Chains Background Paper No. RVC 5, UNCTAD, pp. 3-4.
14. Amita Batra (2007), "South Asia's Free Trade Agreement: Strategies and Options", *Economic and Political Weekly*, 42(38), p. 3878.
15. Nisha Taneja and Aparna Sawhney (2007), "Revitalising SAARC Trade: India's Role at 2007 Summit", *Economic and Political Weekly*, 42(13), p. 1082.
16. Nisha Taneja, Saon Ray, Neetika Kaushal and Devjit Roy Chowdhury (2011), "An Approach to Prune India's Sensitive Lists under SAFTA", *Economic and Political Weekly*, 46(11), p. 15.
17. Asit Ranjan Misra (2013), "Safta members propose to reduce sensitive list", *Livemint*, 17 July; on line source: https://www.livemint.com/Politics/fInJz4wPhBeWZd0WBGz2bO/Safta-members-propose-to-reduce-sensitive-list.html. Accessed on 28 June 2020.
18. Kirtika Suneja (2018), "India-South Asia trade has potential to triple to $62 billion", says World Bank, *The Economic Times*, 24 September; on line source: https://economictimes.indiatimes.com/news/economy/foreign-trade/india-south-asia-trade-has-potential-to-triple-to-62-billion-says-world bank/articleshow/65935340.cms?from=mdr. Accessed on 19 June 2020.
19. Dushni Weerakoon (2006), Jayanthi Thennakoon, "SAFTA: Myth of Free Trade", *Economic and Political Weekly*, 41(37), p. 3922.
20. The World Bank, "Agreement on South Asian Free Trade Area"; on line source: wits.worldbank.org › GPTAD › PDF › archive › SAFTA. Accessed on 2 July 2020.
21. Smruti S. Pattanaik, "Making Sense of Regional Cooperation: SAARC at Twenty", *Strategic Analysis*, 30(1), 2011, p. 148.
22. Amita Batra, "Saarc and Economic Cooperation", *India International Centre Quarterly*, 41(3/4), Winter 2014-Spring 2015, p. 52.

23. Asit K. Biswas (2011), "Cooperation or conflict in transboundary water management: Case study of South Asia", *Journal des Sciences Hydrologiques*, 56(4), p. 664.
24. Ashok Swain (1993), "Conflicts over water: The Ganges Water Dispute", *Security Dialogue*, 24(4), p. 434.
25. Ishtiaq Hossain (1981), "Bangladesh-India Relations: Issues and Problems", *Asian Survey*, 21(11), p. 1118.
26. Haweya Ismail (2015), "Indian River Link Project: Bangladesh Concerned Over Ignored Agreement"; on line source: http://www.futuredirections.org.au/publication/indian-river-link-project-bangladesh-concerned-over-ignored-agreement/. Accessed on 11 June 2020.
27. Hari Bansh Jha (2013), "Nepal-India Cooperation in River Water Management", *Strategic Analysis*, 37(2), p. 229.
28. Saleem H. Ali (2008), "Water Politics in South Asia: Technocratic Cooperation and Lasting Security in the Indus Basin and Beyond", *Journal of International Affairs,* 61(2), p. 171.
29. Gargi Parsai (2011), "India, Pakistan resume talks on Tulbul project"; on line source: https://www.thehindu.com/news/national/India-Pakistan-resume-talks-on-Tulbul-project/article13884916.ece. Accessed on 6 July 2020.
30. The *Hindustan Times* (2019), "Will stop our share of water to Pak, says Nitin Gadkari a week after Pulwama attack"; on line source: https://www.hindustantimes.com/india-news/gadkari-amps-up-pitch-after-pulwama-talks-of-diverting-water-from-3-rivers/story-J4HPN2mflYQz9dl7dT4nMK.html. Accessed on 7 July 2020.
31. Amit Ranjan (2016), "Disputed Waters: India, Pakistan and the Transboundary Rivers", *Studies in Indian Politics,* 4(2), p. 199.
32. Pankaj Kumar Sharma (2012), "Conflict Over Water Between India and Pakistan: Fear and Hopes?", *The Indian Journal of Political Science*, 73(1), p. 134.
33. Paula Banerjee, Sanjoy Hazarika, Monirul Hussain and Ranabir Samaddar (1999), "Indo-Bangladesh Cross-Border Migration and Trade", *Economic and Political Weekly*, 34(36), p. 2549.
34. Zahoor A. Rather (2016), "India-Bangladesh Border Issues: Challenges and Opportunities", *International Studies*, 50(1&2), p. 136.
35. Deepak K. Singh. (2010). *Stateless in South Asia: The Chakmas between Bangladesh and India*, New Delhi: Sage Publication, p. 77.

36. Sangeeta Thapliyal (1999), "Movement of population between India and Nepal: Emerging challenges", *Strategic Analysis*, 23(5), pp. 781-82.
37. Myron Weiner (1993), "Rejected Peoples and Unwanted Migrants in South Asia", *Economic and Political Weekly*, 28(34), p. 1742.
38. Dinuk Jayasuriya (2014), "Drivers of irregular and regular migration from Sri Lanka: Evidence from a large scale survey", *Irregular Migration Research Programme Occasional Paper Series*, p. 13.
39. Vinod Khobragade (2010), "Ethnicity, Insurgency and Self-Determination: A Dilemma of Multi-Ethnic State: A Case of North-East India", *The Indian Journal of Political Science*, 71(4), p. 1159.
40. Manoj Kumar Nath (2004), "Mapping North East on India's Foreign Policy: Looking Past, Present and Beyond", *The Indian Journal of Political Science*, 65(4), p. 640.
41. Myron Weiner (1978), *Sons of the Soil: Migration and Ethnic Conflict in India*, Princeton, Princeton University Press, p. 69.
42. Deepti Sharma (2015). "The Kashmir insurgency: Multiple actors, divergent interests, institutionalized conflict" in Jugdep S. Chima (ed.) *Ethnic Subnationalist Insurgencies in South Asia*, New York, Routledge, p. 16.
43. Robert N. Kearney (1985), "Ethnic Conflict and the Tamil Separatist Movement in Sri Lanka", *Asian Survey*, 125(9), p. 916.
44. David N. Gellner (2007), "Caste, Ethnicity and Inequality in Nepal", *Economic and Political Weekly*, 42(20), p. 1825.
45. Dev Raj Dahal and Yubaraj Ghimire (2012), "Ethnic Federalism in Nepal: Risks and Opportunities", *Georgetown Journal of International Affairs*, 13(1), p. 76.
46. Rita Manchanda (2008), "Waiting for 'Naya' Nepal", *Economic and Political Weekly*, 43(29), p. 25.
47. Pushpita Das (2008), "Towards a Regulated Indo-Nepal Border", *Strategic Analysis*, 32(5), p. 884.
48. Sumanta Banerjee (2006), "The 'Ides' of April: Lessons from Nepal", *Economic and Political Weekly*, 41(19), p. 1832.
49. P. Venkateshwar Rao (1988), "Ethnic Conflict in Sri Lanka: India's Role and Perception", *Asian Survey*, 28(4), p. 419.
50. Sandra Destradi (2012), "India and Sri Lanka's Civil War: The Failure of Regional Conflict Management in South Asia", *Asian Survey*, 52(3), p. 599.

51. Varun Vaish (2011), "Negotiating the India-Pakistan Conflict in Relation to Kashmir", *International Journal on World Peace*, 28(3), pp. 53-80.
52. Balraj Puri (2008), "Jammu and Kashmir: The Issue of Regional Autonomy", *Economic and Political Weekly*, 43(34), p. 10.
53. S.D. Robert (1985), "South Asian conflicts" in Mohammed Ayoob (ed.), *Conflict and Intervention in the Third World*, London, Croom Helm, p. 170.
54. "Siachen: All you should know about the world's costliest battlefield" (2019); on line source: https://economictimes.indiatimes.com/news/defence/siachen-all-you-should-know-about-the-worlds-costliest-battlefield/articleshow/72142137.cms?utm_source=contentofinterest&utm_medium=text&utm_campaign=cppst. Accessed on 13 May 2020.
55. Pavan Nair (2009), "The Siachen War: Twenty-Five Years", *Economic and Political Weekly*, 44(11), pp. 35-40.
56. Andrew North, "Siachen dispute: India and Pakistan's glacial fight"; on line source: https://www.bbc.com/news/world-asia-india-26967340. Accessed on 17 June 2020.
57. Omer Farooq (2006), "Siachen Glacier Conflict: Discordant in Pakistan-India Reconciliation", *Pakistan Horizon*, 59(2), pp. 73-82.
58. Nasreen Akhtar (2015), "Composite Dialogues between India and Pakistan: Challenges and Impediments", *International Journal on World Peace*, 32(3), pp. 49-74.
59. Harsh V. Pant (2007), "Will the Twain Ever Meet?", *Asian Survey*, 47(2), pp. 231-49.
60. Dhananjay Tripathi (2019), "Influence of Borders on Bilateral Ties in South Asia: A Study of Contemporary India-Nepal Relations", *International Studies*, 56(2-3), p. 194.
61. J.W. Garver (1991), "China-India rivalry in Nepal: The clash over Chinese arms sales", *Asian Survey*, 31(10), pp. 956-75.
62. Stephen Groves (2014), "India and Nepal Tackle Border Disputes"; on line source: https://thediplomat.com/2014/09/india-and-nepal-tackle-border-disputes/. Accessed on 19 June 2020.
63. Bishwanath Ghosh, "Anger against India over blockade snowballs in Nepal"; on line source: https://www.thehindu.com/news/national/anger-against-india-over-blockade-snowballs-in-nepal/article8032072.ece. Accessed on 17 June 2020.
64. Rahul Mishra (2018), "From Look East to Act East: Transitions in India's Eastward Engagement" in G. Rozman, J.C. Liow (eds.),

International Relations and Asia's Southern Tier, Asan-Palgrave Macmillan Series, p. 328.

65. Shaun Narine (2008), "Forty years of ASEAN: A historical review", *The Pacific Review*, 21(4), p. 419.
66. Christophe Jaffrelot (2003), "India's Look East Policy: An Asianist Strategy in Perspective", *India Review*, 2(2), p. 2.
67. Shibashis Chatterjee (2007), "Conceptions of Space in India's Look East Policy: Order, Cooperation or Community?", *South Asian Survey*, 14(1), p. 76.
68. Joint Statement of the First ASEAN-India Summit, Phnom Penh, 5 November 2002; on line source: https://asean.org/?static_post=joint-statement-of-the-first-asean-india-summit. Accessed on 25 April 2020.
69. Chietigj Bajpaee (2017), "Dephasing India's Look East/Act East Policy", *Contemporary Southeast Asia*, 39(2), pp. 348-72.
70. Sangeetha Kandavel and Joe A. Scaria (2011), "Look East, and act East, too: US Secretary of State Hillary Clinton to India"; on line source: https://economictimes.indiatimes.com/news/politics-and-nation/look-east-and-act-east-too-us-secretary-of-state-hillary-clinton-to india/articleshow/9299669.cms?utm_source=contentofinterest&utm_medium=text&utm_campaign=cppst. Accessed on 20 April 2020.
71. Ngaibiakching Amba Pande (2019), "India's Act East Policy and ASEAN: Building a Regional Order Through Partnership in the Indo-Pacific", *International Studies*, 57(1), p. 8.
72. "Modi woos investors, lays out Asean vision" (2019); on line source: https://www.hindustantimes.com/india-news/modi-woos-investors-lays-out-asean-vision/story-ewgCs1Is4oLDCI2HTI5JKL.html. Accessed on 2 May 2020.
73. Niranjan Marjani (2020), "Myanmar could be India's gateway to Southeast Asia"; on line source: https://www.aseantoday.com/2020/02/myanmar-could-be-indias-gateway-to-southeast-asia/. Accessed on 11 May 2020.
74. The *Business Standard* (2019), "Govt releases Rs. 193.16 cr fund for India-Myanmar-Thailand highway project"; on line source: https://www.business-standard.com/article/economy-policy/govt-releases-rs-193-16-cr-fund-for-india-myanmar-thailand-highway-project-119010300502_1.html. Accessed on 10 June 2020.
75. Niranjan Marjani (2020), "Myanmar could be India's gateway to Southeast Asia"; on line source: https://www.aseantoday.com/2020/02/myanmar-could-be-indias-gateway-to-southeast-asia/. Accessed on 15 June 2020.

76. Dipanjan Roy Chaudhury (2019), "Northeast India gateway to Southeast Asia under Act East Policy: PM Modi in Bangkok"; on line source: https://economictimes.indiatimes.com/news/politics-and-nation/northeast-india-gateway-to-southeast-asia-under-act-east-policy-pm-modi-in-bangkok/articleshow/71871976.cms. Accessed on 25 April 2020.
77. *Ibid.*
78. *The Financial Express* (2016), "PM Narendra Modi leaves tomorrow for Laos to attend ASEAN, East Asia Summits"; on line source: https://www.financialexpress.com/india-news/pm-narendra-modi-leaves-tomorrow-for-laos-to-attend-asean-east-asia-summits/369429/. Accessed on 28 June 2020.
79. Indrani Bagchi (2016) "Dhaka cancels port to be built by China, India eyes another"; on line source: https://timesofindia.indiatimes.com/india/Dhaka-cancels-port-to-be-built-by-China-India-eyes-another/articleshow/50894554.cms. Accessed on 12 June 2020.
80. Dipanjan Roy Chaudhury (2018), "India to help develop Colombo, Trincomalee Ports: Foreign Secretary S. Jaishankar"; on line source: "https://economictimes.indiatimes.com/news/defence/india-to-help-develop-colombo-trincomalee-ports-foreign-secretary-s-jaishankar/articleshow/61251807.cms?from=mdr. Accessed on 28 June 2020.
81. "BIMSTEC: Transport and communication" (2019); on line source: https://bimstec.org/?page_id=270. Accessed on 23 May 2020.
82. Arijit Mazumdar (2018), "India's Soft Power Diplomacy Under the Modi Administration: Buddhism, Diaspora and Yoga", *Asian Affairs*, 49(3), pp. 468-91.
83. *Ibid.*, p. 471.
84. Junuguru Srinivas (2019), "Modi's Cultural Diplomacy and Role of Indian Diaspora", *Central European Journal of International and Security Studies*, 13(2), p. 85.
85. *The Hindustan Times* (2019), "Modi woos investors, lays out Asean vision"; on line source: https://www.hindustantimes.com/india-news/modi-woos-investors-lays-out-asean-vision/story-ewgCs1Is4oLDCI2HTI5JKL.html. Accessed on 2 May 2020.
86. *The Asian Age* (2019), "Japan's investments in India have not been without pitfalls"; on line source: https://www.asianage.com/india/all-india/150419/japans-investments-in-india-have-not-been-without-pitfalls.html. Accessed on 8 June 2020.
87. "India, S. Korea set sights on $50 billion trade" (2018); on line source: https://www.thehindubusinessline.com/news/world/india-s-korea-set-sights-on-50-billion-trade/article24382091.ece. Accessed on 3 June 2020.

88. The *Times of India* (2019), "Why South Korea needs India more than ever"; on line source: https://timesofindia.indiatimes.com/business/india-business/why-south-korea-needs-india-more-than-ever/articleshow/68090670.cms. Accessed on 16 June 2020.
89. The *Economic Times* (2019), "India, Australia 'natural partnership' registers steady growth in 2019"; on line source: https://economictimes.indiatimes.com/news/defence/india-australia-natural-partnership-registers-steady-growth-in. Accessed on 29 June 2020.
90. *The Business Standard* (2019), "India-Asean bilateral trade may double by 2025 to $300 billion: Study"; on line source: https://www.business-standard.com/article/economy-policy/india-asean-bilateral-trade-may-double-by-2025-to-300-billion-study-119111200547_1.html. Accessed on 22 June 2020.

5

India and the Global South

Souradeep Sen

Indian foreign policy, since independence, has grappled with two inter-related ambitions: to become a dominant and independent mover of global affairs and to exercise leadership of what has come to be known as the Global South (GS). Previously deemed the Third World—primarily owing to the logic of Cold War rivalry—the GS and its myriad historical linkages and colonial disruptions continue to influence India's global identity formation. The Global South rhetoric, beginning with the self-assertion of newly independent countries via non-alignment, still holds currency within policy-making circles despite serious attempts being made to project India as a rising power or middle power no longer sequestered by old Third World or Global South ties.[1] This is not to argue that such an obsession is parochial. But, like all foreign policy ambitions, this too has its limitations.

The GS emerged in the 1990s as a successor term to the Third World, following the demise of bipolarity and the contemporary resurgence of globalization. And despite its overtly geographical connotation, the Global South cannot be territorialized into fixed geographical boundaries. The concept of GS lies more within the precinct of International Political Economy (IPE) than foreign policy *per se*, where it has come to be associated with underdeveloped nations. India's relationship with the Global South thus, would have to be evaluated at the backdrop of the political and the economic, bearing in mind the struggles for decolonization and the consequent state-building enterprises of Third World countries. The achievement of freedom in foreign policy manoeuvering was not only a constituent of that enterprise, but a very tenet of sovereignty.

There are authoritarian, hereditary, democratic, and semi-democratic political systems in the GS, along with diverse economies and cultures. A straightforward definition of the term is quite impossible as it cannot be comprehended as a concrete entity. At best it can be treated, "...as an ideational abstraction, providing a loose term of reference,—mostly economic,—in international relations".[2] Although this chapter would attempt to trace the roots of this concept at greater lengths, suffice it to say here that India—under its post-colonial leadership—was one of the rare Third World countries where the euphoria following decolonization had been succeeded by real nation and state-building projects. Elsewhere in the Third World, such endeavours were frustrated as the leadership largely depended upon authoritarian control instead of democratization and social justice.[3] Thus, it was India's success as a nation which propelled its leadership of the Third World and subsequently, within the GS.

The present chapter comprises three sections. In the first, it would address the conceptual ambits of Global South, following it up with more practical elements of its formation. The second section would deal with India's role in creating the contemporary GS outlook and its implications. The third and final section would focus upon two cases of Indian foreign policy experiences with two large regions of the Global South Africa and Latin America.

From 'Third World' to 'Global South'

The present section would first trace the rise of the GS as a concept in International Relations by fathoming its linkages with the Cold War era demarcation of the Third World. Then it will dwell upon the arguments by which India can be accepted as a pioneer of Global South revivalism. For an influential author on the subject, the GS as a critical concept has at least three significant definitions, thereby creating contentions with regards its meaning, use, applicability, and analytical value.[4] The first definition, used by some scholars and NGOs, regards the GS to comprise countries classified by the World Bank as low or middle income that are located in Asia, Africa, Oceania, Latin America, and the Caribbean. This definition is descriptive and heavily influenced by theories of underdevelopment and their attendant jargons—periphery, less-developed, developing, underdeveloped, or the Third World—to lump together diverse economic, socio-cultural and political histories into an overarching category. By the logic of this nation-state focus, it would be rather possible to neatly demarcate the contours of the GS. It would comprise the countries that do not belong to the Organisation for Economic Cooperation and Development (OECD),[5] with the possible exceptions of Chile, Colombia, and Mexico (see Table 5.1).

The second definition rejects the first and accepts a de-territorialized political economy conceptualization of the term. Based largely upon Antonio Gramsci's essay *The Southern Question*, the focus here is on uneven national processes of economic development and the role of capitalism in creating 'internal colonization' within national societies by means of importing globalization to poorer regions. As one author puts it, "there are Souths in the geographical North and Norths in the geographical South", or there are growing schisms in wealth and power within countries, which must be acknowledged.[6] As the second definition also adduces, the GS is indeed a concept with deep political economy roots. The third definition enables the term to refer to a transnational political subjectivity and subaltern (dominated groups) resistance under contemporary capitalist globalization.[7] This definition is connected with the second and stands diametrically opposed to the geographically determinism of the first definition. It is more abstract than the second and looks beyond specificities of geographical location to identify the social agency of dominated groups.

Table 5.1: OECD Member Countries

Countries	Date of Joining	Countries	Date of Joining
Australia	7 June 1971	Japan	28 April 1964
Austria	29 September 1961	Korea	12 December 1996
Belgium	13 September 1961	Latvia	1 July 2016

Canada	10 April 1961	Lithuania	5 July 2018
Chile	7 May 2010	Luxembourg	7 December 1961
Colombia	28 April 2020	Mexico	18 May 1994
Czech Republic	21 December 1995	Netherlands	13 November 1961
Denmark	30 May 1961	New Zealand	29 May 1973
Estonia	9 December 2010	Norway	4 July 1961
Finland	28 January 1969	Poland	22 November 1996
France	7 August 1961	Portugal	4 August 1961
Germany	27 September 1961	Slovak Republic	14 December 2000
Greece	27 September 1961	Slovenia	21 July 2010
Hungary	7 May 1996	Spain	3 August 1961
Iceland	5 June 1961	Sweden	28 September 1961
Ireland	17 August 1961	Switzerland	28 September 1961
Israel	7 September 2010	Turkey	2 August 1961
Italy	29 March 1962	United Kingdom	2 May 1961
United States	12 April 1961	As of July 2020	37 nation-states

Source: Organisation for Economic Co-operation and Development (2020), "List of OECD Member countries—Ratification of the Convention on the OECD," Paris; https://www.oecd.org/about/document/list-oecd-member-countries.htm (accessed on May 10, 2020).

Thus, there is no clear-cut definition of the GS and one can be content with only the bare outlines of the concept on which a more personalized interpretation can be created. However, a brief overview of the emergence of the term could be provided while bearing in mind the diversity of all three definitions. Each of them has merits. While the first is most descriptive, it provides a link between history and political economy, thereby between global position and economic relations (such as the core, periphery, and semi-periphery; see Fig. 5.1 in contrast with Table 5.1). It also urges scholars to recognize and challenge the structures and processes that generate global inequalities. The second and third definitions are more analytical. These postcolonial conceptualizations of GS focus more on power, uneven resource distribution and the role of race and other variables of identity formation within global capitalism which are invariably important for tracing South-South cooperation (or relations among subaltern groups across national, linguistic, racial and ethnic lines).[8]

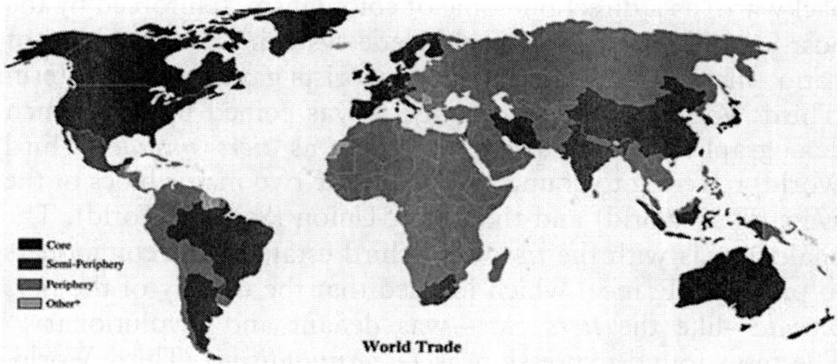

Figure 5.1: The World System
(based upon late 20th century trading status)

Source: Christopher Chase-Dunn, Yukio Kawano and Benjamin D. Brewer (2000), "Trade globalization since 1795: Waves of Integration in the World-System," *American Sociological Review*, 65(1), February, pp. 77-95; on line source: https://www.jstor.org/stable/2657290. Accessed on May 15, 2020. Other* denotes countries with less than 1 million population, which were excluded from analysis.

In his inaugural address (1949), US President Harry S. Truman spoke about the 'underdeveloped areas' of the world which sparked an intellectual debate regarding development and modernization. Although this term was problematic for its narrow focus on economic growth and levels of industrialization—with the assumption of linear progress and the implication that there was a universal measurement of development to be assessed against Western standards—it was telling in its psychological provenance. In political economy, the North is synonymous with technologically advanced post-industrial countries of the first world, whereas South is associated with the Third World. More than a billion people in sub-Saharan Africa, South and Central Asia, Latin America, and Central America live in abject poverty with little or no access to education, sanitation, food, and health care. The North-South divide is a controversial area in the study of IR. The rise of dependency theory in the 1950s challenged modernization theory, holding a mirror to the forcefully extractive and exploitative relationship between the core (economically powerful) and periphery (economically backward) as a direct outcome of colonialism, reinforced by the post-Second World War world trade system.[9] The analogies of Latin American and dependency theorists gave rise to the term 'Third World'. More specifically, it was coined by the French demographer Alfred Sauvy in 1952, as *tiers monde* (Third World) referring to countries outside the two major blocs of the West (First World) and the Soviet Union (Second World). The analogy was with the *tiers état* (third estate of the commoners in pre-1789 France) which implied that the destiny of the *tiers monde*—like the *tiers état*—was defiant and revolutionary.[10] The term found expression as *tercermundismo* (Third World-ism) as a way of improving Latin America's status vis-à-vis the developed countries of the West.[11]

Non-alignment and India's Role in Conceptualizing the Third World

The aforementioned categorization was starkly Western in origin, but there were original attempts to evolve intellectual categorizations from within the Third World as well. The Western manner of mapping the world was premised upon its ideological contention with the socialist bloc. Whereas, the Third World itself had a heterogeneous character which became the impetus behind various self-descriptions of *tiers monde* identity. In 1974, the then Vice Premier of the Peoples' Republic of China, Deng Xiaoping, made a similar attempt in the United Nations by arguing that the First World comprised the United States and Soviet Union (the prime Cold War rivals), the developing countries of Asia, Africa, Latin America and so on form together the Third World; while the developed countries between the two made up the Second World.[12] This seems rather a variation upon Western constructs, while the Indian attitude and formulations on the concept had an interplay between domestic and external factors which stressed upon the emergence of a novel, vibrant and strong Asia, relieved of the clutches of colonization.

It can be argued that India envisioned itself as not only as the champion of Third World solidarity via the Bandung Conference (1955) and subsequently, the first Non-aligned Conference (1961), but also as a rule-maker in international affairs by its independent voice in the UN. Commitments toward creating a world free of war and wants were intrinsic to Nehruvian internationalism. Notions of nationalism and those of India's civilizational credentials were prominent in its Third World engagements. Both went hand-in-glove and were instrumental in the creation of foreign policy objectives, at least under the stewardship of Jawaharlal Nehru. Writing in preparation for the Asian Relations Conference (1947), Nehru stressed the need for Asian countries to stand on their feet and not become stooges of great powers by developing a sense of solidarity among the newly decolonized countries which would help in creating a real inter-Asian foreign policy—as a significant step away from bipolarity.[13] This idea of Asia's emergence would be amplified by Nehru in the Bandung Conference (1955) and subsequently enlarged to include the oppressed countries of other continents in the first NAM Conference (1961). Both summits aimed at decolonizing international practices on question of foreign policy and development by carving out a path to political, social, and cultural emancipation away from the ideologies proffered by the Western and Soviet blocs. Nehru was joined by Ghana's Prime Minister Nkrumah, Indonesian President Sukarno, Yugoslavian President Tito, and Egyptian President Nasser in his efforts to rid the world of military alignments.

Non-alignment was a unique foreign policy initiative of the nascent Indian state. As Nehru had put it, non-alignment was the middle course India has to steer, "...not merely because of expediency but also because we consider it the right course".[14] It was right because, "the very process of marshalling the world into two hostile camps precipitates the conflict which it has sought to avoid".[15] There might seem to be an overt idealism in these words, but the leadership of the NAM and the promotion of Third World-ism definitely involved a sense of realpolitik. Nehru, as one of the founders of NAM, promoted Third World-ism not just out of genuine concerns about peace, but also—very astutely—to serve several narrower interests of Indian foreign policy.

The essence of the *Panchsheel*,[16] which served as the intellectual credo of NAM not only created an Intergovernmental Organization (IGO) which is second only to the UN in membership and world population (see Box 5.1), but cemented India's legacy as the intellectual leader of the Third World. The NAM was conceived not as an isolationist and/or neutralist stance, but as a progressive platform in support of decolonization, detachment from bloc politics—and thereby, as a truly free *tiers monde* voice in international affairs. Insofar as India's foreign policy was concerned, by leading the NAM, Nehru clearly circumvented four issues which might have troubled India otherwise:[17] (i) that overt alignment with one

Box 5.1: The 120 Members States of NAM (as of July 2020)

Algeria, Afghanistan, Antigua & Barbuda, Azerbaijan, Angola, Bahrain, Bahamas, Belarus, Benin, Bangladesh, Barbados, Botswana, Bhutan, Belize, Burkina Faso, Brunei Darussalam, Bolivia, Burundi, Cambodia, Chile, Cameroon, Fiji, Colombia, Cape Verde, India, Cuba, Central African Republic, Indonesia, Dominica, Chad, Iran, Dominican Republic, Comoros, Iraq, Ecuador, Congo, Jordan, Grenada, Cote D'Ivoire, Kuwait, Guatemala, D.R. Congo, Laos, Guyana, Djibouti, Lebanon, Haiti, Egypt, Malaysia, Honduras, Equatorial Guinea, Maldives, Jamaica, Eritrea, Mongolia, Nicaragua, Ethiopia, Myanmar, Panama, Gabon, Nepal, Peru, Gambia, Oman, Saint Kitts & Nevis, Ghana, Pakistan, Saint Lucia, Guinea Bissau, Palestine, St. Vincent & the Grenadines, Guinea, Papua-New Guinea, Suriname, Kenya, People's Democratic Republic of Korea, Trinidad & Tobago, Lesotho, Philippines, Venezuela, Liberia, Qatar, Libya, Saudi Arabia, Madagascar, Singapore, Malawi, Sri Lanka, Mali, Syria, Mauritania, Thailand, Mauritius, Timor-Leste, Morocco, Turkmenistan, Mozambique, United Arab Emirates, Namibia, Uzbekistan, Niger, Vanuatu, Nigeria, Viet Nam, Rwanda Yemen, Sao Tome & Principe, Senegal, Seychelles, Sierra Leone, Somalia, South Africa, Sudan, Swaziland, Tanzania, Togo, Tunisia, Uganda, Zambia, Zimbabwe.

Source: James Martin Center for Nonproliferation Studies (CNS) (2012), "NAM Member States," Monterey; http://cns.miis.edu/nam/about.html (accessed on May 15, 2020).

superpower would undermine India's hard-won independence; (ii) such alignment might have diminished India's ability to diversify economic relationships; (iii) that alignment would lead to entrapment in conflict where India could not afford to participate; and (iv) such alignment will inevitably diminish India's global influence and credentials as a peace-loving and civilizational country.

Although the Nehruvian non-aligned posture soon unraveled following India's war with China—when Nehru had to bite the bullet and acquiesce to an air defense agreement with the US—the step gathered significant praise from realists but did not propel him towards more serious ties with the West. This can be taken as an example of how complex India's relationship with the Global South is in actuality, as the basis of an enduring Indian foreign policy grounded in notions of Third World coalitions is quite impossible. This is due to the significantly stark structural heterogeneity and differentiated interests among this motley group of states.[18]

Prime Minister Indira Gandhi detested the term 'Third World'. Instead she transformed the NAM by propagating themes of inequality and the urgent need for restructuring the global economic order in the Lusaka (1970) and Algiers (1973) Summits (see Table 5.2). This led ultimately to the adoption of the New International Economic Order (NIEO, of which later) by the UN General Assembly in 1974. India's foreign policy journey through Third World realms can be summed as a transition from 'hard realism' from the mid-1960s to the mid-1980s, to economically driven pragmatism since economic liberalization kicked in. However, economic diplomacy—or conflict resolution by economic cooperation—in the wake of liberalization, has hardly diminished the Third World rhetoric in India's policy formulations. On the contrary, that was the time of its transition to the GS rhetoric—to counteract inequitable Western notions on trade, environment, development, intellectual property rights, and so on.[19]

The Emergence of 'Global South' and Indian Foreign Policy

The tripartite division of the globe soon came under scrutiny after India's successful push towards the NIEO. Furthermore, the

Table 5.2: NAM Summits: 1961-2019

No.	Date	Host country	Host city	No.	Date	Host country	Host city
1st	1–6 September 1961	Yugoslavia	Belgrade	10th	1–6 September 1992	Indonesia	Jakarta
2nd	5–10 October 1964	United Arab Republic	Cairo	11th	18–20 October 1995	Colombia	Cartagena
3rd	8–10 Sept. 1970	Zambia	Lusaka	12th	2–3 September 1998	South Africa	Durban
4th	5–9 September 1973	Algeria	Algiers	13th	20–25 February 2003	Malaysia	Kuala Lumpur
5th	16–19 August 1976	Sri Lanka	Colombo	14th	15–16 Sept. 2006	Cuba	Havana
6th	3–9 September 1979	Cuba	Havana	15th	11–16 July 2009	Egypt	Sharm el-Sheikh
7th	7–12 March 1983	India	New Delhi	16th	26–31 August 2012	Iran	Tehran
8th	1–6 September 1986	Zimbabwe	Harare	17th	13–18 Sept. 2016	Venezuela	Porlamar
9th	4–7 September 1989	Yugoslavia	Belgrade	18th	25–26 October 2019	Azerbaijan	Baku

Source: Compiled by the author from different sources. Note: The 'United Against Covid-19' virtual Summit was held on May 4, 2020, was attended by 30 heads of states and other dignitaries. See, Ashutosh Nagda (2020), "India's Renewed Embrace of the Non-Aligned Movement," *The Diplomat*, May 11; on line source: https://thediplomat.com/2020/05/indias-renewed-embrace-of-the-non-aligned-movement/. Accessed on May 15, 2020.

imprecision of the term 'Third World' following the dissolution of the Soviet Union, and its implicit hierarchy of categorizing the world gained detractors by about the mid-1990s. The enormous regional differences in economic growth and poverty made any neat categorization impossible, which was compounded by rising levels of prosperity and related socio-economic developments in countries like Japan and Taiwan. When placed beside the changes in various states' partnership with and participation within the global economy, and when compared against economic underperformances in countries like India and Brazil, it was clear that the 'Third World' can no longer conceptually represent such enormous regional differences.[20] In the late-1990s, the growing homogenization of cultures and societies as a result of globalization was based on similar divisions characterizing the world during the Cold War. The West still continued to hold a disproportionately large share of the world's wealth, trade, investment, and technologies. Despite the end of the Cold War, the narrative was still constructed in the backdrop of the 'West versus the Rest' equation—with the Rest signifying deep troughs of poverty and depravation interspersed with plains of greater or lesser degrees of prosperity.[21] Despite challenges to the tripartite categorization, it was clear that the 'Rest' being too vague to be used for academic analysis, geographical bearings were imperative.

It is not surprising then, that scholars and activists reinvigorated their calls for non-Western analysis of global issues for an informed understanding of regional, national, and local struggles associated with these challenges. There is an interesting hypothesis regarding the origin of the term. The 'South' became a term used by scholars interested in understanding geo-political processes, drawing attention to political struggles led by non-Western peoples and communities placed outside the Western world. The 'South' was meant to center the poorer parts of the world; a term originating from within itself, standing in opposition to previous terms like the 'Rest' and the 'Third World' which *othered* these regions. And following the globalization discourse in the 1990s, the world 'Global' became attached to 'South' to form the contemporary compound term.[22]

Indian foreign policy, at this juncture, was keeping up with this re-conceptualization of space. The dissolution of the Soviet Union and the subsequent proclamation of the 'end of history' by the supporters of liberalism and capitalism marked not only the obsolescence of 'Third World' but questioned the very relevance of NAM as a platform for Third World solidarity. But, non-alignment was not discarded as a theme of Indian foreign policy. Rather it was re-imagined since the Cold War as a way of engaging many nations to meet India's variegated security requirements. Such multilateral initiatives like the BRICS (Brazil, Russia, India, China, and South Africa) forum and India's active participation in the G-20 implies two things: (i) that India has been keen to follow what its self-styled vision document—the Nonalignment 2.0—has dubbed as a move towards reinforcing 'strategic autonomy' in an increasingly multipolar world for pursuing its own interests[23] and (ii) that it is willing to positively engage with the GS agenda, however, with a much less revolutionary content and leadership ambition than what it had previously expressed during the demands for NIEO.[24] For a proper estimation of India's role in setting the trend towards the GS rhetoric, a modicum of historical analysis is warranted, which has to be supplanted with further theoretical investigations into how the term gradually drew more attention at the turn of the millennium.

Foreign Policy of Defiance: India's Role in UNCTAD, G-77 and the Demand for the NIEO

In 2013, the then Indian Finance Minister, P. Chidambaram vented his ire upon the twin international financial institutions—the International Monetary Fund and the World Bank—pointing out India's frequently fraught relations with the IFIs (International Financial Institutions) and their roles in creating an overall unsteady state of global economic governance in the early twenty-first century.[25] But this was not the first time that a minister of a developing country—especially, India—had raised his/her voice against the lopsided policies of IFIs. Created under the stewardship of the West in 1944, the IMF and World Bank are often called Bretton Woods twins—the former focused on macroeconomic imperatives and the latter for nurturing development and poverty eradication. Encompassing domestically, infrastructure building, investment, social sector promotion, and state capacity-building, the World Bank was created primarily keeping in mind the less developed regions of the globe which would need financial assistance from time to time for developmental purposes. But, international monetary relations under the Bretton Woods system soon developed in a trajectory which proved to be nothing but disastrous for developing countries. The system tied national currencies to the US Dollar, backed by it convertibility into gold at an official rate. Following the 'Nixon shock' of 1971, the era of floating exchange rates began. And by the end of the Reagan and Thatcher revolutions which led to an ascendant neo-liberal market fundamentalism, the West could successfully turn these IFIs into their instruments for pushing trade liberalization, privatization of state-owned enterprises, deregulation of labour markets, and for opening up the channels of foreign investment, in lieu of financial assistance to underdeveloped countries. These were called 'structural adjustment' measures: a way to coerce developing countries into adopting a neo-liberal economic framework, leading to tragic consequences in most Asian and African economies.

India has been a founding member of both IFIs and felt entitled to draw funds from both for developmental projects. However, during the 1967 devaluation of the rupee, India was not treated—within the Bretton Woods institutions—with the respect due to a founding member and this led to strained relationships and mutual distrust.[26] India was not to revive cordial ties with the IFIs before 1991, when it had to bite the bullet and liberalize its economy. But, a few other significant developments also took place, leading up to India's estrangement from the Bretton Woods twins which not only firmly cemented its anti-Western—and consequently, pro-Third World—stance, but also justified its pro-Soviet tilt during Mrs. Gandhi's first tenure. India's defiant turn away from the Bretton Woods institutions and towards Third World solidarity had a huge impact upon South-South cooperation and the 'Bandung Spirit' which nurtured it.[27]

South-South cooperation has been a key organizing concept and set of practices in pursuit of liberating communities and nations from the clutches of colonialism, poverty, oppression, and underdevelopment, through a vision of mutual benefit and solidarity among the disadvantaged of the world economic system. It conveyed the hope that development may be achieved by the poorer countries themselves through their mutual assistance to one another, transforming the world order to reflect their mutual interests with regard to the affluent and dominant global North.[28] This emergent movement of Third World solidarity thereby sought to challenge the vertical relations between colony and metropole that served to inhibit relations between countries of the GS. India as a leader of the NAM further developed this solidarity—especially since the mid-1960s, following its brush with Western hypocrisy in the IFIs—to challenge the deepening global inequality while lessening the Third World's economic and political dependence on the global North and its financial institutions.

The year 1964 was more than significant for Indian foreign policy. The demise of Nehru plunged the country into seemingly unprecedented policy myopia. However, it was also the year when countries of the developing world also started to actively challenge the West's invisible hand in the international economic system. It marked the beginning of a fundamental systemic reorientation, whereby the centrality of East-West Cold War bipolarity was gradually replaced by a North-South dichotomy drawn primarily along economic and developmental lines. Two significant systemic developments took place in 1964: (i) the establishment of the United Nations Conference on Trade and Development (UNCTAD), as a permanent intergovernmental body under the UN General Assembly to deal with trade, investment, and developmental issues, with the iconic dependency theorist Raúl Prebisch as its first secretary-general and (ii) the setting up of the Group of 77 (G-77), named after the number of countries present at the founding of the UNCTAD, as a caucus organization of developing states to pursue common goals and develop leverage in UN deliberations.[29] India, for the first time, found an identity of interests with other developing nations in these fora. Especially when it was already struggling in the UN after Nehru's blunders in refusing the permanent membership of the Security Council twice on account of China and other missed opportunities which suddenly brushed it under the high tables of great power politics.[30] Indian diplomats were instrumental along with other representatives, notably from Latin America, in shaping the Third UN Conference on the Law of the Sea (UNCLOS III) during 1973-82. Indeed, India's formal alliance with the Soviet Union in 1971 betrayed the hollowness of its non-alignment, and its subsequent war with Pakistan revealed the shaky foundations of *tiers monde* solidarity. Indian foreign policy, nonetheless, kept up its more intensive involvement within the G-77 and other GS fora. It also stepped up its criticism of the Bretton Woods institutions, especially insofar as these compelled debtor nations to liberalize their economies in lieu of loans.

All these developments in the path leading up to the demands for the NIEO are indeed confusing. But they are all linked in a chronological chain of events (see Box 4.2) which can simplify understanding. The demand for the NIEO originated in the oil crisis of 1973 when developing countries wanted to change the global order in their favour, but the West—through more practised diplomacy—restored the status quo to its advantage.[31] The Organization of the Petroleum Exporting Countries (OPEC) wanted to take advantage of the seeming shifts in the balance of power in favour of developing countries by suddenly deciding to raise the prices of oil.

India's handling of the oil crisis marked its foreign policy's turn toward 'hard realism'.[32] The OPEC raised the price of crude oil three times between 1973 and 1975, cutting oil production and announcing an embargo on supplies to countries which were close friends of Israel—with which most members of the OPEC were pursuing ideological and military conflicts at that time. The United States, being in support of the Israelis were hit hard by the oil crisis in the 1970s. India, on the other hand, understood the strategic importance of the Persian Gulf for its energy needs. Indira Gandhi embarked upon having cordial relations with Iran, Iraq, Saudi Arabia, and the smaller nations

Box 5.2: The Rise and Fall of the NIEO

- 1964—the creation of UNCTAD and G-77.
- 1967—India's setback in IFIs following devaluation.
- 1973—the UNCLOS III, defining rights and responsibilities of nations vis-à-vis their use of the world's oceans; the Conference took place till 1982, signed in the same year.
- 1973—oil crisis by OPEC, India's diplomatic bonhomie with the Persian Gulf.
- 1974—the New International Economic Order demanded by developing countries; the Sixth UN Special Session of General Assembly convened, declaring NIEO.
- 1975—the Seventh UN Special Session developed regulatory mechanisms of NIEO.
- 1981—the Cancun Summit Conference stalled North-South cooperation for lack of consensus, US objections and fragmentations within the GS.
- 1982—the South-South Cooperation Conference was summoned by India in an attempt to coordinate trade policies within the G-77; differences of opinions stalled further solidarity through NIEO.
- 1992—Cartagena Summit of the UNCTAD effectively led to undermining the NIEO process.

Source: Compiled by the author from various sources.

of the Gulf Cooperation Council, but stopped short of a maritime agreement with the Persian Gulf. This reduced the effects of India's energy crisis, but did not endear India to the OPEC to such an extent that it would partner the Gulf countries in negotiations with the West through the North-South Dialogue.[33]

Instead, India became more vocal and active in the UN and NAM summits, focusing on the needs of developing countries in a world economy heavily tilted against them. During the oil crisis, the G-77—with Indira Gandhi as one of its leaders—clamoured for such needs which were condensed into demands for a New International Economic Order. The Sixth UN Special Session of the General Assembly (1974) convened to establish the NIEO in which India played a major role (see Box 5.3). The North-South Dialogue was also established, but soon degenerated into a dialogue and consequent agreements between the OPEC members and the West.[34] However, the NIEO showed initial promise. Calling for better terms of trade, increased access to markets and development assistance, re-negotiation of debts, a code of conduct for transnational corporations, a larger share in the international transmission of information, and an audible voice in the decision-making of multilateral institutions, the NIEO was instrumental in preparing the groundwork for South-South cooperation.[35] India played an important role in amending the rules of international trade to permit developing nations to impose import restrictions for improving their export potentials. The Most Seriously Affected capitals—owing to the oil crisis—hoped that investments from newly enlarged petrodollar funds from the OPEC would cushion their increased oil costs.[36] But, the NIEO soon unravelled for various reasons which will be dealt with subsequently. It is imperative to first discuss the order in some details and dwell upon its achievements.

Box 5.3: India in the Sixth UN Special Session of the General Assembly (UNGASS, 1974)

Speaking at the Special Session, the then Indian Foreign Minister S. Swaran Singh suggested:

- a comprehensive policy for the revalorization of prices of raw materials
- provision for additional liquidity for specially effected countries
- equitable pattern of voting rights in IMF and other IFIs
- provision of external capital for the development of poorer countries
- financial and technical assistance to developing countries.

These recommendations were crystallized into the NIEO during May 1-2, 1974.

Source: United Nations (1974), "Resolutions adopted by the General Assembly during its Sixth Special Session, 9 April-2 May 1974," UN General Assembly, U.N. Doc. A/9559, New York: 2 May; on line source: https://www.un.org/en/ga/sessions/special.shtml. Accessed on June 15, 2020.

The West was suspicious and even inimical to the NIEO right from the beginning. Speaking in California on June 11, 1978, the Indian Prime Minister Morarji Desai implored the US to support developing nations in their quest to achieve self-sufficiency, but to no avail.[37] Playing a pivotal role in UNCTAD IV (1976), India helped in the adoption of global action for improving market structures in international trade in commodities of interest to the developing countries, like tea and jute. It also upheld its suggestions for implementing NIEO, proffered in the Seventh UN Special Session of the General Assembly (see Box 5.4). The 1979 session of the UN General Assembly adopted a resolution which irked the Western countries so much that they collectively blocked any further NIEO discussions within the auspices of the UN. The resolution emphasized the need to conduct global talks within the UN framework on energy, raw materials, trade development, currency, and financial institutions which was effectively opposed by the US, Britain and Germany.[38] This

Box 5.4: India in the Seventh UN Special Session of the General Assembly (UNGASS, 1975)

Speaking at the Special Session, the then Indian Foreign Minister S. Swaran Singh suggested:

- that the developed countries should spend more on development assistance to the Third World rather than on Weapons of Mass Destruction (WMDs).
- less import dependence for developing countries for basic goods like fuel and fertilizers for correcting balance of payments.
- removal of trade barriers and strengthening of supply, production, marketing and distribution of products manufactured in developing countries.
- greater say for developing countries in IFIs, provisions for greater liquidity through IMS to cope with problems of external debt.
- the conduct of transnational corporations be subject to greater regulation for protecting the sovereignty of developing countries from their detrimental effects, also to protect their freedom in the management of natural resources for development.

These resolutions were adopted by the UNGA on September 16, 1975.

Source: United Nations (1975), "Resolutions adopted by the General Assembly during its Seventh Special Session, 1-16 September 1975," UN General Assembly, U.N. Doc. A/10301, New York: 16 September; https://www.un.org/en/ga/sessions/special.shtml (accessed on June 15, 2020).

ultimately resulted in subsequent GS solidarity meetings being held outside the precinct of the UN with the Cancun Summit Conference (1981) and South-South Cooperation Conference (1982) as notable examples of such meetings (see Box 5.5).

Box 5.5: Cancun Summit Conference (1981) & South-South Cooperation Conference (1982)

The 1981 conference was attended by 14 developing and eight industrialized countries, with the USSR refusing to participate.

- The conference could not reach a consensus on major issues like energy security, reconstruction of the international economy because of divergent Third World voices.
- Also, no North-South dialogue was possible because of rigidities of the US and other countries.
- The 1982 conference was summoned by India and attended by 44 developing countries of the G-77.
- The conference discussed food and energy security, strategies for GS negotiations, promotion of collective self-reliance among developing countries, and the need to promote international dialogue on NIEO.
- India, along with other developing countries pledged to donate to a proposed multilateral financing authority with a target of US$ 15-20 million, with an expert group under India's chairmanship which did not materialize.

Source: N. Jayapalan (2001), *Foreign Policy of India*, New Delhi, Atlantic Publishers and Distributors, pp. 469-70.

While Bandung and NAM embodied the political dimensions of South-South Cooperation, the G-77 and its demand for the NIEO was the economic dimension of this solidarity movement.[39] The NIEO was to be achieved through tackling structural unequal exchange by a just and equitable relationship between the export of developing countries and their imports, with an emphasis on sovereignty over natural resources and the right to nationalize key industries.[40] These demands were rooted in the failure of the post-war international order—premised upon the Bretton Woods system—to end colonial legacies and provide adequate space for postcolonial states to establish their own national approach to development. The NIEO and the institutions which engendered it were initially successful in provoking considerable debate within the global North which, more often than not, degenerated into acrimonious name-calling. One analyst called the UNCTAD, 'the poor nations' pressure group'.[41] The West had reasons to feel threatened by the rise of GS solidarity, since for the first time in the post-Second World War scenario, the developing countries were no longer looking at the West for leadership in economic matters. Being exposed of the actual motives behind its economic posturing, the West felt that their basic value and control over the global order eroding under the weight of a resurgent Global South.[42] Indeed, this was propellant enough for it to renegotiate its economic diplomacy vis-à-vis the GS, which became especially easy since the GS was never a coherent or united whole.

India tried hard to create a united GS front by its advocacy of NIEO. In the South-South Cooperation Conference (1982), Indira Gandhi implored developing countries to close their ranks to withstand pressure from affluent nations. But these fell into deaf ears and India's close ties with the Soviet Union were adduced by the West to falsely implicate it as an agent of the socialist world.[43] There were sharp differences of opinion regarding the role of the UN and the IFIs in such dialogues or conferences. There were no concrete decisions in the 1982 conference regarding agricultural support and food security, multilateral financial facilities among the developing economies, technical cooperation and so on, despite such items being in the agenda of the meeting. There was nothing but a unanimous acceptance of a rhetorical cooperation for collective self-reliance, with an ironic call for further North-South economic negotiations and not those along South-South lines.[44]

By the mid-1980s, it was clear that the Third World debt crisis and the rise of neo-liberalism had eclipsed the NIEO project. It was a triumph of the Western lobbies in the UN and the Bretton Woods institutions. Third World solidarity received a further dent in the 1992 Cartagena Summit of the UNCTAD which dropped its demands for the adjustment of international patent system to the developmental needs of the GS. Instead, it adopted a position which diminished its potential to gain through technological transfer and its standing in the World

Intellectual Property Organization and the General Agreement on Tariffs and Trade (GATT).[45] This also served to undermine India's efforts, along with other developing countries, in creating the Global System Trade Preference (GSTP, 1985) which would have secured trade relations among developing countries from unhealthy competition. Henceforth, the UNCTAD became increasingly marginalized by the GATT and its successor, the WTO (more of that later). The UNCTAD's role as a counter-hegemonic organization resisting the dominance of the Bretton Woods institutions was effectively nullified and the North-South Dialogue relapsed into a crony capitalist club of the West and the richer Southern nations, especially those belonging to the OPEC. The activism which promoted the issues of equity and development slacked. But the issues remained, and still remains part of an international agenda which can be treated as a lasting legacy of developing countries and India's role in demanding the NIEO. A re-imagined and inclusive international economic order remained a foreign policy objective for India, even after liberalization, but was soon surpassed by other pressing geo-strategic imperatives which were nonetheless related to issues concerning the greater good of the developing countries.

The GS at the Turn of the Millennium: Contemporary Outlook and Indian Foreign Policy

At the turn of the millennium, there was a widespread desire among developing countries for moving South-South Cooperation once again onto the center stage of global political economy to promulgate a new wave of economic transformation. The rise of key GS countries and the success of some multilateral forums created by them gave impetus to increasing debate and consideration of the potentials of a new phase of challenges, which would relinquish the hegemonic and neo-colonial control of the global North.[46] There were seemingly significant shifts in global production and manufacturing lines from the North to the GS—owing to globalization and its consequent capital flows—which led to economic growth and industrialization in the latter. The Washington Consensus (1989), which contained a set of free-market economic policies supported by the IMF and World Bank, and the US Treasury Department, was initially intended to help developing countries which were in need of economic assistance. However, it proved to be a prime mover of economic globalization in the 1990s, and not a panacea for the economic backwardness of the GS countries. For one author, it at once created and left unanswered several distributional, socio-economic and climate-related crisis which invariably accompany a neo-liberal paradigm of global developmental economic expansionism.[47] It created more jobs in developing societies, thereby increasing the individuals' purchasing power, but fostered a deeply embedded faith in linear material progress through innovation and technological development, with the presumed capacity to create unlimited increases in production and consumption—as preceding arguments in favour of a consumerist culture. Governments in the GS henceforth started to grapple with the issue of managing the tension between global capital expansion and the protection of the rights and welfare of people and the environment.[48] This led to reformulations regarding the role of the West and the rise of the rest—by that it was meant the GS countries.

As has been previously adduced, the Global South has multiple definitions—some descriptive and geographically grounded, and some abstract, analytical and geographically indeterminate. It is a dynamic term and is seemingly there to stay till the North-South divide is present. Inequalities are increasing not just among nations but between and within communities residing within the same country. And the GS is a favourable term than Third World-ism because it is inclusive and is not just a replacement for linear development-oriented terms. For one author, the term, "...functions as more than a metaphor for underdevelopment. It references an entire history of colonialism, neo-imperialism, and differential economic and social change through which large inequalities in living standard, life expectancy, and access to resources are maintained".[49] A de-territorialized use of the term GS draws attention to global struggles and solidarities that result from shared experiences of subjugation under contemporary global capitalism, while providing space for scholars and activists to examine the specificities of issues, processes, and struggles at the national, regional or transnational levels.[50]

Although there can be theorizations on the GS from the standpoints of the leading positivist and post-positivist theories of IR—liberal, realist, Marxist, and constructivist positions—a leading expert has emphasized the inadequacies of such theories to examine the GS position. Revealing the ethnocentric and other biases of such theorizations, he urged instead for the need of more non-Western conceptualizations of GS—which would be true to its heterogeneous socio-political character.[51] Invoking a plethora of Indian and Chinese IR theorists, the same author concluded that the space for oriental ideas in IR theory has been limited, much to the detriment of the academic discipline. He called for a much more gender-sensitized and pluralistic IR theory and foreign policy analysis which would be free from racial and ethnocentric biases, coming from within the GS itself—akin to the *subaltern universalism* of Amitabh Acharya, or the *relational partnership democracy* of Qin Yaqing.[52]

However, a modicum of geographical orientation has proved worthy of the attention of GS analysts. As such bearings are imperative insofar as global governance and positivist IR research are concerned. The IR literature, especially foreign policy analysis, still remains heavily attuned to positivism, as it continues to influence data collection for international action on developmental issues. To exemplify, the GS narrative received added impetus after the publication of the *Millennium Development Goals: A Compact among Nations to End Human Poverty* (2003) by the United Nations Development Programme (UNDP). Also, after its initiative of the same year which brought forth another publication emphasizing 'development cooperation', with the UN acting as the "international machinery for the promotion of the economic and social advancement of all peoples".[53]

The initiative behind the annual publication of the Human Development Reports by the UNDP since 1990, came from the sustained economic research of Amartya Sen and Mahbub ul-Haq—both scholars with roots in developing nations. And the GS got further recognition by the release of the UNDP's 2013 Human Development Report (HDR). Titled, *The Rise of the South: Human Progress in a Diverse World*, it heralded a new standard for looking at the so-called Southern countries, where the combined outputs of Brazil, China, and India (BIC) were pegged as equal to the combined outputs of the longstanding industrial powers—the G-7—for the first time in a century and a half.[54] The HDR looks not only at GDP but also measures the human development index (HDI) of a country based on education, health, gender, and income parameters. The 2013 report for the first time showed a dramatic improvement of HDI scores in countries belonging to the GS such as Bangladesh, Benin, Colombia, El Salvador, Gambia, Laos, Uganda, and Vietnam. Thus, geographical identification of the term became imperative for research designs in global governance and political economy. The report also identified three key drivers for improved HDI scores in GS countries: (i) a proactive developmental state; (ii) tapping of global markets; and (iii) determined social policy innovation. Also, for guaranteeing future success, the Report provided four policy recommendations to the GS countries: (i) enhancing equality, especially gender equality; (ii) enabling greater voice and participation of citizens, including youth; (iii) confronting environmental pressures; and (iv) managing demographic change.[55]

Therefore, there is a close correlation between the need to build national consensus for long-term policies to ensure the gradual integration with the world economy and the imperative to invest in domestic human development to take full advantage of the opportunities provided by external openness. It was clear by 2013 that the South-South rhetoric of the NIEO days was being transformed into a living reality of our times, as a propellant behind not only economic growth but also human development. This cooperation became evident most clearly in trade relations among Southern countries (see Tables 5.3 and 5.4) which contributed to positive HDI among these states even in the 2019 HDR.[56] At the ideational level, developing countries with poorer HDI can learn from those among its ranks with better HDI as their experience is more relevant than those of the OECD countries. And more practically, South-South cooperation in investment, finance, technology transfer, and trade have been the key contemporary drivers of economic growth in the GS.

To exemplify, merchandise trade among GS countries increased from 8.1% in 1980 to 24% in 2018, with Asian countries conducting 59.99% intra-regional trade and 40.01% trade with other continents and developing countries.[57] And there has been the highest average annual HDI regional growth with 1.35% in South Asia (from .441 to .642) and 1.28%in East Asia and Pacific (from .519 to .741)—regions which account for a huge share of South-South trade—in the 1990-2018 period, as per the 2019 HDR (see Table 5.5).[58] This naturally hints at a positive correlation between economic growth due to increased South-South trade and HDI growth in these regions. But, all is not very optimistic in the developing regions, especially with regard to group-based inequalities. There are stark gender inequalities especially in India (rank 122 out of 162 countries in the list of Gender Inequality Index), Sri Lanka (86), Bhutan (99), and Myanmar (106) (United Nations Development Programme (2019), Beyond Income, Beyond Averages, Beyond Today: Inequalities in Human Development in the 21st Century, pp. 316-19).

Table 5.3: Global Merchandise Trade Flows (2018)

Hemisphere	Amount	Percentage of World Trade
North-North	US$ 6.9 trillion	36
North-South	US$ 6.9 trillion	36
South-South	US$ 5.4 trillion	24

Source: United Nations Conference on Trade and Development (2019), "Trade within and between 'hemispheres,'" in *UNCTAD Handbook of Statistics*, New York; on line source: https://stats.unctad.org/handbook/MerchandiseTrade/ByPartner.html. Accessed on June 20, 2020.

While India's HDI ratings have not been that impressive as compared to other GS countries—ranking 129 in the 2019 HDR, with Inequality-adjusted HDI recording a fall from .647 to .477—it has had a more or less impressive economic record since liberalization. This shows India as an exception to the established rule of economic growth leading to higher HDI, for a surfeit of domestic reasons which cannot be discussed at length within the scope of this volume (United Nations Development

Programme (2019), Beyond Income, Beyond Averages, Beyond Today: Inequalities in Human Development in the 21st Century, p. 310). However, from a foreign policy perspective, India's economic diplomacy can be adduced as exemplary in its quest for GS solidarity. India's voice as a representative of the GS triumphed in various rounds of WTO negotiations, where it pitched in favour of better terms of trade for developing countries. But before India's role in the WTO is discussed at length, a few determinants of Indian foreign policy must be touched upon for a holistic understanding of its part in the resurgence of the GS. The coordination of the external and internal agendas of foreign policy making, the changeover from the NAM to 'strategic autonomy', and finally an anticipated move towards 'strategic influence' are such cases in point which would serve as foundations for analyzing the extent of India's influence on the present international trade regime, with special reference to the benefits it accrues for the GS.

Balancing the Internal and External Agendas of Foreign Policymaking: India at Crossroads

As has been argued earlier, India's multilateral engagements through the BRICS forum and its participation in the G-20 fostered a sense of 'strategic autonomy' which the NAM 2.0 (2012) had emphasized for deft foreign policy implementation. However, there are serious external and internal agendas serving as determinants of foreign policy and India's recent successes in this front owe much to the careful management of internal inequalities generated by the state-society gap and its external capability in ensuring regional stabilization in South Asia, if not the entire GS.[59]

India's foreign policy vision document, the NAM 2.0 (2012), attempted to provide solutions for the impending policy issues and challenges, while invariably creating some by itself. As the document had recognized, the concept of 'strategic autonomy' has largely replaced 'non-alignment' as the moniker of Indian foreign policy in the last quarter of a century. However, the desire for 'strategic autonomy' is not something unique insofar as a nation-state is concerned. States seek to maximize their 'autonomy' in the international system to the extent that they can—based upon available resources and the political ambitions of their respective leaderships. With greater economic clout, Indian foreign policy has had greater maneuverability since the early twenty-first century. By the 1990s, it was clear that the NIEO project had collapsed, and India started gaining from its acceptance of the 'Washington Consensus'. By implication, 'strategic autonomy' is nothing more than the flip-side of the 'economic autarky' that India pursued during the Cold War and which resulted in its pro-Third World demands surrounding the NIEO. However, given contemporary circumstances, India's involvements with and championship of the GS rhetoric—especially vis-à-vis international trade regimes—required a much different tact in tune with the critical economic interdependence with the rest of the world.[60] This was based upon two structural changes concerning India in particular, but having larger implications for the GS: (i) despite economic slowdown since 2014-15, India has still been on its way of becoming a major power itself, so it had to come to terms with its emerging strengths and (ii) the huge change in the nature of the Indian economy after two and a half decades of accelerated growth, by which nearly 50% of its economic growth has been increasingly linked with international trade.[61]

These structural changes are significant for the present times—at least as far as pre-eminence within the GS is concerned—with the rise of China having overt neo-imperialist tendencies and its relationship with the US entering a new low during the Covid-19 pandemic. As the NAM 2.0 had predicted, India's attitude towards a potential rivalry or collaboration between China and the US will continue to be an important challenge for its foreign policy. By implication, the smaller GS countries would soon have to align themselves with either India or China, as the trajectory of their relationship has descended towards greater animosity in the aftermath of the recent Galwan valley skirmish. Any India-China bipolarity in Asia would entail substantive security cooperation among India, Japan, and the US, to counteract China. Thus, its obsessions with the concept of 'strategic autonomy'—at least in decision-making circles—only explain the distance between its growing potentials on the one hand, and the inertia of its strategic discourse, on the other. Whereas, for accruing regional and transnational gains, it must focus upon influencing the global order by proactively creating conditions for sustained economic growth. For furthering the interests of the GS, a new external task is necessary, now more than ever, which can be summed up as the quest for 'strategic influence'.[62] What implications will this have upon India's relationship with the GS? To answer this question a few factors of the new South-South cooperation would have to be addressed.

Although the new South-South cooperation has continued the NIEO's call for a fairer trading system, such demands indeed take place within a radically transformed global context. In such a context, it is increasingly difficult for any particular country to assume leadership of the GS as the projects and patterns of enhancing regional influence are now pursued by several expanding Southern economies within a larger complex pattern of global economic transnationalism, transcending any particular geographical region.[63] Now the task for Indian foreign policy is to re-conceptualize its stance vis-à-vis the rest of the GS by coming to terms with the fact that it is one among equals and no longer the preeminent rule-maker of South-South cooperation. Although the NAM 2.0 had made it clear that India was willing to shed this garb, it has become even more imperative in the present times. The rise of myriad regional and global economic re-alignments since the 2008 economic crisis, has led to the beginning of far reaching global structural changes ever since.

The GS rhetoric, at least in the last decade and a half, has been shifting from the rising hope that Southern economies would be liberated from the North's dominance—thereby reflecting a kind of contemporary neo-Third World-ism—to a 'gradual acquiescence' that the South's economic success is intrinsically linked to and subsumed within the existing global capitalist development paradigm. To exemplify, far from rejecting the principles of global free trade, the GS countries see themselves as having little choice but to seek membership of the WTO—since to do otherwise would be to risk marginalization—despite the WTO's stringent policy options for developing countries.[64]

However, it is a feature of the new South-South cooperation to seek reforms of the WTO, and herein the significance of countries like India assume center stage. In such cases, the ability of a country's foreign policy to exercise 'strategic influence' becomes paramount, as 'autonomy' can no longer be defined along conventional lines in the post-globalized age. Whether and where new 'spheres of influence' may be created by an ambitious Southern power is a serious historical question of the present times—having profound implications upon the future world order—akin to the horizontal and vertical spread of Chinese influence throughout Africa and Central Asia by means of its OBOR and other the mechanisms of economic diplomacy.

India in the GATT/WTO: Changing Interests and Orientation

In a way, India's brand of participation in the GATT/WTO has been an example of its advocacy of the contemporary GS rhetoric, based upon the latter's 'gradual acquiescence' to global capitalism. It also exemplifies India's encapsulation of the external and internal foreign policy determinants in furthering its 'strategic influence'. National interest has changed continuously since the 1950s, with consequent changes in India's orientations towards the international trading system. The WTO is perhaps the foremost institution where India has enhanced its influence, till date. India's attachment to the collective causes of the GS has continued to determine the adaptability and flexibility of its international agenda. Insofar as the WTO is concerned, it has adopted a more selective coalition-building strategy agreeing to flexible alliances such as the G-20. This has helped maintain aspects of 'bloc diplomacy'—or diplomacy conducted by groups of countries having similar interests—but has been at once more pro-active and issue-oriented than the missionary zeal of the NAM and the G-77.[65]

The General Agreement on Tariffs and Trade (GATT) traces its origins to the same 1944 Bretton Woods Conference which had created the twin IFIs, and had laid the foundations for the post-Second World War financial system. The International Trade Organization (ITO)—as it was originally conceived—was supposed to serve as the third leg of the system. But, the failure of the US Senate to ratify the ITO draft charter nipped it in the bud, which led to parallel negotiations on a multilateral agreement for reciprocal reductions in tariff barriers. These negotiations resulted in the signing of the GATT on November 30, 1947. And a sufficient number of signatory nations—including India—ratified the GATT for its entry into force on January 1, 1948, under a 'Protocol of Provisional Application'. This led to the GATT surviving the ITO's demise, although it lacked coherent institutional structure, since the negotiators had expected the agreement to be subsumed under the ITO's umbrella. Nevertheless, the GATT became functional as a legal agreement between many countries, whose overall purpose was to promote international trade by reducing or eliminating trade barriers such as tariffs or quotas.[66] In spite of its institutional deficiencies, the GATT managed to function as a *de facto* international organization—sponsoring eight 'rounds' of multilateral trade negotiations from 1947 to 1994 (see Table 5.6). In the first rounds, negotiations were conducted on a product by product basis—known as the 'request/offer' approach—whereby GATT contracting parties exchanged lists of requests and offers on products of interest to them in order to reach agreement on tariff concessions. However, the Uruguay Round (1986-94) entirely changed this practice. It was the largest trade negotiation ever: involving 123 countries, spanning for eighty-seven months, and covering almost all trade. It ultimately culminated in the Marrakesh Agreement (1994) which established the WTO on January 1, 1995. The WTO incorporates the principles of the GATT and provides a more enduring institutional framework for implementing and extending them.

The topmost decision-making body of the WTO is the Ministerial Conference (see Box 5.6), which usually meets every two years. It brings together all members of the WTO—164 members since July 2016[67]—all of which are countries or customs unions. The Ministerial Conference can take decisions on all matters under any of the multilateral trade agreements. Although the GATT also had a similar mechanism, it often faltered due to the lack of consensus. When the GATT ministerial meeting in Geneva (1982) intended to launch a major new

Table 5.6: GATT/WTO Rounds

Name	Start	Duration	Countries	Tabled Items	Achievements
Geneva	April 1947	7 months	23	Tariffs	Signing of GATT, 45,000 tariff concessions affecting $10 billion of trade
Annecy	April 1949	5 months	34	Tariffs	Countries exchanged some 5,000 tariff concessions
Torquay	Sept. 1950	8 months	34	Tariffs	Countries exchanged some 8,700 tariff concessions, cutting the 1948 tariff levels by 25%
Geneva II	Jan. 1956	5 months	22	Tariffs	$2.5 billion in tariff reductions
Dillion	Sept. 1960	11 months	45	Tariffs	Tariff concessions worth $4.9 billion of world trade
Kennedy	May 1964	37 months	48	Tariffs and anti-dumping	Tariff concessions worth $40 billion of world trade
Tokyo	Sept. 1973	74 months	102	Tariffs, non-tariff measures, 'framework agreement	Tariff reductions worth more than $300 billion achieved
Uruguay	Sept. 1986	87 months	123	Tariffs, non-tariff measures, rules, services, intellectual property, dispute settlement, textiles, agriculture, amendment of GATT articles	The round led to the creation of WTO, and extended the range of trade negotiations, leading to major reductions in tariffs, agricultural subsidies, and an extension of intellectual property rights.
Doha	Nov. 2001	Ongoing	159	Tariffs, non-tariff measures, agriculture, labor standards, environment, competition, investment, transparency, patents, etc.	The last agreement to date, the Bali Package, was signed on 7 December 2013.

Source: World Trade Organization, "Understanding the WTO," Geneva; https://www.wto.org/english/thewto_e/whatis_e/tif_e/tif_e.htm. Accessed on August 10, 2020.

negotiating round, the conference stalled on agriculture, trade in services and intellectual property. It was only after the compromise of GS countries vis-à-vis the international patent system—in the 1992 Cartagena UNCTAD Summit—that the Uruguay Round could proceed, albeit without their explicit commitments toward cutting import duties and opening service markets. The delay in resolving every outstanding issue of the Uruguay Round was ultimately profitable for the developed countries in the WTO, and not the GS: the aspects of service and intellectual property leading to the Agreement on Trade Related Aspects of Intellectual Property Rights (TRIPS), and the creation of the WTO itself could not have taken place without the GS compromise on these issues, which effectively negated the NIEO. However, the Uruguay Round contained timetables for new negotiations on several topics which it could not cover. Most notably, on agriculture and services at the turn of the millennium, and the developmental needs of the GS. This led to the Doha Developmental Agenda in late 2001.[68]

Box 5.6: List of WTO Ministerial Conferences

Nur-Sultan, Kazakhstan, on hold due to Covid-19 pandemic
Buenos Aires, 10-13 December 2017
Nairobi, 15-19 December 2015
Bali, 3-6 December 2013
Geneva, 15-17 December 2011
Geneva, 30 November – 2 December 2009
Hong Kong, 13-18 December 2005
Cancún, 10-14 September 2003
Doha, 9-13 November 2001
Seattle, November 30 – December 3, 1999
Geneva, 18-20 May 1998
Singapore, 9-13 December 1996

Source: World Trade Organization, "Ministerial Conferences," Geneva; on line source: https://www.wto.org/english/thewto_e/minist_e/minist_e.htm. Accessed on August 10, 2020.

Although India had been a founding member of the GATT, its domestic philosophy and trade policy—until the late 1980s—were very antithetical to the latter's underlying principle of trade liberalization. India's import-substitution approach to development favoured a system of tariffs and quotas aimed at infant industry protection which coupled well with the NIEO demands and not with the GATT. India's export pessimism resulted from its alignment of trade with the lived experience of colonialism and imperialism. This biased analogy was abjured in the 1990s, in favour of liberalization, when the Indian economy was on the verge of bankruptcy. The coherence of its economic philosophy with the underpinnings of the international trading system is something new. And it exudes India's very own 'gradual acquiescence' to global capitalism. Its recognition of the WTO as a vehicle for trade negotiations has remained resolute, and a more outward-oriented approach has enabled the country to garner the benefits of an open economy. By 2008, India's international trade was twenty times what it had been in 1980.[69] However, its stance vis-à-vis the international trading system always articulated the need of developing countries—particularly their industrialization efforts. After the Uruguay Round, the general feeling among developing countries, and certainly in India, seemed to have been that the TRIPS agreement was not in their best interest, and was acceptable only as part of a larger package wherein developed countries would remove or lower trade barriers in areas of interest to developing countries. However, after 17 years of the Uruguay Round this notion was petering out. When the Doha Round was launched in 2001, it was hailed as a corrective action of sorts, aimed at restoring the perceived imbalances of the Uruguay Round by putting the interests of developing countries at the forefront. Although cynical views have repeatedly questioned the justification of calling the Doha Round a 'development' round, India's participation in it has significantly steered its course towards the developmental concerns of the GS.

To begin with, India was skeptical about the Doha Round's commitment towards development and tried to forestall its launch at the 2001 Doha Ministerial Conference. But, when this round still sailed through, it only made India a major voice within the WTO. It was vocal in the selection of the WTO director-general, by rallying with the developing bloc;

it insisted on the implementation of outstanding issues from the Uruguay Round, and resisted the inclusion of the so-called 'Singapore Issues'—investment, competition, facilitation, and government procurement—into the negotiations; its coalition-building strategy involving the Like-Minded Group—or LMG, a group of GS countries that wanted to block the 'Singapore Issues'[70]—implicitly bestowed upon India a GS leadership role within the institution. However, it eventually had to accept the Doha Development Agenda (DDA).[71]

India exercised greater 'strategic influence', especially through coalition-building, in the Cancun Ministerial Conference (2003). India's influence led to the formation of the G-20, which combined the bargaining weight of Brazil, China, and South Africa. The G-20 exposed the false rhetoric of the Global North on trade liberalization, putting forward an alternative agenda that garnered greater support in the GS. Its influence also provided it the leadership of other coalitions like the Core Group and the G-33. The former demanded the removal of the 'Singapore Issues' from the DDA, and the latter committed to the promotion of greater flexibilities in food security. Together with the GS countries in the WTO, India could counteract the US-EU agenda and its bargaining power vis-à-vis developmental issues of the GS ultimately betrayed the Doha Round's empty promises of development.

The Doha negotiations have repeatedly collapsed and a successful completion of the round is still out of sight. This is not because of India's inflexibility on developmental issues, but due to the North's reluctance towards granting the GS a level playing field in terms of trade through the WTO. Since 2001, India has been in pursuit of just the same, along with securing—realistically—more favourable terms of trade for itself. During the Hong Kong Ministerial Conference (2004), India consolidated its pivotal position within the Five-Interested Parties (United States, EU, Brazil, India, and Australia), and as a member of the G-4 (United States, EU, Brazil, and India). The result was the renegotiation of the DDA to be more in tune with the South's developmental concerns, by retaining only 'trade facilitation' of the 'Singapore Issues'—discarding the rest—and by agreeing to eliminate all export subsidies by 2013.[72]

Till the global economic recession of 2008, India continued with its alliance with the G-20 and other developing countries within the WTO. It refused to concede the US-EU offer on Non-Agricultural Market Access in 2007. In 2008, India also rejected a deal in the critical G-7 meeting on grounds of the inadequacy of special developmental clauses vis-à-vis food security in the GS. In the aftermath of the 2008 financial crisis, India began its proactive engagements in the WTO, but was not entirely keen to embrace its apparent role as a major stakeholder. The latter significantly diminished its rule-making abilities in the organization, unfairly branding the country as an obstructionist negotiator. Henceforth, India adopted a more cautious approach. Reaffirming India's commitment to the GS, the then Commerce Minister stressed that, "development issues, particularly those of interest to LDCs, should be the foremost priority [in the Doha Round].... India was the first developing country to extend duty free quota access to all LDCs."[73]

India's caution translated into a proactive role in the Bali Ministerial Conference (2013) which focused on two major issues: food security and trade facilitation. Negotiations were steered by the Indian delegation's pitch to secure meaningful package on food security for subsistence farmers in India and GS countries. The final deal influence by India reflected its willingness to engage in trade-offs, provided that clear developmental flexibilities were established by which India could buy and stock as much food from its farmers, to implement the National Food Security Act (2013).[74] Since the adoption of the Bali Package (2013), India for the first time was willing to act independently of GS coalitions, and pursue its own path to renegotiate the DDA. It ratified the Trade Facilitation Agreement in April 2016, which came into force in February 2017 when the WTO obtained the two-thirds acceptance from its total membership. India's stance vis-à-vis the WTO, however, needs an urgent re-evaluation in the light of very recent developments such as the Covid-19 pandemic and its national government's adoption of the 'Atmanirbhar Bharat' slogan. Whatever be the nature of impending changes, three generalizations can be formed insofar as the future course of India's trade relations and its fidelity to the GS rhetoric are concerned.

To begin with, India's present stance towards international trade—following 'Make in India for the world' or to alter the terms of engagement by becoming a part of global value chains—would require a considerable increase in domestic industrial output and foreign investment. Now India can no longer be content with removing the domestic constraints that have prevented it from fully garnering the benefits of the international trade system. This has been due to its hitherto underdeveloped domestic regulatory environment and India's inability to fully appreciate the growing relationship among trade, investment, and competition. It must now turn its attention to facilitating convergence between its domestic policy and its foreign policy, at which Prime Minister Modi has hinted in his recent Independence Day speech.[75] A necessary boost to domestic regimes dealing with trade policy would help India integrate itself into global value chains through strategic trade and investment policy instruments, and to align its trade policy with foreign policy. The resultant growth trajectory by adopting 'next generation' reforms would allow India to engage more with trading partners both regionally and globally, and would make its voice stronger in the WTO and various multilateral fora.

Second, with the domestic front clearly linked with its foreign policy, India can significantly augment its standing in the WTO, especially in the light of its previous role as a negotiator of the Doha changeover. The Doha Round has marked the change in the underlying negotiating environment of world trade, where progress was slow in a new, stickier regime of global trade negotiations. India did recognize the importance of staying engaged globally, even if it were only for its political and strategic benefits. Today, developing countries are a part of the multilateral system like never before, and whenever broad consensus or unanimity is required, developing countries have the ability to influence proceedings at the WTO. In most matters economic size trumps country numbers, and this has compelled GS countries to undertake multilateral initiatives—BRICS, IBSA, RIC, SCO, and G-20, more of these later—to counter the Global North countries in the WTO. India has been an intrinsic part of such mini-multilateral groupings, which are perhaps more in the nature of clubs. This new approach to multilateralism can be best described as 'plurilateralism'.[76] India has emerged as a pivot in groupings such as BRICS, IBSA, RIC and BASIC, which have time and again challenged the supremacy of Northern countries in trade regimes. For examples, the developing nations of G-20 demanded concessions on agriculture and governance issues; the India, Brazil, South Africa (IBSA) grouping has similarly criticized the protectionist policies of the G8 and emphasized the need to push ahead with the Doha developmental round; the Brazil, Russia, India, China, South Africa (BRICS) grouping has sought to address several of the issues originally raised by the NIEO, such as the reform of the IFIs to give the rising powers more influence in their operations.[77]

Finally, in order to foster better ties among GS countries, not least to explore new spaces for economic growth, investments in infrastructure, energy security, and the realization of symbiotic social services, India is likely to continue its pursuit of 'strategic partnerships', and trans-continental cooperation and outreach programmes, especially in Latin America and Africa. These have been ensuing for quite some time, being ostensibly based upon three reasons:[78] (a) identity: or the shared history of colonialism and exploitation, which form the bases of their GS identity; (b) interest: to reform global governance in issue areas other than trade, such as the UN; and (c) domestic politics: countries in Latin America and Africa have significant workforce depending upon agriculture and rural activity, so does India, and this converging domestic interest might prevent them from furthering trade liberalization in international fora.

India's Plurilateral Engagements and Global South Outreach

India's current position vis-à-vis the GS revolves around the politics of multilateralism.[79] Or what this chapter has claimed to be 'plurilateralism'. This new trend has been overt in its foreign relations with Latin America and Africa, as only through a foreign policy outreach could India hope to maintain and enhance its economic growth at home and political clout abroad. From the beginning of economic liberalization in the early

1990s, to the economic crisis of 2008 and the period beyond, India's economic diplomacy had never been tasked in such a demanding manner—to ensure economic growth domestically, and to reorient its foreign policy toward regions that had remained neglected or caught up in a historical straitjacket.[80] And, one might add, the task of creating a decent space for GS countries in the global system of exchange. The latter was perceived to foster a symbiosis of sorts among India and its GS partners, especially with regard to their positions in institutions of global governance, not least in the global capitalist order. Such plurilateralism can be best comprehended under the umbrella of India's trans-continental outreach programmes.

The Africa Outreach

Although India's relations with the countries belonging to the continent of Africa dates back to the halcyon days of the NAM and G-77, its recent outreach in Africa is ostensibly based upon some contemporary imperatives. Succinctly, these involve energy and mineral resources, trade and investment, traditional, and non-traditional security threats, diaspora, global governance issues, and most importantly, the emerging competitive dynamic of Sino-Indian relations in third spaces, beyond Asia.[81] India's pitch to counter the growing influence of China in Africa has transformed its involvements within the continent from merely a political stance. India's foreign policy and diplomacy in Africa have made remarkable progress in building mutually beneficial relations in the continent. As a champion of the GS, India has promoted itself as a preferred partner, unlike the path taken by the business-oriented Chinese diplomats in Africa. India has gained from the perception that its companies have been more willing to engage local resources and personnel, with projects and investments in Africa which are responsive to local needs and are not entirely self-interested. India's trade with Africa has grown from US$ 5.3 billion in 2001 to US$ 69 billion in 2019.[82]

It is projected that by the year 2050, Africa's population would have doubled to 2.4 billion. And according to the IMF, it would be home to several of the fastest growing economies in the world, in a few years' time. Economically, the Africans have taken steps towards integration. In March 2018, 44 African nations signed the Continental Free Trade Agreement (AfCFTA). The free trade area aims to deepen the African integration process and will allow free movement of people and trade across the continent. The United Nations Economic Commission for Africa (UNECA) forecasts that this will boost intra-regional trade by 52% in five years. The African Union's initiatives, such as the Programme for Infrastructure Development (PIDA) would reduce infrastructure deficit across the continent by prioritizing its development in transport, energy, and green technologies, trans-boundary water resources, and in the Information and Communication Technologies (ICTs) sector.[83]

Recent initiatives taken by the Indian Government and its industrial sector have also helped in the upward movement of India's trade with Africa. India has always been keen on sharing its development experience, and promoting beneficial development in the GS has always been a driver of India's outreach towards Africa. The Indian Technical and Economic Cooperation (ITEC) Programme was instrumental until the 1990s for sharing India's development experience as part of the South-South cooperation. It included the deputing of technical industry experts and training candidates from Africa in a large number of technical disciplines in Indian institutes, and scholarships for African students in Indian universities. The IBSA forum, as another example, emphasized the common interests of the three continents in the international arena. After liberalization in India, the ITEC programme was expanded to include the funding of pilot projects in specific areas and to cover feasibility studies.[84] After 1991, India has been equally guided by other factors—largely accruing from rapid economic growth—in pursuing more entrenched relations in Africa: such as the needs of the countries involved vis-à-vis their economic growth, and the need to build wider and deeper relations in Africa, given their weight in international institutions.[85]

The close political relationships among India and various African countries are now being buttressed by flourishing trade and investment opportunities. This began with regular India-Africa Forum Summits (IAFS) from 2008 onwards, and various financial and technical instruments focusing on specific groups of African countries. The Export-Import Bank of India (EXIM) in collaboration with Confederation of Indian Industries (CII) made technical and financial assistance available through the India-Africa Project Partnership. In 2002, the EXIM Bank launched the Focus Africa Programme to enhance trade with African countries. Initially, the focus of this programme was limited to sub-Saharan Africa. In 2003, this programme was broadened to include North African countries. The EXIM-CII project has organized 14 India-Africa Project Partnership Conclaves since 2005. The first India-Africa Forum Summit (2008) began the process of structured engagement with African countries by announcing the Duty Free Tariff Preference (DFTP) Scheme for Least Developed Countries (LDCs). The second Summit (2011) discussed bilateral trade issues.[86] Multilateral initiatives—such as the Techno-Economic Approach for Africa-India Movement (Team-9) involving India and African countries like Burkina Faso, Chad, Ghana, Guinea-Bissau, Ivory Coast, Mali, and Senegal—were also launched. Till the UPA II regime in India, the ITEC budget for Africa stood at the US$ 2 billion (2012), with 167 open credit lines of EXIM Bank amounting to US$ 8.57 billion (2013) covering all the major African countries in a multilateral grand design.[87]

India hosted the annual meeting of African Development Bank (AfDB) in 2017. This highlighted the increasing priority given by Indian Government towards promoting economic cooperation with African countries.[88] The EXIM-CII Africa conclaves provide a platform for business leaders from India and Africa to discuss future projects. Similarly, other organizations, such as Federation of Indian Chambers of Commerce and Industry (FICCI) have been promoting trade with the continent.[89]

With the advent of Prime Minister Modi, India-Africa relations have taken a more vibrant turn. There have been 34 outgoing visits to African countries at the Presidential, Vice-Presidential and Prime Ministerial levels. Till the outbreak of the Covid-19 pandemic, there has not been a single country in the continent that has not been visited by at least a Union Minister. To enhance diplomatic engagement, India is opening 18 new embassies in Africa, to take the total number of Indian missions to 47 out of a total of 54 countries in Africa.[90] Trade and investment have also been on the rise. The DFTP Scheme has benefited African nations by extending duty free access to 98.2% of India's total tariff lines. Thirty-eight African countries benefit from the DFTP Scheme. India has become the fifth largest investor in Africa with cumulative investments of $ 54 billion. As the Indian Prime Minister has himself remarked in his 2019 speech to the Ugandan Parliament, India's priority is not just Africa, but all Africans—every man, woman and child in the continent. For the present Foreign Secretary of India, this would go a long way in drawing goodwill from such linkages.[91] And it would indeed cover the distance insofar as GS solidarity is concerned. The latter has been on the ascendant with India's multilateral engagements with perhaps its most favoured strategic partner in the continent, South Africa.

In 2015, the then President of South Africa, Jacob Zuma, visited New Delhi for the third India-Africa Forum Summit, and reinvigorated the urge to participate in the BRICS and the Indian Ocean Rim Association (IORA). Recalling the successes of the IBSA Dialogue Forum—from 2003—in articulating the GS voice on pressing issues of the UN, the IFIs, and the WTO, Zuma was providing impetus to further multilateral initiatives via the BRICS and other fora. This was swiftly taken up by PM Modi during his visit to South Africa in 2016, and led to the signing of four crucial agreements between the countries on ICTs, tourism, cultural cooperation, and the establishment of grassroots innovation in the domains of science and technology. There were agreements to further cooperation in defence, energy, agro-processing, human resource development, infrastructure and technology; with South Africa openly supporting India's entry into the Nuclear Suppliers Group (NSG).[92]

The 2016 Joint Statement was followed by the 2019 Joint Statement when President M. Cyril Ramaphosa visited India. This included relevant multilateral platforms as well, like the G-20, BRICS, IBSA, BASIC, NAM, WTO, and IORA. The leaders concurred that the BRICS agenda has expanded over the years. They recognized the BRICS Forum's valuable contribution in reforming the global financial and economic architecture. Expressing satisfaction at the operationalization of the New Development Bank (NDB), they agreed to continue with the institution-building momentum in BRICS with an aim to further bridge the investment-gap in key economic sectors.[93] The organization of BRICS echoes South African perceptions that it needs India in it to actively confront the economic and political clout of the US and Europe, by attempting to shift the global political and economic center from the developed world to the GS.[94]

Among South Africa's non-traditional partners in the GS, the relationship with India is the most active and holds the greatest prominence. This especially due to the presence of deep Gandhian roots in South Africa—Mahatma Gandhi led his first *satyagraha* in South Africa and later influenced the leader of the country's anti-Apartheid movement, Nelson Mandela—and the presence of the highest number of Indian diaspora in Africa, with a total strength of 1,218,000, thereby constituting 3% of South Africa's total population.[95] India is South Africa's fifth-largest export destination and fourth-largest import origin and is the second-largest trading partner in Asia. Bilateral trade between India and South Africa (see Fig. 5.2) currently stands at US$ 10 billion. In 2016, both countries set a target of doubling bilateral trade and investment to US$ 20 billion by 2021. A recent joint study by Confederation of Indian Industries (CII) and PricewaterhouseCoopers (PwC) published in May 2018, suggested that around 140 Indian companies have invested close to US$ 4 billion in South Africa, thereby creating direct employment for over 18,000 people. The leading Indian companies are Wipro, Coal India, Cipla, HCL Technologies, Tata Motors, Zomato, Mahindra and Mahindra, Vedanta, and Motherson Sumi. South African companies which have invested in India are SASOL, FirstRand, Old Mutual, ACSA, Shoprite, and Nandos.[96] On July 12, 2018, India and South Africa made a joint proposal at the WTO regarding the temporary moratorium on customs duties on electronic transmissions, which can lead to loss of competitiveness among developing countries. This joint India-South Africa report took due note of attempts by the developed world to make commitments more comprehensive

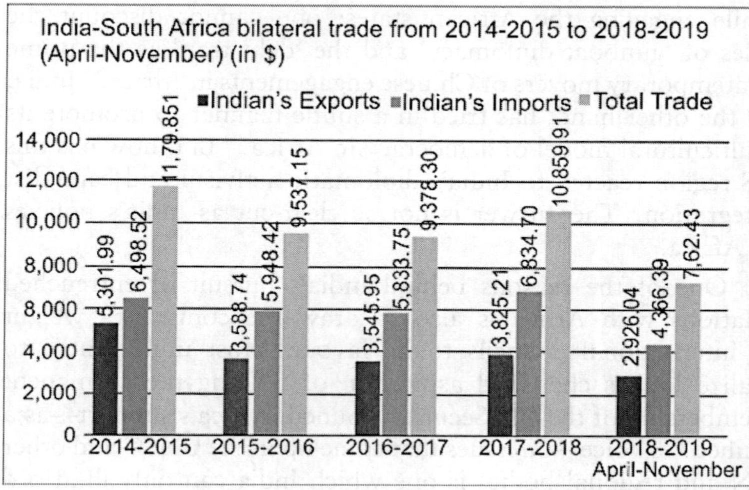

Fig. 5.2: India-South Africa Bilateral Trade Data

Source: Abhishek Mishra (2019), "India-South Africa relations: A perennial bond," Observer Research Foundation, 25 January, https://www.orfonline.org/expert-speak/india-south-africa-relations-a-perennial-bond-47557/ (accessed on August 21, 2020).

and stringent through negotiations on regional trade agreements and multilateral commitments. Relations between India and South Africa have provided a key anchor to these developments, building upon a long-standing history as well as providing a sense of continuity in membership among these formations.[97]

Although India still has some distance to traverse to become a major player in Africa—especially in its bid to counter the long-standing Chinese influence in the region—Indian diplomacy has been largely successful in the region for its human touch. While, the business sector in India has participated along with its government in a joint movement in Africa, following a philosophy which is very different from that of the Chinese. India has been able to leverage its historical role in supporting anti-colonial movements in Africa and has aimed to foster greater regional integration and multilateral cooperation, always with an eye to strengthening the GS bloc. Whereas, China has apparently had only its ambitions as a global hegemon in mind while engaging the African states; one cannot discount the roles of 'gunboat diplomacy' and the 'debt trap' as the prime contemporary movers of Chinese engagements in Africa.[98] India, on the other hand, has tried in a subtle manner to promote its multicultural model of democracy in Africa.[99] But, how has this GS region reacted to India's diplomatic activism and capitalist integration? The answer is not as clear-cut as India's policies in Africa.

One of the reasons behind India's pursuit of entrenched relations with Africa is also to draw the continent's weight in international councils to its favour. Most importantly, to realize India's cherished aspiration of holding the permanent membership of the UN Security Council. Africa's support—as a unified GS voice—on issues that come up in the UNSC and other UN and regional bodies is one which India can only ill-afford to garner, being the continent's long-standing partner. Should the African countries get two seats on a rotational basis in the Security Council—as they have been demanding—India would need to greatly intensify its relations with each of the African countries. African states have welcomed India's relative flexibility and its less didactic stance as compared to the European powers and China. But, neither Africa, nor Latin America—as will be shown subsequently—has expedited India's ambitions in global platforms, which is indicative of the schisms which exist even in the period of renewed South-South cooperation.

India's campaign for permanent membership received a boost with PM Modi's participation in the 47th session of the UNGA (2015). Failure to garner the support of the Africa Group—comprising all members of the AU, demanding two permanent and five non-permanent seats for Africa, abolition of veto—in previous summits meant that the two-thirds majority could not be reached and India's reform proposals were ultimately defeated. This lack of support was not interpreted in a good light and led to diminishment of the GS solidarity, especially when contrasted with India's stupendous contributions towards UN Peacekeeping Operations (UNPKO) in Africa (see Chapter 7). Most of the countries in the GS are averse to India's permanent membership, despite being the beneficiary of India's contribution towards UN peacekeeping missions aimed at these troubled spots. Furthermore, its campaign has been held hostage by the unrealistic demands of underdeveloped countries, especially those subscribing to the Africa Group, the Uniting for Consensus (UfC) group and other GS formations with vested interests in the UNSC reforms. Even the L.69 formation—with 42 developing countries mostly from Africa, Latin America and Caribbean—has opposed the G-4 proposal for UNSC reforms led by India. The dynamics of India-Latin America relations are different from India's Africa outreach, but the outcomes are telling with regard to why it is, after all, befitting for India to come out of its sequestered GS role in the near future.

India and Latin America

The neglect of foreign relations between India and the Latin American states went both ways at least till 1964, when the formation of the UNCTAD and G-77 marked the beginning of a process of fundamental systemic reorientation in international political economy. Latin America featured only sporadically in the history of Indian foreign policy, with the possible exception of Brazil. Brazil clearly stands out as India's principle strategic partner in the region. Both are emerging powers having a variety of common interests pursued generally through bilateral and multilateral mechanisms. The rise of *tercermundismo* or Third World-ism in Latin America led many countries in the region to build ties with important states in Asia and Africa.[100] While the reformulation of South-South cooperation has led India to develop cordial diplomatic relations with almost all Latin American states, some of these partnerships have attained important strategic value for Indian foreign policy.[101]

The year 2014 was particularly eventful for Indian diplomacy in Latin America. The newly elected PM Modi visited Brazil for the BRICS summit, and also engaged in an interactive session with the leaders of Latin America on its sidelines. In view of India's growing demand for energy and its interest in seeking overseas investments, Latin America attracts New Delhi's interest. Three of the G-20 economies are in the region—Mexico, Brazil, and Argentina. In the last two decades, India's trade with Latin American countries has grown substantially and its investments are diversified in sectors such as Information Technology (IT) and manufacturing. The region has also emerged as an important market for the Indian pharmaceutical and automobile industries. The clash with China over the Latin American space was inevitable for India, which all the more necessitated more entrenched relations with these states under PM Modi. Relations with the oil-rich Venezuela was almost derailed when India's leading hydrocarbon entity, the Oil and Natural Gas Corporation (ONGC) found itself in a difficult position owing to the delay in payment of dues by Venezuela's Petróleos de Venezuela, S.A. (PDVSA). Also, when the US threatened economic sanctions against Venezuela, following protests against its President, Nicolás Maduro, in 2019, and India was compelled to develop energy ties with other Latin American countries, such as Mexico.[102]

Mexico is India's second largest trading partner in Latin America and in 2017-18 bilateral trade was valued at approximately US$ 8.30 billion. In 2016, India exported more to Mexico than to some countries in its more immediate neighbourhood such as Thailand, Myanmar, and Iran. Since Mexico opened its oil sector for foreign participation in 2014, New Delhi has viewed it as a viable source of crude oil and associated investments. In part, India's outreach to Mexico under PM Modi derives from the government's move to diversify the country's energy sources.[103]

The Argentinian Government views its relationship with India as 'strategic' in nature. For India, Argentinian support in the WTO negotiations on agriculture has been crucial and both states have come to similar understandings on issues concerning public stockholding, food procurement, and distribution. The 2019 visit of Argentine President, Mauricio Macri to India saw both sides exploring ways to step up cooperation in areas such as defence, nuclear energy, and space. In a step forward, the MoU on defence cooperation between Argentina and India could be significant in view of the former's evolving military cooperation with China. Similar synergy was evident in other strategic areas including civil nuclear energy and space.[104]

The GS angle to India's relationships with Latin American states has been unmistakable. Indian President Ram Nath Kovind, in conclusion of his 2018 Cuba visit, delivered a speech on 'India and the Global South' at the University of Havana. Such deliberations underscore the legacy of India's leadership of the NAM, implying that it continues to influence its engagement with Latin America. Furthering the spirit of GS solidarity in the region, India has now agreed to provide Guyana with a line of credit amounting to US$ 4 million for development of irrigation facilities and of US$ 19 million for the setting up of a super specialty hospital in Guyana. Chile is India's sixth largest trading partner in the region and its advantageous geographical position incentivizes New Delhi to explore broader economic cooperation with the country. India and Peru, meanwhile, are deliberating on a comprehensive free trade agreement for which three rounds of discussions have taken place so far. India is also focusing on developing relations with multiple Latin American nations in the sphere of energy. It is looking at Guatemala to join its International Solar Alliance initiative in which several Latin American countries including Brazil, Costa Rica, Suriname, and Venezuela are members. Likewise, in Peru, the Indian Vice-President has emphasized cooperation in renewable energy. Peru is a founding member of the International Solar Alliance. Panama, on the other hand, has recognized India's growing capabilities in specific areas and seeks to gain from agencies such as the Indian Space Research Organization.[105]

However, one of India's most salient bilateral relationships in Latin America is with Brazil. Both are rising powers looking forward to assume leadership roles in their respective regions; both aspire for high level of economic growth while struggling to bring a huge swathe of their populations out of poverty, both are committed to multilateralism in formulating strategies to confront global challenges evident in their membership of forums such as BRICS, IBSA, and G-20 and, lastly, both wish to have a bigger voice on issues of global governance including permanent membership in the UNSC.[106] With PM Modi's visit to Brazil in 2014, both have intensified their commitment to multilateralism by the final agreement on the BRICS Bank. Bilateralism also flourished with three important agreements: on cooperation in the field of environment, implementing arrangement for cooperation in space for establishing a Brazilian earth station for receiving and processing data from the IRS satellites, and establishment of a consultation mechanism on mobility and consular issues. Brazil was also instrumental in guiding India in the negations for the India-MERCOSUR Preferential Trade Agreement (PTA) under which reciprocal tariff preferences are offered between the signatory countries.[107] Cooperation in key areas like energy has grown slowly in recent times, with bilateral trade standing at US$ 8.2 billion in 2018-19 which is expected to increase to US$ 15 billion by 2022.[108]

These bilateral relationships and dialogues notwithstanding, India is equally keen to the engage the region multilaterally. In 2012, India initiated its maiden dialogue with the Community of Latin American and Caribbean Countries (CELAC), as a corollary move to institutionalize cooperation agreements with regional organizations such as MERCOSUR and the Andean states—the latter comprising Bolivia, Colombia, Ecuador, and Peru. The India-CELAC initiative is being imagined along the lines of the India-Africa Forum Summits and its support has been crucial in India's attempted entry into the Nuclear Suppliers Group.[109] Multilateralism through the IBSA and BRICS has yielded mixed results for India. The lack of ambition during the Lula presidency (2003-10) in Brazil led to the neglect, and near demise, of the IBSA. Nascent cooperation in strategic sectors and industries calls for more attention. India is involved with Brazil bilaterally through purchase of aircraft, civilian and military; in maritime exercises through the IBSA; and on situations of international conflict in BRICS.[110]

The BRICS initiative is now seemingly under attack from China. Although the BRICS Bank was transformed into the New Development Bank (NDB) as the GS alternative to Bretton Woods institutions, China financed the Asian Infrastructure Investment Bank (AIIB) to facilitate projects in the Asia Pacific, particularly along its OBOR project.[111] The BRICS countries will have to promote and integrate financing amongst them to enhance trust, aiming at a broader type of cooperation. Intra-

BRICS cooperation is likely to continue—especially in the wake of South-South trade exceeding North-South trade in the present decade—even after the possible cessation of the North-South contention. Low-income countries have increasingly received South-South foreign aid via BRICS, which shows that the NDB and similar institutions are the result of decades-long process of greater economic engagement by and among developing states.

Conclusion

As adduced by the length of this chapter, the Global South phenomenon has come a long way, from the days of the NAM and G-77 to the period where GS countries themselves have gradually acquiesced to be integrated within the dynamics of global capitalism. India has played a crucial role in formulating the *tiers monde* identity of developing countries through the advocacy of non-alignment. It led from the front during the Third World's demands for the NIEO, being impelled by its own 'economic autarky' and the humiliation faced in the Bretton Woods twin. When liberalization kicked in, India transformed the GS narrative—while still being its most vocal proponent—by negotiating reforms in the GATT/WTO.

Nonetheless, India still has a long way to traverse before being unanimously recognized as a major power in the world and for that Indian foreign policy has adopted a variety of tactics in recent times. Plurilateral initiatives are likely to assume center-stage insofar as India's dealings with the rest of the GS is concerned. Furthermore, as the GS has encountered increasing fragmentation along economic and political lines, the best route for India to maintain cordial bilateral ties with the majority of these countries—while at the same time accruing economic benefits from such relations—is through the mechanism of 'strategic partnerships'. Strategic partnerships are commonly associated with defense or security related issues, but a survey of formal strategic partnerships around the world reveals that they can also cover a wide range in bilateral relations. Such strategic partnerships assert the fact that India is finally out of its non-aligned mould and is contemplating a move beyond 'strategic autonomy': the acceptance, even reluctantly, of its 'strategic influence'.

India has been a strong advocate of multilateralism, which has allowed it to balance its limited material power. But, the debacles surrounding its bid for the permanent membership of the UNSC—propelled by lack of support from its GS partners—must now drive India to shed its 'defensive multilateralism' and adopt a more pro-active stance in global governance, by balancing—if not discounting—its GS identity and role with its enduring global power ambitions. Non-alignment and non-intervention notwithstanding, India must realize that greater clout in global governance would inevitably strengthen its leadership position vis-à-vis the GS, and this would entail often going it alone, given the increasingly fragmented and strategic nature of the Global South narrative and the relationships among GS countries today.

Endnotes

1. Shantanu Chakrabarti (2016), "Global South rhetoric in India's policy projection," *Third World Quarterly*, 38(8), pp. 1909-10; DOI: 10.1080/01436597.2016.1248931. on line source. Accessed on May 15, 2020.
2. Aneek Chatterjee (2012), "Theorizing the Global South in IR: Problems and Prospects," *FGSIS Conference*, France; on line source: https://www.academia.edu/2778363/Theorizing_the_Global_South_in_IR_Problems_and_Prospects. Accessed on May 15, 2020.
3. Samantha Christiansen and Zachary A. Scarlett (2013), "Introduction," in S. Christiansen and Z.A. Scarlett (eds.), *The Third World in the Global 1960s*, New York, Berghahn Books, p. 4.
4. Anne Garland Mahler (2017), "Global South," in Eugene O'Brien (ed.), *Oxford Bibliographies in Literary and Critical Theory*, New York, Oxford University Press.
5. The OECD member countries account for 63 percent of world GDP, three-quarters of world trade, 95 percent of world official development assistance, over half of the world's energy consumption, and 18 percent of the world's population. See, U.S. Mission to the OECD, Government of the United States of America, "What is the OECD?"; on line source: https://usoecd.usmission.gov/our-relationship/about-the-oecd/what-is-the-oecd/. Accessed on May 10, 2020.
6. Anne Garland Mahler (2018), *From the Tricontinental to the Global South: Race, Radicalism, and Transnational Solidarity*, Durham, Duke University Press, p. 32.

7. Anne Garland Mahler (2017), *op. cit.*
8. *Ibid.*
9. Aneek Chatterjee (2012), "Theorizing the Global South in IR: Problems and Prospects," *op. cit.*, pp. 2, 6-7.
10. Marcin Wojciech Solarz (2012), "'Third World': The 60th anniversary of a concept that changed history," *Third World Quarterly*, 33(9), 1561-73; DOI: 10.1080/01436597.2012.720828. on line source: Accessed on May 10, 2020.
11. Varun Sahni (1991), "Latin America and Other Regions," in M. Deas (ed.), *Latin America in Perspective*, Boston, Houghton Mifflin, pp. 293-97.
12. Herbert S. Yee (1983), "The Three World Theory and Post-Mao China's Global Strategy," *International Affairs*, 59(2), Spring, pp. 239-49; on line source: https://www.jstor.org/stable/2619937. Accessed on May 20, 2020.
13. Vineet Thakur (2018), "An Asian Drama: The Asian Relations Conference, 1947," *The International History Review,* pp. 1-23; DOI:10.1080/07075332.2018.1434809. on line source. Accessed on May 10, 2020.
14. Jawaharlal Nehru (1984), in S. Gopal (ed.), *Selected Works of Jawaharlal Nehru, Second Series*, 1, p. 539, New Delhi, Jawaharlal Nehru Memorial Fund.
15. *Ibid.*, 13, p. 371.
16. The *Panchsheel* were the five guiding-principles for Sino-Indian relations, later used as the basis of NAM: respect for sovereignty/ territorial integrity; non-aggression; non-interference; equality; peaceful co-existence. See, Aneek Chatterjee (2010), *International Relations Today: Concepts and Applications*, *First Edition*, New Delhi, Pearson, p. 118.
17. Andrew Kennedy (2015), "Nehru's Foreign Policy: Realism and Idealism Conjoined," in David M. Malone, C. Raja Mohan, and Srinath Raghavan (eds.), *The Oxford Handbook of Indian Foreign Policy*, New Delhi, Oxford University Press, pp. 96-97.
18. Shantanu Chakrabarti (2016), "Global South rhetoric in India's policy projection", *op. cit.*, p. 1915.
19. Sanjaya Baru (2015), "The Economic Imperatives Shaping Indian Foreign Policy," in David M. Malone, C. Raja Mohan, and Srinath Raghavan (eds.), *The Oxford Handbook of Indian Foreign Policy*, New Delhi, Oxford University Press, pp. 330-31.
20. Mark T. Berger (2004), "After the Third World? History, Destiny and the Fate of Third Worldism," *Third World Quarterly*, 25(1),

pp. 9-39; on line source: https://www.jstor.org/stable/3993775. Accessed on May 15, 2020.

21. Peter Dicken (2011), *Global Shift: Mapping the Contours of the World Economy*, New York, Guilford Press, p. 476.
22. Marlea Clarke (2018), “Global South: What does it mean and why use the term?”, *Global South Political Commentaries*, University of Victoria, Canada: 8 August; on line source: https://onlineacademiccommunity.uvic.ca/globalsouthpolitics/2018/08/08/global-south-what-does-it-mean-and-why-use-the-term/. Accessed on May 20, 2020.
23. Sunil Khilnani, Rajiv Kumar, et al. (2012), “Nonalignment 2.0: A Foreign and Strategic Policy for India in the Twenty First Century,” Working Paper, 29 February, New Delhi: Centre for Policy Research, pp. IV, 8, 32; on line source: https://www.cprindia.org/research/reports/nonalignment-20-foreign-and-strategic-policy-india-twenty-first-century. Accessed on May 15, 2020.
24. *Ibid*., pp. 69-70.
25. Jason A. Kirk (2015), “India and the International Financial Institutions”, in David M. Malone, C. Raja Mohan, and Srinath Raghavan (eds.), *The Oxford Handbook of Indian Foreign Policy*, New Delhi, Oxford University Press, p. 609.
26. Sanjaya Baru (2015), *The Economic Imperatives Shaping Indian Foreign Policy*, p. 330.
27. Jacqueline Anne Braveboy-Wagner (2009), *Institutions of the Global South*, London, Routledge, pp. 13-14.
28. Kevin Gray and Barry K. Gills (2016), “South-South cooperation and the rise of the Global South,” *Third World Quarterly*, 37(4), p. 557-74; on line source: http://dx.doi.org/10.1080/01436597.2015.1128817. Accessed on May 10, 2020.
29. Varun Sahni (2015), “India and Latin America: Distant Acquaintance, Rhetorical Solidarity, Strategic Engagement”, in Sumit Ganguly (ed.), *Engaging the World: India’s Foreign Policy since 1947*, New Delhi, Oxford University Press, pp. 375-95.
30. Chinmaya R. Gharekhan (2007), “India and the United Nations”, in Atish Sinha and Madhup Mohta (eds.), *Indian Foreign Policy: Challenges and Opportunities*, New Delhi, Academic Foundation, pp. 193-215.
31. Arundhati Ghose (2015), “India’s Multilateral Diplomacy: The Challenges of Global Governance,” *Public Diplomacy*, in The Ministry of External Affairs (MEA), Government of India, New Delhi: 19 December; on line source: https://mea.gov.in/distinguished-lectures-detail.htm?369. Accessed on June 10, 2020.

32. Surjit Mansingh (2015), "Indira Gandhi's Foreign Policy: Hard Realism?", in David M. Malone, C. Raja Mohan, and Srinath Raghavan (eds.), *The Oxford Handbook of Indian Foreign Policy*, New Delhi, Oxford University Press, p. 112.
33. Kunwar Rajendra Singh (1998), "The Persian Gulf Region", in L. Mansingh (ed.), *Indian Foreign Policy: Agenda for the 21st Century*, 2, New Delhi, Foreign Service Institute/Konark, pp. 102-15.
34. Arundhati Ghose (2015), "India's Multilateral Diplomacy: The Challenges of Global Governance", *op. cit.*
35. Surjit Mansingh (2015), "Indira Gandhi's Foreign Policy: Hard Realism?", *op. cit.*, p. 113.
36. Nils Gilman (2015), "The New International Economic Order: A Reintroduction", *Humanity Journal*, 6(1), 19 March; on line source: http://humanityjournal.org/issue6-1/the-new-international-economic-order-a-reintroduction/. Accessed June 10, 2020.
37. N. Jayapalan (2001), *Foreign Policy of India*, New Delhi, Atlantic Publishers and Distributors, pp. 468-69.
38. Robert W. Cox (1979), "Ideologies and the New International Economic Order: Reflections on some Recent Literature", *International Organization*, 33, pp. 257-302; on line source: https://www.jstor.org/stable/2706612. Accessed on June 10, 2020.
39. Kevin Gray and Barry K. Gills (2016), "South-South cooperation and the rise of the Global South", *op. cit.*, p. 558.
40. Robert Biel (2000), *The New Imperialism: Crisis and Contradictions in North/South Relations*, London, Zed Books, p. 124.
41. Joseph S. Nye (1973), "UNCTAD: Poor Nations' Pressure Group', in Robert W. Cox and Harold Jacobson (eds.), *The Autonomy of Influence*, New Haven, Yale University Press.
42. Arundhati Ghose (2015), "India's Multilateral Diplomacy: The Challenges of Global Governance", *op. cit.*
43. Rudra Chaudhuri (2014), *Forged in Crisis: India and the United States since 1947*, Oxford, Oxford University Press.
44. N. Jayapalan (2001), *Foreign Policy of India*, *op. cit.*, pp. 470-71.
45. Ankie Hoogvelt (2001), *Globalization and the Postcolonial World: The New Political Economy of Development*, Basingstoke, Palgrave, p. 151.
46. Kevin Gray and Barry K. Gills (2016), "South-South cooperation and the rise of the Global South," *op. cit.*, p. 558.
47. John Williamson (2005), "The Strange History of the Washington Consensus," *Journal of Post Keynesian Economics*, 27(2), Winter,

pp. 195-206; on line source: https://www.jstor.org/stable/4538920?seq=1. Accessed on June 20, 2020.

48. Barry K. Gills (2010), "Going South: Capitalist Crisis, Systemic Crisis, Civilisational Crisis", *Third World Quarterly* 31(2), pp. 169-84; on line source: https://doi.org/10.1080/01436591003711926. Accessed on June 10, 2020.
49. Nour Dados and Raewyn Connell (2012), "The Global South," *Context*, 11(1), pp. 12-13; https://doi.org/10.1177/1536504212436479. Accessed on June 15, 2020.
50. Anne Garland Mahler (2018), *From the Tricontinental to the Global South: Race, Radicalism, and Transnational Solidarity.*
51. Aneek Chatterjee (2012), "Theorizing the Global South in IR: Problems and Prospects", *op. cit.*, pp. 12-14.
52. *Ibid.*, p. 14.
53. United Nations Development Programme (2004), "Forging a Global South," New York: 19 December; on line source: http://www.undp.org/content/dam/china/docs/Publications/UNDP-CH-PR-Publications-UNDay-for-South-South-Cooperation.pdf. Accessed on June 20, 2020.
54. United Nations Development Programme (2013), *The Rise of the South: Human Progress in a Diverse World*, Human Development Report, New York, pp. 21-38; on line source: http://hdr.undp.org/en/content/human-development-report-2013. Accessed on June 10, 2020.
55. United Nations Development Programme (2013), *The Rise of the South: Human Progress in a Diverse World, op. cit.*, pp. 4-7.
56. United Nations Development Programme (2019), *Beyond Income, Beyond Averages, Beyond Today: Inequalities in Human Development in the 21st Century*, Human Development Report, New York; on line source: http://hdr.undp.org/sites/default/files/hdr2019.pdf. Accessed on June 15, 2020.
57. United Nations Conference on Trade and Development (2019), "Trade structure by partner," in *UNCTAD Handbook of Statistics*, New York; on line source: https://stats.unctad.org/handbook/MerchandiseTrade/ByPartner.html. Accessed June 20, 2020.
58. United Nations Development Programme (2019), *Beyond Income, Beyond Averages, Beyond Today: Inequalities in Human Development in the 21st Century*, p. 307.
59. Shantanu Chakrabarti (2016), "Global South rhetoric in India's policy projection", *op. cit.*, p. 1916.
60. Rajiv Kumar (2010), "Maintaining Strategic Autonomy in an Interdependent World", *Strategic Analysis*, 34(4), pp. 525-26.

61. C. Raja Mohan (2015), "Foreign Policy after 1990," in David M. Malone, C. Raja Mohan, and Srinath Raghavan (eds.), *The Oxford Handbook of Indian Foreign Policy*, New Delhi, Oxford University Press, p. 142.
62. *Ibid.*
63. Kevin Gray and Barry K. Gills (2016), "South-South cooperation and the rise of the Global South", *op. cit.*, p. 564.
64. Robert H. Wade (2003), "What Strategies are Viable for Developing Countries Today? The World Trade Organization and the Shrinking of 'Development Space'," *Review of International Political Economy*, 10(4), Tenth Anniversary Issue, pp. 621-44; online source: https://www.jstor.org/stable/4177479. Accessed on June 30, 2020.
65. Rajendra M. Abhyankar (2018), *Indian Diplomacy: Beyond Strategic Autonomy*, New Delhi, Oxford University Press, p. 233.
66. Douglas A. Irwin, et al. (2008), *The Genesis of the GATT*, Cambridge, Cambridge University Press.
67. World Trade Organization (2016), "Members and Observers," Geneva: 29 July; on line source: https://www.wto.org/english/thewto_e/whatis_e/tif_e/org6_e.htm. Accessed on August 11, 2020.
68. World Trade Organization, "The Uruguay Round," Geneva; on line source: https://www.wto.org/english/thewto_e/whatis_e/tif_e/fact5_e.htm. Accessed on August 10, 2020.
69. Kamal Saggi (2010), "India at the WTO: From Uruguay to Doha and Beyond", Working Paper No. 425, August, Stanford: Stanford University, p. 4; on line source: https://kingcenter.stanford.edu/publications/india-wto-uruguay-doha-and-beyond. Accessed on August 10, 2020.
70. International Centre for Trade and Sustainable Development (2001), "Like Minded Group Sets Out Positions Before Doha," Geneva: 10 July; on line source: https://ictsd.iisd.org/bridges-news/bridges/news/like-minded-group-sets-out-positions-before-doha. Accessed on August 10, 2020.
71. Rajendra M. Abhyankar (2018), *Indian Diplomacy: Beyond Strategic Autonomy*, *op. cit.*, p. 218.
72. Sungjoon Cho (2005), "Half Full or Half Empty?: The Hong Kong WTO Ministerial Conference has Delivered an Interim Deal for the Doha Round Negotiation", *American Society of International Law*, 9(39), December 29; on line source: https://www.asil.org/insights/volume/9/issue/39/half-full-or-half-empty-hong-kong-wto-ministerial-conference-has. Accessed on August 5, 2020.
73. World Trade Organization (2011), "Address by Shri Anand Sharma Minister of Commerce, Industry and Textiles at the Eight

Ministerial Conference of the WTO", Geneva: 15 December; on line source: https://www.wto.org/english/thewto_e/minist_e/min11_e/min11_statements_e.htm. Accessed on August 15, 2020.

74. Rajendra M. Abhyankar (2018), *Indian Diplomacy: Beyond Strategic Autonomy*, *op. cit.*, p. 220.
75. Pranab Dhal Samanta, "PM Modi's Independence Day message: Make in India for the world", *The Economic Times*, 17 August 2020.
76. Samir Saran (2015), "India's Contemporary Plurilateralism," in David M. Malone, C. Raja Mohan, and Srinath Raghavan (eds.), *The Oxford Handbook of Indian Foreign Policy*, New Delhi, Oxford University Press, p. 623.
77. Kevin Gray and Barry K. Gills (2016), "South-South cooperation and the rise of the Global South", *op. cit.*, pp. 560-64.
78. Originally conceived for Brazil-India relations; see, Vinícius Rodrigues Vieira (2015), "The 'Eastern Brother': Brazil's View of India as a Diplomatic Partner in World Trade," in Kate Sullivan (ed.), *Competing Visions of India in World Politics*, UK, Palgrave Macmillan, pp. 111-27. But these reasons have a much wider ramification, as per the present author.
79. Christopher J. Lee (2015), "From Imperial Subjects to Global South Partners: South Africa, India and the Politics of Multilateralism", in Kate Sullivan (ed.), *Competing Visions of India in World Politics*, UK, Palgrave Macmillan, pp. 79-93.
80. Rajendra M. Abhyankar (2018), *Indian Diplomacy: Beyond Strategic Autonomy*, *op. cit.*, p. 283.
81. Constantino Xavier (2015), "Unbreakable Bond: Africa in India's Foreign Policy", in David M. Malone, C. Raja Mohan, and Srinath Raghavan (eds.), *The Oxford Handbook of Indian Foreign Policy*, New Delhi, Oxford University Press, pp. 569-72.
82. Harsh Shringla, "Why the India-Africa bond matters", *Hindustan Times*, 13 February 2020.
83. Ruchita Beri (2020), "India-Africa Trade", *Diplomatist*, 4 January; on line source: https://diplomatist.com/2020/01/04/india-africa-trade/. Accessed on August 10, 2020.
84. Ministry of External Affairs (MEA), Government of India, "Indian Technical and Economic Cooperation Programme", New Delhi: 21 August 2020; on line source: https://www.itecgoi.in/index.php. Accessed on August 21, 2020.
85. Rajendra M. Abhyankar (2018), *Indian Diplomacy: Beyond Strategic Autonomy*, *op. cit.*, p. 284.

86. Ruchita Beri (2020), "India-Africa Trade", *op. cit.*
87. Rajendra M. Abhyankar (2018), *Indian Diplomacy: Beyond Strategic Autonomy*, *op. cit.*, p. 285.
88. Ruchita Beri (2020), "India-Africa Trade", *op. cit.*
89. Constantino Xavier (2015), "Unbreakable Bond: Africa in India's Foreign Policy," *op. cit.*, pp. 573-74.
90. Harsh Shringla, "Why the India-Africa bond matters", *op. cit.*
91. *Ibid.*
92. Ministry of External Affairs (MEA), Government of India (2016), "India-South Africa Joint Statement during the visit of Prime Minister to South Africa," Pretoria: 8 July; on line source: https://www.mea.gov.in/bilateral-documents.htm?dtl/27001/IndiaSouth_Africa_Joint_Statement_during_the_visit_of_Prime_Minister_to_South_Africa_July_08_2016. Accessed on August 20, 2020.
93. Ministry of External Affairs (MEA), Government of India (2019), "India-South Africa Joint Statement during State Visit of President of South Africa," New Delhi: 25 January; on line source: https://www.mea.gov.in/bilateral-documents.htm?dtl/30952/IndiaSouth_Africa_Joint_Statement_during_State_Visit_of_President_of_South_Africa. Accessed on August 20, 2020.
94. David Harris and Simona Vittorini (2015), "What Does 'Development Cooperation' Mean? Perceptions from India and Africa," in Kate Sullivan (ed.), *Competing Visions of India in World Politics*, UK, Palgrave Macmillan, pp. 94-110.
95. Abhishek Mishra (2019), "India-South Africa relations: A perennial bond," *Observer Research Foundation*, 25 January; on line source: https://www.orfonline.org/expert-speak/india-south-africa-relations-a-perennial-bond-47557/. Accessed on August 21, 2020.
96. Abhishek Mishra (2019), "India-South Africa relations: A perennial bond", *op. cit.*
97. High Commission of India, South Africa, Ministry of External Affairs (2020), "India South Africa Relations," Pretoria: 5 February; on line source: https://www.hcipretoria.gov.in. Accessed on August 10, 2020.
98. "Gunboat and Debt Diplomacy: Harsh Choices for Africa," *The African Executive*, 25 April 2019; on line source: https://africanexecutive.com/article/read/10123. Accessed on August 20, 2020.
99. Rajendra M. Abhyankar (2018), *Indian Diplomacy: Beyond Strategic Autonomy*, *op. cit.*, p. 286.
100. Varun Sahni (1991), "Latin America and Other Regions", *op. cit.*

101. Harsh V. Pant (2016), *Indian Foreign Policy: An Overview*, Manchester, Manchester University Press, p. 192.
102. Ketan Mehta (2019), "India in pivotal geographies: Latin America," *Observer Research Foundation*, 19 August; on line source: https://www.orfonline.org/expert-speak/india-in-pivotal-geographies-latin-america-54551/?amp. Accessed on July 19, 2020.
103. Ketan Mehta (2019), "India in pivotal geographies: Latin America", *op. cit.*
104. Ministry of External Affairs (MEA), Government of India (2019), "State visit of President of Argentina to India," New Delhi: 14 February; on line source: https://www.mea.gov.in/press-releases.htm?dtl/31051/State+visit+of+President+of+Argentina+to+India+February+1719+2019. Accessed on August 10, 2020.
105. Ketan Mehta (2019), "India in pivotal geographies: Latin America", *op. cit.*
106. Harsh V. Pant (2016), *Indian Foreign Policy: An Overview*, *op. cit.*, 192.
107. MERCOSUR comprises Argentina, Brazil, Paraguay, Uruguay, and Venezuela. See, Ministry of Commerce and Industry, Government of India (2003), "MERCOSUR Preferential Trade Agreement (PTA) Negotiations," Paraguay: 17 June; on line source: https://commerce.gov.in/international_nextDetail_WTO.aspx?LinkID=32&idwto=33. Accessed on August 10, 2020.
108. *Business Today* (2020), "Republic Day 2020: India Brazil to have a bilateral trade of $15 billion by 2022", 26 January; on line source: https://www.businesstoday.in/current/economy-politics/republic-day-2020-india-brazil-to-have-a-bilateral-trade-of-15-billion-by-2022/story/394639.html. Accessed on August 20, 2020.
109. *The Economic Times* (2018), "Latin America and Caribbean region critical for our ambition to get NSG entry: India," 12 July; on line source: https://economictimes.indiatimes.com/news/defence/latin-america-and-caribbean-region-critical-for-our-ambition-to-get-nsg-entry-india/articleshow/55688389.cms?from=mdr. Accessed on August 22, 2020.
110. Deepak Bhojwani (2018), "India and Latin America: The Way Forward," *Public Diplomacy*, in The Ministry of External Affairs (MEA), Government of India, New Delhi: 12 April; on line source: https://www.mea.gov.in/distinguished-lectures-detail.htm?747. Accessed on June 10, 2020.
111. Rajendra M. Abhyankar (2018), *Indian Diplomacy: Beyond Strategic Autonomy*, *op. cit.*, p. 264.

6

India and Leading Powers of the World: USA, China

Jayita Mukhopadhyay

A thorough and in-depth analysis of India's international relations calls for a probe of its changing equations with some leading powers of the world. Gradual evolution of India and its emergence as a major power in the arena of world politics can only be understood in the background of such a study and this chapter is dedicated to that objective. The dynamics of India's relationship with leading powers, namely, USA (United States of America) and China are analysed in the following pages.

INDIA AND USA

Relationship between India, the largest and most populous functional democracy of the world, and USA, widely perceived to be the strongest democracy of the world presents a fascinating area of study and analysis as the relationship has oscillated between moments of intense suspicion and mistrust during the Cold War era and periods of close friendship and collaboration after the Cold War.

Relationship in the Cold War Period: An Overview

Historical links between America and India could be traced back to the year 1492, when explorer Christopher Columbus discovered America in the course of his search for a new route to India. During the last quarter of the eighteenth century, several American ships visited Indian ports in connection with trade. Legal authority to Indo-US trade was given by Jay's Treaty of

1794 between England and America. Benjamin Joy of Boston was appointed the first American Consul at Calcutta in 1792. Thereafter, trade, cultural, and religious missionary activities brought the two lands close. When India became independent on 15 August 1947, American President Henry S. Truman sent a message to Lord Mountbatten, Governor General of India, extending his good wishes on the occasion, signalling the beginning of a new era in the relationship between the two countries. Indian Prime Minister Nehru in an address to an American audience remarked: "May I also say that all of us in India know very well, although it might not be so known in public, what great interest President Roosevelt had in our country's freedom and how he exercised his great influence to that end",[1] thus indicating the possibility of future bonhomie between the two countries.

Despite differences in cultural traits, habits, values, race and other factors, two countries were expected to share a bonding on the basis of common factors like long history of fight against foreign domination, yearning for freedom and penchant for liberal democratic principles and democratic governance. However, matters took a different course in the post-Second World War period, when the Cold War started. US policy of containment of Communism and concomitant drive to create its zone of influence, its move towards unprincipled alliance with non-democratic regimes like Pakistan (which often came under military dictatorship), just to contain Soviet Union and thereby protect and further its own national interests led to divergence of foreign policy objectives and courses with India. India's policy of non-alignment and quest for autonomy of decision making was viewed with suspicion by the US administration. John Foster Dulles, US Secretary of State under President Dwight D. Eisenhower, characterized the non-aligned ideal as 'immoral and opportunistic', a view widely shared by successive US governments in Cold War era (1945-91). The US viewed India with suspicion that it was a Soviet partner trying to thwart American interest, particularly in Asia. India, on the other hand, was aggrieved that Washington sided with Pakistan on the Kashmir issue from the very beginning and supplied it arms which were used against India in the 1965 and 1971 wars between India and Pakistan.[2]

Thus, the major points of divergence during the Cold War period were as follows:

(i) India's non-participation in US policy of containing Communism and refusal to become a member of security blocs like NATO (North Atlantic Treaty Organization formed in 1949), SEATO (Southeast Asia Treaty Organization formed in 1954), CENTO (Central Treaty Organization formed in 1955, in 1955) all directed towards limiting Soviet influence.

(ii) America's constant material and financial support to Pakistan as an important frontline US ally in South Asia, and the vexed Pakistan factor which further alienated India from the US.

(iii) Different stands taken by India on various international issues like recognition of the Communist regime of China, the Korean Crisis, the America-Vietnam war, Afghan Crisis, the Palestine question and the creation of Israel, and India's refusal to sign the NPT (Nuclear Non-Proliferation Treaty), alleging it to be unfair, unequal, and discriminatory.

There were differences on many other issues like India's preference for a socialistic model of economic development vis-à-vis America's market-driven economy. However, relationship between the two countries during the Cold War era was never uniformly antagonistic and oscillated between periods of warmth at certain points and apathy, if not antipathy on some other moments. There were occasions when the two countries were on the same page. To illustrate, both India and the United States were on the same side on the Suez Canal issue in 1956. Again in 1959, when President Eisenhower visited India, he was given a tumultuous welcome and the President on his part observed: "The strength of India is our interest." What is even more significant, in October 1962, when China attacked India, America along with Britain came to support India. The Kennedy period was also witness to much bonhomie between the two countries. His successor, President Johnson also kept the cordiality intact by establishing the Tarapur Atomic Plant and by supplying a large quantity of food grains to enable India to fight over the acute shortage caused by the severe drought in 1966-67 (Under US Government's Food for Peace Programme popularly known as PL-480). Again in 1973, as a friendly gesture, the United States wrote off the largest amount of foreign debt ever cancelled in history by liquidating two-thirds of its accumulated rupee holdings (US$ 2 billion) in India acquired in return for wheat shipments under PL-480. It was a case of rare magnanimity on the part of Washington. The tenure of India's Prime Minister Morarji Desai who exhibited pro-US attitude brought some amiability in the relationship between US and India.

The American President Jimmy Carter's official visit to India in 1978, many years after President Eisenhower's visit to India in 1959 marked a significant development in bilateral relations. Carter's visit was followed by a return visit to the US by the Indian Prime Minister, Morarji Desai and brought the two countries closer. However, this affability did not last long when the Congress Party Government led by Indira Gandhi refused to rally on the side of the United States in its anti-Soviet crusade over Afghanistan and advocated the withdrawal of Soviet troops from Afghanistan. The Congress Government was also very vociferous against US naval base in Diego Garcia, an island in the Indian Ocean, as India felt that the base might turn the Ocean into a hotspot of super power rivalry. However, since the early 1980s, even the Congress Government changed its stance, recognizing the rising power of US and the benefits which would accrue to India from close ties with it. India started pursuing a well-planned policy of improving and strengthening relations with the US. The visit of Indira Gandhi to America in 1982 was termed by the American media as 'operation defrost' between the two countries. The feel-good atmosphere continued after Rajiv Gandhi became Indian Prime Minister in 1985. His visit to America in June 1985 was a successful event. Rajiv bonded well with President Ronald Regan and the signing of the Memorandum of Understanding (MOU) on technology transfer was a welcome development. The improvement in the US-Soviet superpower relationship since 1986 removed the Cold War constraints on the upgrading of Indo-US relations, and predictably, the process got accelerated in post-Cold War era.[3]

Relationship after the Cold War: Paradigm Shift

The disintegration of the erstwhile USSR (United Soviet Socialist Republic), the first socialist country of the world, the collapse of socialist bloc in East Europe and the eventual ending of the Cold War in 1991, ushered in some paradigmatic shifts in international political and socio-economic scenario. The disintegration of USSR also opened the door to India-US rapprochement and the eventual formation of the strategic partnership between the two. Also, the end of the Cold War created an atmosphere where the two nations could forge stronger ties. A few factors brought about the convergence of interests and aspirations, objectives, and goals between the two countries. These were:

1. In the altered international political and strategic environment, India could no longer afford to be not on good terms with the world's lone superpower, the USA. It could no longer depend on Russia, the successor state of USSR for supply of arms or monetary support as Russia was undergoing political and economic transformation. Strategic and geopolitical considerations in Asia also underwent noticeable changes. Growing military might, territorial ambitions and assertiveness of China was causing discomfort to the US establishment. In 1989, the People's Liberation Army's decision to crush pro-democracy protestors in Tiananmen Square signalled an end to any quasi-alliance between US and China. Thereafter, gradually the US began to see a rising China as a potential strategic competitor. This led US to forge new partnership with another emerging power, India.
2. Perception about India among the political elites of America also underwent considerable changes. Steady functioning of democratic governance in India, its

commitment to liberal values, its non-aggressive, pro-peace foreign policy slowly made India acceptable to the American political elite. Also, India's acceptance as a 'responsible nuclear power' by the international community, brought about a change of view among US policy makers who found a new ally in stable, peaceful, economically rising India. In 1990, the US imposed sanctions on Pakistan based on the 1985 Pressler Amendment, cutting off aid because of its nuclear weapons program. Throughout 1990s, although US often treated India and Pakistan at par (much to the dislike of Indians), it was becoming evident that a stable democratic Indian polity had the potential to best serve the US post-Cold War interests in South Asia.

3. In the year 1991, liberalisation of India's economic policies, initiated by Prime Minister P.V. Narasimha Rao and steered by the then Finance Minister Manmohan Singh with the objective of making the economy more market- and service-oriented, and expanding the role of private and foreign investment drew the US closer to India. The Liberalisation-Privatisation-Globalisation agenda of India improved its status as an investment destination and since India had a rapidly growing middle class with an enhanced purchasing power, the US was keen to get access to the burgeoning Indian market.
4. The Indian diaspora in the US played a remarkable role in changing the perception of India in the US. The Indian Americans, one of the wealthiest and educated ethnic groups in the US, was also instrumental in gently pushing US towards India.[4]

There were considerable excitements both in the US and Indian administration about the new found bonhomie in the relationship between the two countries and many of them started describing India and US as 'natural allies'. The volume of bilateral trade rose from US$ 5070 million in 1991 to US$

14353 million in 2000, the size of American investment in India also underwent steady increase since 1991 and these were indicative of deepening economic interaction between the two countries which benefited both of them.[5] However, scholars like Stephen Cohen warned against such high expectations about the growing relationship, and pointed out that there would be differences in their foreign policy objectives and interests and complexities would have to be managed through patient and sustained dialogues, mutual adjustments and accommodations.[6]

Relationship during the Premiership of Narasimha Rao (1991-96)

Contrary to expectations, the regime of P.V. Narasimha Rao, the first post-Cold War Prime Minister of India, did not see much progress in bilateral relations. The following were some major areas friction which created obstacles for betterment of ties:

- India's refusal to sign the NPT (Nuclear Non-Proliferation Treaty), and its active perusal of missile technology programme collided with Clinton Administration's efforts to effectively instal an international non-proliferation regime through the passage and acceptance of the CTBT (Comprehensive Test Ban Treaty), the FMCT (the Fissile Material Cut-Off Treaty) and MTCR (the Missile Technology Control Regime). In 1992, India successfully tested the Augmented Satellite Launch Vehicle (ASLV) and the Polar Satellite Launch Vehicle (PSLV); test fired intermediate range missiles Agni and Prithvi in 1994; and announced the launch of Trishul, a surface-to-air missile and Akash, an anti-tank ballistic missile. The US viewed India's opposition to CTBT as an impediment to its non-proliferation agenda and its missile programme as a destabilising factor in the military balance of South Asia.
- The issue of alleged human rights violations by India, particularly in Kashmir, was raked up by Clinton Administration quite frequently to embarrass India.

> A variety of utterances on the part of Bill Clinton and his officials, particularly Robin Raphel, then the newly appointed Assistant Secretary of State for South Asian Affairs bore testimony to this. Raphel questioned the very accession of Jammu & Kashmir (J&K) with the Indian Union. To add fire to the fuel, Clinton also promised India baiters, like Ghulam Nabi Fai, self-styled protagonist of human rights in J&K, to work with him "and others to bring peace in Kashmir." Analysts have observed that such hue and cry on the issue of human rights was intended to create a sense of insecurity in the minds of Indian policy makers over the question of national security.[7]

However, economic relations between the two countries began to improve in the wake of the initiation of economic reforms in India. There was considerable hike in US investments in India during Rao's time. But compared to America's trade with China in 1996, India-US trade remained quite insignificant. The Clinton Administration gave a Most Favoured Nation status in trade to China in 1993 which was denied to India because of differences over non-proliferation and human rights issues.

It is to be noted that despite the lack of an overall policy framework, security cooperation also increased during this period, though at a very moderate pace. During the Gulf War, the Indian Government granted refuelling rights to US military aircraft en route from the Pacific to the Middle East. In 1996 and 1997, the Indian and US navies held joint exercises (the Malabar series) in the Indian Ocean.[8] A Defence Policy Group was established in the mid-1990s. Its activities included high-level exchanges, periodic policy reviews and reciprocal visits by senior commanders.[9]

By mid-March 1994, Indo-US relations went very low. Against this background, Narasimha Rao visited Washington, DC, in May 1994. The outcome of the visit was surprisingly positive. As a result of negotiations between the two, all open criticisms of India's human rights records were withdrawn. Similarly, the pressures created by the US on other security-related issues were also relaxed. As an economic concession to the US, India opened up its telecommunications field for the American business. As a quid pro quo, the US promised flow of funds into Indian industries, particularly in the fields of power and infrastructure development. Thus, Rao's visit considerably boosted bilateral trade. The US soon emerged as the largest investor in India mainly in power, infrastructure, and telecom industries.

However, the US conceded no substantial gains to India in the security arena. The US continued its policy of treating India and Pakistan as equals, particularly when it came to their nuclear weapons programs and the issue of Kashmir. The US urged India to consider holding a plebiscite in Kashmir to determine its future and did not discriminate between the nuclear behaviour of India and Pakistan in cajoling both countries to join the NPT and the CTBT as non-nuclear weapons states. Despite the protests and expression of displeasure by India, the US Government gave to Pakistan military spares and hardware worth $368 million.[10]

Relationship during the Period of two United Front Governments (1996-97)

In keeping with established trends, during the tenure of first United Front Government led by Prime Minister H.D. Deve Gowda, economic relations between India and the US continued to grow and inflow of foreign direct investment from the US also steadily increased. But irritants to the relationship, particularly the non-proliferation issue continued to stall further improvements in ties. I.K. Gujral took charge as the Prime Minister of the Second United Front Government on 21 April 1997. By the time, President Clinton has started his second term in the US. A number of positive trends in both Indian and US administration blended harmoniously to bring about noticeable improvements in the relationship between the two countries. These developments were:

- The introduction and application of 'Gujral Doctrine', helped to improve ties between India and its neighbours and was welcomed by US Administration as it was to some extent relieved by the easing of tension in South

Asia, considered a nuclear-active zone. This made the Second Clinton Administration favourably disposed towards India.

- As the US senate kept the CTBT, sponsored by Clinton Administration under prolonged consideration with strong indication that it might not approve the treaty, the issue lost its importance as an impediment to the betterment of ties between India and the US.
- Politically important reciprocal visits by Indian and US officials brought about better understanding between the two countries. There was growing agreement between the two countries regarding measures to combat terrorism. The US gradually, through a step by step diplomacy, had come to accept India's point of view that Pakistan was promoting cross-border terrorism in Punjab, the north-eastern states in general and more particularly in J&K. Thus, there was a congruence of perceptions over the menace of terrorism between the two countries. The signing of an extradition treaty between the two countries in August 1997 was another welcome development. Several important agreements and MOUs were signed between the two countries which expanded the area of common interests.
- Two-way trade and commerce kept on increasing steadily.[11]

Relationship during Atal Bihari Vajpayee's Government

In the early days of Vajpayee's Second term as Prime Minister of India, Indo-US relations suffered due to India's decision of conducting the nuclear tests in 1998 (Pokhran II) which was viewed by Clinton Administration as a direct affront to its attempt at impose global nuclear non-proliferation regime. Economic sanctions were imposed on India by the US following the tests. However, a resilient Indian economy and the pressure from American business lobby on its government to relax sanctions reduced the impact of sanctions on India. Interestingly, within a month of the tests, in June 1998, India and US engaged themselves in diplomatic dialogues that continued for two and half years. The dialogue between India's External Affairs Minister Jaswant Singh and US Deputy Secretary of State for South Asian Affairs, Strobe Talbot made significant contribution in restoring mutual trust and confidence in bilateral relations. A combination of factors brought about this transformation in bilateral relationship. These were:

- America was much dissatisfied with Pakistan's reciprocal nuclear tests immediately in the wake of India's tests which the US tried to stop desperately and which caused much embarrassment to Clinton Administration.
- Pakistan's connection with the Taliban regime in Afghanistan, and providing territorial space to Al-Qaeda outfit of Osama Bin Laden, already responsible for bomb attacks in US embassies located in Kenya and Tanzania earned for it the displeasure of Clinton Administration.
- The instability in Pakistani politics and growing interference of the army with the decisions of the political executive caused much consternation to the US.
- Pakistan's adventurism in Kargil, which could have resulted in a nuclear war between India and Pakistan was against US interest in the region and consequently, US Administration distanced itself from Pakistan and openly sided with India.
- India's long standing democratic culture, its growing economic potential and huge emerging market must have appeared to be attractive to the US Administration vis-à-vis the shattered economy and unstable polity of Pakistan.

In the backdrop of this growing amiability of relationship took place the historic visit of President Bill Clinton to India in March 2000. This visit marked the beginning of a new era in Indo-US relations and signalled a shift towards acknowledging New Delhi as a potential great power by the US Administration. The 'Vision Statement' signed by President Clinton and Prime

Minister Vajpayee, with its elaborate Addendum, was the most comprehensive document ever signed by India and the US on bilateral relations. In this document, the two countries identified special areas of mutual interest on which they pledged to work together in order to strengthen bilateral relations in the future. While the main portion of the "Vision Statement" referred to the liberalization of the Indian economy, nuclear non-proliferation, joint efforts to preserve the global environment, the role of the Americans of Indian origin in promoting bilateral cooperation; the "Addendum" chalked out different areas of mutual engagement for the future. The "Addendum" had ten sections, where the need for institutional dialogue was highlighted. While Section 1 emphasized the importance of "regular, wide ranging dialogue" between the two nations, Section 2 noted that the President of the US and the Prime Minister of India would hold regular bilateral summits in alternating capitals or elsewhere, and would also use multilateral meetings to review bilateral relations and consult on international issues. The pledge for regular bilateral summits between the two Heads of Government was unprecedented, because never before in their diplomatic relationship, had the two Heads of Government met regularly. It could be noted here that in subsequent years since President Clinton's visit to India, the Indian and American Heads of Government met regularly, either in bilateral summits, or at multilateral meetings, where the two met separately to discuss bilateral relations.[12]

There was change of administration in US while Vajpayee was still the Prime Minister of India as on January 20, 2001, George W. Bush took over as the 43rd President of the United States. Under the new Bush Administration Indo-US relations developed at a steady pace. The Republican Party, which Bush represented, was less didactic and intrusive on non-proliferation issues, compared to the Democrats and that facilitated further cementing of ties between the two countries. In his confirmation hearings before the Senate Foreign Relations Committee, the then Secretary of State designate Colin Powell stated that India had the potential to help keep the peace in the vast Indian Ocean area and its periphery. In a Presidential Determination signed shortly after assuming office, President George W. Bush waived all nuclear-related sanctions on India. The appointment of Robert Blackwill, a confidante of the President as US Ambassador to India was an indicator of the importance that the Bush Administration placed on its relations with India. However, though politico-military ties continued to grow, the trade and investment relationship, despite its enormous potential, continued to flounder if not stagnate. India, after successfully implementing its first round of economic reforms in the early 1990s failed to maintain the momentum due to bureaucratic hurdles and other constraints. India's tariffs and regulatory barriers remained high. Consequently, while India's exports to the United States steadily expanded since the mid-1990s (from US$ 5.7 billion in 1995 to US$ 10.7 billion in 2000), US trade flows to India since 1995 actually stagnated, averaging US$ 3.5 billion during the same period. US investment in India also did not exhibit very successful track record.[13]

The horrific terrorist attack of 9/11 was a point of inflection when the US foreign policy took a new turn with the introduction of its 'War on Terrorism'. In the aftermath of the attack, there was a transformation in America's geostrategic thinking as Afghanistan, the base of the Al-Qaeda, the prime accused in the 9/11 terrorist attack, became the central focus of its war against terror. While Pakistan shares a border with Afghanistan, it was one of the three countries which recognised the Taliban regime while India had never recognised it. While the US needed Pakistan's logistic support, India was perceived as a second line of defence. India was very quick and unequivocal in condemning the 9/11 attacks and in offering support to US in its fight against terrorism. The US took India's help during 'Operation Enduring Freedom' in Afghanistan. The Indian navy escorted and protected high-value American shipping through the Straits of Malacca. India also allowed US flights across its territory and provided refuelling facilities for American aircraft. India's response galvanised the change in military ties between the two countries and led to intensification of cooperation in defence sector and counter-terrorism areas. Understanding for the first time India's concern for terrorism, the Bush Administration banned terrorist groups like the Lashkar-e-Taiba, and condemned underworld mafia don Dawood Ibrahim who was a suspected mastermind behind terrorist attacks in Mumbai. In 2002, the Bush Administration released the National Security Strategy (NSS), a guiding document outlining the transformation of Indo-US relations, and deepening of cooperation between the two. However, despite such positive developments, US was unwilling to include India's fight against terrorism in its own war on terrorism, as it needed more the cooperation of Pakistan to fight Al-Qaeda in Afghanistan.

However, in continuation of process generated by the Vision Statement, the two countries kept working closely in areas like intelligence gathering, law enforcement, dealing with cybercrimes, and promoting mutual cooperation in science and technology, health care and environment. At a meeting of the US-India Defence Policy Group (DPG) in December 2001, the two sides committed themselves to substantially increase the pace of high-level policy dialogue, military-to-military exchanges and other joint activities. As part of the growing India-US military links, the Indian Defence Minister George Fernandes visited Washington in January 2002 and held substantial talks with Defence Secretary Donald Rumsfeld and National Security Adviser Condoleezza Rice. Issues covered included terrorism as well as sharing of military intelligence. The two sides also signed a General Security of Military Information Agreement (GSOMIA) which essentially guarantees that they would protect any classified technology shared between them. It also paved the way for the future sale of US weapons to India.[14]

India and United States reached a milestone in their strategic relationship by announcing in January 2004 the 'Next Steps in Strategic Partnership' (NSSP), designed to increase cooperation in civilian nuclear activities, civilian space programs, high-technology trade, and missile defence. Since January 2004, cooperation under the NSSP progressed through a series of reciprocal steps that built on each other. These steps included expanded engagement on nuclear regulatory and safety issues, enhanced cooperation in missile defence, peaceful uses of space technology, and steps to create the appropriate environment for increased high-technology commerce.[15] Under NSSP, the US made modifications to American export licencing policies that would encourage cooperation in commercial space programmes and permit exports to power plants at safeguarded nuclear facilities.

Relationship during Manmohan Singh's Government

Manmohan Singh took charge as India's Prime Minister in June 2004 and from the very beginning, expressed his keen desire to continue close cooperation with US in the areas of nuclear energy, economic, and security issues. A great development took place in July 2005 when Singh visited Washington, and in a joint statement with George W. Bush, India and the United States agreed to enter into a civil nuclear agreement.

This landmark decision was an implicit recognition, for the first time, of India as a nuclear weapons power. Singh's visit also coincided with the completion of the NSSP which had been announced in January 2004, and which aimed to increase cooperation in civilian nuclear activities, civilian space programmes, high-technology trade, and missile defence.

The core of this agreement was the emphasis on non-proliferation of Weapons of Mass Destruction (WMD). Even though India did not officially join the Non-Proliferation Treaty (NPT), through this agreement, it was afforded the same benefits and advantages as other leading nuclear powers, like the United States. According to the then US Under Secretary of State for Political Affairs, Nicholas Burns, as far as nuclear-related issues were concerned, India committed itself in public, very specifically to a series of actions to which it had not previously committed itself. While the joint statement and related press releases listed a wide range of responsibilities and actions, three essential ones were:

- India would move to separate civilian and military nuclear facilities. India's impetus—which was acknowledged by Bush—to continue developing its nuclear facilities has to do with its increased reliance on fossil fuels to meet is energy needs. Thus, safe, civilian nuclear energy would help in the sustainable development of India's economy.

- India would place these civilian nuclear facilities under the International Atomic Energy Agency (IAEA) safeguards.
- India would refrain from transfer of enrichment and reprocessing technologies to states that do not have them and supporting international efforts to limit their spread.

The US, for its part, would work toward full civil nuclear cooperation with India, including granting India a waiver from the Nuclear Suppliers Group (NSG), which would allow members to trade nuclear material with India, even though it was not a part of the NPT. As part of the earlier sanctions, India had been isolated from the NSG.[16]

President George Bush (Jr) visited India from 1 to 3 March 2006. On 2 March 2006, President Bush and Prime Minister Singh signed the Civil Nuclear Deal (CND) in New Delhi. As per the deal, India promised to place fourteen of its twenty-two power reactors under IAEA safeguards permanently.

India promised that all future civilian thermal and breeder reactors shall be placed under IAEA safeguards permanently. However, New Delhi clarified that the Indian Prime Minister 'retains the sole right to determine such reactors as civilian', implying that India will not be constrained in any way in building future nuclear facilities, whether civilian or military, as per its national requirements. Military facilities and stockpiles of nuclear fuel that India had produced up to then were to be exempted from inspections or safeguards.

India also made some further commitments. These were:

- India agreed to continue its moratorium on nuclear weapons testing.
- India committed to strengthening the security of its nuclear arsenals.
- India agreed to work toward negotiating a Fissile Material Cut-off Treaty (FMCT) with the United

States banning the production of fissile material for weapons purposes.

- India agreed to prevent the spread of enrichment and reprocessing technologies to states that don't possess them and to support international non-proliferation efforts.
- US companies will be allowed to build nuclear reactors in India and provide nuclear fuel for its civilian energy program.

An approval by the Nuclear Suppliers Group (NSG) lifting the ban on India had also cleared the way for other countries to make nuclear fuel and technology sales to India.[17]

Despite opposition from parties in both the countries, Congressional approval for the US-India Agreement for Cooperation Concerning Peaceful Uses of Nuclear Energy (123 Agreement) came in October 2008. Before that, on 25 September 2008, Singh visited Washington and lobbied hard in favour of the imminent completion of the deal. The Indian Prime Minister viewed that for 34 years, India had suffered from a nuclear apartheid. India had not been able to trade in nuclear material, nuclear reactors, nuclear raw materials. He thanked President Bush for proposing the Civil Nuclear Deal and hoped that it would bring the two nations further close.

In 2009, as Barack Obama entered the White House, concerns were voiced about US involvement with Pakistan and China, and how that would affect US ties with India following the Bush Administration. However, during Singh's visit to Washington in November 2009, Obama vowed to uphold the historic nuclear agreement.

In a Joint Statement issued by Singh and Obama, India and US reaffirmed the terms of the nuclear agreement, emphasised their respective moratorium on nuclear testing and the increasing need to work towards global non-proliferation. Manmohan Singh opined during the visit that US-India relations rested on 'Five Es', economy, energy, environment, education, and empowerment. The two leaders looked forward to the Nuclear Security Summit convened in Washington in April 2010, which saw a more urgent call for non-proliferation of nuclear weapons, especially in response to non-state agents acquiring WMD. Singh attended the summit and outlined India's unwavering commitment to non-proliferation and disarmament, and the use of nuclear energy for safe and clean energy. He also announced the establishment of India's Global Centre for Global Energy Partnership. President Obama's official visit to India in 2010 gave a further boost to the fledgling relationship between the two countries.

Relationship during the Modi Government

The relationship has gained accelerated momentum and vigour after Narendra Modi assumed the role of India's Prime Minister in May 2014. Under the stewardship of Modi and Obama, the bilateral relation developed into a 'global strategic partnership'. During a four-day visit to US in September 2014, Modi not only met US President Barack Obama, but also sought to invite investment from prominent CEOs and urged the Indian-American community to take up a greater role in the development of India. Also in New York, Modi announced new visa and travel schemes that would make it easier for people to get to India. He declared that 'People of Indian Origin' (PIO) cardholders would now be able to get lifelong visas for travel to India. Previously, this option had only been open to those of Indian origin who had applied to another scheme, called the Overseas Citizenship of India (OCI). In New York, Modi also met with business leaders and urged them to invest in India. He elaborated on policies he would implement to facilitate investment in India later during his trip in Washington, DC at a speech at the US-India Business Council (USIBC). Modi's remarks were well-received by USIBC and American Government and business leaders.

During the visit, the two sides set up a contact group for advancing the full and timely implementation of the Civil Nuclear Cooperation Agreement. Modi and Obama co-authored editorial in the *Washington Post*. Though somewhat filled with platitudes, the editorial nonetheless suggested several areas where India and the United States could cooperate more concretely in the future.[18]

President Obama's visit to India in January 2015 also generated lot of excitement and enthusiasm. During the visit, the two sides issued a 'Delhi Declaration of Friendship' and adopted a joint strategic vision for Asia-Pacific and the Indian Ocean Region. They renewed the Defence Framework Agreement and proclaimed their intention of deepening cooperation on maritime security. Mr. Obama announced a slew of initiatives that included US$ 4 billion in loans from US banks, US$ 2 billion in financing for renewable energy projects in India and US$ 1 billion from the Exim Bank of the US for project financing.[19]

President Donald Trump assumed office of the American President in January 2017. The new President was interested in making economic deals with India and sustaining the defense relationship, and Prime Minister Modi responded by quickly engaging with Trump. In June 2017, China provoked a military standoff in the Himalayas that brought India and the US closer together. PLA troops moved onto the Doklam Plateau in the Himalayas to build a road that infringed upon the territory of the Kingdom of Bhutan, which had long been under Indian protection. The Indian Army responded by sending troops into the area to block road construction, which led to a 73-day standoff between the Indian Army and PLA. While India demonstrated resolve during the standoff in spite of China's protests, New Delhi was careful to keep the confrontation from escalating into a border war. However, US and Indian officials asserted that Doklam was a 'game changer' and would bring India ever closer to cooperating with the US and its allies. In August 2017, President Trump announced a new US strategy towards South Asia in which the US would increase the number of troops in Afghanistan to more than ten thousand and keep its presence open-ended. The strategy included pressuring Pakistan to do more to stop terrorists from using safe havens within its borders and India providing more economic and development support to Afghanistan. The US Department of Defense under Secretary James Mattis was interested in sustaining and improving defense relations to counter a rising China in the Indian Ocean and Asia.

He opined that the world's two greatest democracies should have the two greatest militaries. This view was repeated by Trump and Modi in November 2017 on the sidelines of the Association of Southeast Asian Nations (ASEAN) Summit in Manila, when the two leaders pledged to elevate India's status as a major US defense partner. As part of the December 2017 National Security Strategy (NSS), the US pledged to "deepen the strategic partnership with India and support its leadership in Indian Ocean security and throughout the broader region". At the same time, the US criticized Pakistan for its military's unwillingness and inability to counter the Afghan Taliban and Haqqani Network operating from its soil. In March 2018, the Trump Administration announced a "Free and Open Indo-Pacific Strategy" (FOIPS) and a "strong coalition of democracies" that replaced President Obama's "Rebalance to Asia" strategy.[20]

After getting re-elected in the year 2019, the Indian Prime Minister Modi visited US in between September 21 and September 27, 2019 during which he addressed the annual U.N. General Assembly session and had a series of bilateral and multilateral engagements in New York. The Indian PM attended an Indian community event 'Howdy Modi' in Houston during the visit. The Houston gathering of the Indian diaspora in the US on a Sunday addressed by Prime Minister Narendra Modi and US President Donald Trump was a resounding success in meeting its stated and implied objectives. Modi had drafted Indian diaspora communities in several countries for advancing his strategic objectives. The diaspora in the US is of pre-eminent significance given its increasing political heft and the centrality of the US in India's strategic architecture. President Trump's appearance at the rally and his effusive support for India were a reflection of the community's influence in US politics. He named fighting 'radical Islamic terrorism' as a key common interest of the two countries, spurring a standing ovation by the audience. During the visit Modi also addressed the 74th session of the U.N. General Assembly (UNGA). As the world commemorated Mahatma Gandhi's 150th birth anniversary, Modi hosted a special event 'Leadership Matters: Relevance of Gandhi in the Contemporary World' on September 24 in the Economic and

Social Council (ECOSOC) Chamber in the U.N. Headquarters. Modi and Trump also emphasised on border security, an important, but controversial issue in both democracies.

President Donald J. Trump's visit to India on 24 February, 2020—the eighth of any US President—was widely lauded by domestic media in India and produced a series of small deals in arms, energy, and nuclear cooperation. The trip failed, however, to produce large or transformative agreements to advance the US-India strategic partnership. The signing of a widely expected 'mini trade deal' was conspicuously absent during the President's visit. Negotiators from both countries have worked for months to resolve a variety of market access and intellectual property disputes that have impeded otherwise steady growth in the bilateral trade relationship. Though the visit was much publicised and the 'Namaste Trump' rally held in Ahmedabad, displayed the friendship between the two countries, trade deal negotiations reached a temporary stalemate which somehow affected the spirit of the visit.[21]

After the outbreak of the Covid 19 pandemic, India shipped in August 2020, 50 million tablets of hydroxychloroquine to the United States, following a personal request by the US President. America thanked India for this warm humanitarian gesture, as hydroxychloroquine was believed to be as a possible treatment for Covid 19 and other respiratory diseases. The US on its part, had also expressed solidarity with India during the recent (late 2020) skirmishes between Indian and Chinese troops in the Galwan region of Ladakh valley of India.

Future Directions

India-US relationship is likely to grow in a positive way in the years ahead for many reasons. The economic dimension is all-important to the US. India, already the third largest economy, could become the second largest by 2030. This prospect makes India an attractive trade and business partner of the US, which the Americans would be unwilling to ignore. The China factor will also play a defining a role in the relationship. India, because of its size and capacities, is the only country in Asia that could be viewed as a counterbalance to China. With US-China ties becoming manifestly adversarial centring around trade disputes and China's dealing of the pandemic, US would tilt more towards India. With China unveiling its ambitious designs to equal if not replace the US as a global power by 2050, India's value as America's strategic partner will increase. India wants to reform the current global political and economic order, so as to have more say in international governance and expects to receive endorsement from US.

Maritime security has become an area of long-term geopolitical convergence between India and the US, encapsulated by the Indo-Pacific concept. The triggers are the unprecedented expansion of the Chinese navy, China's search for maritime outposts and naval bases in the Indian Ocean, and its conduct in the South China Sea. The security of the Indian and the Pacific Oceans is linked because China will first have to push back US power in the western Pacific to be able to expand its presence in the Indian Ocean to threatening proportions. The US has renamed its Pacific Command as the Indo-Pacific Command. India, mindful of Association of Southeast Asian Nations sensitivities about the Indo-Pacific concept and the need to maintain adequate space for engaging China, has diluted the concept's anti-Chinese connotations by clarifying in June 2018 that the Indo-Pacific was an inclusive concept and not a strategy directed against any country.

Defence ties with the US will continue to expand through institutional arrangements such as Logistics Exchange Memorandum of Agreement; Communications Compatibility and Security Agreement (COMCASA); the Industrial Security Annex; Strategic Trade Authorization-1 (STA-1); and Major Defence Partner status. With the Basic Exchange and Cooperation Agreement (BECA) to materialise, and a revamped Defense Technology and Trade Initiative (DTTI), India-US security relations will surge ahead in the future. India's budgetary constraints apart, indigenous defence manufacturing will have to be promoted with US cooperation to sustain long-term growth of defence ties.

Areas of divergence with the US will continue. Trade issues, always contentious, could become more so as economic ties grow and mature. US positions on trade and investment issues are lobby driven and therefore prone to oscillation. With the World Trade Organization (WTO) weakened, US will use bilateral tools to extract concessions. Energy ties with the US will expand. The US, a global power, will always try to fit India into the jigsaw of its interests worldwide. However, India is not in a position to induce the US to cater to its regional interests, be it in Pakistan, Afghanistan, Iran or west Asia. The issue of human rights should not figure in relations between democracies, but the US has a propensity to pass strictures on other countries, including India, on human rights questions, and this could well continue to be an irritant in relations. The US will remain India's most important partner across domains in the future, even as a reconciliation between 'America First' and India's emphasis on a more just and equitable international order to promote its own rise will have to be constantly adjusted by the two nations in the future.

INDIA AND CHINA

India and China are two Asian behemoths who together account for over one-third of the world's population. Both are fast-growing economies having huge potentials of ushering in the much-vaunted Asian century, provided they are able to act in spirit of cooperation or at best, healthy competition. Hence, the relationship between these two nations has tremendous significance for the peace and stability of the world order and progress of humanity as a whole. The course of the relationship between these Asian giants has been like a roller-coaster ride, as the initial high spirit later subsided, leading towards border disputes and military tensions, then again improving through enhanced economic cooperation followed by recent phases of renewed border skirmishes. This study is divided into two sections. First section briefly covers the early years of the relationship till the death of Chairman Mao Zedong, the supreme leader of China. The second section focuses on the dynamic developments in the relationship, starting with the era of Deng Xiaoping till the time of present President of the People's Republic of China, Xi Jinping. An attempt to analyse the probable future direction of the relationship is the intended objective of the study.

Relationship in the Mao Era

Independent India and new socialist state of China began their journey almost simultaneously, India gaining independence in 1947 and China emerging as the first socialist country of Asia in 1949, both inheritors of the rich legacy of rich ancient civilizations. Jawaharlal Nehru, the first Prime Minister of India, having a socialist leaning, welcomed the creation of a socialist China as a victory in the struggle against imperialism and colonialism. When the PRC (People's Republic of China) was declared, India was among the first countries to give it diplomatic recognition. China also expressed willingness to forge friendly ties with India by sending its Premier Zhou Enlai to India and the two countries declared that their friendship would be guided by the 'Panchsheel' (five principles) which essentially called for mutual respect to each other's sovereignty, territorial integrity and the policy of non-interference.[22]

However, China refused to accept British engineered McMahon line as the legally acceptable boundary between India and China, and did not acknowledge sovereign status of Tibet as an independent state between India and China. China claimed Tibet to be a part of its own territory. In 1955, China joined the conference of Afro-Asian nations in Bandung, and supported the initiatives of these countries to lunch Non-Aligned Movement in the backdrop of a sharply polarised world generated by the Cold War. India was appreciative of China's stand in Bandung. Unfortunately, relationship took a turn towards bitterness by late 1950s when differences emerged over border issues and Tibet's accession to China. Both India and China accused each other of illegal occupation of territory. There had been a series of violent border skirmishes between the two countries after the 1959 Tibetan uprising, when India granted asylum to the Dalai Lama, the Tibetan religious leader.

China did not object to Ladakh or Aksai Chin being part of India until a couple of years after 1950, when Indian Constitution adopted the whole of Jammu and Kashmir as its integral territory. The Chinese planned aggression beyond the western boundary of Tibet—which had been taken over by the communist regime in 1950—through a network of three roads to be built under military supervision passing through Aksai Chin. One of these three roads was Highway Number 219 that connected Hotan in Xinjiang to Lhasa in Tibet. Construction activities began only after 1953 when Hindi-Chini Bhai-Bhai was becoming the slogan for India-China initial friendship. But by the late 1950s, claims and counterclaims of territories, and the Tibet issue overshadowed the brotherhood slogan (Hindi-Chini Bhai Bhai). The myth of friendship had been busted by 1959. The then Indian Prime Minister Jawaharlal Nehru was diplomatically asserting India's sovereign right over Aksai Chin that China had for all practical purposes occupied.[23]

India initiated a defensive Forward Policy from 1960 to hinder Chinese military patrols and logistics, in which it placed outposts along the border, including several north of the McMahon Line, the eastern portion of the Line of Actual Control proclaimed by Chinese Premier Zhou Enlai in 1959. Chinese military action grew increasingly aggressive after India rejected proposed Chinese diplomatic settlements throughout 1960-62, with China re-commencing previously-banned "forward patrols" in Ladakh from 30 April 1962. China finally abandoned all attempts of peaceful resolution on 20 October 1962, invading disputed territory along the 3,225 kilometre-long (2,000 mile) Himalayan border in Ladakh and across the McMahon Line. Chinese troops advanced over Indian forces in both theatres, capturing Rezang La in Chushul in the western theatre, as well as Tawang in the eastern theatre. China's victory in the war was decisive. The war ended when China declared a ceasefire on 20 November 1962, and simultaneously announced its withdrawal to its claimed 'Line of Actual Control'.[24]

British Indian Army was manning China-Tibet border, and this mantle fell to Indians after Independence. India knew China border was indefensible. It was not feasible to build logistics and fortifications when China attacked in 1962. It took several weeks to condition soldiers to fight in depleted oxygen levels. Besides, Nehru did not anticipate such treacherous moves from China which explains India's defeat.

The war yielded a few advantages to China:

- It succeeded in teaching a lesson to India on the issue of Tibet.
- It to some extent nullified India's position on the border issue.
- It was a setback for India's design to assume the leadership of the Third World.
- The occupation of Aksai Chin, consolidated during the war, was a significant achievement, described by Chinese leadership as a brilliant move coming out of "the strategic vision of a great man, Chairman Mao Zedong" as they felt that "Aksai Chin is like a Damocles sword hanging over India's head" in addition to being a gateway to Central Asia and an easy route to "easily run over New Delhi, the Indian capital city".
- It was a blow to the image of Nehru, as his miscalculations regarding China's intent precipitated the war.[25]

However, the net gain in terms of territory for China was an insignificant 2,000 square kilometres of alpine desert in Ladakh between the first and second Chinese claim line. A major gain for India was the fact that for the first time the United States announced that the McMahon Line constituted the international boundary in this region. The British, apart from re-confirming the validity of the McMahon Line, took a step further than the US position when the then Foreign Secretary Lord Home told the Foreign Press Association that "we have taken the view of the Government of India on the present frontiers and the disputed territories belong to India". Thus, Chinese aggression on the border paid no substantial political dividends. All the three major powers of the world at that point of time—the United States, the Soviet Union and Britain—openly supported the Indian cause. On the other hand, China lost a sincere friend in Jawaharlal Nehru. From that point onwards in the minds of most of the Indian public the perception of China changed conclusively and it began to be associated with perfidy.[26]

After the 1962 war, diplomatic relations were cut off and the two nations distanced themselves from each other. Consequently, the relation between the two countries reached the nadir. Blood spilled in Indo-China border again in 1967. In summer of 1967, Chinese troops tried to set up installations at Nathu La, just across the Chinese border within the territory of Sikkim. India troops were met by Chinese machine gun fire and gave a fitting response, succeeding in destroying the Chinese installations. After an uneasy ceasefire, Chinese troops made a similar attempt at nearby Cho La, but were again beaten back. That clash in Sikkim, where India got the better of China just five years after defeat in the 1962 war, saw a revival of Indian security policies. Border clashes and sporadic violence continued during much of the 1970s, and bilateral relations touched very low.

Relationship in the Post Mao Period

After the death of Mao Zhe Dong in 1976, Deng Xiaoping gradually became the supreme leader of China and led his country through a series of far-reaching economic reforms, which earned him the reputation as the 'Architect of Modern China'. There was change in the political milieu in India also as Indira Gandhi lost election in 1977 and Morarji Desai became the first non-Congress (party) Prime Minister of the country. Some steps were initiated by new governments in both nations to improve bilateral relations. Officially, both the countries restored their ambassadorial relations in August 1976. After the 1962 war, K.R. Narayanan became the first Indian Ambassador to China. Though India did not hesitate in showing her keenness in repairing the wrecked relations with China, the latter seemed to be in no hurry. In February 1979, A.B. Vajpayee, External Affairs Minister of the Morarji Desai Government, visited China. He was the first Indian leader to visit China after the 1962 war. The visit helped in bringing back normalcy in India-China relations.

The creative solution that Vajpayee and Chinese leaders discussed to resolve the border dispute was that the two countries would not let normalisation of bilateral relations become a hostage to the resolution of the border dispute. The two nations would try to develop bilateral relations in an all-round manner and simultaneously, try to resolve the border dispute through dialogue and by ruling out the use of force to change the status quo along the Line of Actual Control (LAC).[27]

In 1981, Chinese Foreign Minister Huang Hua visited India. On June 28, the Indian Prime Minister Indira Gandhi met Huang Hua. The two sides agreed to further discuss the solution to the border question and related measures to promote bilateral relations by the officials of the two countries at a proper time. As an aftermath of Huang's visit, in December 1981, Chinese and Indian deputy ministers of Foreign Affairs held the first round of talks in Beijing. Since then till November 1987, the two sides held eight rounds of talks. However, as history showed, these talks did not make much difference in India-China relations. China reacted sharply when India granted statehood to Arunachal Pradesh (former NEFA) on 20 February 1987, showing resentment at India's decision. China also stepped up its military activities in the region. This again hampered any possible border negotiations between the two countries.[28]

Relations improved somewhat during Rajiv Gandhi's tenure. He was the youngest Prime Minister when he took over the reins of power in New Delhi in 1984. He visited China in December 1988. During the visit, the two sides issued a Joint Communiqué that stressed the need to restore friendly relations on the basis of Panchsheel. Both the countries agreed to broaden bilateral ties in various areas, working to achieve a 'fair and reasonable settlement while seeking a mutually acceptable solution' to the border dispute. The communiqué also expressed China's concern about agitation by Tibetan separatists in India and reiterated China's position that Tibet was an integral part of China. Rajiv Gandhi signed bilateral agreements on science and technology cooperation, on civil aviation to establish direct air links and on cultural exchanges. The two sides also agreed to hold annual diplomatic consultations between foreign ministers, and to set up a Joint Ministerial Committee (JMC) on economic and scientific cooperation and a Joint Working Group (JWG) on the boundary issue. The latter group was to be led by the Indian Foreign Secretary and the Chinese Vice Minister of Foreign Affairs. The JWG was to determine the LAC in western and central sectors. In eastern sector, the troops used to be deployed generally on either side of McMahon line. It was an important beginning as both sides did not have a mutually acceptable understanding where their troops held ground on the border.

In fact, in May 1987 itself, during the eighth round of border talks it was decided to upgrade the talks from bureaucratic to ministerial levels. The initial steps taken by Rajiv Gandhi appeared to be leading towards easing the relations between the two Asian neighbours. Beginning of 1990s marked the beginning of another new phase in Indian political scenario as well as in the area on Sino-Indian relationship. P.V. Narasimha Rao assumed the office of the Prime Minister of India on 21 June 1991. Chinese Premier Li Peng visited New Delhi in December 1991. Li Peng's five-day visit to India, the first by such a high-ranking Chinese dignitary since Premier Zhou Enlai's visit in 1954, was marked by the signing of three important agreements, relating to resumption of border trade, cooperation in space research and opening of consulate offices in Mumbai and Shanghai. Media hailed the visit as a success. Again, the year 1992 marked a significant chapter in Indo-China relations. Indian President R. Venkataraman visited China. This was the first Head of the State's visit from India to China. Border trade resumed in July 1992 after a gap of more than thirty years, and consulates were reopened in Mumbai and Shanghai. In December 1992, Indian Defence Minister Sharad Pawar visited China in the capacity of Defence Minister. Sharad Pawar was the first Indian Defence Minister to visit China.[29] During his visit, the two defence establishments agreed to develop academic, military, scientific, and technological exchanges and to schedule an Indian port call by a Chinese naval vessel. Six rounds of talks of the Indian-Chinese JWG were held between December 1988 and June 1993 and in the same month, the two sides agreed to open an additional border trading post. After the sixth round of talks was completed, the longstanding border dispute seemed to be easing, as both the countries pledged to reduce troop levels and to respect the cease-fire along the India-China border.

Prime Minister Narasimha Rao visited China in September 1993. A noteworthy development happened as the Agreement on the Maintenance of Peace and Tranquillity along the LAC in the border area was signed during this visit. It provided for both sides to respect the status quo on the border, clarify the LAC where there are doubts and undertake Confidence Building Measures (CBMs). A senior level Chinese Military delegation made a six-day goodwill visit to India in December 1993 aimed at fostering the CBMs between the defence forces of the two countries.

Chinese President Jiang Zemin's visit to India in 1996 was another positive development as it marked the signing of four important agreements. These agreements were on CBMs in the military along the LAC; the maintenance of consulate offices of India in the Hong Kong Special Administrative Region in the PRC; agreement on cooperation for combating illicit trafficking in narcotic drugs and other crimes; and agreement on maritime support.

After Bharatiya Janata Party (BJP)-led government came to power in India some changes in the Indo-China relations happened. The nuclear tests conducted by India on 11 and 13 May 1998 (popularly known as the Pokhran II tests) caused some set-back to bilateral relations as China had strongly objected to these tests. In response to the objection raised by China, Indian Minister of External Affairs Jaswant Singh observed that after the tests undertaken by India in May 1998, India declared that the country shall only maintain a minimum credible deterrent and not engage in any arms race. The role of India's nuclear weapons is defensive; accordingly, India had announced a policy of no-first-use and a policy of non-use against non-nuclear weapon states. However, China was not convinced by such proclamations by Indian policy makers and as a retaliatory move, expressed its support to Pakistan during the Kargil conflict (between India and Pakistan) in 1999.

The new millennium (21st century) brought some positive changes in India-China bilateral relations. Indian President K.R. Narayanan visited China in the year 2000 marking a gradual re-engagement between the two countries which suffered a set-back during Pokhran II tests. This week-long visit of the Indian President from 28 May-3 June had been successful in re-creating a friendly atmosphere, emphasising the historical necessity and the advantage both the countries would be deriving from developing Sino-Indian amity and cooperation. President K.R. Narayanan got a warm welcome from China's President Jiang Zemin. After holding talks with his Chinese counterpart, the President of India also held talks with Premier Zhu Rongji, Chairman of the Ninth National Committee of the Chinese People's Political Consultative Conference (CPPCC) Li Ruihuan and the Chairman of the Standing Committee of the National People's Congress (SCNPC) Li Peng. During his entire itinerary most of the controversial issues were avoided in discussions, especially the nuclear issue. The absence of severe notes on either side and an agreement to set up an Eminent Persons' Group (EPG) to help develop the bilateral relationship—were the highlights of the State Visit. The President remarked in an interaction in Kunming with scholars from the Yunnan Academy of Social Sciences, "In India-China relations, I have the impression that we have reached the stage of criticality. From now on, it is bound to increase in intensity and speed." Informed sources close to the President explained that by 'the stage of criticality', he meant that 'the time of preparation' was over, that it was 'time for action' and that 'objective conditions were favourable' for the resolution of all bilateral problems. On the whole, visit by K.R. Narayanan in 2000 was considered 'a successful atmosphere-building' visit.[30]

Chinese Premier Zhu Rongji visited India in January 2002. The visit took place sometimes after the attack on Indian Parliament by Pakistan-backed terrorists and increase of tension between India and Pakistan. Zhu reiterated the Chinese position that the India-Pakistan dispute should be resolved through negotiations. The Indian Government clarified its stand to him on the issue of attack on Parliament and Prime Minister Vajpayee assured Zhu that the problem with Pakistan would be sorted out through talks. After discussing a wide range of subjects, Prime Ministers of both countries decided on issues like 'enhancing friendship, strengthening mutual ties and expanding economic cooperation'. Both New Delhi and Beijing appeared to favour the creation of a multi-polar world as they expressed common views on many important issues.

In June 2003, Indian Prime Minister A.B. Vajpayee visited China. India had now formally recognised that the area known as the Tibet an autonomous region is part of the People's Republic of China. China, for its part, agreed to start border trade through the north-east Indian state of Sikkim—a move that was being seen as an acceptance by Beijing of India's claim over that area. The year 2004 proved to be a landmark in bilateral relations as the two countries proposed opening up the Nathu La and Jelep La passes in Sikkim which would be mutually beneficial to both countries. In the same year, bilateral trade between them touched US$ 13.6 billion.[31] This was a clear indication of the emergence of the two of them as stronger economies in Asia and the improving trade relations between them.

Chinese Premier Wen Jiabao stressed on Sino-Indian cooperation in high-tech industries during his visit to India in April 2005. Wen Jiabao observed in a speech in Bangalore that cooperation was just like two pagodas (temples), one, hardware and one, software. He also stated that the 21st century will be the Asian century of the IT industry. Though Wen's 2005 visit was very much publicised before and after it happened, nothing new came out of it. Apart from the celebration about economic relations and increasing trade between India and China, all that it yielded was a formal acceptance of Sikkim as a state of India, by Wen. The two sides elevated their relations from a 'constructive and cooperative partnership' to a 'strategic and cooperative partnership'. On 6 July 2006, China and India reopened Nathu La pass after a closure of 44 years. The rest of the world considered this development as positive step towards improving bilateral relations between the two countries.

Chinese President Hu Jintao's visit to India in November 2006 was a big step in bringing understanding and cooperation between India and China on diverse issues. Hu Jintao proposed 'five points' to increase political trust, business cooperation, cultural and social exchanges and multilateral cooperation on the one hand and address the boundary issues on the other. In his interaction with the media, Hu Jintao made it clear that working together to expand cooperation and create a bright future was the primary task for both the countries. But the visit could not yield anything concrete. No clarity was reached on border issues, a perennial problem in bilateral relations.

Similar was the case with the Prime Minister Manmohan Singh's visit to China in January 2008. Chinese Premier Wen Jiabao and Indian Prime Minister Manmohan Singh signed a joint document which was highlighting no new issues. A reference was made to the five principles of peaceful coexistence popularly known as Panchsheel; expressing the view that adherence to such principles was the need of the hour for ensuring peace in the world. These were the very principles violated by China when it attacked India in 1962. The two countries also agreed to promote bilateral cooperation in civil nuclear energy. But when it came to the issue of India seeking permanent seat in the Security Council of the UN, all China said was that it understands and supports India's aspirations to play a greater role.

As the calendar advanced into mid-2009, the underlying differences between the two neighbouring countries could no longer be suppressed. When India applied for a loan from the Asian Development Bank (ADB), for funding an irrigation project in Arunachal Pradesh, China raised serious objections and even tried to stop the loan. It repeatedly told the ADB that loans from an international financial institution cannot be granted for projects meant to be implemented in a 'disputed land', and that Arunachal Pradesh was still a disputed land. However, the loan was granted to India in October 2009 with the intervention of the US and Japan. China not only expressed its displeasure at this but also considered it a manipulation of authority as both the US and Japan held the largest proportions of total shares in ADB. In July 2009, Indian External Affairs

Minister S.M. Krishna said that India had made it clear to all member nations of ADB that political considerations cannot be cited for prohibiting the bank for evaluating any project.[32]

This deterioration of Indo-China relations could be traced back to a development that occurred in 2007. India became part of a four-member international group called the 'Quad Initiative', which was initiated by Shinzo Abe, Prime Minister of Japan. The Quad was founded on the concept of 'democratic peace.' The member countries, USA, Australia, Japan and India held its inaugural meeting on 25 May, 2007. China had earlier sent a demarche (an action or gesture by a diplomat, especially a formal appeal, protest, or the like) to Tokyo, New Delhi, Canberra, and Washington. The demarche demanded to know why such an initiative was being established.[33] Even the joint naval exercises conducted that summer in the Bay of Bengal by the four Quad powers and Singapore, were viewed by China with suspicion. She felt that they were being conducted allegedly under NATO operational procedures which would facilitate access to the American military satellite system. China suspected that India was thoroughly benefiting from these joint naval exercises and could not hide its irritation.

The year 2010 witnessed a noteworthy development when in May the first lady President of India Pratibha Patil paid an official visit to China. This was the first visit by an Indian head of state in ten years. The Chinese side attached great importance to the visit as it marked 60 years of establishment of diplomatic relations between the two countries. Apart from her meetings with President Hu Jintao and other Chinese leaders, Vice-President Xi Jinping attended the reception hosted by the Indian Embassy in China. 'Cultural and people-to-people exchanges and cooperation featured prominently in President Patil's visit to China.' But not much was discussed about the strategic issues some of which were hampering the relations between the two countries. Though economic relations between India and China were not affected much and China remained the biggest trading partner of India, bilateral trade was not proving favourable to India. Alistair Scrutton quoted Srikanth Kondapalli saying, "There are green lines such as trade but there are concerns there as well such as the (trade) imbalance and anti-dumping concerns. There is also a realisation in India that you have to make your displeasure more explicit to be taken seriously."[34]

In an attempt to keep the trade relations moving, the Chinese Premier Wen Jiabao paid another visit to India in December 2010 accompanied by some 400 Chinese business leaders who wished to sign business deals with Indian companies. Prime Minister Manmohan Singh's visit to China in April 2011 also saw some positive changes in relations. Compared to Manmohan Singh's earlier visit to China in 2008, the visit of 2011 was considered a more successful one. Singh attended the third BRICS summit held in the Chinese city of Sanya where he met the Chinese President. Both the leaders reached an understanding to abandon most of the irritants which caused deterioration to bilateral relations. Indian side also agreed to Chinese Premier Wen Jiabao's suggestion that both sides create a working mechanism for consultation and coordination on border issues. According to the National Security Advisor Shiv Shankar Menon, this 'working mechanism' would actually be the formation of a 'Standing Group' that would serve as a medium through which sensitive issues would be dealt with. And this would be done without actually involving New Delhi or Beijing. Both the leaders designated the year of 2011 as the 'Year of China-India Exchange'.

Chinese President Hu Jintao came to India in March 2012 to attend the fourth BRICS summit. On 29 March 2012, he met Indian Prime Minister Manmohan Singh in New Delhi. Both the leaders discussed, among other things, the regional issues of common concern to the two countries and announced the year 2012 as the 'Year of India-China Friendship and Cooperation' pledging to take this opportunity to elevate the Sino-Indian strategic cooperative partnership to a new level.

Chinese Defence Minister General Liang Guanglie visited India in September 2012. The visit was significant for the reason that a Chinese Defence Minister visited India after a gap of eight years. A growing understanding between the two navies operating in Gulf of Aden to combat piracy jointly by establishing an informal understanding over the timings and coordination of escort convoys was discussed. However, the changing scenario of the geo-politics in the Asia-Pacific region where China was sensing encirclement by the US, the growing relations of the latter with India, also formed the backdrop of Liang's visit. And the outcome of this visit too was not altogether different from the previous visits of other leaders. Much was discussed but not much was resolved, especially the issues pertaining to the security at disputed borders.

Indian Prime Minister Manmohan Singh met Chinese President Xi Jinping during the Fifth summit of the BRICS nations held in Durban, South Africa in March 2013. This was the first structured high-level contact between the two countries, since the change of leadership in China. Speaking to reporters after the meeting, Singh said India values its ties with China. The two leaders discussed all contentious issues, including the boundary and Chinese dams along the Brahmaputra River.

Chinese President Xi Jinping visited India and met the new Indian Prime Minister Narendra Modi in late 2014. Continuing to build upon a decade-long pragmatism in managing territorial disputes, the Chinese and Indian leaders set their sights on expanding bilateral co-operation ranging from trade and investment to broader issues such as climate change and development in the global South. Beijing pledged to hike Chinese investment in India. At the same time, Beijing and New Delhi endorsed the establishment of the New Development Bank and the Asian Infrastructure Investment Bank (AIIB). China, together with Russia, welcomed India (and Pakistan) as full members of the Shanghai Co-operation Organisation (SCO).[35] A total of 16 agreements were signed in various sectors including, commerce & trade, railways, space cooperation, pharmaceuticals, audio-visual co-production, culture, establishment of industrial parks, sister-city arrangements, etc. The two sides also signed a MOU to open an additional route for Kailash Mansarovar Yatra through Nathu La. The Chinese side agreed to establish two Chinese Industrial Parks in India and expressed their intention to enhance Chinese investment in India.

Indian Prime Minister Narendra Modi visited China from May 14-16, 2015. Besides meeting with the Chinese leadership, Prime Minister Modi and Premier Li also addressed the opening session of the First State/Provincial Leaders' Forum in Beijing. There were 24 agreements signed on the government-to-government side, 26 MOUs on the business-to-business side and two joint statements, including one on climate change. Prime Minister Modi also announced the extension of the e-visa facility to Chinese nationals wishing to travel to India.

The momentum of meetings at the top leadership level continued in 2016 too. President Pranab Mukherjee made a state visit to China from May 24 to 27, 2016. He visited Guangdong and Beijing where he met with the Chinese leadership. President also delivered a keynote address at the Peking University and attended a Round Table between Vice Chancellors and Heads of institutions of higher learning of the two countries. Ten MOUs providing for enhanced faculty and student exchanges as well as collaboration in research and innovation were concluded between the higher education institutions of the two countries. President Xi Jinping visited India in October 2016 to participate in the BRICS Summit in Goa. The two leaders also met along the sidelines of the SCO Heads of States Summit in Tashkent in June 2016 and in Astana in June 2017.[36] Prime Minister Narendra Modi visited China in September 2016 to participate in the G-20 Summit in Hangzhou and in September 2017 to participate in the BRICS Summit in Xiamen, where he also held bilateral talks with President Xi Jinping.

In recent years, China has ventured beyond its traditional spheres of activities—East and South-East Asia—to the Indian Ocean Region. China's perspectives on the importance of the Indian Ocean to its economic and security interests have been informed and influenced by three sets of key considerations. First, China's perceived maritime interests have expanded and now constitute an increasingly crucial component of the country's overall economic development due to the rising international trade portion of its gross domestic product (GDP) and its growing energy and raw materials imports. Second, Beijing sees a 'Malacca Dilemma' in the form of a potential bottleneck or, at a minimum, a node of extreme vulnerability should a hostile state or states seek to block the transits of energy and other resources headed to China and Chinese exports of manufactured goods. Finally, as its dependence on, and stake in access to, maritime traffic continues to rise, China is witnessing an expanding internal debate about whether it is a continental or a maritime power and, to the extent that it is the latter, about how a balance can be struck between asserting China's maritime rights and interests by developing the necessary naval capabilities to protect them. Consequently, China has become increasingly involved in projects in Myanmar, Pakistan, and Sri Lanka, among other countries, that appear to be aimed at developing alternative land routes for oil transport should maritime passages be disrupted. China is also bolstering its geopolitical influence in the Indian Ocean littorals: Hainan Island; Woody Island in the South China Sea; Chittagong in Bangladesh; the 1,200-km pipeline from the port of Sittwe in Myanmar to Kunming in China's Yunnan Province; the Gwadar Port in Pakistan; a US$ 1 billion port at Hambantota in Sri Lanka.

China's drive towards a greater presence in the Indian Ocean, best illustrated by its massive investments in infrastructure projects and its ambitious plan to develop an economic corridor connecting the Gwadar Port to China's north-western autonomous region of Xinjiang, including the upgrading of the 1,300 kilometre Karakoram, or 'Friendship' Highway and the ambitious US$ 46 billion "China-Pakistan Economic Corridor" (CPEC), launched during President Xi's 2015 visit to Pakistan, have all contributed to India's suspicion and growing anxiety, lending credence to the 'string of pearl' hypothesis, first developed by US analysts, which posits that China is trying to expand its naval presence by building civilian maritime infrastructure along the Indian Ocean periphery, with the objective of encircling India, thereby limiting its zone of influence.[37]

The view that connectivity offers a set of tools to influence other countries' foreign policy choices has become commonplace in analysis about the China-led Belt and Road Initiative (BRI).

The BRI has garnered much attention, positive and negative, since its inception in 2013. It is one of the world's biggest initiatives for promoting connectivity and providing funds to finance infrastructure development. In South Asia, the BRI underscores the growing Sino-Indian competition in the subcontinent and the Indian Ocean region. In its strongest stance on the BRI to date, India marked its protest by not attending the Belt and Road Forum that China hosted in May 2017. In official statements, India questioned the initiative's transparency and processes, and New Delhi opposed the China-Pakistan Economic Corridor (CPEC) due to concerns about territorial sovereignty as the proposed corridor will run through the disputed Pak-occupied Kashmir.[38]

Apart from CPEC, China and Pakistan have been engaged in close co-operation in civilian nuclear programmes, joint fighter aircraft development and anti-ethnic separatist activities, a growing security concern for China. Beijing has also offered diplomatic support to Islamabad at international and multilateral organisations, one example being the alleged Chinese block on India's effort at the United Nations to name JeM chief Masood Azhar and other groups as terrorist organisations. Another is the reported Chinese role in preventing India from joining the NSG, partly driven by concerns over the impact of India's admission on Pakistan. All these have naturally affected Indo-China relations quite adversely.

The 2017-18 revival of the Quadrilateral Security Dialogue, often known as the Quad 2.0, by the new liberal world nexus of Australia, India, Japan, and United States, raised questions about the seeming stability of India-China relations. The Quad as an 'Indo-Pacific' proposition is essentially a consequence of the growing power asymmetry in Asia, and is directed toward achieving equilibrium. By attempting to overcome the trust deficit between countries and by endorsing a multipolar world order, the Quad calls for a renewed commitment to an orderly rule-based global structure. For obvious reasons, China has disapproved these developments. The military border standoff at Doklam in 2017—when India placed troops to prevent China from building a road into territory claimed by its ally,

Bhutan was no ordinary episode in India-China relations. With its potential to escalate into a small-scale war, it tested their diplomatic nerve and skills. Diplomacy was at its core and both sides successfully averted further escalation. India stood proud that the Indian Army successfully faced the People's Liberation Army (PLA) for 73 days, something that few Asian militaries perhaps could do. For New Delhi, it was crucial to stop the PLA from constructing roads in the Doklam tri-junction area, in what it terms a disputed region, without triggering a war. For Beijing, its attempt to inject an element of strategic complexity into a politically stable India-Bhutan relationship was successful, as evidenced by China's ongoing attempts to create divisions between India and its neighbours. Moreover, Beijing sought to test India's diplomatic character and military preparedness in the face of a territorial threat. The resolution of this incident thus illuminated the complexity of India-China relations and how small-scale incidents can spiral without political will.

India-China relations witnessed a new wave of optimism for a progressive and engaging partnership following the Wuhan Summit, the informal 2018 meeting between Narendra Modi and Xi Jinping. Key to this has been continuous exchange of political and official visits from both sides. To maintain "closer strategic communication" was the overarching outcome of the Modi-Xi informal meeting in Wuhan. The Modi-Xi meet on the sidelines of the Shanghai Cooperation Organization (SCO) in Qingdao in June 2018, followed by a meeting against the backdrop of the Johannesburg Brazil-Russia-India-China-South Africa (BRICS) summit in July 2018. This strengthened the notion that India-China relations were fast following a personality-centric engagement process. The Chinese Defense Minister Wei Fenghe's visit to India in August 2018 was more for rebuilding the lost confidence between the two militaries. Establishment of a hotline between their militaries and resumption of annual military exercises and dialogues set the course for reframing the faltering relationship, generating an amount of confidence that was most required. Added to this was the positive change evidenced in their bilateral trade exchanges—the most stabilizing factor in their relations—witnessing an upward trend of 25 percent, to almost US$ 90 billion in 2017-18. To India's concern, the trade ties with China are lopsided, with Beijing enjoying a growing trade surplus. Not to overlook, after the United States, India has the second-largest trade imbalance with China. All initiatives to improve this situation have only increased Chinese dumping in Indian markets.

In 2019, Indian PM Modi and Chinese President Xi Jinping met on an informal summit at Mamallapuram, a coastal town near Chennai, India on October 11-12. During this summit, Modi and Xi reinforced their commitment to improve trade relations. This was one of the key agreements of the Wuhan summit. The leaders agreed to set up new mechanisms to achieve this goal. China promised to address the vexed issue of India's huge trade deficit with China. Modi and Xi agreed that there must be a rules-based and inclusive international order. They agreed that there must be reforms that reflect the new realities of the 21st century. They also agreed that rules-based multilateral trading systems must be supported and strengthened. The nations also reinforced their commitment to work together for open and inclusive trade arrangements that will benefit all countries. They also made a commitment to address global developmental challenges, including climate change and meet the Sustainable Development Goals. To celebrate the 70th year of diplomatic relations between the two nations, the year 2020 will be designated as Year of India-China Cultural and People to People Exchanges, the MEA said. To mark the occasion, many events will be planned, it added.

To celebrate the civilisational ties between the nations, the two leaders have decided to form a 'Sister-state relationship' between Tamil Nadu and Fujian Province. There was also a proposal to set up an academy to study these links. It was hoped that the focus on tourism and contact among the people of both nations will not only boost trade, but it will help in building trust between them. Establishing such confidence-building measures can help integrating the people by removing stereotypes.[39]

Unfortunately, matters took an ugly turn in 2020 between the two Asian neighbours. China started making intrusion in

Galwan valley of Ladakh across LAC in the summer of 2020. China also claimed that Indian soldiers had crossed the LAC, but India dismissed China's accusations. As per reports appearing in international media, the PLA had intruded into the Indian side of the LAC, disrupted normal patrolling, and destroyed posts and bridges on the Galwan Nala at Chang-Chenmo.

Looking at the issue only from the LAC angle would be a mistake. To put things in the perspective, in the wake of the abrogation of Articles 370 and 35A by Government of India in 2019, there was a sudden outburst from Beijing over making Ladakh a Union Territory (UT). China described India's move as 'unacceptable', undermining its 'sovereignty' and raised the issue at the UNSC. India dismissed China's assertion, termed Ladakh's new status as an 'internal matter' having no implication for India's external boundaries or the LAC with China. While India had pursued its core national interests in J&K, China's response was strategic—a shift that was likely to have a lasting imprint on geopolitics.

Tension between the armies of the two countries along the LAC escalated in June 2020, leading to violent confrontation. At least 20 Indian soldiers were killed in a clash with Chinese forces, as per Indian official sources. It was the first deadly clash in the border area in the last 45 years. China did not confirm any casualties, but accused India in turn of crossing the border onto the Chinese side. Though no shots were fired, the battle was fought with rocks and clubs. Local media outlets reported that the Indian soldiers had been beaten to death. There are several reasons why tensions are rising now—but competing strategic goals lie at the root, and both sides blame each other. India had built a new road in the most remote and vulnerable area along the LAC in Ladakh. And India's decision to ramp up infrastructure seems to have infuriated Beijing. The road could boost Delhi's capability to move men and materiel rapidly in case of a conflict.[40]

While there is a significant power asymmetry between India and China, both are experiencing a simultaneous rise. Both sides have greater capacity today than at any point since the formation of the modern Republic of India and the People's

of GDP and growth trajectory. It knows that India is also far behind on military modernisation and overall capabilities. China is ruthlessly resisting India's access to global governance bodies, such as the UNSC and NSG. To keep India tied at that level, China is objecting to India's growing strategic proximity to the US. It is encircling India strategically and economically through its strategic and economic corridors—BCIM (Bangladesh, China, India and Myanmar), CPEC (China-Pakistan Economic Corridor), and the Trans-Himalayan Connectivity Network. It is raising issues like Kashmir at the UN and establishing footprints in the Indian Ocean.

India should take some realistic steps instead of aspiring for strategic equilibrium at the present moment. A self-reliant economy and further modernization of military and social infrastructure could make India nearer to China. Till these goals are achieved, the proper way for India could be to adjust with China, at least tactically, for some time. Such an adjustment could be based on mutual give and take. India must talk to China about reciprocity in bilateral relations. India would concede some if China wishes to concede. Before any proper equilibrium, India needs to be economically and militarily self-reliant. For India's strategic interests, border disputes with China needs to be peacefully settled through dialogues. Any direct confrontation with China should be avoided by all possible means, now and in the near future.

Endnotes

1. The Publications Division, Ministry of Information and Broadcasting, Government of India (1958), *Nehru's Speeches*, Vol. 1, September 1946-May 1949, 2nd ed., pp. 94-95; on line source: https://www.india.gov.in/publications-division-ministry-information-and-broadcasting. Accessed on 24 June 2020.
2. Aneek Chatterjee (2017), *Neighbours, Major Powers and Indian Foreign Policy*, New Delhi: Orient Blackswan, p. 120.
3. J.A. Naik (2000), *A Textbook of International Relations*, New Delhi: MacMillan, pp. 191-93.
4. Stephen F. Burgess (2019), "The Evolution of India-US Relations and India's Grand Strategy", *UNISCI Journal*, January; on line source: https://www.researchgate.net/publication/333832603_

The_evolution_of_India-US_relations_and_Indias_grand_strategy. Accessed on 22 August 2020.

5. United States Census Bureau; on line source: https://www.census.gov/foreign-trade/balance/c5330.html. Accessed on 22 August 2020.
6. Stephen P. Cohen (2005), *Emerging Power-India*, New Delhi: Oxford University Press, p. xv (Preface).
7. P.M. Kamath (1998), "Indo-US Relations During the Clinton Administration: Upward Trends and Uphill Tasks Ahead"; on line source: https://www.idsa-india.org/an-feb-2.html. Accessed on 22 June 2020.
8. *Far Eastern Economic Review* (2000), 30 March, p. 22.
9. *Janes Defence Weekly* (1999), 17 November.
10. Stephen F. Burgess (2019), *op. cit.*
11. Aneek Chatterjee (2017), *op. cit.*
12. Public Affairs Office, US Consulate General, Calcutta (2000), "US-India Relations: A Vision for the 21st Century", *Official Text*, March, p. 1.
13. Ravi Tomar (2002), "India-US Relations in a Changing Strategic Environment", Research Paper No. 20, 2001-02, published by the Department of the Parliamentary Library.
14. *Ibid.*
15. Ministry of External Affairs, Government of India (2004), Press Release; on line source: https://www.mea.gov.in/bilateral-documents.htm?dtl/6789/India+and+United+States+Successfully+Complete+Next+Steps+in+Strategic+Partnership. Accessed on 21 August 2020.
16. *Firstpost*, "India-US nuclear deal"; on line source: https://www.firstpost.com/india/india-us-nuclear-deal-all-you-need-to-know-about-the-landmark-agreement-3596209.html. Accessed on 24 August 2020.
17. Council on Foreign Relations, USA (2010), "The US-India Nuclear Deal", *Backgrounder*, November 5; on line source: https://www.cfr.org/backgrounder/us-india-nuclear-deal. Accessed on 24 August 2020.
18. Akhilesh Pillalamarri (2014), "What Did Narendra Modi's US Trip Accomplish?", *The Diplomat*, 2 October; on line source: https://thediplomat.com/2014/10/what-did-narendra-modis-us-trip-accomplish/. Accessed on 24 August, 2020.
19. *The Hindu* (2015), "Top 10 highlights of Obama's visit to India", January 27.

20. Michael D. Swaine (2018), "Creating an Unstable Asia: The US Free and Open Indo-Pacific Strategy," *Carnegie Endowment for International Peace and Security*, 2 March; on line source: http://carnegieendowment.org/2018/03/02/creating-unstable-asia-US-free-and-open-indo-pacific-strategy-pub-75720.
21. The *Washington Post* (2020), "Trump's India trip didn't produce a trade deal", February 27; on line source: https://www.washingtonpost.com/politics/2020/02/27/trumps-india-trip-didnt-produce-trade-deal-heres-what-did-result/. Accessed on 26 August 2020.
22. Aneek Chatterjee (2010), *International Relations Today: Concepts and Applications*, New Delhi: Pearson, p. 243.
23. Prabash Dutta (2020), "How China captured Aksai Chin", *India Today*, June 22; on line source: https://www.indiatoday.in/india/story/how-china-captured-aksai-chin-1691562-2020-06-22. Accessed on 9 Sept. 2020.
24. Hoffman, Steven A. (1990), *India and the China Crisis*, Berkeley: University of California Press. pp. 101-04.
25. Aneek Chatterjee (2010), *op. cit.*
26. R.S. Kalha (2012), "What did China Gain at the End of the Fighting in November 1962?", *IDSA Comment*, November 21; on line source: https://idsa.in/idsacomments/WhatdidChinaGain%20attheEndoftheFighting_RSKalha_211112. Accessed on 2 Sept. 2020.
27. Sudheendra Kulkarni (2018), "The one who reached out to China: On Atal Bihari Vajpayee", *The Hindu*, September 11.
28. Gareth Price (2007), "China and India: Cooperation and Competition". *Asia Programme Briefing Paper*. ASP BP 07/01, London: Chatham House.
29. Embassy of India, Beijing (2012), "India-China Bilateral Relations-Defense Relations"; on line source: www.indianembassy.org.cn. Accessed on 3 Sept. 2020.
30. N. Ram (2020), "A Successful atmosphere building visit". *Frontline*. Vol. 17 (Issue-12), 10-23 June.
31. Government of India, Ministry of External Affairs (2005), "Report of the India-China Joint Study Group on Comprehensive Trade and Economic Cooperation". 11 Apr; on line source: http://mea.gov.in/Uploads/PublicationDocs/6567_bilateral-documents-11-april-2005.pdf. Accessed on 3 Sept. 2020.
32. *Times of India* (2009), "China objects to ADB funds for Arunachal: Krishna", 09 July.

33. Brahma Chellaney (2007), "Quad Initiative: An Inharmonious Concert of Democracies", *Japan Times,* 19 July; on line source: www.japantimes.co.jp. Accessed on 3 Sept. 2020.

34. Alistair Scrutton (2010), "India PM warns China wants foothold in South Asia". *Reuters*; on line source www.Reuters.com. Accessed on 7 Sept. 2020.

35. Jingdong Yuan (2017), "Sino-Indian Relations in the Modi-Xi Era", *Future Directions International*, 14 February; on line source: https://www.futuredirections.org.au/publication/sino-indian-relations-modi-xi-era/. Accessed on 7 Sept. 2020.

36. Ministry of External Affairs, Govt. of India (2017), "India China Bilateral Relations"; on line source: https://mea.gov.in/Portal/ForeignRelation/China_October_2017.pdf. Accessed on 8 Sept. 2020.

37. Jingdong Yuan (2017), *op. cit.*

38. Darshana Barua (2018), "India's Answer to the Belt and Road: A Road Map for South Asia", *Carnegie India Paper,* August; on line source: https://carnegieindia.org/2018/08/21/india-s-answer-to-belt-and-road-road-map-for-south-asia-pub-77071. Accessed on 8 Sept. 2020.

39. *The Hindu Business Line* (2019), "Modi-Xi informal summit: Key takeaways", October 14; on line source: https://www.thehindubusinessline.com/news/modi-xi-informal-summit-key-takeaways/article29680297.ece. Accessed on 8 Sept. 2020.

40. BBC News (2020), "India-China clash: 20 Indian troops killed in Ladakh fighting", 16 June; on line source: https://www.bbc.com/news/world-asia-53061476. Accessed on 10 Sept. 2020.

41. Manoj Kewalramani (2020), "Arriving at a new normal in India-China relations", *The Hindustan Times*, July 3.

42. John Hurley et al. (2018), "Examining the Debt Implications of the Belt and Road Initiative from a Policy Perspective," *CGD Policy Paper*, March; on line source: https://www.cgdev.org/sites/default/files/examiningdebt-implications-belt-and-road-initiative-policy-perspective.pdf. Accessed on 8 Sept. 2020.

43. Stanly Johny (2020), "Why China is being aggressive along the LAC", *The Hindu*, June 26.

7

India and Important Powers: Russia, Japan

Jayita Mukhopadhyay

INDIA AND RUSSIA

Relations between India and Russia are rooted in history, mutual trust and mutually beneficial cooperation. This is a partnership that has withstood the test of time, and which enjoys the support of the people of both countries. In the period immediately following independence the goal for India was attaining economic self-sufficiency through investment in heavy industry. The Soviet Union invested in several new enterprises in the areas of heavy machine-building, mining, energy production and steel plants. During India's second Five Year Plan of the sixteen heavy industry projects set up, eight were initiated with the help of the Soviet Union. This included the establishment of the world famous IIT Bombay.

A watershed moment in relations between India and the Soviet Union was the signing of the Treaty of Peace and Friendship in August 1971. The Treaty was the manifestation of shared goals of the two nations as well as a blueprint for the strengthening of regional and global peace and security. The nineties were a tumultuous period for both countries. In 1990, India extended loans to the USSR in the form of technical credit and in 1991, India extended food credit and gift of 20,000 tonnes of rice.[1]

After the end of the Cold War, disintegration of Soviet Union and emergence of the Russian Federation as the principal inheritor of Soviet legacy, both India and Russian Federation faced the challenge of adjusting to the post-Cold War New International Order and to recalibrate and rejuvenate their relationship.

Relationship in the Post-Cold War Era

Though India's strategic partnership with the erstwhile Soviet Union was indeed an advantage for developing relationship with the post-Soviet newly independent states, in the changed situation, there was a need to shift its focus, from the larger canvas of the former Soviet Union to a smaller canvas to renew and build close strategic ties with each of these fifteen new Republics and particularly Russia. Since 1991 the strategic relationships between India and these states of former Soviet Union have come a long way, but there are lot more potential that exists for cooperation which needs to be nurtured by both the sides. Russia is one country that India could not afford to ignore, as it is the only trusted partner with whom India had mutual compatibility and a close political, military and economic partnership for decades. Russia and the former Soviet Union, contributed to creating India's key strengths and capabilities in the nuclear, defence, space, and heavy industry sectors when no other country was willing to support India's endeavours to modernize.

For the newly created Russian Federation also, adjustment to the post-Cold War order was an uphill task. Russia, the most prominent among the successor states of the former Soviet Union, in spite of inheriting the formidable military power of its predecessor, found itself suddenly reduced to a regional power. Economic chaos and political uncertainty at the internal level further compounded its predicament. Besieged as they were by the domestic constraints, the new rulers of Russia were initially not in a position to clearly define the foreign policy goals of the nascent state and ascertain its position in the post-Cold War International Order. With the ideology as the 'guiding principle' of the state policy having been abandoned, the new Russian ruling elite, in order to carve out a new international role for Russia, found itself suffering from a priority cleavage.

It was clearly pulled between a declining nostalgia for past relations with countries like India and a growing proclivity towards cultivating closer ties with the west. However, it is worth recognizing that after getting over their initial confusion and hesitation, India and Russia could soon get into the process of rediscovering their bilateral level common interests which are multidimensional in nature.

In early nineties, there was a growing appreciation for each other in both these countries as both are multinational, multi-ethnic, and multi-linguistic states. Boris Yeltsin, first President of newly formed Russian Federation lauded India as a major democratic federal state of the world, and observed that consensus was necessary to transform any society to avoid conflicts and to adjust to economic, political, technical, and military realities of the post-Cold War era. He affirmed that Russia attaches great importance to India's efforts to balance different interests as well as linguistic and religious groups, Yeltsin also declared that India's motto of 'unity in diversity' could be an effective formula for solving endemic social and political problems of the post-soviet Russia.[2]

When Russian President, Boris Yeltsin came to India in January 1993, his words and observations presented a summary of the then bilateral relations between the two countries. In his speech to the Indian Parliament on 29 January 1993, he admitted the difficulties for which he had to look to the West to pull Russia out of the morass in which the country found itself. Hence, in this phase India and Russia found entangled in a wed of controversies and differences, e.g. cryogenic deal, arms transfer, rupee-rouble exchange, Kashmir issue, etc. The Commonwealth of Independent States (CIS) which came into being after the disintegration of USSR, did not accord privileged position to India which it enjoyed earlier. However, Yeltsin clarified that all the commitments made to India with regard to supply of military hardware spares of various types by the earlier government would be honoured. This provided great relief to India. During his two-day visit, Yeltsin signed a series of agreements with Indian leaders that sought to end differences on economic and military cooperation. A central issue over the last years had been the size of India's debt to Russia, which had been in dispute because of the rapidly falling value of the Ruble.

Under the terms of the new settlement, India's debt fell from about US$ 11 billion to about US$ 8 billion. Shiv Mukherjee, an Indian spokesman, said, "As part of the economic package, India and Russia scrapped a 15-year agreement that permitted trading in rupees and rubles. Instead, they will now conduct trade in hard currency." The rupee-ruble arrangement developed as an integral part of Indian-Soviet relations and helped India, as a specially favoured trading partner, pay for MIG fighter jets and other Soviet military equipment with its own currency, saving tens of billions of dollars in foreign exchange at the time. Moscow had been the largest sellers of arms to India. India and Russia agreed to increase military cooperation and develop joint military production projects. The supplies of spare parts and equipment, which had slowed in preceding years, were to be hastened under this accord. Mr. Yeltsin said the two sides were also negotiating the purchase of advanced jet trainer fighters for the Indian Air Force.[3]

The high point of his visit was a Peace and Friendship Treaty signed with Prime Minister P.V. Narasimha Rao which pledged co-operation in the economic, political and other fields. The forerunner of this treaty was the historic Indo-Soviet Friendship Treaty initialled between Indira Gandhi and Leonid Brezhnev. However, the new treaty did not contain the strategic security clause under which the erstwhile Soviet Union and India were committed to each other's defence. Russia again offered full support to India on the Kashmir issue and asserted that Kashmir was an integral part of India. Further Russia ruled out third party intervention in bilateral matters and agreed to implement the agreement on space cooperation, including supply of cryogenic engines.[4]

Narasimha Rao, the first Prime Minister of India to assume office after the Cold War, visited Russia in July 1994. Rao's visit to Russia removed several bottlenecks in defence, strategic, and trade ties. At a joint press conference in Moscow, Rao talked about how the prospects for Indo-Russian relations are "very bright" and Yeltsin chipped in with "we have a smoothly running mechanism for cooperation". Various agreements, agreements and proposals were signed during the visit. The important ones are:

- Two declarations and nine agreements covering mutual strategic interest, defence—extending an $830 million credit—trade, and technology, among others.
- An agreement for setting up a ₹ 40-crore joint venture for upgrading and servicing Russian aircraft.
- Proposals to streamline trade and business ties, promoting joint ventures and upgrading port facilities, possibly using part of India's ₹ 30,000-crore debt.[5]

Political observers saw the visit of Russian Prime Minister Viktor Chernomyrdin to India in December 1994 that occasioned the signing of the eight agreements as a sign of a return to the earlier course of warm relations between New Delhi and Moscow. In March 1995, India and Russia signed agreements aimed at suppressing illegal weapons smuggling and drug trafficking.[6]

Relationship in the New Century

Indo-Russian relations continued to be strengthened by Putin and Vajpayee Governments. President Putin paid a highly successful visit to India in October 2000. The two countries chalked out steps to set their bilateral relationship on a new footing reworking past agreements on bilateral cooperation. Putin and Vajpayee signed the overreaching declaration on Strategic Partnership. Since the signing of "Declaration on the India-Russia Strategic Partnership" in October 2000, India-Russia ties acquired a qualitatively new character with enhanced levels of cooperation in almost all areas of the bilateral relationship including political, security, defence, trade and economy, science and technology, and culture. Under the strategic partnership, several institutionalized dialogue mechanisms started operating at both political and official levels to ensure regular interaction and follow up on cooperative activities. This was in addition to ten other agreements signed by the two countries setting out the building blocks for further cooperation. President Putin "breached the long standing international nuclear blockade against India by committing Russia to expand atomic energy cooperation with India". Both the countries committed the two countries to "non-participation in any military, political or other alliances or associations or armed conflicts directed against the other side, or in any treaties agreements or understandings infringing upon the independence, sovereignty, territorial integrity or national security interests of the other side."[7]

Besides strategies partnership and trade and cultural cooperation, the two countries also pledged to fight international terrorism. Addressing the Indian Parliament, Putin said that Indian was as much a victim of "terrorist international" in Kashmir as Russia was in Chechnya. Condemning terrorism, President Putin said that, it was often the same individuals, the same terrorist organization who were conducting terrorist act from "the Philippines to Kosovo including Kashmir, Afghanistan and Northern Caucasus". Prime Minister Vajpayee described terrorism as one of the major challenges and pledged to fight it at all levels. India and Russia, victims of international terrorism, have had productive cooperation in combating the scourge terrorism. They coordinate their activities of combating cross-border terrorism on the basis of the Moscow Declaration signed by them in November 2001 and in the framework of the joint working group on combating international terrorism. Both sides, holding the view that international terrorism is a threat to peace and security, a grave violation of human rights and a crime against humanity, maintained that there can be no justification whatsoever for any act of terrorism, and that multi-ethnic democratic countries like India and Russia are especially vulnerable to acts of terrorism which are attacks against the values and freedoms enshrined in their societies. Pointing an accusing finger towards Pakistan, the joint statement condemned the states that aid, abet or shelter terrorists, charging them with being guilty of acts terrorism as their actual perpetrators. In the aftermath of September 11, 2001 terrorist attack in New York and Washington, DC, Russia, like India, fully supported international struggle to defeat terrorism, though neither of the two countries contributed troops to the US-led coalition.[8]

In their own ways, both India and Russia struggled to define their relations with other major players on the global stage in a post-11 September global context where the rules of international politics were in a state of flux and where the terms of the economic interaction between nations were being re-set. Therefore, their continued affirmation of a long-standing friendship assumed more than just a symbolic importance. There was a real-convergence of perspectives on issues as vide ranging as the promotion of multipolarity in global politics, the scourge of terrorism, nuclear proliferation and security issues facing south, central and west Asia. During Putin's visit to India in December 2002, while India, agreed to intensify the strategic partnership with Russia, the latter supported India's position on Pakistan and asked it to end support for cross-border terrorism. The Russian endorsement of the Indian position on terrorism on Pakistan reflected its desire to maintain traditional goodwill in relations by showing sensitivity to India's security concerns. India and Russia shared identical views on the situation in Afghanistan, situated in the common neighbourhood of both the strategic partners, and focused on economic reconstruction of the war-ravaged nation. The joint statement could not have been more explicit with the two sides expressing concern over the deteriorating security situation in Afghanistan, and emphasizing that successful stabilization in that country. Both sides underscored the importance of stepped-up action by the international security assistance force in combating production and trafficking of illegal narcotics in Afghanistan. Both countries agreed to expand their relations in the aerospace sphere, an area of traditional cooperation for decades. Apart from the Russian assistance in the Chandrayan-2 manned space mission, a youth satellite, India would participate in the GLONASS Satellite navigation programmed. Under a deal India would receive high-precision navigation signals from GLONASS for civilian as well as military purposes; this would help India in its socio-economic development and fight against cross-border terrorism. GLONASS is the Russian equivalent of the United States' global positioning system that permits users to determine a near precise position of any object within meters. Since 1991, both India and

Russia launched market reforms. The Indian economy recorded an impressive annual growth at an average rate of about 7 percent. Its forex reserve touched about US$ 200 billion mark. Similarly, the Russian economy especially after 1998 registered tremendous growth mainly due to high energy prices. However, in spite of tremendous boost in economy of both the countries and in spite of having huge potentials of economic cooperation, the relation did not witness any substantial achievement in economic front.

Indian Prime Minister Manmohan Singh's visit to Moscow from December 4-6, 2005 highlighted the continued importance of Indo-Russian cooperation in a changing geopolitical scenario. Beginning with President Vladimir Putin's first visit to India in October 2000, bilateral summits between the Indian Prime Minister and the Russian President, alternatively in each other's capital, become an annual feature. In contrast, President Putin's predecessor President Boris Yeltsin visited India only once, in January 1993. Undoubtedly, the coming to power of President Putin reinvigorated India-Russia ties. In a statement to the press at the conclusion of his visit, Manmohan Singh spoke of the need "to anticipate what measures we need to take to meet new and emerging opportunities for further strengthening of our strategic partnership, in meeting our respective national priorities as well as in pooling our efforts in sharing global responsibilities". Manmohan Singh gave the assurance of India's support for Russia's accession to WTO (World Trade Organisation) and emphasised that the bilateral Accession Agreement shall be concluded at the earliest. President Putin responded by stating that "Russia welcomes the fact that India has the status of observer in the Shanghai Cooperation Organisation. We intend to work closely with our Indian partners in the multilateral organizations in the Asia-Pacific region." Russia had also been persistently pushing tripartite interaction among the three largest states of the continent: Russia, India, and China. Consequently, a mechanism of regular interaction among the foreign ministers of the three countries during the UN General Assembly sessions in September of each year was established.[9]

Upon conclusion of the Summit-level talks, the following documents were signed:

- Agreement between the Government of India and the Government of the Russian Federation on Reciprocal Protection of Intellectual Property Rights in the field of Military-Technical Cooperation.
- Agreement between the Government of India and the Government of the Russian Federation on Safeguard Technologies while implementing long-term cooperation in the area of joint development, operation and use of the GLONASS System for peaceful purposes.
- Agreement between the Indian Space Research Organization and the Federal Space Agency of the Russian Federation on Cooperation in the field of solar physics and solar-terrestrial relationships within the framework of the Coronas-Photon Project.

The two countries took stock of progress in the implementation of the agreements reached during the official visit of the President of the Russian Federation to India in December 2004. Expressing satisfaction at the results achieved, they agreed that the range and depth of bilateral cooperation could be further expanded, particularly in priority areas such as energy security, trade and economic, high technologies, exploration of outer space, peaceful uses of nuclear energy and military-technical cooperation.[10]

The maiden visit of President Dmitry Medvedev to India in December 2008 yielded significant results. He was the first world leader to visit India after the 26/11 terrorist attack on Mumbai and hence, discussion on countering terrorism was placed on the top of the agenda. Expressing strong solidarity with the Indian Government and people, Medvedev pledged to "work with India on a whole spectrum of the problem and provide support in all directions". The Joint Declaration, signed by President Medvedev and Prime Minister Manmohan Singh, urged the international community to provide all assistance to bring to justice the organisers of the latest terrorist attack on India's financial capital. The statement called upon all countries to actively cooperate with India in its effort to find the perpetrators, masterminds, sponsors and everyone connected with the barbaric act. One of the major achievements of the visit was the new thrust that Indo-Russian peaceful nuclear cooperation received as a result of the summit. Apart from signing an agreement for construction of four more reactors at the Kudankulam Plant in Tamil Nadu where Russia was already in the final stages of building two reactors, both sides expressed the desire to build additional reactors there as well as go for new nuclear plants elsewhere in the country, particularly in the east coast of India. A site would soon be identified on India's east coast where Russia would build six reactors. Russia would not only build these reactors, but it would also provide guarantee for lifetime supply of nuclear fuel to them.

During Medvedev's visit both countries signed a deal worth US$ 700 million for Russian nuclear fuel supply to India. These deals, coming as they did in the aftermath of the much-hyped Indo-US nuclear agreement, signified that Delhi and Moscow were poised for some sort of strategic partnership in the sphere of nuclear cooperation.[11] Dmitry Medvedev held talks with Indian Prime Minister Manmohan Singh on a wide range of issues when Singh was Russia on an official visit in December 2009. The talks focused on key areas in Russian-Indian economic cooperation: energy, transport, the metals sector, information technology, the pharmaceutical industry, biotechnology, and military technical cooperation. Current international affairs were also on the agenda. Moscow and Delhi both supported speedy adoption of an international convention on combating terrorism, and the creation of a new global financial security architecture.

A joint declaration on deepening the two countries' strategic partnership in the aim of countering global challenges was adopted at the talks' conclusion. This document assessed the importance of the Russian-Indian strategic partnership and presented a common vision on establishing a polycentric international system for the twenty-first century. Medvedev and Singh presided over the signing of intergovernmental agreements on the 2011-20 military technical cooperation programme and post-sales service and maintenance of arms and military equipment supplied to India, and also a protocol to the intergovernmental agreement on cooperation in developing and manufacturing a multipurpose transport plane. An agreement between the Russian and Indian Governments on cooperation in the peaceful use of nuclear energy was initialled, and the 2010-12 cultural exchange programme between the two countries was approved. The talks also saw the signing of a loan agreement between Russian State Corporation Bank for Development and Foreign Economic Affairs (Vnesheconombank) and the Export-Import Bank of India.

Medvedev and Singh made press statements and answered journalists' questions following the talks. The latest summit was the third meeting between Medvedev and Singh this year: the two leaders met in June at the SCO and BRIC summits in Yekaterinburg, and in September at the G20 summit in Pittsburgh.[12] During the visit of the Russian President Medvedev's visit to India in December 2010, the Strategic Partnership was elevated to the level of a "Special and Privileged Strategic Partnership."[13]

Manmohan Singh described Indo-Russian relations as "special and privileged partnership" that produces steady benefits to both countries in "defence, space, hydrocarbons and nuclear energy" ahead of his visit to Russia in 2011. India and Russia signed several agreements covering defence, energy and trade during their 12th annual bilateral summit. "Both sides are also working to put in place a system to ensure rapid commercialization of R&D that is being done in laboratories. This includes the establishment of India-Russia Centres of Science and Technology in each other countries," the Prime Minister said. The Russian part of the centre was inaugurated in Moscow just hours before the PM's flight landed in Moscow. The Prime Minister assured Russia that India would fulfil all its commitments on bilateral nuclear cooperation while according top priority to safety issues and concerns raised by people in Kundankulam.

Manmohan Singh praised Indo-Russian defence cooperation as "an important pillar of our strategic partnership" and "an essential link in our multifaceted relations." He described Russia as "a most reliable partner" in defence. The Prime Minister noted convergence of views between the two sides on international issues like the revival of the global economy, cooperation within BRICS, the situation in West Asia and North Africa and the challenges in Afghanistan.[14]

The President of the Russian Federation, Vladmir V. Putin, paid an official visit to India on December 24, 2012 at the invitation of Prime Minister of the Republic of India Manmohan Singh for the Annual Summit between two countries. The Prime Minister of India and the President of the Russian Federation stressed the importance of further progressing the special and privileged strategic partnership between the two countries. They expressed satisfaction that the year 2012 was marked by an intense bilateral dialogue, regular top and high-level meetings and multifarious cultural activities to mark the 65th anniversary of the establishment of diplomatic relations between India and the Russian Federation.[15]

Ten bilateral documents were signed during Putin's visit. The Memorandum of Understanding (MoU) to establish an Indo-Russia Joint Investment Fund, worth US$ 2 billion, was created to encourage direct investment and acquisition of assets in critical infrastructural, manufacturing and hydrocarbon extraction sectors. The Joint Venture (JV) to set up a modern industrial facility for the manufacture of Russian helicopters in India was promote the development of a high technology-based domestic aerospace industry. The joint collaboration to manufacture pharmaceuticals in Russia along with the IT agreement for developing software, systems integration and emergency response systems was to help India in producing niche products. The pilot project to assess the feasibility of the Global Navigation Satellite System (GLONASS) in areas such as disaster management, telephony and long distance communications was to give India a useful alternative for the American Global Positioning System (GPS). The two contracts for the supply of 71 Mi-17 helicopters and 42 Sukhoi-30 MKI fighter jets worth US$ 3.5 to 4 billion were signed which further boosted India-Russia defence cooperation. While there are many areas of cooperation between the two countries, yet some irritants continued to trouble the relationship. It is important to highlight some of these, which need to be addressed in order to further cement bilateral ties. India's weapons diversification policy also remains a matter of concern for Russia since India accounts for close to 30 per cent of Russian revenues from arms exports. In certain quarters in the Russian establishment, this issue is looked at through the broader framework of India's perceived drift towards the West. From India's perspective, the repeated delay in the delivery of the aircraft carrier Vikramaditya and reports of technical problems affecting the leased Akula nuclear submarine were issues of concern. Bilateral trade continued to be the most unsatisfactory part of the Indo-Russian partnership, with total trade standing at less than US$ 10 billion. While there had been a 30 per cent increase in trade in 2012 as compared to the previous year, the true economic potential remained untapped. Thus, there was positive outcome of Putin's visit as well as unresolved issues which needed attention. Nevertheless, Manmohan Singh's statement about 'Indo-Russian partnership having a special place in the hearts and minds of Indians' and his 'commitment to further strengthen ties' did hold promise for the future and underscored that India and Russia cannot afford to dilute their bilateral relations as they both require each other.[16]

In 2014, India saw a change of government with Narendra Modi of BJP taking over as prime minister. For Russia, it was a year when its focus was firmly on the domestic situation after the Ukrainian crisis and annexation of Crimea, and the resulting deterioration of ties with the West. Both these events would influence the foreign policy trajectories of the two governments in the coming years, albeit in different ways. For Russia, this led to a growing dependence on China both economically and strategically. India, responding to a rising power in its backyard, had already been moving towards building closer ties with the US, which had introduced its own pivot to Asia. This focus was carried forward by the newly-elected Modi Government, witnessed in a steady rise in economic and defence ties between

India and the US. India also strengthened its relations with Japan, West Asia and the immediate neighbourhood in the five-year period. In a nutshell, PM Modi's foreign policy has been marked by whirlwind visits across the globe aimed at revitalising ties with a host of countries. This sense of exuberance, however, was missing in the country's relations with Russia in the years immediately following Modi's assumption to the prime ministership.

At the systemic level, the period 2014-18 saw a continuation of the changes underway in the global order, with the decline of US primacy and the rise of other emerging powers, particularly China. This has led to an attempt by these powers to shore up their influence, especially in Asia reflected in China advancing its Belt and Road Initiative (or BRI, which India opposed), the enunciation of the 'Indo-Pacific' (opposed by Russia and China) and Russia's aim of a "greater Eurasian partnership."[17]

Political Relations

Political relations between India and Russia, as has already been noted, have historically been steady and cordial. The two countries have had the advantage of what analysts refer to as a "problem-free environment" despite a weak economic base. A total of 19 annual summits have been held uninterrupted, alternately in India and Russia, since they were first instituted in 2000. The leaders of the two countries also meet regularly at the meetings—or on the side-lines—of various multilateral organisations like the grouping of Brazil, Russia, India, China, and South Africa (BRICS), the Shanghai Cooperation Organization (SCO) and G20. Indeed, it was Russia that pushed for India's entry into SCO; India became a full member in 2017. A major reason for this was Moscow's desire to prevent the organisation from being dominated by China, a concern that was shared by the Central Asian states as well. China, while initially resistant to the idea, agreed on the condition that Pakistan too joined the multilateral body.

The two sides also signed the 'Strategic Vision for Strengthening Cooperation in Peaceful Uses of Atomic Energy' in 2014 and agreed on the 'Partnership for Global Peace and

Stability' in 2016. In early 2019, Russia bestowed the Order of St Andrew the Apostle on PM Modi for his "distinguished contribution to the development of a privileged strategic partnership between Russia and India and friendly ties between the Russian and Indian peoples".[18]

Economic Relations

The 2014 joint statement issued by India and Russia—meant to provide a vision for the coming decade for their relationship—identified the areas of energy, technology, and innovation and economic cooperation as focal points. Some of the recommendations included participating in oil, gas, petrochemical and power projects in each other's countries, joint design and development of technology in areas like space, defence, aviation, IT, new materials as well as an increased focus on high-technology sectors—while declaring that they will "facilitate the full realization" of "enormous untapped potential in bilateral trade, investment and economic cooperation."

Nevertheless, the balance of trade remains in favour of Russia and the deficit has risen two times in the last decade to reach $ 3.1 billion in 2014. The energy sector saw a certain

Table 7.1: India-Russia Bilateral Trade (2010-20)

Year	Bilateral Trade (US$ Billion)
2010	8.5
2011	8.9
2012	11.04
2013	10
2014	9.51
2015	7.83
2016	7.71
2017	10.17
2018	8.40
2019	8.11
2020	6.50

Source: Ministry of External Affairs, Indian Embassy in Moscow.[19] Also, Exim Data Bank, Ministry of Commerce and Industry, Government of India.

degree of forward movement in 2015, with an MoU signed regarding exploration and production of hydrocarbons in Russia. Important agreements in the field of nuclear energy were finalised during 2014 and 2015.

Table 7.1 shows the slow growth in the bilateral trade, which has hovered between US$ 7-10 billion for almost a decade now. There are several factors that have contributed to this weakness in India and Russia's economic ties: lack of involvement of the private sector; absence of logistics; poor connectivity; and more recently, the stalling of the International North-South Economic Corridor, resulting in higher costs.

Defence and Cultural Relations

While India and Russia's economic relationship has been a weak point in the post-Cold War period, the most glaring sign of the stagnation may yet be that in 2014, the US emerged as the top arms supplier to India, pushing Russia to the second position based on data for the preceding three years. At the same time, India became the top foreign buyer of US weapons in 2014. Given that the military-technical ties were historically the bedrock of India and Russia's relationship, a drop in the sector was a clear matter of concern.

While in overall terms, Russia remained India's top supplier of defence items during the period 2014-18, the total exports fell by 42 percent between 2014-18 and 2009-13. Russia still commands 58 percent of total arms imports by India, followed by Israel and the US at 15 and 12 percent, respectively. This figure, however, is a step down from 2010-14 when Russia had a share of 70 percent of the Indian defence market. Despite this, Russia's market share ensures that the country remains a critical supplier to India, both of new arms and spare parts. The military-technical cooperation that includes transfer of technology and joint production is a unique relationship that is extremely valuable to India.

The first ever Tri Services exercise under the annual INDRA format and joining of India as a full member of SCO were positive developments of 2017. The year 2017 was especially significant, being the 70th anniversary of establishment of diplomatic relations between the two countries. India participated as Guest Country in the St. Petersburg International Economic Forum-2017. The Prime Minister of India Shri Narendra Modi was the Guest of Honour. During this time the 18th Annual Bilateral Summit was also held, which saw the adoption of the historic St. Petersburg Declaration: Vision for the 21st Century, and signing of 12 Agreements in economic and political areas. Both countries celebrated the 70th anniversary by organizing events across the length and breadth of the countries reflecting the deep and multifaceted relationship.[20]

There are 20 educational institutions across Russia that teach Indian languages. Latest figures suggest that about 11,000 Indian students are studying in Russia, primarily in medical and technical courses. The number of tourists from Russia to India has been on the rise, and in 2017 it was the eighth largest source of foreign arrivals to India.

The Sochi Informal Summit

In May 2018, it was announced that PM Modi will meet President Putin for an informal summit at Sochi, the first interaction in such format with the Russian leader. The announcement came just a month after the Wuhan informal summit between PM Modi and Chinese President Xi Jinping. While the latter had followed the Doklam standoff in July-August 2017, with an aim to remove "misconceptions", and seek areas of cooperation, no specific reason was given for the summit with Russia except for "further strengthening our Special and Privileged Strategic Partnership." Coming only four months before the October 2018 annual summit between India and Russia, the Sochi Summit was an acknowledgement of the need to bring about a change in the relationship. The change was reflected in the joint statement, titled "Enduring Partnership in a Changing World", that contained several concrete plans for the year: the "conclusion of the contract for supply of S400"; first meeting of India's NITI Aayog and Russia's Ministry of Economic Development; start of talks on a free trade agreement (FTA) between Eurasian Economic Union (EAEU) and India; launch of single-window service in Russia for Indian companies; launch of Russia Plus in India to help Russian companies invest in India; holding of the India-Russia Business Summit; setting up of the Far East Agency in Mumbai; signing of the India-Russia Economic Cooperation: The Way Forward (March 2018); and the beginning of LNG supply from Gazprom (contract with GAIL). There were over 50 ministerial level visits to enhance the ties. Apart from the US$ 5.2-billion S400 deal, the year also saw the finalisation of four frigates—two to be purchased from Russia (US$ 950 million) while two will be made at Goa Shipyard Limited (US$ 500 million).

The US$ 400 deal, despite the threat of it attracting Countering America's Adversaries through Sanctions Act (CAATSA), was a sign of India's desire to maintain its strategic autonomy as well as build on its strong defence relationship with Russia.[21]

Some of the defence deals signed with Russia in 2019 included a US$ 3-billion deal for a nuclear submarine to replace INS Chakra, the approval for purchase of 464 T-90 tanks for $ 2 billion, and the launch of the joint project to manufacture of AK-203/103 rifle in Amethi in the state of Uttar Pradesh. Further, under emergency procurement, the defence ministry approved the purchase of US$ 1.47 billion 'Igla-S Very Short Range Air Defence Systems' (VSHORAD) from Russia. There was also an attempt to shore up the bilateral economic relationship with PM Modi being invited as the main guest for the Eastern Economic Forum in 2019. The first India-Russia Strategic Economic Dialogue was held in November 2018 to find ways to improve economic ties. It must be noted that several mechanisms already exist at the bilateral level with regard to trade issues, but they are not very effective even as they have been around for more than a decade. Therefore, it remains to be seen if the latest initiatives would lead to a qualitative change in economic ties with Russia or merely follow the older pattern of inertia.

Changing International Context Affecting the Relationship

The Indo-Russia relationship faces increasing stress from the evolving international scenario characterised by the rise of China and the impact it has on the broader regional and global order. India and Russia have followed remarkably different policies in dealing with this phenomenon, most visibly in Asia. In 2012, President Putin had called India a "key strategic partner in the Asia-Pacific region," which assumed significance in light of an Asia "where China is looming increasingly large," leading the two to "revise their relationship."[22] This was also the year when Moscow's pivot to Asia was confirmed through the APEC summit, a concept in which India occupied an important position. However, subsequent events have led to a deepening of Russia-China strategic partnership due to a commonality of interests in political, economic and strategic domains while a similar level of engagement with other countries of Asia has not been realised. India is by no means an exception to this broader Russian policy drawback in Asia. However, given that Russia has a long history of relations with India since its independence—unlike the case of East Asia where it was largely side-lined during the Cold War period—bilateral reasons are inadequate in explaining why the potential of the strategic partnership has not been realised. In this case, Sino-Russian relations have been an important factor. Russian Sinologist Alexander Lukin argues that the Russian officials have accepted that "cooperation with the West cannot be fully restored" after 2014, leading to a "methodical and deeply rooted pivot to China." Apart from the bilateral trade which touched over $ 100 billion in 2018, Russia also needs Chinese investment to fund its development needs. The two also share a common opposition to US hegemony and a focus on sovereignty, territorial integrity, non-interference in internal affairs, equality, and mutual benefit. The imposition of Western sanctions after the Ukrainian crisis and annexation of Crimea meant Russia had to look for a "strong external partner," leading to a "more ambitious pivot to China." On the ground, this meant sales of S400 air missile defence system and Su35 fighter jets (overturning a decades-old policy), which will directly "affect the balance of power in Taiwan" as well as beginning of joint naval exercises (2015).

On the economic front, Russia overtook Saudi Arabia as the leading oil supplier to China at certain points in 2015-16, reducing the restrictions around Chinese investment in the energy and infrastructure projects, signing of the largest ever

US$ 400 billion gas deal, proposal to connect Eurasian Economic Union to the Belt and Road Initiative after initial Russian hesitation regarding the latter as well as increase in cooperation in Central Asia. The 2016 Foreign Policy Concept of Russia also describes the "common principled approaches" of the two countries as one of the key elements "of regional and global stability." Russia concluded that in the prevailing scenario, a burgeoning relationship with China would best suit its national interests. It also needs to be acknowledged that in comparison, India would be hard-pressed to extend similar support to Russia due to its own economic limitations and strategic goals. Moreover, these developments in Sino-Russian relations happened at a time when India was decisively reaching out to the US, distancing itself from the "rhetoric of non-alignment" to lead to one of the "most intense bilateral engagements that New Delhi enjoys with any nation." India became a major defence partner of the US (2016), began the 2+2 dialogue (2018), and signed the Logistics Exchange Memorandum of Agreement (LEMOA, 2016) as well as the Communications Compatibility and Security Agreement (COMCASA, 2018). The idea of 'Indo-Pacific', too, had been gaining ground at this time, with the Indo-US joint statement of June 2017 officially including the nomenclature in the bilateral document. Meanwhile, the allegation of Russian interference into the 2016 US presidential elections caused further divide between the two. In other words, Russia has directed its policy so as to counter the US predominance, one that India has shown no interest in backing due to its desire to improve its economic status and further relations with all major powers.

Indeed, India has ramped up its engagement with other major powers like Japan, Israel, Germany, and France. In the case of Japan, which was building its own idea of Free and Open Indo-Pacific (FOIP), it has consisted of an increased focus on relationship with India. Fuelled by economic complementarities and concerns over a rising China, the two countries have taken important steps to build a 'Special Strategic and Global Partnership.' The two are also collaborating on various connectivity projects in Asia and Africa (Asia-Africa Growth Corridor)—finding synergies in India's Act East policy and

FOIP. These developments have taken place alongside regular meetings of foreign secretary level trilateral of Japan, Australia, India since 2015; the first 'formal official level discussions' under the Quad Framework (2017) and the maiden meeting of leaders of Japan, America, India (JAI) in 2018 on the side-lines of G20 summit. Interestingly, the meeting of JAI was followed by the first trilateral summit of Russia, India, China (RIC) in 12 years—at the initiative of Moscow. But the trilateral (RIC), which meets regularly at the level of foreign ministers, has seen only 'nominal', levels of cooperation, hobbled as it is by differences between India and China.[23]

Thus, foreign policy trajectories of India and Russia have been marked by widening divergences in recent years. This has been most prominently reflected in the Russian displeasure over the idea of the Indo-Pacific, with Russian Foreign Minister Sergei Lavrov calling it an "artificially imposed construct" being promoted by the US, Australia, and Japan to contain China. It became evident that Moscow's interpretation of the concept is different from that of New Delhi. The remarks, made in February 2019, came despite the fact that several months earlier in June 2018, PM Modi in his Shangri La speech made it clear that the concept of Indo-Pacific for India is based on "inclusiveness, openness and ASEAN centrality and unity" and not "as a strategy or as a club of limited members." Specifically mentioning Russia, the PM hailed it as a "measure of our strategic autonomy that India's Strategic Partnership, with Russia, has matured to be special and privileged." The Prime Minister also clarified that Indo-Pacific is not "directed against any country" and that India seeks to build through dialogue a common rules-based order in the region, "based on the consent of all, not on the power of the few."[24]

It must be noted that Russia has been sceptical about the Indo-Pacific as enunciated by the US, favouring the description as 'Asia-Pacific' instead. While the two countries still regard each other as valued partners with a friendship built on "deep mutual trust," their foreign policy goals are taking them in different directions. Russia needs China for its national interests; India has its own policy aims. As New Delhi seeks to increase its influence in Indo-Pacific through its Act East policy, it needs partners in a region where Russia has a much weaker presence. Russia's role in the Indo-Pacific will depend on how successful it is "in dealing with the fundamental problems hindering its economic development," making it only natural for India to look for partners that can help it achieve its goals in the region. The situation has also been complicated by their failure to find convergence on issues like multipolarity and the role of SCO. Russia's increased engagement with Pakistan has also not been received well in New Delhi. In 2014, Moscow removed the arms embargo imposed on Pakistan and sale of Mi-35 helicopters and engines for JF-17 Thunder went through. The two sides also began joint military exercises—much to the dismay of India—especially in 2016 when it was reported by Russian state-run news agency TASS that the drills would be held in Gilgit-Baltistan, an area India considers as being illegally occupied by Pakistan. To a certain extent, this was a message to India for its growing closeness to the US; at the same time, Moscow is looking at Pakistan with reference to its policy on Afghanistan and wider stability in Central Asia and Caucasus—where differences have now emerged with New Delhi. Zamir Kabulov, Russia's special representative to Afghanistan, has gone on record to say that it would not be possible to eliminate terrorism "without the cooperation of Pakistan." India does not agree with Russia's treatment of Pakistan as "part of the solution rather than part of the problem."[25]

Future Trends

India and Russia continue to share a common strategic rationale for their relationship: apart from bilateral synergies, the two are members of various multilateral organisations including BRICS, RIC, G20, East Asia Summit and SCO—where avenues for cooperation on issues of mutual importance exist. There is also a need for cooperation in areas like counterterrorism, cyber security, the Afghanistan conflict, outer space, and climate change. The fact that Russia holds a permanent seat at the UN Security Council and has been a supporter of India on various issues including Kashmir at the international forum is of critical importance for New Delhi.

India would do well to take steps to shore up its relations with Russia to prevent it from becoming more dependent than it already is on China. At the same time, Russia would also benefit from diversifying its relations across the region, including India, so as to prevent its pivot to Asia becoming a pivot to China.

India and Russia will have to diversify their areas of cooperation beyond energy and defence. The trade relationship remains weak and needs active intervention to take advantage of policies like 'Make in India'. Also, concrete proposals in the areas already identified by the two countries need to be identified and implemented on a priority basis, including start-ups, infrastructure, shipbuilding, river-navigation, high speed railways, space, food processing, and high-technology products.

China and India's current impasse poses a huge political challenge for Russia; staying out of border tensions between the two countries is in line with Moscow's interests in forging diversified political contacts. Russia, as already noted, has established long-term strategic ties with both India and China, and would not want to jeopardise it by lending support to either country. When India announced on August 30 that it will not participate in the Kavkaz-2020 military exercise in southern Russia, the official reason New Delhi provided for this decision was difficulties associated with the COVID-19 pandemic. But, according to experts, the real reason for India to skip the event is due to the participation of the Chinese military in the exercises.[26]

Many foreign policy experts are of the opinion that India should not fear the closeness in Russia-China ties, as it is of temporary nature and a result of the current geopolitical setup. Russia is seeking to regain its status as a great power therefore it will continue to view China as a potential strategic adversary of the future. A problematic area for cooperation between China and Russia is that of the Eurasian Economic Union. Economic integration in Eurasia was originally pursued by Russia with no immediate concern and/or interest for China. However, it is becoming clear that China has developed strong interests in this region. While each country has pursued independent projects in Central Asia, they will both struggle for domination in the region and hence conflict of interest is inevitable between them.

Further, China does not recognise Crimea as part of Russia, and Russia takes a neutral stance on China's claims in the South China Sea.[27]

Indian Defence Minister Rajnath Singh visited Russia in June 2020 for the 75th Victory Day parade. He was in Moscow again on September 4 to attend the SCO Defence Ministers' Meeting. These visits saw detailed discussions around furthering the India-Russia defence relationship alongside the promise to accelerate certain supplies based on New Delhi's requirements. The September visit coincided with the biannual Indo-Russian naval exercises, INDRA, in the Andaman and Nicobar Islands, in the strategically crucial waters of the Indian Ocean. India's External Affairs Minister S. Jaishankar attended the online BRICS foreign ministers meeting on September 4 and also travelled to Moscow for the SCO Foreign Ministers meeting (September 9-10). These multilateral forums are useful tools to foster continued India-Russia cooperation at the bilateral and multilateral levels. While increasingly divergent foreign policies of its members pose challenges of agenda-setting and overall scope, it also underscores that at this moment of flux, India and Russia are keeping all their options open. Mr. Jaishankar has noted that we live in a 'curious world' where one cannot view engagement with different parties as a 'zero-sum game'. By implication, worsening India-China ties or a burgeoning China-Russia relationship does not automatically mean a breakdown of the India-Russia strategic partnership. In fact, India and Russia have spent the past few years strengthening their partnership, particularly since the 2018 Sochi informal summit. From substantive defence engagement to regional questions in Central Asia, Afghanistan and West Asia, a conversation with Moscow remains an important element of Indian foreign policy.

India and Russia are pragmatic players looking at maximising their strategic manoeuvrability, which understandably has led them to align with different powers based on their respective geopolitical positioning. Both recognise the value of having a diversified portfolio of ties. The relationship cannot flourish on defence and historical linkages alone. With systemic changes underway in international relations, new dimensions of cooperation need to be found to build a strong economic and strategic partnership. Both India and Russia will have to learn to navigate their relationship amidst challenges emerging not just from bilateral factors but also regional and global ones, as both countries seek to strengthen their position at a time of flux in the international order. In this context, it may be noted that the Russia-Ukraine war in early 2022 will not affect India-Russia relations much. Stable and burgeoning cooperation between the two countries is in the best of interest of both these countries and their citizens.

INDIA AND JAPAN

Relationship between India and Japan, two leading parliamentary democracies of Asia, dates back to the 6th century AD with the introduction of Buddhism in Japan. Through history, scholars and pilgrims travelled between the two countries and linked together the mind and spirit of people through socio-cultural exchanges. Japan's contribution in India's struggle for freedom directly or indirectly has been considerable. The victory of Japan over Russia in 1905 inspired the nationalist leaders of Asia particularly India who had launched an organized movement for the liberation of their country from British rule. Japan played an important role in providing shelter and place for refugees. It also cooperated to the Indian revolutionaries who had to escape from their country to avoid arrest by the British Government.

Relationship in Post-Independence Era

After the Second World War, Japan and India signed a peace treaty in 1952, with a declaration that "there shall be firm and perpetual peace and unity between India and Japan" and established diplomatic relations.[28] Pandit Jawaharlal Nehru visited Japan from 2 to 4 October 1957 and was warmly welcomed by Japanese people as well as its leadership. Summing up the result achieved by the visit, *The Hindu* wrote, "It appears to foreshadow an era of real cooperation between two Asian countries which had followed divergent paths in the past. Political cooperation is likely to follow in wake of economic collaboration and it will be a Red Letter Day for Asia, where the three leading nations of Asia, i.e. Japan, China and India establish friendly relations and help in raising the living standard of the less developed countries of South East Asia". For some time after the war, raw materials from India, particularly coal and iron ore helped in Japan's industrialisation programme and recovery from the devastation of war. After Japanese Prime Minister Nobusuke Kishi's visit to India in 1957, Japan started providing aid loans to India since 1958. In 1985, Prime Minister Rajiv Gandhi paid a visit to Japan which rekindled the spirit of friendship between the two countries. Since 1986, Japan has remained India's largest aid donor.

Japan adopted a pacifist constitution and refrained from playing interventionist role in world politics. Consequently, during the Cold War period, Indo-Japan relationship was on an even kill.

Soon after India launched its 'Look East' policy and the policy of economic liberalization, the policies received much encomium from Japan. This was reflected in the generous grant of Japanese loans in the early 1990s which helped the Indian economy in its time of crisis. The impact of the Look East policy is also reflected in India's negotiating free trade agreements with Japan, China, Thailand, Singapore and with ASEAN as a whole.

However, India's nuclear tests in 1998 was not received well by Japanese leadership and following US posturing, Japan imposed economic sanctions on India.

Relationship in the New Millennium

Relationship between the two countries was poised to improve considerably as in beginning of the new millennium as there was a perceptible softening in Japan's attitude towards India. Analysts pointed out that the warming of Indo-US relations did certainly bring about a major thaw in the Japanese attitude. Japanese Prime Minister Yoshiro Mori came to India in August 2000, on a four-day visit to India that marked the beginning of renewed India-Japan ties in security, economics, trade, and information technology. Mr. Mori declared with his Indian counterpart Mr. Atal Bihari Vajpayee that "Japan and India are global partners." The two nations signed an important agreement entitled "Japan-India Global Partnership in the 21st Century". This agreement called for enlargement of exchange and cooperation in economic fields, including information technology, between the two nations. Since Mori's visit, annual meetings of the top leaders of the two countries have been taking place regularly.

Prime Minister Vajpayee's visit to Japan in 2001 was again a landmark in the development of political engagement between India and Japan given that it marked the first visit to Japan by an Indian Prime Minister in almost a decade. The last official visit of an Indian Prime Minister was in 1992 when the Congress Party Prime Minister Narasimha Rao visited Japan. Mr. Vajpayee's visit was particularly significant in the context that the visit took place in the aftermath of the 9/11 terrorist attacks in the United States and the October 1, 2001 militant attacks on the Legislative Assembly of Jammu and Kashmir, perpetrated by Pakistan-based militant organizations. The Joint Declaration resulting from the interpersonal dialogue between the two Prime Ministers indicated that Japan had acquired a more realistic appreciation of India's threat perceptions and security concerns. This was evident in the 11-page Joint Declaration issued at the high level meeting between the Japanese Prime Minister Junichiro Koizumi and Mr. Vajpayee. The declaration talked about India and Japan working together for stability and prosperity in Asia, regularly exchanging views in all security-related matters, increasing military-to-military contacts, and working for the total elimination of terrorism in all regions, while extending the fight against terrorism to those who provide support and sustenance and safe haven to terrorists.

Some highlights of this declaration are:

- The two countries share the ideas of democracy and market economy, the spirit of tolerance, receptivity to diversity and the wisdom to benefit from the distinctive characteristics of their civilizations and cultures. In this perspective, the two leaders announced the common resolve that Japan and India should strengthen cooperation in order to contribute towards the stability and prosperity of Asia and the world in the 21st century.

- The two leaders renewed their recognition of the need for holding regular exchange of views at high levels, in order to facilitate the cross-sectoral dialogue on bilateral, regional, and international issues including regional cooperation. They confirmed to hold, in principle, Foreign Minister-level meetings once a year, making use of appropriate opportunities at multilateral meetings. They also confirmed their intention to further promote exchanges between their Defense, Economic and Finance Ministers.
- The two leaders acknowledged broad as well as deepened economic relations as an essential underpinning to strengthen the bilateral relationship. They shared the view that India's continuing economic reforms, Japan's recovery through structural reform and the existing complementarities between the two economies, will provide a solid foundation for further enhancing their economic relations. Both sides confirmed that it is necessary to reduce impediments to bilateral trade and investment and to encourage economic growth with due consideration to environmental preservation.
- The two leaders recognized that unbounded opportunities exist especially in the area of Information and Communication Technology in which there are extraordinary strong complementaries between Japan and India. They strongly encouraged the interactive efforts in the private sector, such as visits of business delegations, human exchanges, and closer dialogues on IT.
- At the onset of the 21st century, the two leaders confirmed their intention to strengthen the historical and amicable links between the two countries through the promotion of exchanges in culture, education, and science and technology. To that end, India will set up an Indian Cultural Centre in Tokyo. They also placed emphasis on encouraging a wide range of people-to-

people exchanges in all areas including exchanges between local bodies and the youth of both countries.

- The two leaders firmly maintained their position that terrorism cannot be justified wherever, whenever and for whatever reason. They also resolutely condemned terrorism in any form. They believed that the fight against global terrorism has to be comprehensive and sustained, with the objective of total elimination of terrorism in all regions. They shared the view that the fight is not only against the perpetrators of terrorist acts, but should encompass those who provide support, sustenance, and safe haven. In this regard, they shared the view on the importance of the implementation of UN Security Council Resolutions pertaining to terrorism and the twelve UN Counter-Terrorism Conventions. They condemned the barbaric terrorist attacks on 11 September in the USA that posed a grave challenge to the international community as a whole and had given them and the international community fresh cause to work together to counter terrorism with firm resolve. They recognized the importance of strengthening the international legal framework against terrorism.
- Both sides emphasized the need for constructive efforts on non-proliferation of weapons of mass destruction and their means of delivery.
- The two leaders confirmed that for long-term peace and stability in Afghanistan, the future government should be broad based, with fully representative of different ethnic and religious groups, should respect international law, establish good relations with all countries and should not be allowed to export terrorism.
- The two leaders acknowledged the vital importance of the role of the United Nations in world peace, stability, and prosperity, and reaffirmed their intention to work together for the early realization of UN reforms, starting with the reform of the Security Council,

including the expansion of both permanent and non-permanent membership.

- The two leaders recognized the importance of cooperation in matters pertaining to safety and security of international maritime traffic. The two leaders shared a strong commitment for an open and non-discriminatory rule-based multilateral trading system.
- Addressing global environmental problems, including protection of the global climate system, is one of the biggest challenges facing the human kind. Both sides welcomed the agreement reached on rules, procedures and modalities to implement the Kyoto Protocol.[29]

An important outcome of the Vajpayee visit was that India and Japan recognized that they have a convergence of national interests which supersedes any temporary irritant arising out of India's nuclear tests of 1998.

The Japanese Prime Minister Junichiro Koizumi's visit to India in April 2005 was another milestone in the trajectory of India-Japan relations. The April 2005 joint statement issued by the two Prime Ministers proclaimed the cooperation of the two states in promoting the stability of Asia and tackling environmental and other global-scale problems. The joint statement signed by Mr. Koizumi and Dr. Manmohan Singh laid down a concrete "eight-fold initiative" for strengthening the Indo-Japanese partnership. It provided an action plan of specific measures to strengthen relations in eight areas, including the economy, security, culture, and academia. The Japanese Prime Minister attached special importance to Japan's relations with India as Mr. Koizumi said:

> "I recognise that India is stridently emerging as a global power, aided by a robust economic growth, and that it has become a major country essential for peace, stability and prosperity of Asia and beyond. It is good to note that Japan and India are bound by shared values and principles, such as democracy, as well as the convergence of strategic interests. Therefore, Japan and India need each other as a strong, prosperous and

dynamic partner." Prime Minister Koizumi's choosing India as the first port of call in his four-nation visit to Asia and Europe (India, Pakistan, Luxembourg and Netherlands) indicated the rising status of India in Japan's foreign policy calculus. The Deputy Foreign Minister of Japan, Mitoji Yabunaka perceived that India is poised to become a critical partner of Japan in the emerging geopolitical scenario in Asia and it is in the interest of Japan to vigorously pursue its policy of engagement with India both at the bilateral and the multilateral levels.

Following the 2005 visit of Prime Minister Koizumi to India, the Indian Prime Minister Manmohan Singh visited Japan in December 2006. The visit of Manmohan Singh to Japan can be considered as a watershed in India-Japan relations. This is because for the first time the two countries forged a strategic partnership. The December 2006 Joint Statement issued by the Japanese Prime Minister Shinzo Abe and Indian Prime Minister Manmohan Singh, outlined a broad array of issues including political, defence, and security cooperation; development of infrastructure in India and promotion of bilateral trade and investment; comprehensive economic partnership including human resource development for the promotion of manufacturing; a science and technology initiative and people-to-people exchange.[30]

Prime Minister Shinzo Abe, who succeeded Junichiro Koizumi, has been perceived by analysts across the political spectrum in Japan and India as the most Indophile Prime Minister Japan ever had with a genuine interest in an emerging India. Abe came to India on an official visit in August 2007, as a part of an agreement between the two nations to have regular annual summits. Notable is that Japan has no similar summit mechanism with any other country. Abe was in India at a time when a big transformation was taking place in the region's geo-politics. Japan, a nation perceived so far as a political dwarf but an economic giant, was revamping its defence, security, and foreign policies, more independently than before; the rise of

China, North Korea's belligerence, and fresh compulsions arising out of energy security, were the main contributory factors.

Tokyo's revised foreign policy concept had come to centre round the 'arc of freedom and prosperity', encompassing the wide region in the outer rim of the Eurasian continent—extending from North Europe to the whole of Asia as well as Australia and New Zealand. On its part, a rising India was making efforts to play a role in Asia and the world, commensurate with its growing strength. Its Look East policy in particular assumed wider connotations, to cover the whole of Asia. India's stated vision evolved to be shaped in terms of creating an 'arc of advantage and prosperity across the Asian continent'. Foreign Secretary Shiv Shankar Menon's assurance that India's ties with Japan and China will not be a zero-sum game, indeed provided a positive atmosphere to Abe's visit.[31] During the visit, two Joint Statements on "The Roadmap for New Dimensions to the Strategic and Global Partnership between India and Japan" and on the "Enhancement of Cooperation on Environmental Protection and Energy Security" were signed. During this visit, Abe delivered the now-famous "Confluence of the Two Seas" speech—laying the foundation for his concept of Indo-Pacific. This concept has now become mainstream and one of the main pillars of India-Japan ties.[32]

Prime Minister Manmohan Singh paid an Official Working Visit to Tokyo from 21-23 October 2008 when a Joint Declaration on "Security Cooperation" and a Joint Statement on the "Advancement of Strategic and Global Partnership between India and Japan" were signed. Prime Minister Yukio Hatoyama visited India for the Annual Summit from 27-29 December 2009 during which a Joint Statement on "New Stage of Japan-India Strategic and Global Partnership" was signed.[33] The two Prime Ministers reiterated the importance of continuing the annual summit meetings. Both sides confirmed that the Economic Partnership Agreement (EPA) negotiations would be accelerated. Both sides confirmed that the Indian Institute of Technology Hyderabad (IITH) would become the model of Japan-India cooperation in the field of academic exchanges. Both sides also affirmed that bilateral cooperation on energy conservation and other fields will be promoted through the Japan-India Energy Dialogue. The two Prime Ministers welcomed the renewed international attention to the total elimination of nuclear weapons. On the issue of Climate Change, the two Prime Ministers welcomed the Copenhagen Accord and affirmed their resolve to continue to closely cooperate with each other in countering climate change. On the UN Security Council Reform, international finance and global economy, the Doha Development Round of the World Trade Organization (WTO) and counter-terrorism, the two ministers exchanged views and ensured cooperation between the two countries.[34]

Prime Minister Manmohan Singh paid an Official Working Visit to Tokyo from 24-26 October 2010 for the Annual Summit. During this summit meeting, the Indo-Japan strategic relationship reached a new height when Prime Minister Naoto Kan with his Indian counterpart decided to "steadily expand security and defence cooperation between India and Japan" and pledged to "cooperate to enhance their capacity in responding to security challenges such as maritime security which entails the safety and freedom of navigation and counter piracy, humanitarian assistance and disaster relief and response, inter alia, through bilateral and multilateral exercises, information sharing, training and dialogue". A Joint Statement "Vision for India-Japan Strategic and Global Partnership in the Next Decade" and a Joint Declaration on the India-Japan Comprehensive Economic Partnership Agreement (CEPA) were signed by the two Prime Ministers in Tokyo in October 2010.

The statements signed by the two countries and commitments made during the years suggested the fact that both countries saw each other as an important nation to safeguard for each country's national security. In Japanese strategic thinking India started figuring as an important partner as it realized that its security ally the US was overstretched with military missions in Iraq and Afghanistan and thus it was not focusing much on East Asian regional security. Japanese defence planners also noted that with the rise of China there had been a relative decline of US power in the region. Thus, they needed someone to fill the void. India certainly fitted in that calculation. Interactions between the two countries in subsequent years reflected this trend.[35]

Prime Minister of Japan Yoshihiko Noda paid a State visit to India from 27-29 December 2011 and the two Prime Ministers signed a Joint Statement entitled "Vision for the Enhancement of India-Japan Strategic and Global Partnership" upon entering the year of the 60th Anniversary of the establishment of diplomatic relations.

The year 2012 marked the 60th anniversary of establishment of diplomatic relations between India and Japan. During the year-long celebrations, more than 150 commemorative events were organized including performing arts, photo and art exhibitions, traditional crafts and textiles, fashion shows, food festivals, tourism fairs, literary and academic seminars and business promotion in more than 60 cities and 25 prefectures of Japan in co-ordination with Indian Council for Cultural Relations (ICCR) and other Indian and Japanese cultural organizations. ICCR sent three exhibitions and sponsored the visit of seven cultural troupes, comprising 100 outstanding Indian artistes to Japan during the course of the year.[36]

Manmohan Singh's 2013 visit to Japan also was a very fruitful one. The joint statement issued by Dr. Singh and Japanese Prime Minister Shinzo Abe, "Strengthening the Strategic and Global Partnership between India and Japan beyond the 60th Anniversary of Diplomatic Relations", delineated the major thrust areas of mutual cooperation. Some key areas were:

- The two Prime Ministers expressed satisfaction at the steady growth of political exchanges, dialogue, and policy coordination at all levels.
- The two Prime Ministers welcomed the expanding defence relations between the two countries based on the Joint Declaration on Security Cooperation between India and Japan.
- The two Prime Ministers expressed satisfaction that the first bilateral exercise between the Indian Navy (IN) and the Japan Maritime Self-Defense Force (JMSDF) was held in June 2012 off the coast of Japan and

decided to conduct such exercises on a regular basis with increased frequency. They decided to establish a Joint Working Group (JWG) to explore modality for the cooperation on the US-2 amphibian aircraft.

- Prime Minister Singh expressed his appreciation to the government and people of Japan for their continued and unwavering support to India's development. Prime Minister Abe reaffirmed that Japan would continue its Official Development Assistance at a substantial level to encourage India's efforts towards social and economic development, including in the area of infrastructure and human resource development. Noting that the Comprehensive Economic Partnership Agreement (CEPA) has given a fillip to economic and trade relations, the two Prime Ministers stressed the importance of continued efforts to further enhance trade in goods and services as well as investments.
- The two Prime Ministers reaffirmed the importance of civil nuclear cooperation between the two countries, while recognizing that nuclear safety is a priority for both governments.
- The two Prime Ministers reaffirmed their resolve to further promote people-to-people exchanges between the two countries, particularly youth exchange.
- The two Prime Ministers reiterated the commitment of India and Japan to the freedom of navigation and unimpeded commerce based on the principles of international law, including the 1982 United Nations Convention on the Law of the Sea (UNCLOS). They noted ongoing bilateral exchanges on maritime security including counter-piracy activities, participation in bilateral and multilateral exercises as well as sharing of information, and in this context, welcomed the joint exercises between the Coast Guards of India and Japan held off Chennai in January 2012 and in Tokyo Bay in November 2012. They expressed their expectations to

further promote bilateral and multilateral cooperation on maritime issues.

- The two Prime Ministers reaffirmed their support for the East Asia Summit (EAS) as a forum for dialogue on broad strategic, political, and economic issues of common interest and concern with the aim of promoting peace, stability and economic prosperity in East Asia.[37]

The initiation of the Prime Ministership of Narendra Modi heralded the beginning of a new, promising chapter in Indo-Japan relationship. Prime Minister Shri Modi visited Japan from 30 August-September 3, 2014 for the 9th Annual Summit Meeting with PM Abe. During the visit, the two sides upgraded the relationship to a 'Special Strategic and Global Partnership'. Both sides also agreed to establish the 'India Japan Investment Promotion Partnership'. Some important highlights of the visit are:

- Japan promised to give US$ 35 billion to India through public and private funding over the next five years for developmental projects, including building of smart cities and clean-up of river Ganges.
- Both sides signed five pacts covering defence exchanges, cooperation in clean energy, roads and highways, healthcare and women.
- Japan has lifted the ban on six Indian entities including Hindustan Aeronautics Limited (HAL) which was imposed in the aftermath of 1998 nuclear tests.
- The two sides agreed to enhance their defence and strategic cooperation to a new level and also decided to speed up negotiations on a civil nuclear deal.
- In Kyoto, a pact was signed under which Modi's Lok Sabha constituency Varanasi will be developed on the pattern of Kyoto 'smart city' with the help of Japan.
- Tokyo promised to help India in providing financial, technical, and operational support to introduce Bullet trains, a project that Modi has been actively pursuing.

- Prime Minister Modi has asked NRIs to visit India at least once a year to boost tourism.
- Both sides signed a MoU for cooperation in heritage conservation, city modernisation and cooperation in the fields of art, culture, and academics.
- Both countries decided to build a strong, deep, and strategic relationship under the India-Japan Cooperation framework.
- India decided to set up a Special Management Team directly under the PMO to facilitate proposals from Japan.[38]

PM Abe of Japan visited India for the 10th Annual Summit with PM Modi of India from 11-13 December 2015. Sixteen agreements/MoUs were signed/exchanged during the visit. In a special gesture, India also announced "visa on arrival" scheme for all Japanese travellers, including for business purposes, from March 1, 2016. PM Abe, accompanied by PM Modi also visited the city of Varanasi, which signed a partnership agreement with the city of Kyoto in August 2014. PM Modi visited Japan for the 11th Annual Summit from 11-12 November 2016. Following their meeting, the two Prime Ministers issued a Joint Statement and a Fact Sheet. Ten agreements/MoUs were signed/exchanged in a wide range of areas, including cooperation in the peaceful uses of nuclear energy, manufacturing, skill transfer programme, outer space, marine, earth and atmospheric science and technology, agriculture and food-related industry, transport and urban development, textiles, cultural exchange, and sports.[39]

India's and Japan's co-envisioned Asia-Africa Growth Corridor (AAGC) was announced at the 52nd Annual Meeting of the African Development Bank (AfDB) summit in Gandhinagar, India, on May 22-26, 2017. During the announcement, Prime Minister Narendra Modi stated that both India and Japan aim to achieve closer developmental cooperation in Africa. The presence of African and Japanese representatives at this meeting made the announcement significant. Noteworthy too was that it was made amidst the backdrop of China's Belt and Road Forum (BRF) meeting held on May 14-15, 2017, in Beijing. Indeed, many comparisons have been drawn between the AAGC and

China's Belt and Road Initiative, since both encompass Africa and the Indian Ocean as key constituents. Chinese strategic circles have responded critically to the AAGC initiative, arguing that the AAGC is a "duplication of the freedom corridor" that was originally proposed by Japanese Prime Minister Shinzo Abe during his 2016 meeting with Modi in Tokyo. A vision document was released during the May 2017 AfDB summit in Gandhinagar. This document unveiled India's and Japan's strategically ambitious proposition in the Indo-Pacific region, factoring in Africa and the Indian Ocean. According to the vision document, the AAGC will focus on four key target areas: (i) development and cooperation; (ii) "quality infrastructure" and digital and institutional connectivity; (iii) enhancing capabilities and skills; and (iv) establishing people-to-people partnerships. The overriding goal is to enhance "growth and interconnectedness between and within Asia and Africa."[40] A reading of this vision document suggests that the AAGC aims to attain three general objectives: first, advancing both India's and Japan's individual and mutual outreach towards the African continent, focused mainly on developing "quality infrastructure investment"; second, linking Africa with the Indian Ocean Region within an intercontinental context of Asia-Africa cooperation, whereby Japan and India are envisaged as playing leading roles, with African countries also becoming a part of the decision-making process; and third, to shape a liberal and value-based Indo-Pacific order as per their proposed Vision 2025.[41] Although denied by Japan and India, analysts have observed that the Free and Open Indo-Pacific policy as enshrined in the AAGC also provides a counter narrative to China's Belt and Road Initiative (BRI). The BRI like the AAGC, seeks to connect Asia and Africa through large-scale infrastructure projects. Japan with its emphasis on freedom and openness is attempting to differentiate from China's opaque and hegemonic strategy. Similarly, there is no doubt that India's hesitation to join the Belt and Road project is primarily due to transparency and sovereignty issues. India has often rebuked China for its blatant violation of India's sovereignty in the context of China-Pakistan Economic Corridor (CPEC). The Asia Africa Growth Corridor provides a transparent and inclusive alternate to the countries of Africa. It builds on Japanese ethos of working with quality and India's long and historic people-centric partnership with African countries and presents a promising area of mutual cooperation with convergence of interests.[42]

PM Abe visited India again for the 12th Annual Summit on 13-14 September 2017. During the visit, he and the Indian PM Modi oversaw the ground-breaking ceremony for the Mumbai-Ahmedabad High Speed Rail Project. India and Japan concluded 15 MoUs or agreements in panoply of areas ranging from connectivity, investments, civil aviation, Japanese language training, disaster risk management, science and technology, and sports. PM Modi visited Japan for the 13th Annual Summit from 28-29 October 2018. Japan's announcement of joining the International Solar Alliance (ISA), Exchange of Notes concerning the provision of seven Yen loan projects including the Project for the Construction of MAHSR, Currency Swap Agreement, India Japan Digital Partnership and Implementing Arrangement for deeper cooperation between Japan Maritime Self Defence Force and Indian Navy were among the 32 MoUs/agreements signed during the Annual Summit. PM Shri Narendra Modi visited Japan on 27-29 June 2019 to participate in G20 Summit held in Osaka. On the side-lines, he held a bilateral meeting with PM Abe and discussed broad range of topics of mutual interest, such as Japan's assistance to India for the coalition on disaster resilience infrastructure, fugitive economic offenders and anti-corruption measures, and infrastructure works of Japanese companies in the North East. PM Abe and PM Modi also met on the side-lines of G7 Summit in Biarritz (August 2019), and Eastern Economic Forum in Vladivostok (5 September 2019). PM Modi and PM Abe also met on 4 November 2019 in Bangkok during their visit to Bangkok to attend ASEAN-related summit meetings. They exchanged views regarding measures for strengthening Japan-India relations, including defense cooperation, bilateral cooperation in third countries, and collaboration on investment promotion.[43]

Apart from the Annual Summits, the annual Foreign Minister-level Strategic Dialogue, Defense Ministers Meeting and other bilateral dialogue mechanisms ensure regular high level and functional engagements between the two countries. India-Japan Defense and Security partnership has evolved over the years and today forms an integral pillar of the bilateral ties. Exchanges between the two countries have strengthened due to growing convergence on strategic matters; and its significance is growing from the common outlook on issues of peace, security, and stability of the Indo-Pacific Region. The Tri-Service Exchanges between Japan and India have been institutionalized completing the triad. Coast Guards have regular annual exchanges since 2006.

Japan is regarded as a key partner in India's economic transformation. In the recent past, the India-Japan relationship has transformed to a partnership of great substance and purpose. The bilateral trade between India and Japan for FY 2019-20 (April-December) totalled to US$ 11.87 billion.[44]

Recent Trends and Future Directions

In November 2019, India's withdrawal from the RCEP (Regional Comprehensive Economic Partnership), the proposed free trade deal which now aims to bring together the 10-member Association of Southeast Asian Nations (ASEAN), China, Japan, South Korea, Australia, and New Zealand was a setback for Japan's Indo-Pacific policy. Indian Government said the proposed agreement was unacceptable to India in its current form as it did not accommodate New Delhi's concerns and core interests. The RCEP has been viewed as key to regional economic integration in Asia. With India as a member, it would have brought together about half of the world's people and 30% of global GDP. The trade deal figured prominently in New Delhi's "Act East" foreign policy.

But a big concern for India was that it would be flooded by goods from China and elsewhere. India already has a massive trade deficit with China, amounting to US$ 53 billion (€ 48 billion). It's the biggest deficit India has with any country. Japan was appreciative of India's concern and no bad blood was created between the two countries because of India's decision.[45]

Japan is today unquestionably one of India's closest friends with a robust Special Strategic and Global Partnership that encompasses economic and defence cooperation. One of India's biggest investors, Japan is present in virtually every large infrastructure and developmental project in India. It is a permanent partner since 2015 in the tri-lateral Malabar naval exercise, along with India and the US. A military logistics agreement, known as the Acquisition and Cross-Servicing Agreement (ACSA), is under discussion.

In a statement issued after the June 15 clash between the Indian and the Chinese troops in Galwan, the spokesperson of Japan's Ministry of Foreign Affairs expressed hope that the "situation will be resolved peacefully through dialogue between the concerned parties". Japan's Ambassador to India, H.E. Satoshi Suzuki, stated in a tweet on 3 July that Japan "hopes for a peaceful resolution through dialogues". More relevantly, he emphasised that "Japan opposes any unilateral attempts to change the status quo".[46] India and Japan, the two key adversaries of China, signed a key defence agreement for reciprocal provision of supplies and services between their defence forces as Prime Minister Narendra Modi and his Japanese counterpart Shinzo Abe held their annual summit over the phone today.

The Acquisition and Cross Servicing Agreement (ACSA) between Japan's Self-Defense Forces and India's armed forces was signed by Japanese Ambassador Satoshi Suzuki and Defence Secretary Ajay Kumar in New Delhi on 10 September 2020. The agreement comes at a time when India is locked in a tense military stand-off with China at eastern Ladakh and there is an ongoing row between Japan and China over the disputed Senkaku/Diaoyu islands. The agreement establishes the enabling framework for closer cooperation between the armed forces of India and Japan in reciprocal provision of supplies and services while engaged in bilateral training activities, UN peacekeeping operations, humanitarian international relief and other mutually agreed activities, the Defence Ministry said in a statement. The agreement will also enhance the interoperability between the armed forces of India and Japan thereby further increasing the bilateral defence engagements under the special strategic and global partnership between the two countries. The two Prime Ministers held their summit in a unique fashion on phone today lasting 30 minutes during which Abe informed Modi that he would resign from his position due to health reasons and expressed his gratitude and for the friendship and the relationship of trust built with the Indian leader. The two leaders welcomed the signing of the agreement for reciprocal provision of supplies and services between the armed forces of their two countries. They concurred that the agreement will further enhance the depth of defence cooperation between the two countries and contribute to peace and security in the Indo-Pacific region. The two leaders reviewed the status of ongoing cooperation, including the Mumbai-Ahmedabad High Speed Rail project, under the framework of the India-Japan Special Strategic and Global Partnership. They agreed that the strong and enduring partnership between the two countries will play a critical role in charting the course for the global community in the post-Covid world.[47]

Relationship between the two countries has deepened during the Premiership of Shinzo Abe and one hopes that his successor, Yoshihide Suga continues his legacy. Indian leadership, on its part, are expected to continue further the blossoming of relationship between the two democracies committed to a peaceful, steady, prosperous, and non-hegemonic order in Asia.

Endnotes

1. Embassy of India in Moscow (2020), "70 years of India-Russia Relations: A Historic Milestone"; on line source: https://indianembassy-moscow.gov.in/70-years-of-india-russia-relations-a-historic-milestone.php. Accessed on 20 Sept. 2020.
2. Anand P. Mavolankar (2008), "The Changing Matrix of Indo Russian Cooperation', in P.L. Dash and Andrei M. Nazrkin (ed.) *Indo-Russian Diplomatic Relations: Sixty Years of Enduring Legacy,* Delhi: Academic Excellence, p. 486.
3. Sanjoy Hazarika (1993), "Despite U.S., Yeltsin Backs Rocket Deal with India", *The New York Times,* January 30; on line source: https://www.nytimes.com/1993/01/30/world/despite-us-yeltsin-backs-rocket-deal-with-india.html. Accessed on 20 Sept. 2020.

4. "Yeltsin was for pragmatic ties with India" (2017), *The Outlook*, 23 April; on line source: https://www.outlookindia.com/newswire/story/yeltsin-was-for-pragmatic-ties-with-india/467629. Accessed on 20 Sept. 2020.
5. Sunil Dasgupta and Sudeep Chakravarti (1994), "Narasimha Rao's visit to Russia removes bottlenecks in defence, strategic and trade ties", *India Today,* July 31; on line source: https://www.indiatoday.in/magazine/special-report/story/19940731-narasimha-raos-visit-to-russia-removes-bottlenecks-in-defence-strategic-and-trade-ties-809444-1994-07-31. Accessed on 20 Sept. 2020.
6. See, "India Russia Relations"; on line source: https://www.globalsecurity.org/military/world/india/forrel-ru.htm, accessed on 20 Sept. 2020.
7. Indian Embassy, Moscow (2019) "India Russia Relations"; on line source: https://www.indianembassy-moscow.gov.in. Accessed on 20 Sept. 2020.
8. Arun Mohanty (2011), "Indo Russian Strategic Partnership: A Reality Check", *Mainstream*, April, p. 26.
9. Jyotsna Bakshi (2005), "Prime Minister's Moscow Visit", *Strategic Analysis*; on line source: https://idsa.in/strategicanalysis/PrimeMinistersMoscowVisit_jbakshi_1005. Accessed on 21 Sept. 2020.
10. Ministry of External Affairs, Govt. of India (2005), "India-Russia Joint Statement on the outcome of the Official Visit of Prime Minister Dr. Manmohan Singh to the Russian Federation", December 07; on line source: https://mea.gov.in/bilateral-documents.htm?dtl/7105/IndiaRussia+Joint+Statement +on+the+outcome+of+the +Official+Visit+of+Prime+Minister+Dr+Manmohan+Singh+to+the+Russian+Federation. Accessed on 21 Sept. 2020.
11. Arun Mohanty (2008), "Medvedev Visit to India: A Significant Indo-Russian Summit", *Mainstream*, December 20; on line source: https://mainstreamweekly.net/article1090.html. Accessed on 21 Sept. 2020.
12. The Kremlin, Moscow (2009), "Dmitry Medvedev held talks with Indian Prime Minister Manmohan Singh, who is in Russia on an official visit", December 7; on line source: http://en.kremlin.ru/events/president/news/6258. Accessed on 21 Sept. 2020.
13. Indian Embassy, Moscow, "Bilateral Relations: India-Russia Relations"; on line source: https://indianembassy-moscow.gov.in/bilateral-relations-india-russia.php. Accessed on 21 Sept. 2020.
14. Vladimir Radyuhin (2011), "Expanding Indo-Russian cooperation in India's interest: Manmohan", *The Hindu*, December 16;

on line source: https://www.thehindu.com/news/national/expanding-indorussian-cooperation-in-indias-interest-manmohan/article2716903.ece. Accessed on 21 Sept. 2020.

15. Embassy of India, Moscow (2012), "Joint Statement on the 13th India-Russia Annual Summit: Partnership for mutual benefit and a better world"; on line source: https://indianembassy-moscow.gov.in/visit-of-president-of-russia-h-e-mr-vladimir-putin-to-india-24-december-2012.php. Accessed on 22 Sept. 2020.
16. Rajorshi Roy (2013), "Putin's India Visit: A Review', January 4, *IDSA Comment,* on line source: https://idsa.in/idsacomments/PutinsIndiaVisit_rroy_040113. Accessed on 22 Sept. 2020.
17. Nivedita Kapoor (2019), "India-Russia ties in a changing world order: In pursuit of a 'Special Strategic Partnership'", *ORF Occasional Paper*, October 22; on line source: https://www.orfonline.org/research/india-russia-ties-in-a-changing-world-order-in-pursuit-of-a-special-strategic-partnership-56877/. Accessed on 22 Sept. 2020.
18. *Ibid.*
19. Ministry of External Affairs (MEA), Govt. of India (2017), "India-Russia Relations, July 2017"; on line source: http://www.mea.gov.in/Portal/ForeignRelation/India_Russia_May.pdf. Accessed on 22 Sept. 2020.
20. Embassy of India, Moscow, "Ambassador Pankaj Saran's visit to Chechnya Republic"; on line source: https://indianembassy-moscow.gov.in/70-years-of-india-russia-relations-a-historic-milestone.php. Accessed on 22 Sept. 2020.
21. MEA press release (2018), "Informal Summit between India and Russia", May 21; on line source: https://mea.gov.in/press-releases.htm?dtl/29908/. Accessed on 22 Sept. 2020.
22. Harsh V. Pant (2013), "India-Russia Ties and India's Strategic Culture: Dominance of a Realist Worldview", *India Review,* 12 (1).
23. Nivedita Kapoor, *op. cit.*
24. Ministry of External Affairs, "Prime Minister's Keynote Address at Shangri La Dialogue"; on line source: https://www.mea.gov.in/Speeches. Accessed on 23 Sept. 2020.
25. Devirupa Mitra, "Pakistan Critical to Defeating ISIS, Says Russian Special Rep to Afghanistan", *The Wire*, on line source: https://thewire.in/external-affairs/pakistan-isis-afghanistan-russia. Accessed on 23 Sept. 2020.
26. Sumitra Nair (2020), "Why Russia will always take a neutral stand on India-China clash", *The Week*, September 3; on line source:

https://www.theweek.in/news/world/2020/09/03/why-russia-will-always-take-a-neutral-stand-on-india-china-clash.html. Accessed on 23 Sept. 2020.

27. *The Hindustan Times*, "The Moscow Reset", Editorial, 25 June.
28. "Indo Japan Relations", *India Quarterly*, Vol. LVII, No. 1 Jan-March, 2001, p. 95.
29. Japan-India Joint Declaration, Tokyo, December 10, 2001, https://japan.kantei.go.jp/koizumispeech/2001/1210india_e.html. Accessed on 15 Sept. 2020.
30. Ministry of Foreign Affairs of Japan, "Joint Statement Towards Japan-India Strategic and Global Partnership," Tokyo, December 15, 2006; on line source: https://www.mofa.go.jp/region/asia-paci/india/pdfs/joint0612.pdf. Accessed on 15 Sept. 2020.
31. D.S. Rajan (2007), "Shinzo Abe is an admirer of India", August 22; on line source: https://www.rediff.com/news/2007/aug/22guest.htm. Accessed on 15 Sept. 2020.
32. Shubhajit Roy (2020), "Explained: Why New Delhi will miss Shinzo Abe, who gave new shape to Japan's India ties", *The Indian Express*, August 29.
33. MEA, Govt. of India (2013), "India-Japan Relations, Strategic and Global Partnership"; on line source: //www.mea.gov.in/Portal/ForeignRelation/Japan_Relations_-_Jan_2013.pdf. Accessed on 15 Sept. 2020.
34. Ministry of Foreign Affairs of Japan; on line source: https://www.mofa.go.jp/region/asia-paci/india/pmv0912/outline.html. Accessed on 16 Sept. 2020.
35. Shamshad Ahmad Khan, "Indo-Japan Strategic Cooperation: Issues, Expectations and Challenges"; on line source: https://www.academia.edu/5233213/Indo_Japan_Strategic_Cooperation_Issues_Expectations_and_Challenges. Accessed on 16 Sept. 2020.
36. Ministry of External Affairs, Govt. of India, on line source: https://www.mea.gov.in/Portal/ForeignRelation/Japan_Relations_-_Jan_2013.pdf. Accessed on 16 Sept. 2020.
37. Ministry of External Affairs, Govt. of India (2013), "Joint Statement on Prime Minister's Visit to Japan", May 29; on line source: https://www.mea.gov.in/bilateral-documents.htm?dtl/21755/Joint+Statement+on+Prime+ Ministers+visit+to+Japan+Strengthening+the+Strategic+and+Global+Partnership+between+India+and+Japan+beyond+the+60th+Anniversary+of+Diplomatic+Relations. Accessed on 16 Sept. 2020.

38. *India Today* (2014), "10 highlights of Modi's visit to Japan", September 3; on line source: https://www.indiatoday.in/india/north/story/10-highlights-of-modi-visit-to-japan-206964-2014-09-03. Accessed on 17 Sept. 2020.
39. Ministry of External Affairs, Govt. of India (2019), "India Japan Relations"; on line source: https://mea.gov.in/Portal/ForeignRelation/India_japanBilateral_Brief_September_2019.pdf. Accessed on 17 Sept. 2020.
40. Economic Research Institute for ASEAN and East Asia (2017), "Asia Africa Growth Corridor: Partnership for Sustainable and Innovative Development: A Vision Document", African Development Bank Meeting, Ahmedabad, India, 22-26 May; on line source: https://www.eria.org/Asia-Africa-Growth-Corridor-Document.pdf. Accessed on 17 Sept. 2020.
41. Jagannath Panda (2017), "The Asia-Africa Growth Corridor: An India-Japan Arch in the Making?", *Focus Asia Perspective & Analysis*, No. 21, August; on line source: https://isdp.eu/publication/asia-africa-growth-corridor-aagc-india-japan/. Accessed on 17 Sept. 2020.
42. Ruchita Beri (2017), "Asia Africa Growth Corridor: Towards a Shared Philosophy", *IDSA Publication*, June; on line source: https://idsa.in/africatrends/asia-africa-growth-corridor-rberi. Accessed on 17 Sept. 2020.
43. Ministry of External Affairs, Govt. of India (2020), "Brief Note on India-Japan Bilateral Relations", February; on line source: https://mea.gov.in/Portal/ForeignRelation/India-Japan_Bilateral_Brief_feb_2020.pdf. Accessed on 17 Sept. 2020.
44. *Ibid.*
45. Rahul Misra, "Why India pulled out of the RCEP free trade deal"; on line source: https://www.dw.com/en/why-india-pulled-out-of-the-rcep-free-trade-deal/a-51137128. Accessed on 17 Sept. 2020.
46. Sujan R. Chinoy (2020), "The Cartographic Route to Deeper Strategic Partnerships", July 3; on line source: https://idsa.in/policybrief/cartographic-route-to-strategic-partnerships-srchinoy-030720. Accessed on 17 Sept. 2020.
47. *The Statesman*, Kolkata (2020), "China foes India, Japan sign key defence accord as Modi-Abe hold virtual annual summit", September 11; on line source: https://www.thestatesman.com/india/china-foes-india-japan-sign-key-defence-accord-modi-abe-hold-virtual-annual-summit-1502923165.html. Accessed on 17 Sept. 2020.

8

India and the European Union: Changing Dynamics

Udayan Das

The profile of India-European Union (EU) relations have grown in stature with time. Traditionally, India and EU have enjoyed unhindered relations which are free from irreconcilable issues. This has been furthered over the last three decades broadly by two set of factors. First, the birth and growth of the EU, in its present form, has coincided with the rise of India's economic power. In the early 1990s, two different developments were taking place in two different quarters of the world. Fraught with internal rivalries which conceded two devastating world wars, Europe was starting to consolidate internally to avoid another.[1] The foundations of that were laid in a Europe which was still divided by Cold War. Popularized by ideational imageries like the "Iron Curtain" and real barriers like the Berlin Wall, the political and economic integration was separated. As the Cold War ended, Europe had a chance to regroup and leave the legacy of rivalries behind. The European Union is a supranational project which has managed to produce lasting peace against this backdrop and bind the continent of Europe in institutional terms. With time, EU gained in size and stature and became an economic powerhouse in the international order.[2] Simultaneously, India's rise was a recognizable shift from its past.

In the first four decades after its independence, India was primarily an inward-looking economy with a very modest growth rate. A watershed moment came in 1991 with the new economic reforms taking over India marked by a thrust towards liberalization and the undoing of the license raj.[3] With India opening its economic doors for the rest of the world, its foreign policy priorities also changed. New Delhi started looking for more reliable relationships that would complement financial partnerships. As the growth trajectories became stronger, India and EU were turning out to be opportunities to each other for more engaging and sustained trade by serving each other with big and growing markets. Incidentally, this economic complementarity largely continues to define the core of the India-EU relations even today.

Secondly, while both India and EU were growing in stature economically, opening up opportunities for each other, their approach to global issues matched with their growth stories. Several common threads emerged to complement the partnership and they continued to feature and dominate the joint declarations and vision documents. These convergences in ideals have also become a long-lasting feature in the partnership. A shared confidence in democratic ideals and values, upholding multilateralism, growing interest in clean and renewable energy, scientific research, synergies in issues of climate change and people-to-people contacts are some of the major highlights. In other words, India and EU have gradually identified each other through mutual goals and common approaches that aided the relations to grow further.

These twin factors of growing economic prowess and shared beliefs have taken the India-EU relations forward. In the present times, India-EU relations have been marked by strong economic ties and a nascent strategic partnership. Both the parties have developed a matrix of high-level political interactions around a growing framework of relations. These relations have now encompassed political, economic, security aspects. However, there have been heavy criticisms that India and EU relations are not a priority to both the parties which is reflected by the non-binding and open-ended nature of their commitments. As a result, despite overlapping visions and endless opportunities, the relationship is mostly about unrealized potential.[4] Adding to it, relations between India and EU have also assumed a degree of uncertainty due to the exit of United Kingdom from EU through

Brexit.[5] Against an emerging backdrop of the changing power distribution of the international order, India-EU are required to calibrate their relationship which has also seen a considerable downward slope in the last decade. Structural changes and bilateral differences are standing against the potential of a flourishing relationship between the two parties.

The present chapter will look at five aspects in explaining the changing dynamics of India-EU relations. First, it would look at an overview of the origin of the European Union. Second, it would briefly explore the evolution of India-EU relations from its inception to present. Third, it would discern the dimensions of the contemporary India-EU's relationship in understanding its political, economic, and security aspects. Fourthly, it would deal with the question of Brexit implications on India-EU relations. Finally, it would predict what future holds for India-EU relations based on the emerging trends of their relationship.

Origin of the European Union

While the formal establishment of EU is understood through the Treaty of Maastricht in 1992, the genesis of the idea of EU dates back to the post-war period. EU is best understood as a gradual evolution and not a stroke of an agreement. Its multilateralism evolved and expanded with time having a central focus on establishing a supranational entity that serves primarily two objectives—peace and security in the region and producing economic growth. Its initial impulse was to bind together the economies and create an interdependence among the member states in which war becomes self-destructive and obsolete. In effectively implementing this through policies, EU has come up with numerous treaties and agreements in order to regroup and reorganize itself from time and time, as and when felt necessary. This has also resulted in rearranging of institutions to accommodate newer members and enlarged bodies, reorient itself with global realities and align its vision accordingly.

The political and economic union was as much a need as it was a cherished goal. Traditionally, bitter rivalries within Europe, especially France and Germany, had not only barred peace from the time of the empires but had also resulted in two major modern catastrophes in the 20th century. For a war torn and broken Europe at the end of the Second World War, there were very few options left open but to align their interests and cooperate to avoid the future possibilities of a war. Along with that, it was also difficult for countries alone to economically stabilize themselves and grow in isolation. Even if the states did not want to support a federal supranational entity at the cost of undermining themselves, it was essential for their survival.[6] Interdependence among each other and partnerships were essential not only to grow but to sustain as a state against the prevailing nature of circumstances.

The idea of integration was first placed through the Schuman Plan and the foundation of the European Coal and Steel Community (ECSC) led by Jean Monnet. These plans surfaced in the form of post-war reconstruction of the region. The idea behind the community was to intertwine economies and cooperate intensively so that "war not only becomes unthinkable but materially impossible".[7] Initially signed by six members, Italy, Germany, France, Belgium, Luxembourg, and Netherlands, the main aim was to cooperate on the free movement of coal and steel within these countries to ensure a single market. Although it started with a narrow sector, the members had expectations of gradually forming a wider community. Influenced by David Mitrany's functionalist approach of integration, the model sought to start with narrow and specialized technical areas of cooperation which would in time have a 'spillover' and cause cooperation in other areas as well.[8] Soon the ECSC was supplemented by the two new communities by the treaties of Rome—the European Economic Community (EEC) and the European Atomic Energy Commission (EAEC) or the Euratom. The 1960s and 1970s saw a successful economic community attracting further enlargements. In 1973, Denmark, Ireland, and United Kingdom joined while by mid-1980s, Greece, Spain, and Portugal were a part of the community.[9] Simultaneously, there was continuous growth of the institutions, such as the European Council and the Parliament. A significant thrust towards a more comprehensive single market was ensured with the Single European Act signed in 1986. The Schengen Area negotiations which started during the same time were an additional push in implementing an unrestricted space for the people to move freely without any stringent passport and visa controls divulging hard national borders.

From the 1950s to the lead up to the Treaty of Maastricht, there have been three important aspects marking the formation of the European Union in its present form. First, a deep abiding faith in Europe as a single economic space and community. With the visions and policy measures of ECSC and EEC, there was a growing consensus for the removal of trade barriers and ensuring free movement of labor and goods. The satisfactory growth trajectory firmed the foundational stone of Europe as a market space. Second, there has been a steady growth of institutions that would cater to the demands and sustenance of this growing community. The emergence of the European Council (EC) along with broader powers and legitimacy of public voting to the Parliament are some of the significant changes that took place during this time. Thirdly, as peace and security were important objectives alongside economic growth, the supranational body ensured that its commitment towards democracy, human rights and effective multilateralism is not compromised.

As the cold war came to an end, Europe was reconstituted in many ways. Germany was reunified and the division across the east and west of Europe withered away in practically no time. In 1992, the Treaty of Maastricht formally established the European Union. The multilateral body subsequently had multiple waves of enlargement to integrate with the erstwhile European states of the Soviet circuit.

The EU is marked by seven institutions and four freedoms. These four freedoms classified as—freedom of goods, capital, services, and persons are termed to be the essence of European Union as a project.[10] In the years after this, EU has been preoccupied with its enlargements in Eastern Europe and subsequent revisions in its treaties and agreements to calibrate itself.[11] Amidst being the most successful multilateral body, the EU has a complex mesh of institutions with two central difficulties at its heart. First, ensuring a balance between EU as

Box 8.1: Timeline of the Evolution of the European Union[12]

1951: Treaty of Paris led to the formal establishment of the European Coal and Steel Community (ECSC) which brought together six countries: Germany, Italy, France, Luxembourg, Netherlands, and Belgium. The main aim was to set up a common market for coal and steel.

1957: Treaties of Rome established the European Economic Community (EEC) and the European Atomic Energy Community (EAEC) or Euratom.

1965: The Treaty of Brussels was also signed, known as the 'Merger Treaty', bringing together the executive bodies of the ECSC, EEC, and EAEC.

1985: Schengen Agreement was signed and was put into effect a decade later. The main objective was to do away with the passport and border controls, allowing people to move freely within the countries of the Schengen Area.

1986: Single European Act was signed in order to implement a common market to ensure a flow of goods and services without the restriction imposed by internal borders.

1992: Maastricht Treaty or the Treaty on European Union was signed which established the European Union and formalised its institutions, aims, and objectives. The treaty introduced the three pillars of the EU: EU Communities, Common Foreign and Security Policy (CFSP), and the Police and Judicial Cooperation in criminal matters.

1997: Treaty of Amsterdam was signed as a subsequent amendment to the Treaty of Maastricht to strengthen and modify the EU institutions. Parliament was given more powers and majority qualified voting was incorporated to multiple areas in place of unanimous voting which was resulting in deadlocks.

2001: Treaty of Nice was signed to reform the EU institutions for effective functioning against the prospective enlargement of the EU in 2004.

2007: Prominent changes in the institutional functioning were introduced with the signing of the Treaty of Lisbon. The aim was to make EU institutions more democratic and efficient to deal with global challenges competently. It amended the Treaties of Rome and Maastricht and gave EU full legal personality.

2020: United Kingdom formally left the European Union.

a supranational body and its constituent members as individual states. There is a constant balancing and rebalancing between EU and independent member states, as states continue to be primary actors in international relations. Second, a much more logistical problem of accommodating a range of states—big and small powers, within the ambit of EU.

Box 8.2: EU's Institutional Framework[13]

Executive:

European Council: Comprised the top political leaders representing the EU states.

European Commission: The regular executive body of commissioners appointed by the Council and approved by the EU Parliament.

Legislature:

European Parliament: The body is directly elected by the people and is proportionally representative of each state's population.

Council of Ministers: Comprised of government ministers of all EU states divided according to their areas.

Judiciary:

Court of Justice of the European Union: Highest judicial body of the EU which is responsible for interpreting EU law.

European Court of Auditors: Agency which audits the budget.

Financial:

European Central Bank: Regulates the European financial system and manages the currency Euro.

Evolution of India-EU Ties

It is important to understand the evolution of India-EU relations to gauge how three factors have changed over the years—perceptions, interests, and policies. These changing factors have given rise to the present context of relations that we now see.

The initial beginnings of the post-war European integration were not perceived very well by India. New Delhi did not show much enthusiasm in deepening relations with the ECSC and the EEC. A possible reason was that Europe did not occupy primary position in India's foreign policy imagination and was relegated as second priority to neighborhood and great powers. India was skeptical about the economic integration of the Western European states as it believed that it went against the rules of non-discrimination established by General Agreements on Tariffs and Trade (GATT). As India was voicing the concerns of the postcolonial states during that period, it flagged the issue that a coterie of preferential trade agreements within the European states would firm the divide between the developed and the less developed states. Moreover, India had better connections with Britain as a result of historical reasons and when Britain initially showed interest to join the EEC in early 1960s, India was to lose the preferential trading relations with the Commonwealth nations as the EEC trading rules would then takeover. India raised the issue of the future of the Commonwealth nations. The attempt was to secure an associational agreement with the EEC like what was done for erstwhile colonial countries of Africa. However, the EEC perceived this problem as not their own but Britain alone. It did not pay attention to such demands and characterized India as "Britain's Baby" and all South Asian states as "non-associable".[14]

Even though Britain's merger in 1960's was stalled by France and UK joined the EEC a decade later, India took the cue from the situation and understood that it had to develop its relations with West European states, more importantly EEC, independently and irrespective of Britain. The foundation of that relationship was, however, done on the recognition of being equal partners. India became one of the first developing countries to establish relations with the EEC, dating back to the 1962. A decade later, the first Commercial Cooperation Agreement (CCA) was signed between India and EEC from where India and EEC only expanded their trade.[15]

With the formation of the EU and India's increasing push towards diversifying its foreign and economic relations, 1990s was a decade of opportunities for both to cement their ties beyond economic transaction. The 1993 Joint Political Vision and the Cooperation Agreement signed in 1994 marked the beginning of a broader framework of engagement between India and EU. It defined the institutional arrangement of the ties through annual ministerial meetings and dialogues at various levels.[16] The agreement underscored that India and EU would coordinate and build their partnership in technical, economic and cultural matters for the mutual benefit of both.[17] The growing convergence further pushed India and EU to structure an annual summit, the first of which was held in 2000. A watershed moment in the relationship came in 2004 when the parties decided to enter into a strategic partnership with each other. The impetus for EU to enter into a strategic partnership with India was a result of broadly two factors. First, there was a lack of unanimity in EU's Common Foreign & Security Policy (CFSP) which was exposed during the 2003 Iraq War. In the face of the situation, different states in EU had different positions due to their relations with US. As a result, EU had to regroup and organize a more coherent framework to have a voice on global security matters. This led to a renewed CFSP with a much more global mandate and an active engagement agenda with major actors, focused on five central issues, alongside trade, namely terrorism, proliferation of WMDs, regional conflicts, state failure and organized crime.[18] Secondly, given that EU has been looking for a broader global role, deepening relations with India is an indispensability to have a strong footing in the economic and security matters of a changing Asia.[19] As a result of this, EU also recognized India's centrality in the region and the need to engage with it widely. For India, EU's inclination served not only economic and investment opportunities but was also a welcome gesture validating India as a rising and important power.

The evolution of India-EU relations serve to note how systemic and domestic factors have shaped the relationship. While the need for domestic growth has always been an incentive for enhancing trading ties, it found more momentum with India's growing economic clout. As the relationship moved into the post-cold war era, EU's inclination for a broader role in international matters led Brussels to have better engagement with India in the broader context of changing South Asia. India's idea of parity also changed over the years as it started to grow. In the earlier years, India morally stressed on partnership as equal sovereigns as it stood against the exploitation of postcolonial and less developed states. In the post-Cold War scenario, India's emphasis on equal partnership and mutual respect was rather because of its recognition of its own rise and importance in the international order. In other words, for India, the earlier appeal for equal partnership was a moral call for recognition in the international order while now it has transitioned into a more confident power-based appreciation. Throughout the evolution of India-EU relations in the post-Cold War period, EU's growing assertiveness for a broader role and India's focus on equality in the partnership have been two important mainstays, the third one being the non-binding nature of commitments.[20] The third one, non-binding nature of commitments and the use of rhetoric without substantial gains has been a strong criticism of the relationship till the present.

Box 8.3: Evolution of India-EU Relations[21]

1962: India establishes relations with the European Economic Community.

1973: India and EEC sign Commercial Cooperation Agreement.

1981: India and EC signed the Agreement for Commercial and Economic Cooperation.

1993: India and EU release Joint Political Statement.

1994: India and EU sign the Cooperation Agreement.

2000: First Annual India-EU Summit at Lisbon.

2004: India and EU enter into a strategic partnership.

2005: Joint Action Plan adopted by India and EU.

2007: India-EU launch negotiations for Free Trade Agreement (FTA).

India-EU Relations: Economic, Political and Security Aspects

Trade and investments form the backbone of India-EU relations. In 2019, EU was India's largest trading partner. The trade amounted to 80 billion Euros, approximating 11.1% of total Indian trade. In terms of foreign investments as well, EU has a hefty share in India, accounting to more than 68 billion Euros in 2018.[22] India is also EU's ninth largest trading partner in the world.

While the growing numbers suggest positive trends in the economic cooperation between India and EU, the economic relationship has been strained considerably in the last decade. The main reason for this is the deadlock over the Free Trade Agreement. While the negotiations had begun in 2007, there has been no solution in a final agreement. Despite high-level trade dialogues resuming between India and EU, FTA looks an unlikely possibility in the near future.[23] There has been no timelines set for the negotiation to be completed. This long stagnation in financial engagement highlights that there is a dire need to work on the economic relations as well which is the strong point in the partnership. The main issue of the deadlock is that New Delhi believes that the FTA would not be beneficial for India according to the terms unilaterally set by Brussels. Given that India always insists on parity in terms of consensus building, it is unlikely that the talks would proceed until both the parties have adequate room to negotiate and arrive at a consensus. Two of the major reasons that have led to the deadlock are the disagreements over the technicalities and modalities, particularly in the domain of trade in services, and the excessive bureaucratization over the decision-making process.[24]

A lot of attention has been given to the political and security dimensions of India-EU relations in the last decade because of the upgradation and elevation of their ties to a strategic partnership since 2004. The idea of strategic partnership enumerated the resolve to cooperate in the following areas:

1. Cooperating on global issues—multilateralism, peace and security, human rights, counter-terrorism, non-proliferation of Weapons of Mass Destruction (WMD).
2. Improving commercial and economic interaction in technical and sectoral areas.
3. Cooperation in areas related to climate change and sustainable development.
4. Enhancing civil society linkages and people to people contacts.[25]

The strategic partnership did yield dividends for both in terms of cooperation in fields of scientific research, climate change, and sustainable development.[26] However, there are hardly real deliverables associated with major tenets of multilateralism, global governance, democracy, and human rights. The lacunae in tangible outcomes is a result of the differences of the two parties when it comes to these categories. While broadly both the parties agree to democracy and human rights, India believes in the practice of democracy by "not promoting, not exporting", but by capacity building.[27] Similarly, in the field of human rights, New Delhi does not like to be told what is normative as it is very sensitive of such issues relating to governance and sovereignty. India's record of multilateralism is also very fuzzy as it balances between pragmatism and normativity. On the other hand, EU's multilateralism is primarily concerned with the efforts within its immediate neighborhood. Instead of these significant conceptual and executional differences, there has been blanket convergence on these issues which have formed the basis of the strategic partnership. As a result, the policy deliverables have evaporated beyond discussions and talks. This nature of strategic partnership without solid outcomes has been criticized as nothing more than a "charade".[28]

The present nature of India-EU relations is devised on a vision document which puts forward a road map for 2025.[29] The document lays out the plans for India-EU strategic cooperation in more than twenty fields, broadly ranging across foreign policy and security, multilateralism, democracy and human rights, governance, research and technology, climate change, sustainable development and people-to-people contacts. However, like the persisting problems, the document also reveals that there are no financial and legal obligations for either of the parties, making the vision document vague and imprecise.

India and EU: Brexit and Beyond

In a bid to reclaim its national sovereignty, the United Kingdom officially withdrew from EU in January 2020 and entered into negotiations to finish the transition period for the rest of the year. Through a long-drawn Brexit campaign that started almost five years back, UK's primary complaint was that being in EU did not serve its primary national interests. Among the list of its chief complains, the most prominent one was about immigration. The issue of migration led to a significant contradiction between UK and the essence which formed EU that stressed on the freedom of free movement of goods, services, capital, and people. Britain's significant allegation was that the last of the freedoms is creating an influx of immigrants into UK which is deterring the interests of its people and economy. This anxiety coupled with fears of political, economic, social, and cultural insecurity. Adding to it was a perception of EU's institutional incompetency which characterized Brexit to be making UK more secure, sovereign and economically dynamic.[30] The dominant theme of Brexit is that UK would be better off being outside of EU rather than being in it.

Presently, the UK and EU are in a stretch of negotiations to decide the future pattern of engagements between each other. This would include negotiations on the future of trade relations and security and law enforcements.[31] The hard negotiations would mean that each of the parties would attempt to extract the best of the deals possible out of the situation. It is still unclear whether what would be nature of the Brexit and what would the nature of relationship between the two at the after 2020.

How would Brexit impact India and its relations with both UK and EU? Most foreign policy analysts feel that even though in the long run a Brexit would weaken both UK and EU, it would not have significant ramifications for India.[32] However, until the negotiations and deals do not work out between the EU and UK, India needs to play its options carefully and not rush. There are two issues because of which such an approach becomes important. First, a considerable amount of India's business and connections with EU goes through UK. The volume of India-Britain trade is more than one-third of the entire India-EU trade volume. A disjointed market, which was previously a single market would obviously open up newer adjustments and challenges for India to evolve in the region. This would further be problematic as India's strength lies with trade in services. Since immigration is a long-standing issue for the UK, immediate solutions are likely to be elusive to India's disadvantage.

Nevertheless, India's best options are to buy time and keep channels of engagement open with both EU and UK simultaneously. First, India's relations with both the entities would depend on the nature of Brexit. Once the terms of Brexit are finalized, India can have a clearer picture as to what would affect its businesses of things and how. Within this period, both EU and UK would look to expand their base and get in more states to cooperate with them. For instance, EU has emphasized on signing the Bilateral Trade and Investment Agreement with India,[33] while UK is looking for new partners to validate their decision of leaving EU and following their independent course of actions.[34] For India, the task is to assess its interests without prematurely jumping to bandwagon with any of the blocks. While these overtures seem impressive, any deal needs to be arrived after a consensus of mutual interest with considerable scrutiny. Secondly, the most suitable option is to operate a two-channel trade parallelly with both UK and EU. Marginalizing any of the two would harm the scope of India's economic and political interests. The business voices from India are interested in carrying out trade with EU and UK, irrespective of Brexit.[35]

The Future of India-EU Relations

Despite many positives, India-EU relations have been criticized for not having enough political will to go beyond the existing challenges. There are three broad challenges that has furthered these deficits of expectation and reality alongside potential and performance. First, India and EU do not feature in their immediate priority areas of concern which prevents greater cooperation that goes beyond rhetoric. Geographical separation is a cause of that. India is primarily engaged with its immediate periphery of South Asia and its extended neighborhood of Southeast Asia and the Middle East. Similarly, EU is mostly concerned about the North Atlantic region and its eastern borders which end at the Middle East. Secondly, complemented with this geographical distance is the lack of substantial geopolitical standing that the two states lack in each other's regions. In other words, India is not an important geopolitical player in the politics of Europe, neither EU is a major stakeholder in the region of South Asia. In comparison to US and China, both of whom are important actors for India and EU, New Delhi and Brussels do not perceive each other as major players in their respective regions. Thirdly, India has considerably good relations with the constituent members of the EU. When it comes to India's energy security and global power ambitions, these member states bring more value to the table than the EU does.[36] These individual relations also date back to periods before that of India's relations with EU. With three states—France, Germany, and United Kingdom (member of EU till 2020), India had entered strategic partnerships before it had with EU. On the other hand, in contrast with its member states, EU is yet to develop a strong foreign policy which would comprehensively respond to an international order increasingly becoming power driven.[37] On India's part, it is easier to directly deal with the nation states who have a more decisive take on foreign policy, unlike EU who are driven by consensus. Simultaneously, India can also avoid the quagmire of institutions that the EU has as a supranational body, a complexity that traditional states do not have.

It is often quoted and reiterated that India and EU are 'natural partners' by several leaders across time.[38] This is a dictum based on the belief in shared principles of democracy, human rights, multilateralism, and peace. However, it is often criticized that the perception and execution of these ideals differ largely with both, leading to lack of sustained outcomes. While on paper there are many initiatives, in practice the output is scarce. Mostly, the combination of dialogues and meetings are unable to produce any important decisions that take shape of policies.[39] There is also a perception of EU regarding India that it is not "sufficiently speedy and inefficient".[40] This also partly explains the problems of delivery deficit and the widening gap between promise and execution. In terms of democracy and multilateralism as well, there are differences. While EU depends on normative and institutional strength of multilateralism to secure its interests going beyond the immediate state borders and boundaries, India has always held sovereign autonomy very significant.[41] Adding to it, India's approach toward multilateralism has been very selective and arbitrary over the years. In other words, while EU is more driven towards cooperating on economic and technical issues through multilateralism, India's tough neighborhood and security conditions demand a more power-based approach. As EU's foreign policy is still developing a strategic culture when compared to its constituent states, India's priorities and approaches are different. Strategic partnership has not been able to further multilateralism due to such differences between the two parties as their foreign policy traditions are not only different but is shaped by varied forces.[42]

Against the backdrop of these opportunities and criticisms, the future of India-EU relations are dependent on a range of factors. First, the economic future of the relationship has to be decided and should not be delayed further. As economic framework is still the cornerstone of the relationship, the sooner both the parties are able to rejuvenate and re-energize economic relations, the better the direction the relationship would receive. Second, EU's stature in Asia would depend on its choices and stands on geopolitical issues. It would be crucial as to what kind of relations EU would have with China and Pakistan vis-à-vis India. Thirdly, better relations with EU would also depend on its better visibility in the Indian media. The onus would also rest on EU to strengthen its image in the media and amongst the people with which it seeks to better its relations with.[43] Fourthly, EU as an actor is largely marginal to the Indian foreign policy in comparison to the United States and China. This is also because EU is not like any other state in terms of its evolution and functioning. Its evolution suggests that it started off with the objective of creating long-lasting peace through sectoral cooperation amongst the member states. Even in today's international order, states hold primary responsibilities of managing their foreign policies. Hence, developing a strong foreign policy would need a careful maneuvering and balancing within EU. It is also subject to the fact whether the states would recede their claims on foreign policy making, a possibility which seems very unlikely given the nature of prevailing power politics.

The presence of these challenges and the dispassionate nature of relationship has given India-EU relations the tag of a "loveless arranged marriage".[44] The relationship seems to function but there are long-standing challenges which are not addressed. Political and diplomatic rhetoric is dominant rather than time-bound policy solutions and cooperation. If India-EU relations are to realize its potential, there needs to clear and identified tenets on which the parties can reach consensus and cooperate. In the recent past, there have been growing consensus on emerging non-traditional security threats like climate change along with sectoral and technical issues like science technology and space.[45] These would bridge misperceptions about each other and complement the existing nature of engagements.

India-EU relations show us that despite available frameworks of engagement and a host of diplomatic meetings, ties may be hindered by the lack of pressing requirements, mismatch between idea and practice and a lack of resolve to manage outstanding issues. However, this does not mean that the talks are not at all productive. It only means that the existing nature of engagements need to be relooked in a fresh lease and given new directions.

Endnotes

1. EUROPA, "The history of the European Union"; on line source: https://europa.eu/european-union/about-eu/history_en. Accessed on 03 July 2020.
2. Kalin Anev Janse (2015), "Is Europe outperforming the US?", *World Economic Forum*; on line source: https://www.weforum.org/agenda/2015/10/is-europe-outperforming-the-us/. Accessed on 20 July 2020.
3. Arvind Panagariya (2004), "India in the 1980s and 1990s: A Triumph of Reforms", *IMF Working Paper*, WP/04/43, https://www.imf.org/external/pubs/ft/wp/2004/wp0443.pdf. Accessed on 17 July 2020.
4. Bernd von Muenchow-Pohl (2012), "India and Europe in a Multipolar World", *The Carnegie Papers*; on line source: https://carnegieendowment.org/files/india_europe.pdf. Accessed on 18 July 2020.
5. Nayanima Basu (2019), "Deal or no deal, Brexit uncertainty gives India Inc. the hitters", *ThePrint*; on line source: https://theprint.in/economy/deal-or-no-deal-brexit-uncertainty-gives-india-inc-the-jitters/180481/. Accessed on 19 July 2020.
6. Martin J. Dedman (1993), *The Origins and Development of European Union 1945-95: A History of European Integration*, London and New York: Routledge, p. 13.
7. EUROPA, "The Schuman Declaration – 9 May, 1950"; on line source: https://europa.eu/european-union/about-eu/symbols/europe-day/schuman-declaration_en. Accessed on 04 July 2020.

8. Alasdair Blair (2005), *The European Union Since 1945*, London: Pearson Longman, pp. 16-18.
9. EUROPA, "The 27 Member Countries of Europe"; on line source: https://europa.eu/european-union/about-eu/countries_en#tab-0-1. Accessed on 07 July 2020.
10. Wolfgang Munchao (2017), "Europe's four freedoms are its very essence", *Financial Times*, November 12.
11. Herman Lelieveldt and Sebastian Princen (2011), *The Politics of European Union*, Cambridge: Cambridge University Press, pp. 18-22.
12. EUROPA, "EU Treaties'; on line source: https://europa.eu/europeanunion/law/treaties_en. Accessed on 14 July 2020.
13. James Mcbride (2020), "How does European Union Work", *Council on Foreign Relations*; on line source: https://www.cfr.org/backgrounder/how-does-european-union-work. Accessed on 09 July 2020.
14. Rajendra M. Abhyankar (2009), "India and the European Union: A Partnership for all Reasons", *India Quarterly*, 65 (4), pp. 394-96.
15. Ministry of External Affairs (MEA), Govt. of India (2015), "India and the European Union: Future Perspectives", February 23; on line source: https://mea.gov.in/in-focus-article.htm?24797/India+and+the+European+Union+Future+Perspectives. Accessed on 23 July 2020.
16. *The Hindustan Times* (2005), "India-EU Relations"; on line source: https://www.hindustantimes.com/india/india-eu-relations/story-Q7DqJlerVn3e1Wa646jiRI.html. Accessed on 16 July 2020.
17. EUROPA, Treaties Office Database (2013), "Summary of the Treaty"; on line source: https://ec.europa.eu/world/agreements/prepareCreateTreatiesWorkspace/treatiesGeneralData.do?step=0&redirect=true&treatyId=352. Accessed on 23 July 2020.
18. Ummu Salma Bava (2010), "India and the European Union: From Engagement to Strategic Partnership", *International Studies*, 47 (2-4), pp. 377-78.
19. Gulshan Sachdeva (2015), "Evaluation of the EU-India Strategic partnership and the potential for realisation", European Parliament, Directorate general for external policies, Policy Department.
20. Emilian Kavalski (2008), "Venus and the Porcupine: Assessing the European Union-India Strategic Partnership", *South Asian Survey*, 15(1), pp. 72-74.

21. Ministry of External Affairs (MEA), Govt. of India (2015), "India and the European Union: Future Perspectives", February 23; on line source: https://mea.gov.in/in-focus-article.htm?24797/India+and+the+European+Union+Future+Perspectives. Accessed on 23 July 2020.
22. European Commission, Countries and Regions, "India"; on line source: https://ec.europa.eu/trade/policy/countries-and-regions/countries/india/#:~:text=The%20EU%20is%20India's%20largest,the%20total)%20after%20the%20USA. Accessed on 27 July 2020.
23. *The Wire* (2020), "No Sign of EU-India FTA Talks resuming, New High-level dialogue established"; on line source: https://thewire.in/diplomacy/india-eu-summit-trade-talks. Accessed on 27 July 2020.
24. Gulshan Sachdeva (2009), "India and the European Union: Time to de-bureaucratize strategic partnership", *Strategic Analysis*, 33 (2), p. 203.
25. EUR-Lex, European Union Law (2008), "EU-India Strategic Partnership"; on line source: https://eur-lex.europa.eu/legal-content/EN/TXT/?uri=LEGISSUM%3Ar14100. Accessed on 26 July 2020.
26. Christian Wagner (2015), "Western Europe" in David Malone, C. Raja Mohan and Srinath Raghavan (Eds.) *The Oxford Handbook of Indian Foreign Policy*, New York, Oxford University Press.
27. Ian Hall (2017), "Not promoting, Not Exporting: India's Democracy Assistance", *Rising Powers Quarterly*, 2 (3), p. 81.
28. Christophe Jaffrelot (2014), "India and European Union: The Charade of a Strategic Partnership", CERI-Sciences Po, hal-01065630; on line source: https://hal-sciencespo.archives-ouvertes.fr/hal-01065630/document. Accessed on 14 July 2020.
29. Ministry of External Affairs (MEA), Govt of India (2020), "India-EU Strategic Partnership: A Roadmap to 2025"; on line source: https://mea.gov.in/bilateral-documents.htm?dtl/32828/IndiaEU+Strategic+Partnership+A+Roadmap+to+2025. Accessed on 19 July 2020.
30. James McBride (2019), "What Brexit means", *Council on Foreign Relations*; on line source: https://www.cfr.org/backgrounder/what-brexit-means. Accessed on 19 July 2020.
31. Peter Barnes (2020), "Brexit: What happens now?", *BBC*, on line source: https://www.bbc.com/news/uk-politics-46393399. Accessed on 29 July 2020.
32. Radha Kumar (2016), "The EUGS after Brexit: A View from India", *The International Spectator, Italian Journal of International Affairs*, 51 (3), p. 32.

33. Elizabeth Roche (2020), "EU seeking ambitious bilateral trade and investment agreement with India", *Livemint*; on line source: https://www.livemint.com/news/india/eu-seeking-ambitious-bilateral-trade-and-investment-agreement-with-india-11594732637986.html. Accessed on 21 July 2020.
34. Srijan Shukla (2020), "UK wants 5G alliance of 10 countries, including India, to avoid reliance on Chinese Huawei", *ThePrint*, https://theprint.in/world/uk-wants-5g-alliance-of-10-countries-including-india-to-avoid-reliance-on-chinese-huawei/431735/. Accessed on 18 July 2020.
35. *The Business Standard* (2019), "Fuzzy Brexit? High stakes for India over impact on the ties with UK, EU"; on line source: https://www.business-standard.com/article/international/fuzzy-brexit-high-stakes-for-india-over-impact-on-ties-with-uk-eu-117080400338_1.html. Accessed on 17 July 2020.
36. Shashi Tharoor (2012), "Reconsider relations with the European Union", *India Today*; on line source: https://www.indiatoday.in/opinion/shashi-tharoor/story/european-union-india-ties-india-eu-joint-action-plan-102549-2012-05-18. Accessed on 09 July 2020.
37. Stefan Lehne (2017), "Is there hope for EU Foreign Policy", Carnegie Europe: Carnegie Endowment for International Peace; on line source: https://carnegieeurope.eu/2017/12/05/is-there-hope-for-eu-foreign-policy-pub-74909. Accessed on 09 July 2020.
38. Ministry of External Affairs (MEA), Govt. of India (2006), "PM's Statement at the Press Conference at the 7th India-EU Summit"; on line source: https://www.mea.gov.in/Speeches-Statements.htm?dtl/2349/PMs+Statement+at+the+Press+Conference+at+7th+IndiaEU+Summit, accessed on 16 July 2020. Also, *The Hindustan Times* (2020), "PM Modi says India and EU are natural partners, committed to deepen relations", July 15; on line source: https://www.hindustantimes.com/india-news/pm-modi-says-india-and-eu-natural-partners-committed-to-deepen-relations/story-8hfqsVIQrgraRGDjFpXW1I.html.
39. David Malone (2011), *Does the Elephant Dance? Contemporary Indian Foreign Policy*, New York: Oxford University Press, p. 229.
40. Jyontindra Nath Dixit (2019), "India and Europe: Perceptions and Misperceptions", in Rajendra K. Jain (eds.) *Changing Indian Images of the European Union*, Singapore: Palgrave Macmillan, p. 56.
41. Emilian Kavalski (2016), "The EU-India Strategic Partnership: Neither very strategic, nor much of a partnership", *Cambridge Review of International Affairs*, 29(1), pp. 196-201.

42. Rajendra K. Jain (2014), "India-EU Strategic Partnership: Perceptions and Perspectives", NFG Working Paper, No. 10; on line source: http://www.asianperceptions.fu-berlin.de/system/files/private/wp1014-india-eu-strategic-partnership_0.pdf. Accessed on 19 July 2020.
43. Rajendra Jain and Shreya Pandey (2012), "The Public Attitudes and Images of the European Union in India", *India Quarterly*, 68 (4), pp. 340-41.
44. Gauri Khandekar (2011), "The EU and India: A Loveless Arranged Marriage", FRIDE Policy Brief, No. 90; on line source: https://www.files.ethz.ch/isn/132670/PB_90_EU_and_India.pdf. Accessed on 15 July 2020.
45. NDTV (2020), "India EU to step up Cooperation in Climate Change, Science and Technology and Space", July 16; on line source: https://www.ndtv.com/india-news/india-eu-to-step-up-cooperation-in-climate-change-science-and-technology-space-2263569. Accessed on 13 July 2020.

9

India and the United Nations

Souradeep Sen

India is a founding member of the United Nations, signing the UN Charter along with fifty other countries, on 26 June 1945. Even before it achieved independence, India has been one of the leading advocates of global peace, disarmament, decolonization, and sustainable development, thanks to the internationalist outlook of its pre-eminent freedom fighters. After achieving independence, the reflection of the same internationalism and pacifism at the world stage allowed the country to have a commanding role in shaping the various international institutions forming the UN and bestowing it with the leadership of the Non-Aligned Movement. In recent times, the country's repositioning in global governance as an insider in certain global forums, has led to significant successes for Indian diplomacy. It views itself as a champion of the Global South; also as the protector of the interests of developing countries, and this has been a recurrent theme of Indian foreign policy serving as the backdrop for interactions in global governance institutions. With the evolution of global governance, the UN has become the final court of appeal for innumerable 'problems without passports'—or those having no frontiers, requiring solutions that cross all frontiers—such as proliferation of weapons of mass destruction (WMDs), environmental degradation, poverty and starvation, human rights and human security, mass illiteracy and displacement, and the governance of global commons (or the earth's shared natural resources).[1] Additionally, in our present times, the foremost challenge to global governance is being posed by contagious diseases such as the novel coronavirus (Covid-19) global pandemic.

India has asserted that the democratization of global governance is imperative, being contingent upon recognizing the growing role of emerging powers and developing regions. But often, it has failed to reimagine its international behaviour in such institutions, to the detriment of its otherwise strong case for UN Security Council permanent membership. For some experts, the rigidity of certain organizations against institutional change and the inertia of Western powers to move against their established positions, have affected India's perception of itself in institutions of global governance.[2] For others, India's ambivalence results from the lack of a 'grand strategy' to deal with the ever-changing international arena in its foreign policy discourses. Thus, despite its activism in various international institutions, India seems to be reluctant to embrace its prospective influential role as a prime mover of reforms in different institutions of global governance. Perhaps this derives from the belief that India is yet to achieve great power strength in these institutions enough for unilaterally engineering reform proposals without considerable backlash.[3] For this, despite India's substantial contributions toward the UN (including its participation in peacekeeping operations and all the specialized agencies for over seventy years) it continues to form coalitions with other emerging powers and developing countries to promote reforms in the UN, especially those aimed at the Security Council.

The present chapter aims to analyze India's relationship with the United Nations, with special reference to its role in United Nations Peacekeeping Operations (UNPKO) and the politics surrounding India's bid for the UNSC permanent membership. By focusing upon these two aspects of India's relationship with the UN (as a framework for global governance and security) a more or less clear understanding of its successes and missed opportunities in the international arena can be gauged, only by keeping in mind the backdrop of India's colonial/postcolonial experiences and philosophical legacy. For this, the present chapter would first discuss the foundation of UN and its legal framework, along with a brief history of and reasons behind

India's proactive participation in the international organization since its inception. This will be followed by an analysis of how India turned (almost ironically, due to cold war rivalries) into one of the foremost peacekeepers of the world and the political advantage this gave the country towards achieving great power status. The latter, although being within reach, has till date remained only a distant dream for a country which has already invested so greatly toward a permanent seat of the UNSC. The chapter would conclude by raising some issues (such as non-proliferation, climate change and healthcare) which continue to be relevant insofar as India's foreign policy choices vis-à-vis the UN. Furthermore, it seeks to comment on why the UNSC permanent membership is important for the country and the ways in which India's leadership of the Global South and its global role could still be viable diplomatic leverages for achieving the same.

Formation of the UN

The United Nations was established on 24 September 1945, by fifty-one countries as a result of a joint initiative taken by the United States of America, United Kingdoms and the Soviet Union at the end of the Second World War. The term was coined by then US President Franklin D. Roosevelt in 1942. The UN is composed of a group of international institutions, including the Headquarters located in New York, and the specialized agencies, such as the World Health Organization (WHO); the Programmes and Funds, like the United Nations Development Programme (UNDP) and so on. The UN was conceived along the lines of a just and peaceful global community. Its legitimacy derives from universal membership (currently there are 193 member states)[4] and an obligation which ranges from elements of traditional and non-traditional security to economic and social development, environmental, and human rights protection.

When joining, member states agree to accept the obligations of the UN Charter, which is an international treaty underlining the basic principles of international relations. Since its inception, the UN has expanded its activities to address conditions within states, improved its capacity for socio-economic aid, and increased its moral standing in the world—although not without significant challenge. The UN addresses threats to global security coming from both inter-state conflicts and non-state actors, as well as those emanating due to existing political, social and economic conditions within states. Enshrined in the UN Charter are four purposes for its existence:[5]

- Maintenance of international peace and security
- Development of friendly relations among nations
- Achievement of international cooperation in solving international problems and encouraging respect for human rights
- To be a centre for harmonizing the actions of nations.

The UN Charter served as the blueprint for a new international organization that would be at the heart of sustainable peace, to replace the failed League of Nations. It also referred to the needs and interests of peoples as well as those of states. But the UN was created by states for the community of states, and the dialectic between state sovereignty and the protection of the needs and interests of people has not been resolved till date.[6] While initially the UN General Assembly (UNGA) was to be the organization's centre of gravity, the veto power accorded to the Security Council (UNSC) ensured that major decisions depended upon the commanding power concentrated in the five permanent members of the council (p. 5). Although India had supported the veto as a founding member, for its role in fostering great power impartiality and commitment to participation, the success of the US and the UK in bypassing the UNSC for the war in Iraq (2003) was just one of the instances of its disillusionment.

The UN has time and again been questioned with regard to its relevance and effectiveness. But the troubled aftermath of the Iraq war (where its legitimacy was seriously questioned for not being sanctioned by the UN) revealed that it has indeed acquired a sort of moral status in international society. The UN Charter prepares the organization to decide upon the legitimacy of international action in case of threats to peace, breaches of peace and acts of aggression. It also empowers the UN to settle disputes peacefully (relevant Articles in this regard are in Box 9.1). The structure of the UN has six main organs: the Security Council, the General Assembly, the Secretariat, the Economic and Social Council, the Trusteeship Council, and the International Court of Justice (Fig. 9.1). These are intended to achieve international peace and cooperation, by avoiding the problems faced by the League of Nations.

India in the UN

Although India's role in the Cold War has received a rather dismissive treatment owing to its policy of non-alignment, it was actually quite influential in the first two decades of its existence which coincided with the emergence of bipolar hostilities.[7] Since its inception, the Cold War was described by leading Indian politicians as the ultimate culmination of the violence born out of rabid nationalism. For Jawaharlal Nehru, independent India's first Prime Minister and Mahatma Gandhi's hand-picked successor, this type of nationalism was engendered by the zest of European states to acquire spheres of influence, supremacy, and military control. Whereas, anticolonial nationalism demanded liberty and the right to self-determination for colonized people.

Nehru's *internationalism* was a synthesis of his Fabian socialist ideas and the then prevalent subcontinental critique of nationalism. It evolved from a broad cosmopolitanism whereby the best ideas of each civilization would be synthesized into a world federation, and specifically, into federal world government. Nehru envisaged a world that will not be beset by war again, where its people would have the freest possibilities of achieving their maximum potential. This was an idealist position with realist undertones, as Nehru not only left vague the details of such a world government, but also opined that advancing internationalism would suit narrower Indian interests as well.[8] A world government did not undermine the requirement for political responsiveness to local needs, inasmuch as necessitating a standardization of individual, community and national demands into universal principles of human dignity. This initiative found expression in the post-war discourse on human rights, where India played a pivotal role in developing consensus around new norms and creation of novel instruments aimed at their legality and popularization.[9] It was in the Universal Declaration of

Box 9.1: Some Representative Articles of the UN Charter

Preamble: We the peoples of the United Nations [are] determined... "to save succeeding generations from the scourge of war...to reaffirm faith in fundamental human rights...to practice tolerance and live together in peace with one another...to unite our strength to maintain international peace and security..."

Chapter I: Purposes and Principles

Article 2: The Organization and its Members shall act..."on the principle of the sovereign equality of all its Members...shall settle their international disputes by peaceful means... Nothing contained in the present Charter shall authorize the United Nations to intervene in matters which are essentially within the domestic jurisdiction of any state...but this principle shall not prejudice the application of enforcement measures under Chapter VII."

Chapter VI: Pacific Settlement of Disputes

Article 33: "The parties to any dispute, the continuance of which is likely to endanger the maintenance of international peace and security, shall, first of all, seek a solution by negotiation, enquiry, mediation, conciliation, arbitration, judicial settlement, resort to regional agencies or arrangements, or other peaceful means of their own choice."

Chapter VII: Action with Respect to Threats to the Peace, Breaches of the Peace, and Acts of Aggression

Article 39: "The Security Council shall determine the existence of any threat to the [sic] peace, breach of the [sic] peace, or act of aggression and shall make recommendations...to maintain or restore international peace and security."

Article 42: The Security Council may... "take such action by air, sea, or land forces as may be necessary to maintain or restore international peace and security. Such action may include demonstrations, blockade, and other operations by air, sea, or land forces of Members of the United Nations."

Article 43: All Members of the UN shall make available to the Security Council... "armed forces, assistance, and facilities, including rights of passage, necessary for the purpose of maintaining international peace and security."

Article 51: "Nothing in the present Charter shall impair the inherent right of individual or collective self-defence if an armed attack occurs against a Member of the United Nations, until the Security Council has taken measures necessary to maintain international peace and security."

Chapter XV: The Secretariat

Article 99: "The Secretary-General may bring to the attention of the Security Council any matter which in his opinion may threaten the maintenance of international peace and security."

Source: United Nations, "Charter of the United Nations"; on line source: https://www.un.org/en/charter-united-nations/index.html. Accessed on 19 April 2020.

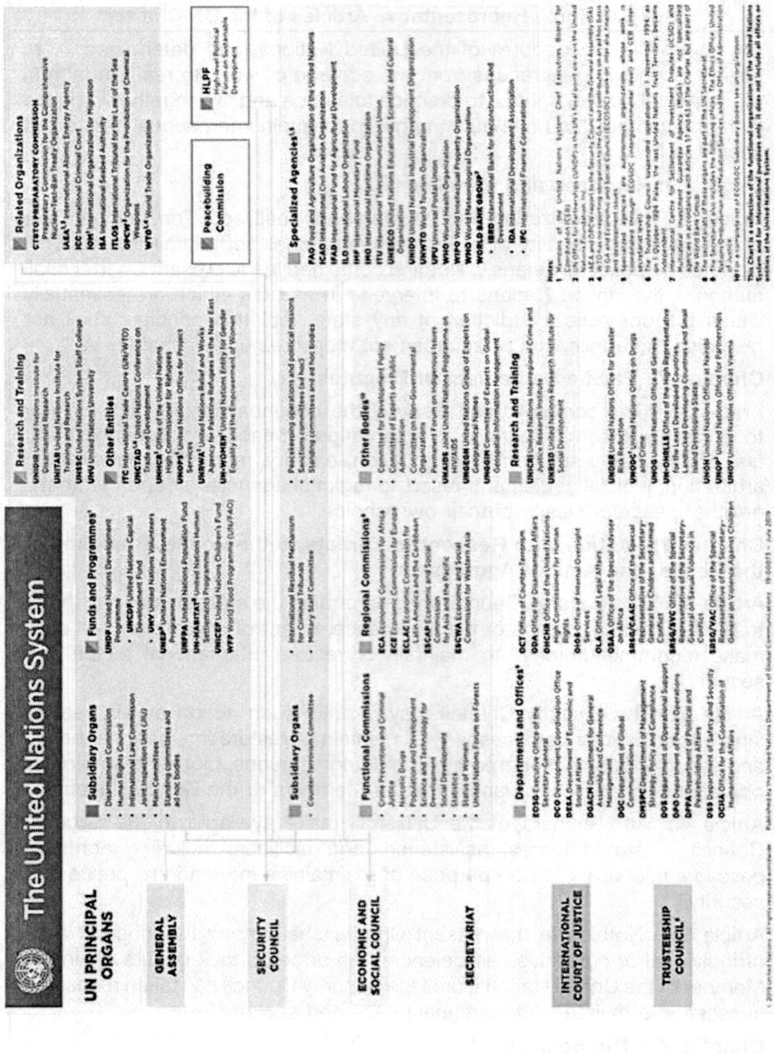

Fig. 9.1: The United Nations System

Source: The United Nations Global Marketplace; on line source: https://www.ungm.org/Shared/KnowledgeCenter/Pages/VBS_UNSystem. Accessed on 19 April 2020.

Human Rights Drafting Committee that India found its footing for the first time within the UN. By its advocacy of economic, social, and cultural rights at par with political and civil liberties, India became a champion of decolonizing countries at the global stage.

India's earliest UN representatives were trained products of the British Indian bureaucracy. India pursued the dual mission of providing moral high ground to and playing global peacemaker for the UN. In the human rights Drafting Committee, India successfully synthesized apparently antithetical sets of rights by the principle of diversity. And it was India that led the effort to bifurcate the legally binding covenant that followed the 1948 Universal Declaration of Human Rights, reflecting negative (political and civil liberties) and positive (economic, social and cultural) rights. 1953 saw the death of Joseph Stalin and the election of Madam Pandit to the presidency of the UNGA, with the unanimous support of the US, USSR, and the Commonwealth countries. This established India as a trusted superpower go-between, especially with its diplomatic involvement in the Korean War (1950-53). At this juncture, Nehru really believed that a turning point had been reached, not just in bilateral relations with the superpowers, but in broader Cold War terms as well.[10]

However, that was not to be. Persistent problems soon derailed India's relationship with the UN and the great powers at its helm. Discouraged from direct intervention against Pakistan by then British PM, Clement Attlee, and despite Article 51 of the UN Charter, Nehru took Pakistan's invasion of Kashmir to the Security Council in 1947. This made it incumbent to accept the decisions of the UN Commission on India and Pakistan (UNCIP). Although India's international prestige grew slightly until its border confrontation with China in 1962, the UNCIP threw the Kashmir issue into a long-term hyperbole.[11] In the 1960s, India championed the causes of South Africa's anti-apartheid struggle, decolonization, global, and comprehensive disarmament. It also assisted the UN peacekeeping efforts in Middle East, Congo, and Cyprus. Non-alignment had already cemented India's position as a leader of the Third World, but its fall from lofty heights was relatively abrupt. India's military takeover of Goa, Daman and Diu and the protracted (even by erstwhile standards) stalemate over Kashmir showed the distance between what it practised and what it preached.

Internationally, India took some missteps as well. Although the Chinese invasion could be attributed to a plethora of reasons, there is no denying that it fundamentally exposed India's utter helplessness against a more powerful adversary and its unfulfilled expectation that the Western powers would come to its aid. Also, India's support to the Soviet occupation of Hungary and its fumbling over the Suez crisis revealed the contradictions of its first Prime Minister and dented its reputation as a champion of peace. India soon realized that the UNSC's power structure was a game of great power politics in which India was no longer welcome at the table. Significantly, it had refused the permanent membership of the council twice in the 1950s (more of this later). With that ship having sailed, India gave paramountcy to its national interest by more openly hitching its star to the Soviet Union after Nehru's demise. Resultantly, it reaped the benefits of the Soviet veto on the Kashmir issue.[12] With the end of the Cold War, power gravitated exclusively towards the UNSC and the rest of the organization was soon marginalized in conflicts ranging from Yugoslavia to Rwanda. With the UNSC now seen as a front for US-driven policies best illustrated in cases such as Libya and Syria, unique spectacles continue to emerge in the UN which have time and again provided fillip to clarion calls for reform. India is one such country in favour of reforms, having participated in all the specialized institutions of the UN and not least, having contributed substantially to the UN's initiatives for the preservation of global peace.

Presently, there are twenty-six organizations of the UN System serving in India.[13] But all are foreshadowed by India's participation in and contribution towards UN peace efforts. India participated in such peace efforts even before gaining independence, often playing a pivotal role in shaping UN peacekeeping, ironically because of the stalemate caused by Cold War bipolar rivalry. Not only has it shaped UN peacekeeping by becoming one of its most ardent advocates, but it has also contributed the largest number of peacekeepers to the UN, both during and after the Cold War. Its significant leadership in peacekeeping operations is often seen as providing the legitimacy for India's reform proposals within the UN. However, India could not capitalize greatly upon its role as the world's 'accidental' peacekeeper, instead remaining a disgruntled rule taker (adhering to existing international norms made by others) in almost every other arena.[14] The following section would scrutinize these issues closely.

India and UN Peacekeeping Operations

India's contributions to the UN Peacekeeping Operations (UNPKO) have been underscored by the professionalism, experience, and sheer numerical strength of its armed forces. By 1945, it stood at a stupendous 2.5 million men, the largest volunteer force in history. India is the largest contributor of troops to the UNPKO, with more than 200,000 troops serving in 49 out of 71 operations undertaken so far.[15] But, before discussing the details of India's participation in peacekeeping for over 70 years, it is imperative to focus on the historical and ideational drivers which propelled the country in this direction.

The Inception of UNPKO

The first UNPKO was launched in Jerusalem (1948). Presently, with approximately 100,000 peacekeepers engaged in fourteen different operations, the UN spends nearly $ 7 billion annually to bring lasting peace around the world. However, nowhere in the XIX chapters of the UN Charter does the word 'peacekeeping' appear.[16] There is a mention of collective security under the leadership of the UNSC (Art. 43) which had remained moribund during the Cold War owing to superpower rivalries. The proposal for a so-called UN Guard came from its first secretary-general, Trygve Lie, as a small force sufficient to prevent localized outbreaks threatening international peace.[17] This, however, did not come to see the light of day. The UN agreed upon a *post factum* definition of peacekeeping after then Secretary-General Boutros Boutros-Ghali described four different types of operations in 1992 (Box 9.2). One expert defines peacekeeping as "traditionally involving military personnel as monitors/observers under restricted rules of engagement (ROE) once a cease-fire has been negotiated."[18]

Box 9.2: Boutros-Ghali's Four Types of Peace Operations in *An Agenda for Peace* (1992)
Preventive diplomacy: Action to prevent disputes from arising between parties, to prevent existing disputes from escalating into conflicts, and to limit the spread of the latter when they occur.
Peacemaking: Action to bring hostile parties to agreement, essentially through such peaceful means as those foreseen in Chapter VI of the UN Charter.
Peacekeeping: The deployment of a UN presence in the field, hitherto with the consent of all parties concerned, normally involving UN military and/or police personnel and frequently civilians as well.
Peacebuilding: Action to identify and support structures which will tend to strengthen and solidify peace in order to avoid a relapse into conflict.

Source: Boutros Boutros-Ghali (1992), "An Agenda for Peace," *Report of the Secretary-General*, U.N. Doc. A/47/277-S/24111, New York: 17 June; on line source: https://digitallibrary.un.org/record/144858?ln=en. Accessed on 20 April 2020.

Dag Hammarskjöld, the second Secretary-General coined the term *peacekeeping*. Mentioning it to be mid-way between Chapters VI and VII of the UN Charter, Hammarskjöld opined that the military organ of the UN, albeit not a conventional military, would have decisive influence over troubled areas.[19] Hammarskjöld's four principles for UN peacekeeping (Box 9.3) were in tune with Gandhi's idea of Peace Brigades in British India of the 1930s. As a matter of fact, pacifists like Nehru and Jayaprakash Narayan were ideationally supportive of Hammarskjöld's principles right from the beginning, thus bringing India closer to the UNPKO. During the Cold War, UNPKO also served the objective of decolonization, and as such these operations were more likely to succeed if they were conducted primarily by countries not engaged in Cold War rivalry. Nehru was quick to grasp the symbiotic relationship between UNPKO and India's established policy of non-alignment. For him, the success of decolonization depended upon UN membership for newly independent states; and for the UN to succeed, peacekeeping was imperative and contingent upon the NDCs.[20] Consequently, non-aligned India along with other neutral countries played a crucial role in the theory and practice of UNPKO. At UN Headquarters, Major General Indar Jit Rikhye, the only military adviser to the Secretary-General (1960-68), worked closely with Hammarskjöld and his successor, U Thant, to develop the peacekeeping doctrine of the UN. While in the field, Indian troops were involved in peacekeeping operations in Korea, Egypt, Lebanon, Congo, West New Guinea, Yemen, Cyprus, and Dominican Republic.

Box 9.3: Dag Hammarskjöld's Four Principles for UN Peacekeeping (1958)
Deployment and presence of UN force is entirely dependent upon the consent of the host state.
Deployment of troops neutral to both East-West conflict and to the specific conflict at hand.
Troops were to maintain absolute impartiality and not meddle in the political outcome of a conflict.
Troops were to remain lightly armed and use force only for their own self-defense.

Source: Dag Hammarskjöld (1958), "Report of the Secretary-General", UN General Assembly, U.N. Doc. A/3942, New York: 8 October; on line source: https://digitallibrary.un.org/record/844803?ln=en. Accessed on 20 April 2020.

India's Role in UNPKO: Historical and Military Reasons

By 1945, India was one of the fifty-one countries to possess a military expeditionary capability required to conduct operations under the UN flag. This force was ironically the product of its colonial legacy, as by the end of the Second World War, the Indian army swelled into a 2.5 million strong land force with field experience in both World Wars. Although by the time of independence, the Indian army had shrunk to 500,000 troops, it was still not only one of the most experienced, but also one of the largest forces outside Cold War blocs. The latter fulfilled the prime requirement for being deployed under UNPKO. Even before independence, Nehru envisaged a continuing global role for India's military, especially in the resolution of South

Asian, Middle Eastern and South-East Asian security problems. However since independence, India's postcolonial leaders were more interested in carving out its non-aligned credentials. And at the global front, it was hard to conceive of a proper role for India's armed forces in decolonization without explicit command from the UN.[21]

But, Nehru was resolute in forwarding every possible support towards the organization for its development into some kind of world government. With provisions in the Constitution of India (Art. 51) and a large, experienced standing army, India had reasons enough to play a normative and material role in the evolution of UNPKO.[22] With this, it participated in some of the most complex and difficult peacekeeping missions around the world. In hindsight, none of these would have been possible for India had there been no superpower rivalry. Had the UNSC been active during the Cold War, Article 43 of the Charter (which provides collective security arrangements) could have been invoked for the maintenance of international peace and security. In its absence, the world has witnessed eight phases of peacekeeping operations (Box 9.4) and billions of dollars spent by the UN for such protracted and often failed operations. The phases in Box 9.4 are indicative of the rise and fall of UN peacekeeping operations during the Cold War and its aftermath. The odd-numbered phases are periods of little new operations (ranging around three new cases per phase) and the even-numbered periods are when peacekeeping literally went over

Box 9.4: Phases of Peacekeeping (1946-Present)
1. the Nascent Period 1946-56 2. the Assertive Period 1956-67 3. the Dormant Period 1967-73 4. the Resurgent Period 1973-78 5. the Maintenance Period 1978-88 6. the Expansion Period 1988-93 7. the Contraction Period 1993-99 8. the Unrealistic Expectations Period 1999-Present

Source: Dennis C. Jett (2019), *Why Peacekeeping Fails*, 2nd edition, Switzerland: Palgrave Macmillan, p. 38.

the roof (with around 15 to 20 new cases per phase). The use of peacekeeping was determined by superpower rivalry, interest of other major powers, and the evolution of conflicts in various zones.

The first two periods of expansion were a result of the wars in the Middle East, where peacekeeping was confined mostly to the continuation of ongoing missions. A third cycle of expansion began in 1988 with the end of the Cold War, where UNPKO were tasked with curbing civil wars. The Contraction Period (1993-99) was short-lived and led to increased intervention to address humanitarian disasters caused by ongoing civil wars in African and East European states. Following the 9/11 attacks, terrorism also added a new dimension to peacekeeping. By March 2020, there were 3928 fatalities among peacekeepers and the decade-wise fatality has increased progressively since 1988. Currently, 69,638 troops and military observers and about 8,756 police personnel are posted around the world in UNPKO. The total number of personnel presently serving in different capacities stands at 95,536.[23]

India has the highest number of fatalities in UNPKO. Till March 2020, as many as 170 soldiers have lost their lives to peacekeeping operations, with the most number of Indian soldiers achieving martyrdom in Egypt and Congo.[24] Despite the glaring gender inequality in UNPKO, India stands out as the first country to contribute an all women contingent, the Formed Police Unit from India (FPU), to the United Nations Observer Mission in Liberia (UNMIL) in 2007.[25]

Of the 71 missions undertaken under UNPKO so far, 13 are still active (Table 9.1), including the earliest UNPKO in the Middle East (United Nations Truce Supervision Organization, May 1948). The latest successfully concluded mission was in Haiti (United Nations Mission for Justice Support in Haiti, October 2017 to October 2019). The total approved budgets (from July 1, 2019 to June 30, 2020) for the 13 operations presently underway is an astounding US$ 6.5 billion.[26]

Table 9.1: List of UN Peacekeeping Missions (1948-2019)

ACRONYM	MISSION NAME	START DATE	END DATE
UNTSO	United Nations Truce Supervision Organization	May 1948	Present
UNMOGIP	United Nations Military Observer Group in India and Pakistan	Jan 1949	Present
UNEF I	First United Nations Emergency Force	Nov 1956	June 1967
UNOGIL	United Nations Observation Group in Lebanon	June 1958	Dec 1958
ONUC	United Nations Operation in the Congo	July 1960	June 1964
UNSF	United Nations Security Force in West New Guinea	Oct 1962	April 1963
UNYOM	United Nations Yemen Observation Mission	July 1963	Sept 1964
UNFICYP	United Nations Peacekeeping Force in Cyprus	Mar 1964	Present
DOMREP	Mission of the Representative of the Secretary-General in the Dominican Republic	May 1965	Oct 1966
UNIPOM	United Nations India-Pakistan Observation Mission	Sept 1965	Mar 1966
UNEF II	Second United Nations Emergency Force	Oct 1973	July 1979
UNDOF	United Nations Disengagement Observer Force*	June 1974	Present
UNIFIL	United Nations Interim Force in Lebanon*	Mar 1978	Present
UNGOMAP	United Nations Good Offices Mission in Afghanistan and Pakistan	May 1988	Mar 1990
UNIIMOG	United Nations Iran-Iraq Military Observer Group	Aug 1988	Feb 1991
UNAVEM I	United Nations Angola Verification Mission I	Jan 1989	June 1991
UNTAG	United Nations Transition Assistance Group	Apr 1989	Mar 1990
ONUCA	United Nations Observer Group in Central America	Nov 1989	Jan 1992
UNIKOM	United Nations Iraq-Kuwait Observation Mission	Apr 1991	Oct 2003

ACRONYM	MISSION NAME	START DATE	END DATE
MINURSO	United Nations Mission for the Referendum in Western Sahara	Apr 1991	Present
UNAVEM II	United Nations Angola Verification Mission II	June 1991	Feb 1995
ONUSAL	United Nations Observer Mission in El Salvador	July 1991	Apr 1995
UNAMIC	United Nations Advance Mission in Cambodia	Oct 1991	Mar 1992
UNPROFOR	United Nations Protection Force	Feb 1992	Mar 1995
UNTAC	United Nations Transitional Authority in Cambodia	Mar 1992	Sept 1993
UNOSOM I	United Nations Operation in Somalia I	Apr 1992	Mar 1993
ONUMOZ	United Nations Operation in Mozambique	Dec 1992	Dec 1994
UNOSOM II	United Nations Operation in Somalia II	Mar 1993	Mar 1995
UNOMUR	United Nations Observer Mission Uganda-Rwanda	June 1993	Sept 1994
UNOMIG	United Nations Observer Mission in Georgia	Aug 1993	June 2009
UNOMIL	United Nations Observer Mission in Liberia	Sept 1993	Sept 1997
UNMIH	United Nations Mission in Haiti	Sept 1993	June 1996
UNAMIR	United Nations Assistance Mission for Rwanda	Oct 1993	Mar 1996
UNASOG	United Nations Aouzou Strip Observer Group	May 1994	June 1994
UNMOT	United Nations Mission of Observers in Tajikistan	Dec 1994	May 2000
UNAVEM III	United Nations Angola Verification Mission III	Feb 1995	June 1997
UNCRO	United Nations Confidence Restoration Operation in Croatia	May 1995	Jan 1996
UNPREDEP	United Nations Preventive Deployment Force	Mar 1995	Feb 1999
UNMIBH	United Nations Mission in Bosnia and Herzegovina	Dec 1995	Dec 2002

ACRONYM	MISSION NAME	START DATE	END DATE
UNTAES	United Nations Transitional Administration for Eastern Slavonia, Baranja and Western Sirmium	Jan 1996	Jan 1998
UNMOP	United Nations Mission of Observers in Prevlaka	Jan 1996	Dec 2002
UNSMIH	United Nations Support Mission in Haiti	July 1996	July 1997
MINUGUA	United Nations Verification Mission in Guatemala	Jan 1997	May 1997
MONUA	United Nations Observer Mission in Angola	June 1997	Feb 1999
UNTMIH	United Nations Transition Mission in Haiti	Aug 1997	Dec 1997
MIPONUH	United Nations Civilian Police Mission in Haiti	Dec 1997	Mar 2000
UNCPSG	UN Civilian Police Support Group	Jan 1998	Oct 1998
MINURCA	United Nations Mission in the Central African Republic	Apr 1998	Feb 2000
UNOMSIL	United Nations Observer Mission in Sierra Leone	July 1998	Oct 1999
UNMIK	United Nations Interim Administration Mission in Kosovo	June 1999	Present
UNAMSIL	United Nations Mission in Sierra Leone	Oct 1999	Dec 2005
UNTAET	United Nations Transitional Administration in East Timor	Oct 1999	May 2002
MONUC	United Nations Organization Mission in the Democratic Republic of the Congo	Nov 1999	June 2010
UNMEE	United Nations Mission in Ethiopia and Eritrea	July 2000	July 2008
UNMISET	United Nations Mission of Support in East Timor	May 2002	May 2005
MINUCI	United Nations Mission in Côte d'Ivoire	May 2003	Apr 2004
UNMIL	United Nations Mission in Liberia	Sept 2003	Mar 2018
UNOCI	United Nations Operation in Côte d'Ivoire	Apr 2004	May 2017
MINUSTAH	United Nations Stabilization Mission in Haiti	June 2004	Oct 2017

ACRONYM	MISSION NAME	START DATE	END DATE
ONUB	United Nations Operation in Burundi	June 2004	Dec 2006
UNMIS	United Nations Mission in the Sudan	Mar 2005	July 2011
UNMIT	United Nations Integrated Mission in Timor-Leste	Aug 2006	Dec 2012
UNAMID	African Union-United Nations Hybrid Operation in Darfur	July 2007	Present
MINURCAT	United Nations Mission in the Central African Republic and Chad	Sept 2007	Dec 2010
MONUSCO	United Nations Organization Stabilization Mission in the Democratic Republic of the Congo*	July 2010	Present
UNISFA	United Nations Organization Interim Security Force for Abyei	June 2011	Present
UNMISS	United Nations Mission in the Republic of South Sudan*	July 2011	Present
UNSMIS	United Nations Supervision Mission in Syria	Apr 2012	Aug 2012
MINUSMA	United Nations Multidimensional Integrated Stabilization Mission in Mali	Apr 2013	Present
MINUSCA	United Nations Multidimensional Integrated Stabilization Mission in the Central African Republic	Apr 2014	Present
MINUJUSTH	United Nations Mission for Justice Support in Haiti	Oct 2017	Oct 2019

Source: United Nations Peacekeeping (2020), "Data," New York: 31 March; on line source: https://peacekeeping.un.org/en/data. Accessed on 21 April 2020. United Nations Peacekeeping (2020), "India," New York: 31 March; on line source: https://peacekeeping.un.org/en/india. Accessed on 21 April 2020. *denotes India's present involvement in missions.

India's Role in UNPKO and Peacebuilding

The sheer size and professionalism of its armed forces, the lack of such forces in other developing countries after the Second World War and India's neutral stance during the Cold War ensured that it not only remained the most acceptable option for host countries, but the most popular choice among states participating in peacekeeping.[27] India's contribution in the field is well documented. In 1950, the 60 Parachute Field Ambulance of the Indian Army was sent to provide medical cover to US/ROK and UN forces engaged in the Korean War. It remained in Korea for three and a half years (from November 1950 to May 1954), and remains the longest single tenure by any military in UNPKO. From November 1956 to May 1967, eleven infantry battalions from India served by rotation in the UN Emergency Force (UNEF 1) to ensure the withdrawal of France, UK, and Israel from Egyptian territory and to sustain the peace between Israel and her Arab neighbours. During the Congo crisis, two Indian brigades participated in ONUC (July 1960 to June 1964). And it was under India's leadership that the rules of UNPKO were altered by then Secretary-General Hammarskjöld to cater to use of force in defence of the mandate, in carrying out humanitarian tasks, and in countering mercenaries.[28]

The role of Indar Jit Rikhye and Krishna Menon in creating these norms and in ensuring their implementation on the ground while tip-toeing the dangerous Cold War political landscape often remains under appreciated by Western experts. India has also, so far, provided 15 Force Commanders in various UNPKO. Presently, Major General Jai Shankar Menon, VSM, is serving as the Force Commander in UNDOF (Golan Heights). India has provided two Military Advisors to the Secretary-General, two Divisional Commanders and seven Deputy Force Commanders to UNPKO.[29] The Expansion Period of UNPKO (1988-93) saw the mushrooming of crises after the end of the Cold War. More than 20 new missions were deployed from 1989 to 1994. Several others began by 2017, and India's contributions in all these could be clubbed into three broad areas:[30]

- **The use of UNPKO for peaceful political transition:** Such operations include UNPROFOR (former Yugoslavia, under Lieutenant General Satish Nambiar); UNTAC (Cambodia); ONUSAL (El Salvador); ONUMOZ (Mozambique); UNOSOM (Somalia); UNAVEM (Angola); UNAMSIL (Sierra Leone); UNMEE (Ethiopia-Eritrea); and UNMIT (East Timor).

- **Augmenting peacebuilding activities by national governance institutions:** Indian troops in the UN has encouraged and mentored in strengthening national governance institutions. The UNTAG saw Indian peacekeepers assist in the creation of the institutions of independent Namibia. India became the first country to demonstrate the effectiveness of women as UN peacekeepers in peacebuilding with the deployment of the first female FPU to Liberia in 2007.
- **Leading the ground-level response to new challenges:** This especially while the UN Security Council remains ineffective in implementing its decisions. The protection of civilians caught in intra-state conflicts is one issue where India's UN peacekeepers have made a positive difference, especially in complex operations like MONUSCO (Congo) and UNMISS (South Sudan). Indian forces have also volunteered medical services, including veterinary support, and engineering services in operations like UNIFIL (Lebanon), contributing to the sustained livelihood of conflict-ridden local communities.

Although the Cold War constrained India's actions, in many cases compelled it to follow rules established by others which were not in its interests, India has reaped several tangible benefits from its rule-shaping role in UNPKO:[31]

- UN peacekeeping has allowed India a high-profile diplomatic and military role, despite the tiny space left for developing countries by great powers, especially during the Cold War.
- As peacekeeping became linked to decolonization, India's influence in the UN increased, especially when NDCs joined the organization and looked to India for leadership.
- It also allowed India to retain its global expeditionary capabilities without being perceived as a threat.

India and UNPKO: Subsidiary Conclusion

The chapter has so far argued that during the Cold War, India ironically became a rule shaper for UN peacekeeping for two fundamental reasons: Nehruvian internationalism and the defunct nature of Article 43 of the UN Charter. The latter took shape in the aftermath of the US involvement in Korea, the Suez involvement of Britain and France, and Russia's invasion of Hungary. Then Secretary-General Dag Hammarskjöld had a reliable ally in India as it fulfilled all of his requirements for a successful peacekeeper: a country with military skills and experience, with no political or economic interests in the Third World areas of conflict, no colonial territories, an identification with active and independent internationalism, and lastly, a strong support for the UN's peace and security functions.[32]

The UN in general and peacekeeping in particular offered India an ideal opportunity to shape rules which served a greater global public good, while providing a head start to New Delhi's strategic interests—even if it could not capitalize in the long run. However, despite its historically warranted contributions and impressive record as the world's foremost peacekeeping nation, India has not been able to translate these into great power status either during the Cold War or ever since. Despite its sacrifices to peacekeeping, India could not further its economic or political interests or garner greater support for its demand of the UNSC permanent membership. Ironically, some countries that benefited from India's peacekeeping contributions remain indifferent or opposed to its global ambitions. Also, India continues to face challenges in the field from terrorists and insurgents in its zest to restore peace in the world. In the Golan Heights, Indian UN military officers were the first to confront such challenges by the Jabhat al-Nusra terrorist group which took UN peacekeepers hostage in 2014. Moreover, staying outside the UNSC, with huge number of personnel on the field throughout the world, deprives India of taking decisions regarding its own troops. This despite Article 44 of the UN Charter (involving decisions of the UNSC concerning troop deployment by allowing the contributing country to the table). India continues to fall prey to a great power tactic to keep developing countries off the nerve centre of the UN.[33] Thus, India remains an 'accidental' global peacekeeper.[34] More so, as it declined, on multiple occasions at the beginning of the Cold War, the coveted permanent membership (instead urging the superpowers to serve it up to the then nascent Peoples' Republic of China) till it abruptly slipped away and became entwined with its own economic vacillations in the international arena. The remainder of the chapter would analyze the politics surrounding permanent membership of the UNSC, and discuss ways to salvage the still unrealized aspiration.

India and the UN Security Council

Chapter V of the UN Charter provides for the composition, functions and powers, voting, and procedure of the Security Council. The council comprises five permanent (China, France, Russia, United Kingdom, and United States of America), and ten non-permanent members to be elected by the General Assembly for a term of two years. While choosing the latter, due regard must be paid to the contribution of members toward the goals of the UN, and also to equitable geographical distribution.[35] What makes the P5 special is that they possess the right to veto (Box 9.5) or nullify any proposal or resolution put to vote in the council. India has held the non-permanent membership of the council for seven times in the past: 1950-51, 1967-68, 1972-73, 1977-78, 1984-85, 1991-92, 2011-12. And in 2019, it has been elected for the eighth time for a similar term in 2021-22, with the unanimous support of all the 55 countries in the Asia-Pacific Group. This is significant, as even Pakistan and China came out in its support, for what India's Permanent Representative to the UN, Syed Akbaruddin, has called a phenomenal success of its quiet and effective diplomacy.[36] This is ironic as there was a time when India could have been firmly established on the other side of the Security Council, had it not been for the miscalculations of its own leaders and diplomats. A little bit of history is warranted here.

Box 9.5: The Right to Veto of the Permanent Members of Security Council
The creators of the United Nations Charter conceived that five countries—China, France, the Union of Soviet Socialist Republics (USSR) [which was succeeded in 1990 by the Russian Federation], the United Kingdom and the United States—, because of their key roles in the establishment of the United Nations, would continue to play important roles in the maintenance of international peace and security. They were granted the special status of Permanent Member States at the Security Council, along with a special voting power known as the "right to veto". It was agreed by the drafters that if any one of the five permanent members cast a negative vote in the 15-member Security Council, the resolution or decision would not be approved. All five permanent members have exercised the right of veto at one time or another. If a permanent member does not fully agree with a proposed resolution but does not wish to cast a veto, it may choose to abstain, thus allowing the resolution to be adopted if it obtains the required number of nine favourable votes.

Source: United Nations Security Council (2020), "Voting System"; on line source: https://www.un.org/securitycouncil/content/voting-system. Accessed on 23 April 2020.

India, China and the UNSC Permanent Membership

During the halcyon days of the 1950s, when India was already a non-permanent member of the UNSC and one of the leading lights in the UN, it began a serious push towards nuclear disarmament. It was seen as an impartial advocate of global peace and in the persons of Madam Pandit and Nehru, as trenchant activists for decolonization and disarmament. Indeed, Robert Oppenheimer, the architect of the atomic bomb, implored Madam Pandit and Nehru to save the world from impending nuclear holocaust, as at that time, only they possessed the stature and goodwill necessary to convince both superpowers. Thus, while the Korean War was still on, India quietly established a disarmament subcommittee through the UNGA to address this issue.[37] However, this came at the same time India was busy investing in its own nuclear energy programme. Such contradictions seemed to reach a peak in the mid-1950s, when India was grappling with the UN and its prospective leadership of the Third World through NAM.

Although both superpowers still believed that India was an honest superpower go-between, its leadership of the NAM seemingly alienated the Western powers at the cost of a very vocal endorsement by the USSR. In 1950, India was offered the permanent membership of the UNSC by the US in place of the newly communist China. In 1955, a similar offer was made by the USSR, which was at that time hosting Nehru on a state visit. Both offers were turned down by him for reasons which have now become clear. But, how could such endorsements be made when there were already five permanent members by 1950 and the UN Charter clearly forbade anymore? The offers were valid for technical reasons.

The Republic of China (ROC) or nationalist China was an original member of the Big Four or the victors of the Second World War (along with the US, Britain, and USSR). In recognition of its longstanding fight against aggression, China was accorded the honour of being the first country to sign the Charter in June 1945.[38] With the support of the US, and despite opposition from other victors, the ROC became a permanent member of the UNSC. In 1949, the Communist Party of China was finally victorious over their enemies, thus drawing the Chinese Civil War to an end and establishing the People's Republic of China. The PRC, according to Mao Zedong was the sole legitimate government of China, especially in the wake of the CPC's domination of the Chinese mainland and the ROC government retreat to Taiwan, Quemoy (Kinmen) and Matsu (Kinma) islands (see Fig. 9.2). As ideology prevented the Western powers from admitting another communist country into the Security Council, they blocked the representation of China by PRC for over two decades. The Soviet Union boycotted the UN, in protest of PRC's exclusion. So, the Chinese seat was technically vacant till 1971, when ironically, by allying itself with Nixon's America,

PRC was finally admitted to the Security Council as the sole legal representative of China, vide General Assembly Resolution 2758.[39] This forced the ROC to join international organizations under other names, especially Chinese Taipei. Its recent request for admission in the organization was also blocked in 2007.[40]

Nehru, on the other hand, had not only rejected the offers for India's permanent seat, but also rallied Third World leaders in support of PRC's permanent membership. For Nehru, in shutting out an established government because it was communist, the West was repeating the fatal mistake it had made in treating the USSR as a pariah, with dire international consequences.[41] Nehru wanted to prevent the West from fomenting the same insecurities which then plagued the USSR, warning that by isolating and outlawing the PRC, it would behave in a predictable manner without any international obligation. The one point where he was absolutely correct is that by asking India to take the Chinese seat in the Security Council, the superpowers were inadvertently creating space for more intense rivalry between India and China.[42] Nehru's reply to both offers, thus, was resounding: not at the cost of the fragile stability and viability of the UN as an institution, and more importantly, not at the cost of China.[43]

The Security Council: India's Dilemma

India's advocacy of PRC and its subsequent sloppy international behaviour did not bode well for the country. It alienated the bulk of the Security Council by being soft towards the Soviet Union's Hungarian invasion, while condemning in no less unequivocal terms the British and French involvement in Egypt. Although diplomatically there seemed to be amity between India and China, the latter contested portions of the border. Through the 1950s, Chinese intentions became clear with the construction of infrastructure in the Aksai Chin region. Nehru was convinced that this was all a misunderstanding, despite remaining firm in defending India's national interest. Referring the matter to the UN, India hoped for neutral arbitration. But, in the wake of the Dalai Lama's daring escape to India and its subsequent approval to provide asylum to him and his retinue in 1959, the UN's pro-India findings were nullified.

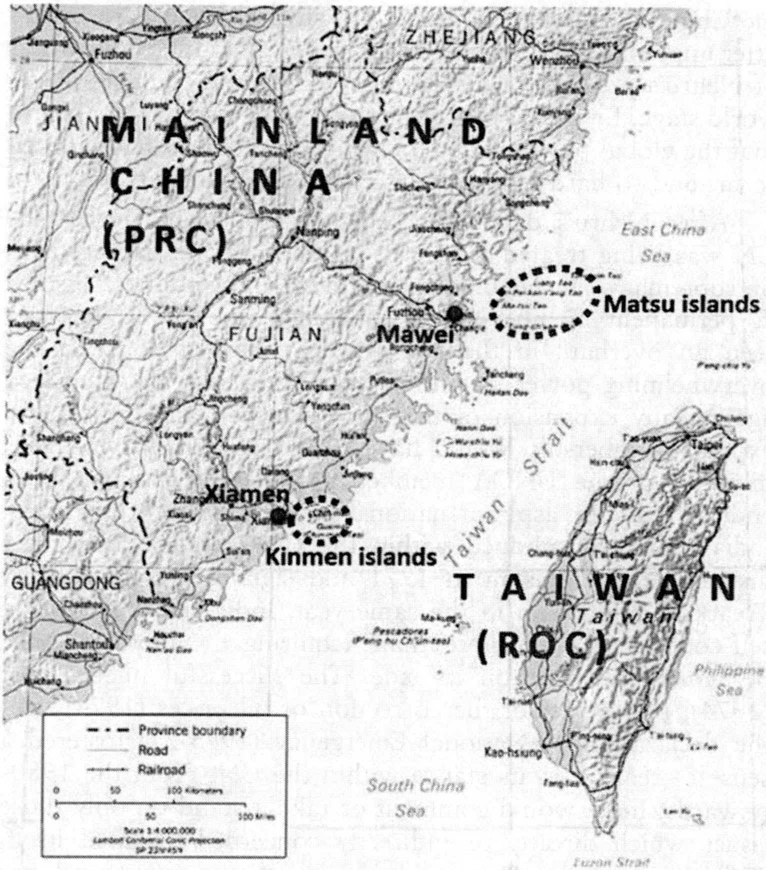

Fig. 9.2: ROC and PRC Placements (1949)

Source: Ling-I Chu and Jinn-Yuh Hsu (2018), "Cold War islands and the rebordering of the nation/state: Kinma in the Taiwan Strait"; on line source: https://www.focaalblog.com/2018/06/18/cold-war-islands-and-the-rebordering-of-the-nationstate-kinma-in-the-taiwan-strait/. Accessed on 26 April 2020.

After the Central Government's hostile takeover of Goa and Krishna Menon's tirades against China, India was gradually losing its international standing as a peaceful country. Things gradually slipped out of Nehru's grasp and ultimately led to the Chinese invasion in 1962.[44] The invasion laid bare India's utter unpreparedness to face a stronger rival and the hollowness of Nehru's pro-India rhetoric, discrediting the country on the world stage. By now it was clear to an aging and hapless Nehru that the global power status for which his country had worked so far and so hard was already a missed opportunity.

After Nehru's demise, it became clear to India that the UN was being treated by the P5 as the ultimate battleground of supremacy in the bipolar world of bloc politics. Insofar as permanent membership is concerned, the UNSC has not seen an overhaul in the last seventy years or so. And the overwhelming power stemming from 'veto' has also militated against any expansion of the same. Further, any decision to expand membership would have to be ratified by two-thirds majority of the UNGA membership, thereby making it an endless road for aspirant nations. In the post-Nehruvian era, India remained subdued within the UN councils. But, after dismembering Pakistan in 1971 and signing the Indo-Soviet Treaty of Friendship in the same year, India regained its lost self-confidence with more than acquiring a valuable UNSC permanent member on its side. The successful nuclear test (1974), the impact of the correction of oil prices (1974), and the declaration of National Emergency (1975-77) fostered a sense of realism in its stance within the UN. From the 1980s onwards, India would comment or take a stand on only those issues which directly or indirectly concerned/benefited itself, with the exception of decolonization, disarmament, military bases, and non-proliferation.[45] Although it participated in all economic forums and voiced concern regarding traditional and non-traditional security threats, India since 1990 has remodeled its external relations on a wider international network, in tune with its economic liberalization and market imperatives. For example, after the Cold War, India started moving closer to the US and its allies, such as Israel (since 1992), despite its support to the Arab cause and friendship with Russia—all attributed to overarching economic imperatives.

India's position in the UN and its legitimacy for permanent membership of the UNSC has periodically been linked to its economic fluctuations. Its economic success in the last two decades has been synonymous with international political stature and ability to assume responsibility only as a UNSC non-permanent member. The 2006 US-India civil nuclear agreement was also seen as a step forward in recognizing the country as a power in its own right, breaking it free of the claustrophobic India-Pakistan regional box. But the international recognition due to these developments during the Manmohan Singh era did not translate into the global recognition that India craved. With the economic and political levers turning towards Asia-Pacific in the last decade or so, and India's role in the Indian Ocean Region (IOR) as a net security provider, the country has found itself at the crossroads of its relation with China and the United States. China's intentions have been particularly clear with the String of Pearls and Belt and Road Initiative (OBOR). And with Indian Navy's nuclear submarines (SSBNs) eternally locked in a trilateral (along with China and Pakistan) security competition in the Indian Ocean, a move towards more friendly relations with the US seemed to be on the cards until at least the last two years.[46] The latter, if sustained, could have given it certain political advantages at the UN. However, the Covid-19 pandemic of 2020 has opened up a plethora of newer diplomatic challenges for India which should foster an even stronger sense of realism in its foreign policy, especially vis-à-vis institutions of global governance. It is perhaps offering the country with an opportunity to evaluate its list of fair-weather friends, foremost in the light of diplomatic pressures pertaining to the supply of prophylactic drugs to great powers. It is, thus, time for India to accept that it is fundamentally alone in a world driven by self-interest. And any initiative towards great power status would have to come from its own international standing, with success dependent upon its ability to persevere in the face of sustained opposition from established powers. With the devolution of Western economies in the post-Covid scenario, the rise of China seems inevitable.[47] India's UN dilemmas notwithstanding, the opportunities this would open up for Asian economies in the days to come must be harnessed if India wants its present G-4 (Brazil, Germany, Japan, and India) bid for UNSC permanent membership to reap any tangible benefits. The 2021-22 non-permanent membership platform seems most opportune for realizing India's global ambitions.

India's Security Council Reform Proposals

India's campaign for permanent membership received a boost with Prime Minister Narendra Modi's participation in the 47th session of the UNGA (2015). Its initial bid for reform and expansion of the UNSC was officially launched in 1994, in collaboration with the G-4 which culminated in 2004-05 by an attempt to mobilize support to gain the required two-thirds majority vote in the critical General Assembly World Summit (2005). The G-4 spearheaded by India demanded an expansion of both permanent and non-permanent memberships which would be inclusive and representative of the interests of both developing and developed countries.[48] It was also willing to settle for a permanent membership without 'veto' for itself, but failure to garner the support of the Africa Group in the 2005 Summit meant that the two-thirds majority could not be reached and the proposal was ultimately defeated.[49]

Despite significant ideational and material contributions to UN peacekeeping, and its membership of all major international, regional and sub-regional organizations, the dominant rhetoric links India's permanent membership to its global economic prowess.[50] India's bid at the UNSC suffered in September 2016, following which the G-4 resolved on launching text-based negotiations during the 72nd session of the UNGA (2017). The negotiating text, though adopted, saw serious opposition from the Uniting for Consensus (UfC) group led by Pakistan and Italy. This came against the backdrop of India and Pakistan again being at loggerheads on Kashmir in 2017, with the Pakistani Prime Minister urging the UNSC to appoint a special representative on Kashmir and the Indian External Affairs Minister accusing Pakistan of supporting jihadist elements. Similar tensions between the two countries plagued India's activism for the permanent membership even as late as 2019, with the Pulwama terrorist attacks before India's general elections and the revocation of Article 370 by the Indian Government, that very year.

Rising regional tensions dropped the permanent membership issue in the backburner despite Japan's reiteration of India's three clusters of reform for the UNSC (Box 9.6), in February 2019. Analysts have attributed this to China's pivotal role in steering anti-India rhetoric in the council. Although the present Secretary-General, Antonio Gutierrez attempted to bring both parties to an agreement, the Indian foreign ministry took a firm stand stating that bilateral matters have to be dealt bilaterally. But, the Kashmir issue continues to have an adverse effect on India's prospects of its permanent membership.[51] India's reform bid within the G-4 conforms to all the tenets of the formerly adopted Decision 62/557 of the UNGA (2008) which defines five broad issues of reform. But, it has often led to more acrimonious debates than consensus largely because of factionalism within the UNGA, where several groups of countries (Table 9.2) with definite vested interests, have stalled the reform process by deliberately blocking two-thirds majority.[52] For one expert, the situation is comparable to an imaginary rugby match where each player (or country) wants to grab the ball (of reforms) and pass it to the direction of its own self-interest, which ultimately results in chaos, indecision and stalemate.[53]

India's Contemporary Involvements in the Security Council

The seven times that India has been on the Security Council, its performance has been technically sound. It has eschewed statements on the burning issues of the day, unless absolutely necessary, in order to not antagonize the P5. Its handling of the Kashmir issue in the UNSC has ensured that it does not come up in a major way. And even when it does, remains confined to a bilateral issue in tune with the Shimla Agreement (1972), despite Pakistan's efforts to revert it to the council.

Box 9.6: India's Three Clusters of Reforms Reiterated by Japan (February 2019)
Categories of membership: The G-4 and other states are convinced that an expansion of both permanent and non-permanent categories of membership would be truly representative and overcome the current imbalance of influence and legitimation crisis of the Security Council.
Regional representation: Giving due regard to geographical representation to correct historical injustices to regions with no permanent members. Representation of small- and medium-sized members, island nations with cross-regional arrangements.
Veto power: New permanent members must be vested with veto-right only after 15 years of holding seat, after reform comes into force. Alternatives were also open for discussion.

Source: Yasuhisa Kawamura (2019), "Joint G4 Statement Delivered by H.E. Ambassador and Deputy Permanent Representative of Japan to the UN", Second IGN on Security Council Reforms, New York: 25 February; on line source: https://www.un.emb-japan.go.jp/itpr_en/kawamura022519.html. Accessed on 27 April 2020.

Table 9.2: Interested Parties in UNSC Reforms

Grouping	Countries	Agenda
G-4	Germany, Japan, India, Brazil	Mainly seek permanent seats for themselves, but are willing to forego their veto rights for fifteen years or possibly even longer.
Uniting for Consensus (UfC)	Prominent members include Italy, Pakistan, Spain, Argentina, Canada, Mexico, South Korea	Opposes G-4 and the addition of any new permanent seats. Instead supports non-permanent addition and abolition/ restriction of P5 veto.
Africa Group	All members of the African Union (AU)	Seeks two permanent and five non-permanent seats for Africa, abolition of veto.
L.69	42 developing countries from Africa, Latin America and Caribbean, Asia and Pacific	Seeks six new permanent seats and six new non-permanent seats balanced across UN regions, abolition of veto.

Arab Group	22 members from Middle East, such as, Iraq, Jordan, Kuwait, Lebanon, Oman, Palestine, Saudi Arabia, UAE and so on	Demands a permanent Arab seat, criticizes veto but does not wish to abolish it.
ACT	21 smaller member states, such as, Ireland, Switzerland, Peru, Uruguay and Liechtenstein	Focuses solely upon improving the working methods, such as, accountability, coherence, and transparency of the Security Council, so that all UN members can take part in it.
P5	China, Britain, France, Russia, United States	Generally hesitant towards reform, despite agreeing in principle (2008). Britain and France are most open to reforms, but not the other members.

Source: Ville Lättilä (2019), "A New Proposal for UN Security Council Reform," *Oxford Research Group*, London: 28 May; on line source: https://www.oxfordresearchgroup.org.uk/blog/a-new-proposal-for-un-security-council-reform. Accessed on 27 April 2020.

The role played by Indian diplomats in its last stint at the Security Council (2011-12) could be a case in point for evaluating the country's contemporary involvements in the same. India's non-permanent membership, coming at the height of the G-4 initiative, proved to be a testing ground for its demand of the permanent seat. India's priorities during that tenure were developmental concerns, eradication of poverty, Millennium Development Goals (MDGs), inclusive growth, terrorism, and Security Council reforms.[54]

However, that was also the time for great international upheavals in the wake of the Arab Spring and its fallouts. India's voting patterns vis-à-vis Libya and Syria proved to be nationally beneficial but internationally neutral. It abstained from voting along with Brazil, South Africa, and Lebanon on the UNSC resolution threatening sanctions against Syria. Indeed, India spared itself from entering into a diplomatic mess by abstaining to vote on the Libyan resolution—also not attracting the ire of the US. In both cases, the Indian position stressed the need for complete respect of a nation's sovereignty, unity, and territorial integrity. In the beginning of 2012, India voted for a new resolution on Syria, with the explicit precondition that any references to regime change, threats of sanctions, and military intervention would be removed. During the same tenure, India also supported Iran's use of nuclear technology with the rider that it is a state's right to use the same for peaceful purposes. It urged Iran to resolve all outstanding issues diplomatically for restoring international confidence in its peaceful nuclear programme.[55] India's voting behaviour as a non-permanent member during 2011-12 showed its willingness to champion solidarity with developing countries, while at the same time exercising restraint at the great powers' front by speaking softly on issues which concern their international role.

India's recent role in the UNSC has raised skepticism on its ability to act as a responsible and active power. Despite treading softly, experts have interpreted its advocacy of Global South countries as an overt anti-Western stance, impacting domestic public opinion. They have often maligned India's risk-averse strategic culture, which according to them, jeopardizes greater recognition and endorsement by the P5—except China.[56] However, it is true that India's latest stint at the UNSC has proved that when the opportunity presents itself, it has to step up its game and take a firm stand on issues in the impending non-permanent tenure. Neutrality would not be an option open to India. And as the UNSC permanent membership continues to be the ultimate currency for effective international leadership, India might have to forsake its attachments to the Global South (which has for so long stereotyped its participation) and take a position which is solely in tune with its own diplomatic-strategic imperatives. Perhaps, under the active leadership of PM Modi, a more resurgent and forthcoming Indian participation in the council is on the cards for 2021-22.

There are various reasons for India to come out of its sequestered Global South role. Most of the countries which comprise this conceptual space are averse to India's permanent membership, despite being the beneficiary of India's contribution towards UN peacekeeping missions aimed at these troubled spots. Furthermore, its campaign has been held hostage by the unrealistic demands of underdeveloped countries, especially those subscribing to the Africa Group and the L.69. India's neutral stance or its obverse (advocacy of developing countries) is often interpreted as a lack of commitment to liberal internationalist values. And as such this precludes the West from inducting another country from Asia which for them has the potential to undermine the effectiveness and legitimacy of this international order. Suffice it to say that with regard to its bid for the UNSC permanent membership, India now has two interrelated objectives before itself: the achievement of self-reliance and economic clout at the global stage, and with that capital, the assumption of more space and responsibility in great power politics.

Other Potential Issues Influencing India's Global Role

As argued in the introduction, the UN has, in the last seven decades, become the port of call for global problems requiring global solutions. By that it has evolved as the hub of global governance. India's role in this organization needs an immediate revision if it has to emerge as a great power, having a significant influence on global governance, in the post-Covid world. Global governance is an amorphous term, loosely used to describe the processes and institutions by which the world is governed. In the lack of a world government, the UN seems to be the only institution capable of exercising global governance—by imposing a sense of order on a world without an organized system of government—based upon the legitimacy it derives from world-wide membership.[57]

How will India come to have a greater say in global governance, in the foreseeable future? The answer is nuanced. By taking a firm stand in global financial and political forums, based primarily upon its national interest. This can take place by participating more openly and more predominantly on the burning issues of the day, whereby it would be recognized as a 'rule-maker' in fields such as climate change and global commons, non-proliferation, and an entirely revamped global healthcare system which is inevitable after the WHO is overhauled in the post-Covid world.

During the months of global ordeal when major countries, following common sense and the directives of WHO, went under lockdown due to the coronavirus pandemic, the global economy had plummeted. India, with its present GDP of ₹200 lakh crores had been predicted to gain significant strategic advantages in a post-Covid world order, where it could mould dialogue for a more multipolar global order. According to one prediction, the global economy would encounter a major overhaul and India can find more space for its industries and supply chains in the new order.[58] Moreover, with its impending non-permanent tenure, it can attempt to steer dialogue in major fronts where its soft power credentials are already quite established. In this regard comes climate change and the global commons.

India formally ratified the Climate Change Agreement (Paris Agreement) in October 2016, agreeing to reduce its carbon footprint to 35 per cent by 2030. Stressing on the application of concepts such as 'Equity' and 'Common but Differentiated Responsibility', it benefitted from participating in the meeting of the Committee of Parties (COP 22), at Marrakesh on 8 November 2016. It has estimated a requirement of US$ 206 billion for action on 'adaptation' of climate-friendly industrial technologies and processes. Its commitment to a strong climate agreement has strengthened its claim for the UNSC permanent seat, especially with the US and China backtracking on their commitments toward the climate in the recent past.[59] Another related challenge is the governance of global commons. International law identifies four global commons: the High Seas, the Atmosphere, Antarctica, and the Outer Space. India, with its new tenure of the Security Council's non-permanent membership would have a seat at the high table of shaping rules vis-à-vis the governance of global commons. The UN has already established that the guiding principle of such spaces happens to be the common heritage of mankind. It has also related the preservation of global commons with sustainable development, environmental protection, peace and security.

Lastly, it has endorsed the preservation of the global commons for future generations under its own auspices and has constituted the UN System Task Team (2013) for that purpose.[60]

India with its ongoing technological revolution and enhanced naval role in the Indo-Pacific could transform the governance of global commons, especially with the help of the Indian Space Research Organisation (ISRO) and the Defence Research and Development Organisation (DRDO).[61] Another domain where India has recognized technological prowess pertains to nuclear proliferation. Nuclear energy is key to India's delivering on the commitments made at the Paris Climate Summit. India's status as a responsible nuclear power has been endorsed by no less than the US which gave the country (vide the 2006 civil nuclear deal) certain facilities not usually available to non-NPT countries or to ones possessing nuclear weapons. India has till date refused to sign the Nuclear Non-Proliferation Treaty (1970, extended indefinitely in 1995) on grounds of its explicit bias—which recognizes only the P5 countries as legitimate nuclear powers. The US-India Civil Nuclear Agreement (2006) has been viewed in India as an endorsement by the US of its views on the NPT. It enabled the country to participate in global nuclear commerce under the aegis of the International Atomic Energy Agency (IAEA) safeguards. Also as a step forward, it brought India to the high tables of nuclear export control and missile control regimes.[62] These have a direct bearing upon rule making vis-à-vis non-proliferation. Membership of the Nuclear Suppliers Group (NSG), the Missile Technology Control Regime (MTCR), and the Wassenaar Arrangement would ensure India unhindered growth of its nuclear power, for meeting both its civil and military requirements. But, even as late as July 2019, China continues to block India's membership in such groups, especially in the NSG.[63] India's recognition as a nuclear power by the NPT seems unlikely, as it would mean granting it a status at par with the P5. It would also inflame China and Pakistan, especially if the rest of the permanent members of the Security Council endorse India on this matter. However, with the perils of nuclear proliferation in South Asia and with toothless Confidence Building Measures (CBMs) and Nuclear

Risk Reduction Measures (NRRMs) between itself and Pakistan, India must convince the world of its potentials as a great power, if not for anything but the sake of credible nuclear deterrence. For that, certain diplomatic achievements are as crucial as crude nuclear capabilities.[64] Thus, it might endeavour to continue its quest for access to the restricted non-proliferation regime and for recognition by the NPT (even if it is not needed) to reaffirm its status as a legitimate and responsible nuclear power. This shall also, in effect, pave the way for other smaller countries waiting for similar recognition. India can thereby directly affect a more multipolar global order, thereby making it imperative to revamp contemporary global governance agencies.

Finally, a new area where India's global ambition could be realized and its grasp around the UNSC permanent membership strengthened happens to be within the World Health Organization (WHO). In the post-Covid world, ensuring global health security and stable healthcare facilities world-wide would inevitably be prioritized. The WHO is the UN's specialized agency for health (refer to Fig. 9.1) and is the coordinating body for international cooperation with regard to health. Although it is an organization with a large and unwieldy mandate, it has come under severe criticism in the past for being too political and West-centric, when it was supposed to be simply a scientific and medical body delimited to an advisory fiat.[65] However, during the 2020 pandemic, it has been derided by the Trump Administration as being slack in response to the disease and pro-China in outlook. Hinting at possible reforms of the organization, the White House remained vague on details.[66] And this is where India might have a serious role to play for cementing its legacy in the scientific echelons of the UN. Since the WHO is part of the UN System, any reform would require diplomatic expertise and credibility. India with its skilled diplomatic corps can lead a multilateral approach by rallying like-minded member states to bestow supranational authority upon the WHO akin to those of the World Trade Organization (WTO). Thereby, the WHO can exercise a combination of enforcements and incentives upon its member states for a range of scenarios vis-à-vis its global health directives.

Conclusion

The present chapter has discussed India's relationship with the UN as a framework for global governance. At length it has described India's past foreign policy dilemmas with special reference to the UN. It has, by way of explanation, discussed the formation, purposes and legality of the various agencies and platforms of the UN. Furthermore, a large part of it has been devoted to India's role in UN peacekeeping and the missed opportunities for securing the UNSC permanent membership. Since the inception of the UN, India has been unequivocal in its advocacy of decolonization, human rights, disarmament and global peace. And till 2020, it has been globally the largest contributor of troops, also accruing the most casualties in UNPKO. Ironically, for Cold War rivalries, India became a superior rule-maker and rule-executor for peacekeeping in the global arena. Following a historical narrative, the chapter could show how India's sacrifices for the promotion of global peace and its ideational contribution towards the UN's peacekeeping framework could not translate into its much sought after global power status. This has been linked with India's historic blunder of rejecting the UNSC permanent seat twice in the 1950s.

The chapter, however, takes a positive stance towards India's recent involvements in the Security Council. It has remained hopeful about what the future beholds for Indian foreign policy vis-à-vis the UN, by highlighting three issue-areas where it could make a significant impact upon global governance, in the post-Covid world order. The UNSC permanent membership, although elusive so far, could be a very real possibility for India if it can be as assertive in the international front as it continues to be domestically. A strong leadership with astute diplomacy is ostensibly the way forward. Axiomatically, India needs to balance its global ambition with its leadership of the Global South. Not least, to make its bid for the council's permanent seat credible and acceptable for the powers that be.

Historically, India has been a strong advocate of multilateralism, which allowed it to balance the limitations of its material power. India's increasing need for material resources, especially its bid to secure energy resources has the potential to derail both its search for major power status and its leadership of the Global South. Through the UN and its various institutions (especially with the opening now in the WHO), India must attempt to strike a balance between its sovereignty and the adoption of a proactive stance in global governance. Reversing its 'defensive multilateralism' (which has so far confined India to a position of a selective rule-taker) could help the country to engage more robustly with global governance processes. Defensive multilateralism reflects diplomatic infirmities of a country which cannot unilaterally enunciate and promote reforms in international institutions without facing backlash from other major powers. For a former diplomat, this is a limitation imposed upon the country by its own diplomatic elite where on the contrary, the West was rather expectant that with the rise of India they would have an additional system-shaper in a multipolar order.[67] Indian officials misunderstood Washington's pro-India stance in the WTO and International Financial Institutions (IFIs) as a mechanism for imposing further responsibilities upon India which will force it to undertake commitments that it was not yet ready to uphold. By that, a coterie of Indian diplomats meant forsaking its moribund non-aligned credentials and the leadership of the Global South. The failure to do either ultimately led to one debacle after the other in India's 2011-12 non-permanent tenure.

Although non-alignment and non-intervention has been the cornerstones of India's multilateral engagements, it must realize that greater role in global governance would invariably strengthen its leadership position in the Global South, and not the obverse. Its participation in trans-continental alliances, IFIs, and the WTO augments its capacity to shape international outcomes, striving for just redistribution of resources and recognition of developing countries. This would be more effective if India can escape the dilemma of having a proactive approach which would necessitate a partial detachment from the Global South. This re-evaluation and re-ordering of accepted strategies seems to be inescapable and imperative for augmenting India's status in global governance agencies like the UN, in contemporary times.

However, it would not be long before the three levels of international politics (personal, national, and systemic) compel India to rethink its foreign policy objectives and global governance potentials.[68] At the personal level, the dynamic leadership of PM Modi would be vital to propel India out of its past diplomatic dilemmas. Nationally, there is a shared emphasis on the need for sustaining economic growth and military clout. Finally, at the systemic level, the decline of American power in the post-Covid world will inevitably open up newer avenues for Asian countries. India's hopes of having greater freedom of manoeuvre vis-à-vis the UN, based upon its national size, political stability, and material capabilities may well be realized in an increasingly multipolar world order.

Endnotes

1. Shashi Tharoor (2013), *Pax Indica: India and the World of the 21st Century*, Gurgaon: Penguin, p. 375.
2. Ministry of External Affairs (MEA), Government of India (2013), "India and the United Nations," New Delhi: 23 September; on line source: https://mea.gov.in/in-focus-article.htm?22231/India+and+the+United+Nations. Accessed on 16 April 2020.
3. Bharat Karnad (2015), *Why India is not a Great Power (Yet)*, New York: Oxford University Press.
4. South Sudan, following its independence from the rest of Sudan in 2011, is the latest member of the UN. See in this connection, United Nations (2020), "Member States"; online source: https://www.un.org/en/member-states/index.html. Accessed on 19 April 2020.
5. United Nations (2020), "Charter of the United Nations: Chapter I"; on line source: https://www.un.org/en/sections/un-charter/chapter-i/index.html. Accessed on 19 April 2020.
6. Manu Bhagavan (2015), "India and the United Nations or Things Fall Apart', in David M. Malone, C. Raja Mohan, and Srinath Raghavan (eds.), *The Oxford Handbook of Indian Foreign Policy*, New Delhi: Oxford University Press, pp. 596-608.
7. Manu Bhagavan (2013), *India and the Quest for One World: The Peacemakers*, UK: Palgrave Macmillan.
8. Andrew Kennedy (2015), "Nehru's Foreign Policy: Realism and Idealism Conjoined", in David M. Malone, C. Raja Mohan, and Srinath Raghavan (eds.), *The Oxford Handbook of Indian Foreign Policy*, New Delhi: Oxford University Press, pp. 92-103.

9. Manu Bhagavan (2013), *India and the Quest for One World: The Peacemakers*, *op. cit.*, pp. 65-74.
10. Manu Bhagavan (2013), *India and the Quest for One World: The Peacemakers*, *op. cit.*, pp. 105-16.
11. Chinmaya R. Gharekhan (2007), "India and the United Nations", in Atish Sinha and Madhup Mohta (eds.), *Indian Foreign Policy: Challenges and Opportunities*, New Delhi: Academic Foundation, pp. 193-215.
12. Rajendra M. Abhyankar (2018), *Indian Diplomacy: Beyond Strategic Autonomy*, New Delhi: Oxford University Press, pp. 206-07.
13. United Nations in India (2020), "UN Agencies in India"; on line source: https://in.one.un.org/page/about-us/. Accessed on April 20, 2020.
14. Waheguru Pal Singh Sidhu (2019), "The Accidental Global Peacekeeper", in Manu Bhagavan (ed.), *India and the Cold War*, Gurgaon: Penguin Viking, pp. 79-99.
15. Ministry of External Affairs (MEA), Government of India (2019), "UN Peacekeeping: India's Contributions," New Delhi: 08 November; on line source: https://www.mea.gov.in/articles-in-indian-media.htm?dtl/32014/UN_Peacekeeping_Indias_Contributions. Accessed on 10 April 2020.
16. Dennis C. Jett (2019), *Why Peacekeeping Fails*, 2nd edition, Switzerland: Palgrave Macmillan, pp. 1-2.
17. Trygve Lie (1950), "Development of a 20 Year Programme for Achieving Peace through the United Nations: Note by the Secretary-General", UN General Assembly, U.N. Doc. A/1304, New York: 26 July; on line source: https://digitallibrary.un.org/record/822344?ln=en. Accessed on 20 April 2020.
18. W. Lewis (1994), "Peacekeeping: Wither U.S. Policy?" in Dennis J. Quinn (ed.), *Peace Support Operations and the U.S. Military*, Washington, D.C., National Defense University Press, p. 185.
19. Dag Hammarskjöld (1959), "Do We Need the United Nations?" Address before the Students' Association, Copenhagen: 2 May, UN Press Release SG/812; https://www.un.org/Depts/dhl/dag/docs/needun.pdf. Accessed on 20 April 2020.
20. Waheguru Pal Singh Sidhu (2019), "The Accidental Global Peacekeeper," *op. cit.*, pp. 81-82.
21. Baldev Raj Nayar and T.V. Paul (2003), *India in the World Order: Searching for Major Power Status*, Cambridge: Cambridge University Press, p. 133.

22. Waheguru Pal Singh Sidhu (2019), "The Accidental Global Peacekeeper", *op. cit.*, p. 84.
23. All current troops and total fatality figures are from, United Nations Peacekeeping (2020), "Data," New York: 31 March; on line source: https://peacekeeping.un.org/en/data. Accessed on 21 April 2020.
24. United Nations Peacekeeping (2020), "India," New York: 31 March; on line source: https://peacekeeping.un.org/en/india, Accessed on 21 April 2020.
25. Ministry of External Affairs (MEA), Government of India (2019), "UN Peacekeeping: India's Contributions," New Delhi: 08 November; on line source: https://www.mea.gov.in/articles-in-indian-media.htm?dtl/32014/UN_Peacekeeping_Indias_Contributions. Accessed on 10 April 2020.
26. United Nations Peacekeeping (2020), "Data," New York: 31 March; on line source: https://peacekeeping.un.org/en/data. Accessed on 21 April 2020.
27. Dipankar Banerjee (2008), "South Asia: Contributors of Global Significance", in Donald C.F. Daniel, Patricia Taft, and Sharon Wiharta (eds.), *Peace Operations: Trends, Progress, and Prospects*, Washington, D.C., Georgetown University Press, p. 192.
28. Ministry of External Affairs (MEA), Government of India (2019), "UN Peacekeeping: India's Contributions", New Delhi: 08 November; on line source: https://www.mea.gov.in/articles-in-indian-media.htm?dtl/32014/UN_Peacekeeping_Indias_Contributions. Accessed on 10 April 2020.
29. United Nations Peacekeeping (2020), "India," New York: 31 March; on line source: https://peacekeeping.un.org/en/india. Accessed on 21 April 2020.
30. Ministry of External Affairs (MEA), Government of India (2019), "UN Peacekeeping: India's Contributions", New Delhi: 08 November; on line source: https://www.mea.gov.in/articles-in-indian-media.htm?dtl/32014/UN_Peacekeeping_Indias_Contributions. Accessed on 10 April 2020.
31. Waheguru Pal Singh Sidhu (2019), "The Accidental Global Peacekeeper", *op. cit.*, pp. 93-94.
32. Larry L. Fabian and Indar Jit Rikhye, "Some Perspectives on Peacekeeping Institutions," *The American Journal of International Law*, 64(4), The United Nations: Appraisal at 25 Years, September 1970, p. 13; on line source: https://www.jstor.org/stable/25660345. Accessed on 23 April 2020.
33. Ministry of External Affairs (MEA), Government of India (2019), "UN Peacekeeping: India's Contributions," New Delhi:

08 November; on line source: https://www.mea.gov.in/articles-in-indian-media.htm?dtl/32014/UN_Peacekeeping_Indias_Contributions. Accessed on 10 April 2020.

34. Waheguru Pal Singh Sidhu (2019), "The Accidental Global Peacekeeper", *op. cit.*, p. 92.

35. United Nations (2020), "Charter of the United Nations: Chapter V"; on line source: https://www.un.org/en/sections/un-charter/chapter-v/index.html. Accessed on 19 April 2020.

36. Sriram Lakshman (2019), "UNSC non-permanent seat: India's candidature receives unanimous endorsement by Asia-Pacific group," *The Hindu*, 27 June; on line source: https://www.thehindu.com/news/national/unsc-non-permanent-seat-indias-candidature-endorsed-by-55-countries-including-pakistan/article28142769.ece. Accessed 23 April 2020.

37. Nayantara Sahgal (2011), *Jawaharlal Nehru: Civilizing a Savage World*, New Delhi: Penguin, pp. 40-42.

38. United Nations (2020), "Milestones 1941-1950"; on line source: https://www.un.org/en/sections/history/milestones-1941-1950/index.html. Accessed on 19 April 2020.

39. UN General Assembly (1971), "Restoration of the lawful rights of the People's Republic of China in the United Nations," Resolution 2758, U.N. Doc. A/RES/2758(XXVI), New York: 25 October; on line source: https://digitallibrary.un.org/record/192054?ln=en. Accessed on 23 April 2020.

40. *The New York Times* (2007), "UN rejects Taiwan application for entry", 24 July; on line source: https://www.nytimes.com/2007/07/24/world/asia/24iht-taiwan.1.6799766.html?_r=0. Accessed on 23 April 2020.

41. Nayantara Sahgal (2011), *Jawaharlal Nehru: Civilizing a Savage World*, *op. cit.*, p. 135.

42. Nabarun Roy (2017), "In the Shadow of Great Power Politics: Why Nehru Supported PRC's Admission to the Security Council", *The International History Review*, 40(2), pp. 376-96; doi:10.1080/07075332.2017.1329156; on line source. Accessed on 23 April 2020.

43. Anton Harder (2015), "Not at the Cost of China: New Evidence Regarding US Proposals to Nehru for Joining the United Nations Security Council," *Cold War International History Project*, Working Paper No. 76, March, pp. 1-16; on line source: https://www.wilsoncenter.org/publication/not-the-cost-china-india-and-the-united-nations-security-council-1950. Accessed on 10 April 2020.

44. Srinath Raghavan (2019), "A Missed Opportunity? The Nehru-Zhou Enlai Summit of 1960", in Manu Bhagavan (ed.), *India and the Cold War*, Gurgaon: Penguin Viking, pp. 100-25.
45. Rajendra M. Abhyankar (2018), *Indian Diplomacy: Beyond Strategic Autonomy*, *op. cit.*, pp. 208-09.
46. Souradeep Sen (2018), "The Nuclearization of the Indian Ocean Region: Toward a Security Paradox?" in D. Ganguly and P. Chatterjee (eds.), *India and Indian Ocean: Present, Past and Future*, New Delhi: Mittal Publishers, pp. 221-44.
47. Aneek Chatterjee (2020), "China after COVID-19: Projections and Reality," *Diplomatist*, 24 April; on line source: http://diplomatist.com/2020/04/24/china-after-covid-19-projections-and-reality/. Accessed on 24 April 2020.
48. UN General Assembly (2005), "Question of equitable representation on and increase in the membership of the Security Council and related matters," U.N. Doc. A/59/L.64, New York: 6 July; on line source: https://electthecouncil.org/timeline-post/the-g4-resolution/. Accessed on 26 April 2020.
49. Rajendra M. Abhyankar (2018), *Indian Diplomacy: Beyond Strategic Autonomy, op. cit.*, p. 213.
50. R. Jagannathan (2015), "India's permanent UNSC membership will only be possible in 2020-25 despite Modi pitch," *Firstpost*, 27 September; on line source: https://www.firstpost.com/world/despite-modis-pitch-indias-permanent-unsc-membership-will-only-be-possible-in-2020-25-2446222.html. Accessed on 27 April 2020.
51. R. Jagannathan (2019), "After UNSC meet on J&K, China says members concerned about human rights situation; India slams Pakistan's 'alarmist' approach", *Firstpost*, 18 August; on line source: https://www.firstpost.com/india/after-unsc-meet-on-jammu-and-kashmir-china-says-members-concerned-about-human-rights-situation-india-slams-pakistans-alarmist-approach-7176061.html. Accessed on 25 April 2020.
52. UN Security Council (2008), "Question of equitable representation on and increase in the membership of the Security Council and related matters", UNGA Decision 62/557, New York: 15 September; on line source: https://www.securitycouncilreport.org/atf/cf/%7B65BFCF9B-6D27-4E9C-8CD3-CF6E4FF96FF9%7D/Decision%2062_557.pdf. Accessed on 27 April 2020.
53. Aneek Chatterjee (2009), "The UN at Sixty three: Problems and Prospects of Reforming a Veteran," *Journal of Management and Social Sciences*, 5(1), pp. 22-29; on line source: https://www.

academia.edu/1092546/The_UN_at_Sixty_Three_Problems_and_Prospects_of_Reforming_a_Veteran. Accessed on 06 May 2020.

54. Rajendra M. Abhyankar (2018), *Indian Diplomacy: Beyond Strategic Autonomy*, *op. cit.*, p. 210.
55. Ministry of External Affairs (MEA), Government of India (2013), "India and the United Nations," New Delhi: 23 September; on line source: https://mea.gov.in/in-focus-article.htm?22231/India+and+the+United+Nations. Accessed on 16 April 2020.
56. *The Economic Times* (2020), "Major differences among UN members over India's permanent membership in UNSC: China", 16 January; on line source: https://economictimes.indiatimes.com/news/politics-and-nation/major-differences-among-un-members-over-indias-permanent-membership-in-unsc-china/articleshow/73304888.cms?from=mdr. Accessed on 27 April 2020.
57. Shashi Tharoor, *Pax Indica: India and the World of the 21st Century*, *op. cit.*, pp. 375-78.
58. Sandeep Phukan (2020), "India needs to open economy in a measured and clever way: Raghuram Rajan," *The Hindu*, 30 April; on line source: https://www.thehindu.com/news/national/we-need-to-think-about-opening-up-the-economy-says-raghuram-rajan-to-rahul-gandhi/article31469174.ece. Accessed on 01 May 2020.
59. Rajendra M. Abhyankar (2018), *Indian Diplomacy: Beyond Strategic Autonomy*, *op. cit.*, pp. 224-28.
60. United Nations (2013), "UN System Task Team on the Post-2015 UN Development Agenda" New York: January; on line source: https://sustainabledevelopment.un.org/post2015/index.php?page=view&type=400&nr=843&menu=35. Accessed 01 May 2020.
61. Gateway House (2018), "India in the Global Commons," New Delhi: 15 August; on line source: https://www.gatewayhouse.in/india-global-commons/. Accessed on 01 May 2020.
62. Rajendra M. Abhyankar (2018), *Indian Diplomacy: Beyond Strategic Autonomy*, *op. cit.*, p. 216.
63. *The Economic Times* (2019), "China rules out India's entry into NSG without 'consensus' on allowing non-NPT countries", 21; on line source: https://economictimes.indiatimes.com/news/defence/china-rules-out-indias-entry-into-nsg-without-consensus-on-allowing-non-npt-countries/articleshow/69893448.cms?from=mdr. Accessed on 01 May 2020.
64. Souradeep Sen (2018), "The South Asian Nuclear Rivalry: The Quest for Deterrence Stability," in K.C. Sarkar and M.T. Islam

(eds.), *Human Security, Peace and Development: South Asian Perspective*, Kolkata: Readers Service.

65. Jen Kirby (2020), "How to fix the WHO, according to an expert," *Vox*, 19 April; on line source: https://www.vox.com/2020/4/19/21224305/world-health-organization-trump-reform-q-a. Accessed on 01 May 2020.
66. Julian Borger (2020), "White House demands WHO reforms but is vague on details, diplomats say," *The Guardian*, 17 April; on line source: https://www.theguardian.com/world/2020/apr/17/trump-world-health-organization-reforms-china. Accessed on 01 May 2020.
67. Rajendra M. Abhyankar (2018), *Indian Diplomacy: Beyond Strategic Autonomy*, *op. cit.*, p. 232.
68. Sumit Ganguly (2019), "The Genesis of Nonalignment" in Sumit Ganguly (ed.), *India's Foreign Policy: Retrospect and Prospect*, New Delhi: Oxford University Press, pp. 3-5.

10

India's Connect with West Asia, Israel and Afghanistan: Evolving Strategies

Gouri Sankar Nag

India's relationship with West Asia is time-tested, durable, and mutually complementary. It is not only at the higher level of official visits that sustain it through vicissitudes, but it is mutually reinforcing in terms of elaborate economic engagements and cultural signals. Indian diaspora and regular people-to-people contacts have invigorated this multi-faceted relationship for a long time. So, while this relationship is, on the one hand, historical, going back to the rulers who invaded India in eleventh and twelfth century or even before; on the other hand, we have to examine the evolving trajectory of this relationship in the contemporary context of geopolitical tensions surfacing in the region. Some experts think that there are four major aspects and determining considerations which served as the bedrock of our policy in the West Asian region since the early period. These are: (i) the historical links with the region; (ii) the Israel factor and the fact that certain principle was involved in extending support to the Arabs; (iii) quest for oil; and (iv) the continuing tussle with Pakistan for support among West Asian states and the effort here was to neutralise positions if outright support was not forthcoming.[1] Over the years, Indian foreign policy in West Asia had been a mix of all the four aspects.

Indian foreign policy towards the West Asian region needs to be viewed in the historical perspective mediated by the long stretch of pre-colonial connections with India which was more of trading and cultural in nature rather than postcolonial relations when the British withdrawal from the region created a vacuum and the US wanted it to be filled by a local power friendly to its interests. So for India, it was not narrowly commodity trade or just crude oil supply, which was to be ensured, but India had to navigate its relations in the region with cautious balance. After independence India was pragmatic enough to uphold nonalignment as her worldview joined by Nasser's Egypt and as many as 11 other states of the region in the 1950s; while it was not sensible on India's part to interfere in the conflict-prone region. This does not mean either India's detachment or reluctance to follow the developments in the region as it unfolded since the late 1940s. That is why we have seen India's policy towards West Asia has been one of careful study and response resembling what one author dubbed as "a fine balance" with tough choices between values and strategic interests.[2]

There were highs and lows in the relations when our policies from initially pro-Israeli stance with sympathies for the Jews as victims of extreme xenophobia in Nazi Germany that led them to consolidate their position in the British protectorate of the Arab land, had changed into a growing perception and realisation in India that the Jewish settlement was creating a new ground of colonization for the Palestinians. So, "initial sympathy waned and withered and India became strongly opposed to Israeli policies".[3] This became important in terms of our policy legitimacy and particularly at home where the Palestine issue remained critically important till date for its symbolic value of safeguarding the interests of not only India's domestic Muslim population but also for its emotive implications for Pan-Islamic solidarity. A point to be noted here is that such championing of the Palestinian cause by India emanated from the strong underpinnings of India's foundational value adherence to oppose colonialism and to support the democratic struggles of people against undue oppression. Yet it was disappointing due to the fact that "there was no reciprocity and many Arab countries were either lukewarm or extended indirect support to Pakistan (even when that country had not shown such a strong mind in its responses towards the Middle

Eastern conflicts)".[4] It was clear when India's unease became palpable in 1971 in the wake of mounting political crisis in the then East Pakistan and the compulsive circumstances that paved the way for India's humanitarian intervention leading to the creation of independent Bangladesh. It was a period when India's relations with the West Asian countries, particularly with Iran became a bit strained until the Shah of Iran was finally convinced that India's intervention was not motivated by any ulterior design to cause dismemberment of Pakistan. Similarly, the Arab-Israeli crisis in early 1970s had also cast a looming impact on the energy importing countries including India when the latter was not only adversely affected by the sudden hike in the price of the crude oil, but also had to initiate efforts to offset the cost of such oil imports through more intensive and commercial exchanges.

Besides, there were three major events which had cast considerable impact on India-West Asia relations. These were: (i) the Revolution in Iran in 1979 that stirred the strategic balance in the region; (ii) military aggression of Saddam Hussein's Iraq on Kuwait in 1990 which evoked the US policy of "Dual containment of Iraq and Iran"; and (iii) the 2010-11 outbreak of Arab Spring which was a mass upsurge against authoritarian regimes. In some countries like Egypt it had far-reaching impact while the uprisings in Bahrain had limited direct effect on the structure of the government. It was the period when the entire region witnessed unprecedented mobilization of youth and social activists brought together by economic crisis, anti-government sentiments and influx of refugees. Even when the government thought of using security forces, it created a boomerang effect because the unrest turned highly confrontational. The unrest in Syria assumed particular importance due to international involvement. The Assad regime complained that it was facing a combined conspiracy of Turkey, Saudi Arabia and Qatari regimes to covertly support the opposition to remove it with the intent to establish a Sunni-backed government in Syria as well as to weaken Iran's key ally in the Arab world. On the other hand, the US and the EU decried the role of Russia and China in blocking a series of UN Security Council Resolutions aimed at condemning the Syrian regime's use of brute force against civilians. The situation in Syria continuously deteriorated throughout 2011 and thereafter till 2019, with civilian casualties multiplying and death toll of military personnel mounting. In this backdrop India had to cautiously adjust her stance towards this politically volatile region.

We find both continuity and change in our stance which cannot be captured either from the historical lens of past events, although they are no less important or merely from the perspective of rise in interest in strategic affairs in contemporary setting. In other words, it ought to be a multi-factor analysis to bring out different facets of the complexity in our dealings with West Asia especially with Iraq and Israel. So, while apparently India's relations with West Asian countries like Saudi Arabia are strengthened, at the same time such euphoria is not applicable to India's relations with some other nations of the region. Put in this backdrop, India's foreign policy initiatives in West Asia may be systematically explored.

Section I: India and West Asia

Before we delve into deeper analysis, it is equally important to keep in mind two factors which might divert our attention from putting emphasis on veritable factors that cement our mutual engagements. One is sort of reductionism and an air of ethnocentrism that creates a mistaken impression about the culture of the region couched in heterogenetic values and their distaste of democracy as well as rejection of concomitant tenets of liberalism. This type of hypothesis is only biased and falsified as evident in the experience of developments that led to Arab Spring movements during 2010-11. Another, perhaps more deleterious tendency or hidden agenda of America's neoconservative plan for remaking the whole of West Asia emanates from its "policy for the region in which the Islamic right wing was to be honed as a main force at the disposal of Euro-American power and the reactionary Gulf monarchies as the great bulwark against communism and secular Arab nationalism".[5] This clearly exposes the contradictory American posture toward West Asia which cannot be relied upon as a credible guide for India's outreach to the region. It is important to keep in mind that India houses around 195 million Muslim population and has her own compulsion apart from her dependence on the Gulf oil to meet "growth-induced energy demand", whereas dependence of the West on Gulf oil has progressively diminished.[6]

Another contemporary factor in Indian foreign policy discourse is India's Look East policy. Given China's belligerent approach in the South China Sea and America's growing interest in the Indo-Pacific, what we find is a kind of vigorous interest not only in terms of recalibrating our eastern outreach but also strengthening our ASEAN connect and resilience to fend off Chinese pressure such that the balance of Indian foreign policy can be said to have little tilted. It is this understanding that tells us that we cannot remain nebulous or coy about our vision and need for rapid engagements with the economic zone of West Asia because 21st century would require a holistic approach vis-à-vis a multipolar regional systems in which India cannot fight shy of her responsibility to play a more constructive role in Russia-dominated central Asian landscape or in the conflict prone ebullient West Asia. Turkey has already started asserting itself and has developed strong ties with President Morsi's Muslim Brotherhood government. Turkey's projected activism is twin tracked, to embolden the Islamists and simultaneously to strengthen the demand for democracy in the Middle East that in turn produces immense suspicion especially among the Saudi-influenced political circles. There are allegations that Turkey (along with Qatar and Pakistan) is involved even in colluding with the Islamic State and al Qaeda affiliated groups inside Syria.[7] Militant approaches by different stakeholders in West Asia are responsible for political volatility of the region. This was the reason why Arab-Israel negotiation or Israel-Palestinian peace process could not be advanced without taking into account the positions adopted by relatively smaller but nonetheless important regional groups like Hamas or the Islamic Jihad. They always played role to sabotage such rapprochement to gain political ground by preaching uncompromised stand vis-à-vis Israel on this issue. Thus, a ground was deliberately created to undermine the moderate elements so that the extremist forces could make their presence strongly felt.

Today, if we are witnessing Turkish hunger for power and accordingly its strategic priorities in the Middle East having gone bullish, it is largely because taking advantage of the regional geopolitics a middle power like Turkey is able to vie with major power mongers like the US, France, and Russia for more influence in the region, basically to fulfil its ambition in Syria for which it outreaches to Iran for wielding remote control over the Syrian regime, the protégé of Iran, and has left behind Saudi Arab, a potential player in regional politics. Thus, a very interesting picture is emerging which is contradictory but nevertheless a happening reality. It is contradictory in two senses: one is Turkey's enthusiastic posture towards Iran in contrast to noticeable divergence in approach between Turkey and UAE. This is why one commentator al-Buluwi has aptly observed "the current 'cold war' in the Middle East has taken two forms. It involves the Shiite-Sunni war being fought in Iraq, Syria, Lebanon and the Gulf, as well as a parallel Sunni-Sunni conflict involving Turkey, Saudi Arabia and political Islamic forces to control and dominate the politics of Sunni Islam".[8]

But seen from another perspective, the situation in the Middle East reflects sort of thinning out of sectarian divide and returning back of politico-strategic considerations. According to one author, "Suggestion in recent years of a Sunni-Shiite schism across the Middle East and Persian Gulf appears much less a factor than jockeying of the key actors with the most military, financial and diplomatic muscle who are trying to shape the region in their image..."[9]. It became evident from the contradictory stances taken by Saudia Arabia and Turkey. While Saudi Arabia saw the YPG (YPG refers to 'People's Protection Units') as an efficient actor to stop Turkey's military advance to the north of Syria and supported the PKK affiliated group as evidence of its pro-US stance, Turkey's military, on the contrary, fought hard to put an end to the YPG's control of Afrin in March 2018. After this Saudi Arabia's Crown Prince Mohammed bin Salman (MbS), described Turkey, Iran and the Muslim Brotherhood as a "triangle of evil". This openly showed that Turkey's gain was perceived to be Saudi Arabia's loss in the region and it highlighted how Ankara and Riyadh's agendas in Syria were becoming increasingly incompatible with each other.[10]

So what can be inferred from the above is the tendency that the impact of sectarian affiliation is undergoing a perceptible change in the regional politics. Although it would be too early to conclude that sectarian identity behind regional hostilities has lost its salience and it has been replaced by new issues of oppression or transparency. Nevertheless Turkey's activism and its opposition from the own camp followers of Sunni Gulf allies—the Saudis and Emirates, distinctly show that belonging to same sect is no longer the major common denominator of political configuration of alliance or balance of power. As an expert observes, "On the contrary, the Jerusalem factor in the deterioration of relations was noteworthy as it became evident with the low-profile response by the Saudi-led axis of the UAE, Egypt and Bahrain to the US's recognition of Jerusalem as the Israeli capital".[11] But for Turkey's Erdogan it was a historic moment to rise to the occasion to champion the Palestinian cause as he affirmed that "Jerusalem is a red line for Muslims". He even convened an emergency Jerusalem summit of the Organization of Islamic Cooperation (OIC) but here again the Saudi-led axis abstained. This remarkable turnaround became clear in the statement of the Bahrain's Foreign Minister that "It's not helpful to pick a fight with the US over side issues while we together fight the clear and present danger of the theo-fascist republic".[12] So, this shifting position is an important signal for India to reset her relations with the Arab states in contemporary context, particularly from the point of view of India's bold move to reorganise the state of Jammu and Kashmir—India's only Muslim majority state. It is needless to say that Indian Prime Minister Modi's 2019 visit to UAE and Bahrain—the two powerful Sunni states commanding significant clout over Pakistan was a calculated move to blunt the spearhead of the propaganda against the Indian move by Pakistan which was trying frantically to internationalise the issue. It reflects India's firm stand on Kashmir.

India's position became clear from India's successful diplomacy in the West Asian region. As one commentator aptly stated that "by hosting Modi both countries not only made their position clear that it was a domestic matter and relations with Pakistan were to be dealt with bilaterally between India and Pakistan".[13] She analysed deeply the intriguing point as to why Bahrain and UAE extended PM Modi such a cordial welcome. According to her, although these visits were already decided, "the Gulf states have their own reasons for wanting to provide Modi this cover".[14] By quoting the words of Abdul Nabi Al Shola, Bahrain's former Minister for Labour that unlike cultural, trade, and commercial relationships with India in the past, they now look forward to cooperate in areas related to security and defence, she described the security scenario in the region as it lay sandwiched between widening footprints of Iran and its continuous backing of political Islam as well as increasing closeness with Sunni Turkey and Qatar, abetting the Muslim Brotherhood leading to growing anxiety for the GCC (Gulf Coordination Council) countries and frustrating policies of the US as both former presidents of US Obama and Donald Trump dithered to take action.[15] Moreover, this perception of insecurity from the standpoint of regime survival multiplied when President Bashir of Sudan was overthrown and stalemate of Libya persisted. It was an alarming signal for the GCC countries that Iranian proxies might covertly endanger the political status quo. So in a situation when the Middle East can no longer count on its Western allies, "the region", according to the commentator, "has increasingly been looking east—Russia, China, India, South Korea".[16] Against such a backdrop it becomes easier to forge closer ties with India given the country's closeness and proximity to the Gulf region, with its ties dating back centuries, strengthened especially during the British raj, believes the commentator.[17] India's impressive growth trajectory and its sprawling market became added attractions for the whole of Middle East. So, it was no gimmick that "Soon after Modi's announcement of his Kashmir move, Saudi Aramco signed a $15 billion USD agreement with India's Reliance Industries Ltd".[18] But above all, the region in the face of looming ISIS threats wants India's cooperation in counter-terrorism, in defence modernization, intelligence sharing—all of which cover different facets of a security dialogue and flow from deeper realisation of shared mutual interests.

Different approaches to solve the long-bedevilled Palestine conundrum are being explored in the region. Bahrain recently hosted a workshop on an economic peace plan mooted by Jared Kushner to settle the conflict between Israel and Palestine by trying to explore how economic transactions between the two sides could be opened up so that in the process a coveted momentum is generated leading to better relations and eventually peace with Israel. No doubt a benign idea although it raised many eyebrows when Bahrain issued visas for Israeli journalists to travel to cover the event. So, there is no gainsaying the fact that the Israel-Arab divide is far from over although new ideas are being tried to achieve some breakthrough amidst the diehard nature of the old conflict.

Of course, any headway in the regional politics is not possible unless the calculations of the extra-regional powers keep changing and favouring some positive outcome. As currently we are witnessing that the Middle East conflict is assuming newer dimensions with Putin's Russia becoming penchant to fill the vacuum created by the US withdrawal from Iraq and its discredited policies in Yemen and Syria. Also a new understanding between Israel and the UAE and Bahrain has surfaced recently following the Abraham Accords. It has brought about a new equation because both Israel and the UAE consider Iran as an 'existential threat'. However, the UAE and Bahrain's normalisation deals with Israel are hardly useful for achieving lasting peace in West Asia. Iranian network with Turkey vis-à-vis Saudi-led coalition with Israel might change all our hitherto notions of contending phalanx in the region. Accordingly, sabre-rattling with Iran has prompted Saudi Arabia to pump plenty of money in the regional politics making it an attractive war zone.

Thus, contending geopolitical calculus including the resource issue along with the urgency to side either with a radical experiment or a right-wing authoritarian state veneered by pro-democratic stance like Erdogan's Turkey seems to be reshaping the old cartography of regional settlement in the

Middle East. In the circumstances, India needs to make a choice and it seems that given India's proximity to Saudi Arabia, India would not be eager to befriend Ankara right now. In fact, India's policy in the Middle East is currently guided by pro-Saudi line or more precisely by India's goodwill posture towards Saudi Arabia's de-facto ruler, crown prince Mohammed bin Salman (popularly, MbS) which has developed into a good chemistry. So, India needs a new approach to balance her relations with Iraq, Turkey and Iraq. Such thought for India's West Asia policy adjustment is crucial at the present juncture because else it can have deeper ramifications as outright support for Kurdish issue could mean endorsement of secessionist politics while at the same time it is also important for India to keep watching the developments if that fructify and crystallise into referendum and to play an important role as a peace mediator among the Kurds, Iraq, and Turkey. At the same time it is particularly important because no regional power or even extra-regional big powers like the US, Russia, or China command enough legitimacy to play such a constructive role in post-ISIS era. However, if we keep aside the point of Sino-Indian competition in the Middle East and get back to the point, it becomes pretty clear that both rise in India's stature coupled with Modi's strong leadership and interest towards renewal of India's West Asia connect have created a spirit that is there to stay. It is also evident from the urge expressed by the Palestinian President Mahmoud Abbas to the Indian PM Modi in February 2018 to seek multi-country peace mediation after Trump recognised contested Jerusalem as Israel's capital in December 2017. So, irked by Washington's handling of the issue and its failure to broker Israeli-Palestinian partition deal, Palestinian President said, "we count on India, with its status as a great power, its historical role in the non-aligned movement and in international forums...to achieve a just peace".[19] No doubt, it was a tribute to India's position as a great power; and a possible broker in the Middle East peace process.

It is also important to acknowledge that the UN, while playing an important part has not been that much effective in solving the Middle East crisis especially the Palestine issue. So, the present situation is also a historic opportunity for India to work assiduously for breaking the impasse. It may be noted that in the past "Perturbed by widespread criticism against the UN inefficiency in the face of Israeli intransigence, Secretary-General Boutros Boutros-Ghali had to ask the Security Council to take 'whatever measures were required' to force Israel to comply with UN Resolution 799. This opened up the possibility of imposing sanctions against Tel Aviv which naturally put the UN and Israel on a collision course. In fact, the non-aligned states had prepared a draft to impose sanctions against Israel".[20] But today the situation has altered to a great extent. India's engagement with non-aligned movement is not only getting revised but PM Modi's camaraderie with PM Benjamin Netanyahu is so visible that today India is definitely in a better position to "play a bigger role in the resolution of the Palestine issue". This enhanced role expectations of India has received acclaim even from current the UN committee on Palestine.[21]

However, what is important to understand here is the political nature of the knot which has to be taken into account. It is because situation in large parts in the Middle East especially due to massive devastations in Syria and ongoing fighting in Yemen and Libya where clashes are erupting, are no doubt calling for relief efforts for the survival of inhabitants. Yet it is not the way to deal with the deeper political and intractable territorial issues, rather humanitarian dimension, if overplayed, might indirectly help to linger or even obscure the political angle of it. So today while it is important to put the UN mission in charge for alleviating the plight of an estimated 7.4 million Yemenis who don't know how they would eke out their next meal. India may consider to initiate back-channel talks between Palestinian and the Israeli officials as in the past she organised such exchange between Saudis and Israel to discuss issues of regional concerns and threats. So we think of India's ability of diplomatic outreach to the contending sides of the Middle East and to bring them together in sync with proportionate increase in India's stature with her elevated position as the newly elected non-permanent member of the Security Council in 2020.

We can find India's stakes mainly from two sides: one is that continuation of the Palestine imbroglio might unleash regional instability in the Middle East which is very crucial from the standpoint of India's energy security. Breakdown of talks actually occurs mainly from trust deficit that results in hard and tough attitude of either or both sides. It is important therefore that India thinks of engaging herself as a facilitator of any broad-based multi-lateral or multi-level initiative of negotiations. Now she enjoys special support of the US owing to latter's Indo-Pacific strategy that lends India additional strength which she can use to leverage to refashion her Western outreach despite reservations to the contrary. Secondly, India has also to be cautious so that India's dual focus on bonding with Israel and Sunni Arab countries might not endanger India's third leg in the Middle East, i.e. its strategic closeness to Shia Iran which is the prime adversary of both Israel and the GCC nations. In August 2015, Indian Security Adviser Ajit Doval was reported to have discussed the possibility of a more long-term base for the Indian navy in Iran. It was planned that India would invest US$ 150 million to develop Iran's Chabahar port as a connectivity imperative for India's sea-land access to Afghanistan and Central Asia. Although this idea to turn India a more consequential power in the Middle East has recently received a jolt as reports revealed that Tehran might exclude New Delhi from the Chabahar project and it was rather interested to strike a long-term comprehensive deal with Beijing. Subsequently, however, Iran's 'Twitter Diplomacy' and meeting at the ambassadorial level made clear that they were still interested to cooperate with India which revealed their understanding of the US pressure on India especially after the US adopted a confrontational posture towards Iran. American hard stance on Iran in recent times had facilitated the entry of Beijing in Iran's strategic space. It was worrisome for India because foothold in Iran could provide India some guarantee to protect her strategic interests in the adjoining Eurasian and Central Asian map. But as correctly observed by a commentator that "unlike in the past, this time, there has been greater convergence of interests between Iran and China. While the sanction-ridden Iran was looking for a lifeline, China, which is engaged in a trade war with the United States, was ready to defy the US sanctions".[22]

According to one expert, Syrian Government was hesitant about inviting India to participate in the reconstruction of this war-raged state. It was due to PM Modi's visit to Israel which was perceived by the state elites in Damascus as India's shift from her hitherto pro-Palestinian bent to befriend Israel, a colonial force.[23] It reveals how much caution India needs to sustain her image in the emotive plane of the Middle East where one mistake would not only mean loss of appeal but also giving an edge to the Chinese side. In fact, there is a strong perception in Syria and other Arab countries that the Israeli-Arab conflict is the root cause behind the protracted war in Syria that triggered huge displacement and refugee conundrum. However, war and population displacement could not dissuade India to continue investing in projects in Syria and India's humanitarian aid to the Syrian regime. Not only this, India's position on the Palestinian issue remains consistent as India voted in solidarity with the cause along with 127 countries in favour of the UN General Assembly resolution in December 2017 that collectively registered opposition to Trump's decision to shift the US embassy from Tel Aviv to Jerusalem. In fact, if we examine India's high level official visits to the different countries in the Middle East ranging from M.J. Akbar's visit to Syria in 2016 to Manohar Parrikar's 2016 visit to the UAE followed by Modi's visits to Ramallah via Jordan, all would signify that India's intention was firstly to de-hyphenate India's mutually distinct relationships with the Arab states on one hand, and with Israel on the other. Secondly, in the words of one author, "These visits were infused with personal bonhomie and warmth between the leadership of these key players—with the Foreign Secretary Vijay Gokhale noting that 'exceptional courtesies' were extended to Mr. Modi".[24]

Therefore, any preconceived cultural notion or our over-enthusiasm nurtured under American guided strategic vision could impede the calculus of our effective network with the Middle East. Our relations with Iran, Syria, Israel, or UAE must not follow any American viewpoint for this region. To India close diplomatic connect with West Asia is also important to control and regulate the flow of alleged international terror-funding.

Hence, it requires cooperation as well as pressure to keep on Saudi Arabia and other West Asian countries so that financial monitoring system could be strictly followed and intelligence sharing mechanisms could be acted upon. For example it may be mentioned that the India-Oman joint statement at the time of PM Modi's visit in February 2018 expressly condemned terrorism in "all its forms and manifestations" and it emphasized on "the need to isolate the sponsors and supporters of terrorists" and highlighted the India-Oman model of "building inclusive societies" as effective tools "to counter extremism and radicalization".[25] But since the route of flow of fund could be very circuitous and difficult to check when operated through hawala, it is important that India should take 'a long-term and strategic view on Islamic militancy'. In doing so, our counter strategy may be based on media and academic projections in West and South Asia on both modernism and the syncretic-moderate aspects of Indian Islam.

So, ideologically, India's effort should be to encourage liberal heritage of Islam and to showcase its patronage to Islamic liberalism and her pluralist tradition abroad through public diplomacy. In this quest, winning support of West Asian regimes might add to the credibility of such projects. Although in the fertile land of Middle East which is fed by lump sum donation or other financial mechanisms that attracts and continue to allure local jobless youth and even foreign jihadi elements, it is difficult to defeat the fierce enthusiasm altogether for Islamic Caliphate. So even if the caliph has retreated after the death of Abu Bakr al-Baghdadi in US military operation, its umpteen sleeping cells are still alive and the ideological appeal of resurrecting the Caliphate seems to be important as it may yet serve a useful purpose in faraway places like Chechnya or Xinjiang. So this holistic understanding is very important especially because the challenge is to counter the projection of political Islam.

The political and ideological nature of political Islam needs to be comprehended well which is responsible for and contributing to the rise of sectarian politics in the region. Since it plays to indoctrinate minds not only in the mosques but even in colleges and universities, it is important to undertake thorough retooling of India's cultural diplomacy. Simultaneously, India should also think of empowering civil society organizations and the academia to focus on organizing such seminars or conferences which can project the successful image of Indian Muslims. Otherwise if adverse policies evoke humiliation or frustration among the Muslim youth, that could turn them to extreme piety and such conclusion that they have been betrayed under the modern secular system which is in fact an oppressive status quo; hence what is needed is to regain the ability to fight back for achieving the true path of their religion. Although this pure Islamic dream is apparently benign, it is radical and exclusive. Hence, it may be noted that many of West Asian countries are themselves victim of radical Islam bent on imposing its own model and annihilating others considered as apostates. Apparently, the rebel groups and internal militias fed by respective warring communities pitted against the repressive regimes want to usher in change in the regional order that oscillates at the intersection of orthodoxy and conservatism on the one hand and rare voices emancipation for transformation, on the other.

Section II: India and Israel

This section analyses India's evolving relations with Israel, which constitutes an important plank of India's West Asia policy. It has already been stated how India's ties with Israel has been oscillated by predominant concern for Palestine since the time of Jawaharlal Nehru. As one of the architects of the Non-Aligned Movement, India's strong official allegiance remained with her Arab allies. It may be noted here that in 1974 India recognised the Palestine Liberation Organization as the sole, legitimate representative of the Palestinians; it was the first non-Arab country do so. India has stood unwaveringly with Palestine's struggle for independent and complete statehood. To say this is not to imply that in reality India-Israel relationship has been troublesome. Rather two points need to be kept in mind to put things in perspective. One is the purported de-hyphenation of India's ties with Israel and Palestine has not reduced the compulsion of seeing the relationships as tightly interlinked. Hence, India's growing Israeli connect cannot be an exclusive policy orientation, something divorced from India's overall approach towards the region. That is why, Israel or vice versa Palestine is crucial from Indian perspective of balanced engagement in the Middle East. Hence, there is no question of enhancing India's footprint in the Middle East by sacrificing her interests and partnership with Israel. However, the talk of such balance could not be thought of prior to the 1990s when India's West Asia policy was predominantly pro-Palestinian and not friendly towards Israel. Even today how far such critical balance can be maintained in the world of excessive media coverage is a matter of continuous efforts towards adjustments. Hence, what is required inevitably means fusion of caution and sensitivity in India's approach rather than media-friendly optics that might spin out unhelpful exaggerated stories to create mistaken images in the circle of the Saudis as well as for Israel. The history teaches how America has experienced the adverse consequences of too-much intimacy in the Middle East and in turn, now gradually withdrawing from the position of excessive commitment and intervention in the region.

Secondly, in India's engagements with the region we can trace three shifting lines. As pointed out by an author, "too much of political grand-standing marked India's engagement with the region before the Cold War", whereas New Delhi "appeared too timid since the 1990s".[26] This timidity can be explained by an attitude to keep safe distance from the "perennial tinderbox" that the Middle East politics was, resulting in reluctance to actively pursue a line in the region, although "close economic links persisted" by outweighing "local governance factors in India's relations with Gulf capitals and West Asia generally".[27] This explains why there is so much of dilemma and dithering in India's approach towards Israel despite the fact that she had recognised Israel as a state in 1950 but took inordinately long time to establish diplomatic relations in 1992. Even thereafter it took more than two decades till 2014 for the warmer ties to become clearly manifest. Even the current bonhomie between India and Israel is not merely the product of strong political leadership in India; rather it is the result of the present situation which is altogether different from the past. The compulsion during the Cold War years was such that it was inconceivable to turn to Israel tied to the Western allies at that time. To quote one expert, even in the early 1990s, "Lalit Mansingh, then deputy head of India's embassy in Washington (and later Indian Ambassador to USA) recalls some nervousness that based on the sentiments of India's Muslim community, Prime Minister Rao might veto the move, but he did not.... But in deference to India's close ties to many Arab states, the relationship with Israel remains an ostensibly low-key one".[28]

Now to understand India's growing ties with Israel, we need to appreciate one noticeable trend that at present when religion remains an important factor, pan-Islamism is no longer a dominant force in the region. Consequently, what we find today is that the previous conflict between Arab-Israeli sides is taking a backseat while the Sunni-Shiite hostilities are getting stronger day by day. It thus offers the scope to improve the India-Israeli relations and to realise the new opportunities that lay beyond the traditional defence-centric relations. As one commentator puts it, bilateral relations are now "going to acquire more BITE—Business, Innovation, Technology and Entrepreneurship, bringing the Start-up Nation and the world's fastest growing economy in a tighter embrace".[29] In the post-Cold War period as India's security challenges started mounting, so did its demand for sophisticated arms, and Israel was there to provide it. As a result, the expansion in the Indo-Israeli relations became gradually less secretive. When India conducted nuclear weapons tests in 1998, it faced international condemnation. But while the Clinton Administration imposed economic sanctions and banned the export of US weapons and military technology, Israel refrained from criticizing India. During the Kargil War in 1999, it supplied the Indian Air Force with much needed UAVs and surveillance systems. Israel also upgraded India's aging, Soviet-era MiG-21 fighter jets and supplied Laser Guided Bombs and 160-mm mortar shells.

Today, Israel is second only to Russia as India's largest weapons supplier. But while Russian supplies fell by 47 percent in 2015-19, weapons imports from Israel increased by 175 percent. Both countries are part of the Joint Working Group on Counterterrorism and have signed agreements on mutual legal assistance in criminal matters, cooperation in homeland security, protection of classified material, and cyber-security. Indian Police Service trainees visit the Israel National Police Academy every year for training. The Indian Border Security Force uses Israeli-developed smart fencing systems as well as radar and surveillance technology in the volatile Kashmir valley. In the midst of the ongoing pandemic, the Indian Ministry of Defence and its Israeli counterpart are also collaborating on developing a rapid testing system. And to this end, an Israeli delegation collected 20,000 samples from Indian Covid-19 patients in early August 2020.

India's overtures toward Israel are no longer a low-key affair. It is something that India's Government and many Indians celebrate. In 2008, following the Mumbai attacks, many Indian political leaders were proposing the Israeli approach to fighting terrorism. The strategic ties between the two nations were further bolstered by the visit of Israeli Prime Minister Ariel Sharon in 2003 to India. It is worth highlighting that despite steady blossoming of relations between the two countries, successive Indian governments time and again reaffirmed that their ties with the Arab nations remained intact. In intelligently balancing ties with Israel, India's approach has always been influenced by a sense of pragmatism. That is why, during Israeli Prime Minister Benjamin Netanyahu's 2018 visit to India, his last evening in the country was marked by a special event attended by the stars of Indian film industry. At the event, Netanyahu declared, "We believe in Bollywood. The world loves Bollywood. Israel loves Bollywood. We want Bollywood in Israel".[30] *Drive*—the Indian version of *Fast & Furious*—was released in November 2019 on Netflix; it is the first Hindi movie to be filmed in Israel. The scenes were shot in Tel Aviv and partly funded by the Israeli Prime Minister's Office and the Ministry of Tourism, with the expectation that a positive portrayal of Israel in Hindi films would boost tourism from India.

Officially, India now considers Israel a strategic partner as both countries position themselves as bastions of progress and democracy while surrounded by not-so-friendly nations. In this sense, they consider each other to be natural allies, engaged in a historic struggle against terrorism and Islamic fundamentalist forces. It is no surprise then that 'Stand With Us', an American pro-Israel advocacy organization and the Israeli Consul General for South India supported the Citizenship Amendment Act (CAA), proposed by the Indian Government. India, for its part, displayed the extent of its alliance with Israel when in June 2019 it voted against granting Palestinians consultative status in the UN's Economic and Social Council. Responding to the vote—a historic turnaround in India's usually expected pro-Palestine tilt at the UN Netanyahu in turn thanked Prime Minister Modi and India in his tweet message, for standing with Israel at the UN.

Recently in August 2020 a landmark normalization of relations between seven-decade-old adversaries—UAE and Israel—was formalised through the 'Abraham Accord'. It brought sudden cheer to India, because it would facilitate bonhomie with Israel, an 'all-weather friend' for India. Be it defence expertise, agriculture know-how or recent scientific advancement sharing, the Israeli people have shown unwavering support for India. It is also to be noted that Israeli businesses have invested in various sectors such as renewable energy, telecommunication, water technologies, and production units in India. Although Israel is ranked the 43rd investor in India, with the gradual expansion of collaborations, there is bright scope that Israeli investments in India would expand more.

On the other hand, the UAE has been steadfast in its support to India, be it on trade, human resource development or the Kashmir issue. India gets huge remittances from UAE as roughly 40 percent of the Emirate's population is Indian. Due to income-tax-free provisions of the gulf country, a majority of the money is remitted to the families in India which in turn strengthens the Indian economy. UAE has also served as a venue of Indian Premier League (IPL) and other cricket tournaments. Bollywood and south Indian cinema are overwhelmingly popular in the UAE and contributes to cultural diplomacy. Moreover, in the context of India's abrogation of Articles 370 and 35(A) and implementation of Citizenship Amendment Act (CAA), and Israel's rapprochement with the UAE is a blow to Muslim unity because it signals that issue of Palestinian Muslims is no longer coming in way of normalizing ties with Israel. Some other countries are also expected to move forward towards signing similar peace agreements with Israel. The Israel-UAE peace pact is good news for India because if Israeli stubbornness on Palestinian question has not deterred Arab countries, then it is a signal that perhaps time and situation have greatly altered.

But India's predicaments can be located at two areas, one is a premonition whether Israel fits well with India's quest for partners of moderate temper for which India advocates the path of negotiated settlement of the Palestine issue and makes a favourable projection in sync with liberal Islam. There is a surmise as to how far Israel could be a benign and moderate player befitting India's wish. Secondly, as stated by the expert quoted earlier, "An Israeli strike on Iran would test the limits of flexibility in Indian policy and doubtless provoke widespread criticism in India. Thus, the bilateral relationship, while serving both countries well, could encounter road bumps ahead which would require careful management".[31]

Section III: India and Afghanistan

This section discusses India's relations with Afghanistan. The strategic importance of Afghanistan becomes clear from Afghanistan's geographical position. It is a gateway to Middle East and has been regarded as belonging as much to West Asian and Central Asian region as it equally tilts on the shoulders of South Asia. Yet with its direct land borders with Iran and its strategic location populated mostly by believers in Sunni Islam (though Afghan society is fragmented between Pashtuns supplying the Taliban leadership who belongs to the Hanafi sect as distinct from Wahhabism of Saudi Arabia and non-Pashtun ethnic groups like Tajiks, Hazaras nurturing deep suspicion towards Pashtuns, making it problematic for united Afghan nationalism to emerge), it acts both as a vital bridge and a barrier to its vast Western backyard connecting it with the Middle East. Not only that but also it is important to appreciate how Afghanistan, from Indian perspective, is crucial for countering Pakistan. As an author points out, "working on the principles of real politic as enunciated from Kautilya to Machiavelli and

Hans Morgenthau—Afghanistan should have been one of our closest friends in the region".[32] In addition, Afghanistan is also important from the point of India's relations with Kashmir. According to the author, "in the early years after independence India hoped that after the ceasefire in Kashmir, relations with Pakistan would enable the continuation and even reinforcement of the historical bonds between the two peoples".[33]

Needless to say, such benign expectation could not be met due to Pakistan's Afghan strategy which was to keep Afghanistan "in such an unsettled state that there is little prospect of the former Mujahedeen returning to peacetime occupations, a large pool of battle-tested persons would become available for use in Jammu and Kashmir as also elsewhere in India".[34] Obviously, therefore, monitoring over Afghanistan is vital for strengthening India's hold over Kashmir and it can only be done by combating terrorism and insurgency through continuous reconstruction paving the way to unity and integrity of Afghanistan. That is why, even when America has started decreasing its troops in Afghanistan and "many in India believe another kind of darkness looms ahead as the US and the Taliban signed an Agreement for bringing peace to Afghanistan".[35] However, there is no question of India's quitting the ground. In fact, deeper analysis reveals a 'catch-22' situation for the US and the West in Afghanistan. Accordingly, systematic elimination of Al-Qaeda bases depends upon relying on the power of local warlords but this can backfire because the latter can take advantage of the situation to mount attack on the central government as happened in the past during the Karzai (2004-09 and 2009-14) and Ghani led Presidential form of government (2014 onwards). But there were two other problems: one was the growing menace of drug trafficking and another was surfacing of bitter relations between Karzai and the US Government after 2010.

This deterioration in Karzai's relations with the US culminated in a standoff in 2013-14 during which the Afghan President refused to sign an agreement authorizing US troops to remain in the country beyond their scheduled withdrawal at the end of 2014. It does not, however, mean that Afghanistan is now strong enough to protect itself and deliver welfare measures confidently. On the contrary, the biggest challenge faced by Afghanistan is the security situation, along with strong and effective leadership that can restore morale not only among the members of the ANDSF (Afghanistan National Defence and Security Forces), but also for common people who are in despair due to lack of safety and want of civil amenities.

So, India should ramp up its scope of activities and there is still lot to be done for the amelioration of severe impact of the Pandemic on trade, economy and health sectors. Besides, there are two other factors: One is our knowledge of how the formation of Taliban government in Afghanistan in 1996 led to make the country a safe home for Al-Qaeda which was responsible for the 9/11/2001 attacks in the United States. A point to be noted here is that India was already a worst victim of Pakistan-sponsored terrorism but she failed to elicit US response until the horrible attack on the World Trade Centre opened the eyes of the world about how Pakistan played the role of midwife of the Taliban regime in Afghanistan. So, India's interest in Afghanistan remains valid till date—to rebuild the Afghan state and adding to its capacity through infrastructure projects and training programme for its security personnel so that it does not become yet again a launch pad of terror attacks. However, suicide bombings are continuing in Afghanistan backed by different terror outfits linked either to Taliban or Pakistan playing through some proxies. This is one of the reasons why Government of India or a section of diplomatic community in India believes that there is no use in talking to Taliban because ultimately it would be tantamount to deal with surreptitious designs of Pakistan working from behind, hence wastage of time and resources. It is also well-known that Pakistan desires to control Afghanistan with its deeper motive of creating a strategic depth so that in case of future Indian army attack its political elites can take refuge into such belly of strategic depth into Afghanistan.

Secondly, India's presence in Afghanistan is also important because the call for stationing India's peace-keeping troops came repeatedly from within the government circles of Kabul. This amply explains how India can engage and render help to rebuild the ANDSF. But going back to historical annals, it is not the narrow lens of bilateral strategic relations, but their historical and cultural bond, time-tested bonhomie and recognition of each other's interests in the post-colonial scenario in Asia which has been sustained by persistent diplomatic and economic exchanges. Apart from the ancient Silk Route between South Asia and Central Asia, the 3000-km long Grand Trunk Road (known as GT Road) pioneered by Afghan emperor Sher Shah Suri in 16th century, which links India, Pakistan and Afghanistan, is a prime example of the grand vision of collective prosperity in South Asia.

The key to any strategic calculation in South Asia is to work out to revive this glory of togetherness and close co-operation in spite of inimical external interference as we have seen during the Cold War era when Pakistan joining the Western bloc invited the Cold War tension in the South Asian region. Also, in dealing with invasive designs of Pakistan in Kashmir, India had to devise her Afghan strategy in such a manner that such strategy's Pakistan-centric orientation was actually to keep Pakistan engaged on both fronts and thereby to bring sort of relative relief on India's western border. India's western frontier bordering Pakistan has been a potential conflict zone compared to her eastern theatre which is less-militarised and less-tensed. Hence, such policy was India's strategic imperative. So, this is an important component of the conceptual framework that would be posited here.

Since independence Kashmir has been India's persistent trouble spot requiring her to play cautious and constructive role. But often being unable to tackle the situation prodigiously India's resort to securitization of Kashmir problem has been responsible for the backlash from the Muslim world. This partly justifies India's increasing commitment and engagement in Afghanistan as a strategic tool to create a favourable international opinion and thereby to create a space useful enough to discourage militancy in Kashmir vis-à-vis Pakistani tactics to use Afghanistan as its 'strategic depth'. Hence, Kashmir angle in India's Afghan strategy cannot be ruled out.

Another dimension of India's Afghan strategic thinking is her understanding of Afghanistan's crucial geo-economic location which is instrumental for India's growing western surge for energy and commercial benefits. On one side, Afghanistan is a corridor to reach out to the natural resource-rich central Asian republics and on the other hand, Afghanistan can be India's triumph card to tag Iran and to create an alternative corridor to avoid China's ambitious One Belt One Road (OBOR) initiative. Keeping this in view, what is noteworthy is that although traditionally India is not a donor country, it has started providing and pledging huge economic assistance to Afghanistan, making it the fifth largest bilateral donor in Afghanistan.[36]

The pivotal importance of a Strategic Partnership Agreement between India and Afghanistan needs to be appreciated in this perspective. The treaty was signed in 2011. It provided for assistance to help rebuild Afghanistan's infrastructure and institutions, education and technical assistance to rebuild indigenous Afghan capacity in different areas. However, the challenge of maintaining India's growing footprint in Afghanistan includes continuous threat posed by unabated terror attacks on Indians in Afghan soil, which is part of hostile design to compel India to pull back from the stabilization-cum-reconstruction process in Afghanistan. An attack on a gurdwara in Kabul, in March 2020—for which the IS-K (Islamic State- Khorasan) claimed responsibility—is a recent example of the very real security threats that festers India's footprint in Afghanistan. Therefore, India's Afghanistan strategy must have a Triangular Conceptual Framework as put in Fig. 10.1:

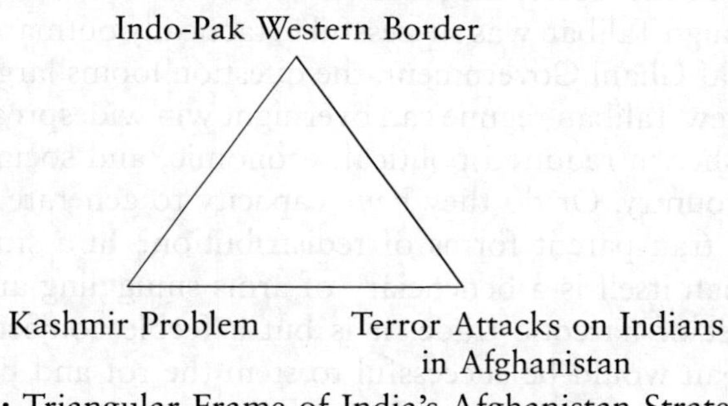

Figure 10.1: Triangular Frame of India's Afghanistan Strategy

Now let us briefly highlight major areas of India's current approach vis-à-vis the Afghan peace process. First, already when the talk of phased withdrawal of USA from Afghanistan was in the air of which India was apprehensive another point arose within the South Block of New Delhi of whether India should engage with the Taliban. It was because the looming spectra of the US military pull-out would drastically change the geopolitical reality of South Asia. For Afghanistan which was already much weakened due to long period of recurrent violence, conflicts and internal power struggle that paved the way for the resurgence of the Taliban, the signal of US military pull-out was very ominous because take-over of state power by the Taliban could not reverse the crisis conundrum of Afghanistan standing at the verge of state failure awaiting chaos and anarchy. It was evident in a number of video clips in social media of how the ordinary Afghans were trying to flee desperately when Kabul fell in the hands of the Taliban in mid-August 2021. It was a clear indicator of conspicuous absence of people's trust on Taliban forces for safety and security—two most important political goods people expect from the state. In the circumstances, we have seen that India's situational response was to evacuate her panic-stricken nationals from Afghanistan. But as regards the point of her foreign policy approach India is yet to accord recognition to the new Taliban regime which seized the state power by ousting the elected government and without intra-Afghan talks to evolve a unified nation state. India firmly stuck to the position that the peace process should be Afghan-led and Afghan-controlled without privileging Taliban at the expense of both the elected Afghan Government and its civil society. So although Taliban was successful in tactically outmanoeuvring the Ashraf Ghani Government, the question looms large as how far the new Taliban regime can overnight win widespread credibility to usher in required political, economic, and social stability in the country. Or do they have capacity to generate revenue and have transparent forms of redistribution? In a situation when Taliban itself is a beneficiary of arms smuggling and the illegal racket of narcotic trade, it is but a feeble conjecture that the Taliban would be successful to stem the rot and bring about a revolutionary transformation in Afghanistan. Rather the new regime would be much more dependent on Pakistan for both political support and trade while partly drawing upon the Salafi regime of Saudi Arabia and its coffer of dinars with which the latter wants to mould and grease this Iranian backyard for fomenting its radical Wahhabism as an alternative to the Iranian Revolution. So the advent of Taliban means full play of orthodox tendencies of declaring minor Muslim sects and groups as out of Islam. As such violent purging and ethnic dictation targeting both the minorities and creating a situation of ethnic separatism loom large. If it happens then regional stability would be jeopardised and India would need to urgently rethink her options—stopping the credit flow and development assistance even at the cost of increasing risk that could imperil India's Central Asia connection and simultaneously to beef up the security through the regional and multilateral forums since disaffected Taliban hardliners might jump into the ISIS Khorasan, a branch established in 2015 to oversee Afghanistan and nearby regions or that ISIS could join hands with Al-Qaeda. So, India's Afghanistan policy was integrally linked with her Kashmir policy and India for all practical purposes could not stay away from Afghanistan.

Secondly, another point of serious consideration for India's imperative for probable reset of her Afghan connect emanates from the fact as stated by scholars is that "Relying primarily on the Afghan Government for stability may have sufficed as a strategy until a decade ago, when discussions on withdrawal began...at present, it is simply untenable. Ashraf and Abdullah provide no real equities for our [India's] long-term interests in Afghanistan...".[37] So in the changed context if India wants to play a role in Afghanistan, she needs to build new equities. It means if India wants to protect her fundamental interests—of remaining engaged in Afghanistan and being able to support an independent government—it will have to make some uncomfortable choices and reposition its strategic actions with a view to mitigating the risks identified by its own officials and diplomats. In this connection, they are two choices before the Indian Government, believe the scholars. First, it can "wait and watch" to closely follow the developments during the transition period and if it paves the way for a degree of political stability. Second, given the "enormous instability" that looms large, in order to remain "engaged in Afghanistan in the future," India may have to build "new equities." This will require India to be "actively involved".[38]

Two more points we shall take into account here. First, while it is uncertain whether India will shift its position decisively at the current juncture and will engage with Taliban or not, the point remains that only through continuous monitoring to arrive at a moment when opening our channels of communication or broadening the net can India expect to have her concerns and voice heard in the future governing circle in Afghanistan and thus retaining the advantage of building bridges. Second, US Special Representative for Afghan reconciliation Zalmay Khalilzad's visit to India in May 2020 and his meeting with Foreign Minister Subramanyam Jaishankar and Ajit Doval was purported to get India to 'take a more active role in the peace process'. Khalilzad publicly made it clear that India was an important force in Afghanistan and even opined that India ought to engage with all the key Afghan players, including the Taliban. The point here is not the US pressure or urge but what is important above all is that India must make a net assessment of the political costs to its interests. In the aftermath of Taliban takeover of Afghanistan, India's active interests in Afghan affairs becomes evident from her dual steps: sending an official team to attend the Moscow process of talks on October 20, 2021 that will include the Taliban Government's Deputy Prime Minister and also New Delhi's official invite to all regional National Security Advisers to Delhi for a meeting in November 2021 including Pakistan's NSA Moeed Yusuf, in a rare departure from otherwise bitter bilateral ties.

Conclusion

India's West Asia policy is getting increasingly matured. But it is not the issue of exclusive Modi factor which is acting to throw aside previous lacklustre legacy of connecting to West Asia. India has to think about the changed context, the new players, emerging risks and ways to deal with those threats without compromising her regional stakes and balance. This requires India to develop and improve institutional mechanisms like special envoy or special advisor for interrelated issues like political Islam, counter-terrorism, cultural diplomacy, etc. Without bureaucratic restructuring of India's Ministry of External Affairs (MEA), it is difficult to accomplish the goal and also what is important is to accord autonomy to the higher level officials in the MEA. Our long-term objective in the region is not to poke nose in the regional power struggle but to maintain our balanced approach while ensuring our rising energy needs in sync with our rapid growth trajectory.

Broadly speaking, our West Asia policy after Cold War follows from our vision and confidence in the emergence of a benign multipolar world in which there could be competitions but no supercilious omnipotence. Only such an order would enable India to elevate her international stature from her current image as a South Asian hegemon. That is why India needs wider and better networked relations with all the countries in the Gulf and MENA (Middle East and North Africa) region. No doubt, in this quest the test of our diplomacy is how can we counter Pakistani narratives on Kashmir and India's engagement with Israel. But situation is altering fast as we have noted. The US is withdrawing its troops from different theatres of the Middle East and new treaties like Abraham Accord provide a new opportunity and greater scope to India to proliferate mutual bonhomie with different regimes of the region. India believes in peaceful dialogue to seek solutions of the geopolitical problems. Particularly, Middle East is known as a hotspot of terrorist extremism. Hence, India needs sustained engagement so that she can secure place in the regional peace process.

As far as West Asia is concerned, India needs sustained attention and to deliver according to her pledged commitments. At the same time, she should also realise that mere optics of high level visits or treaties might not salvage her interests. Instead what India needs most is credibility and not divisive policies because experience of manoeuvring with such policies has in effect alienated the US and eroded its appeal. A point to be noted is that different nations in West Asia are perceived by India as an extended part of our neighbourhood. So, naturally both West Asian nations and India are welcome to invest in each other's industrial corridors. But it is not simply a buyer-seller relationship. Some experts hint that West Asia is increasingly turning into an important strategic pocket for India with crucial maritime lanes like the Strait of Hormuz on which the US, China and other powers are focussing their military attention. But as a former Indian diplomat noted, "India has long had serious reservations about military alliances, military solutions to political disputes and extremely manipulated regime change".[39] This again reflects that the undercurrents of India's West Asia policy lie in India's roadmap of navigating relations based on mutual trust without any overt political ambition, recognition of their proud identity and of course, the shifting waves of regional and global geopolitics. Taken together, we can speak of India's current approach of working with multiple partners on different policy issues, especially her preference to engage with middle powers like Iran, Israel, Saudi Arabia, and Iraq, which reflects multi-alignment in today's world of multi-polarity.

Endnotes

1. See in this context, V.P. Dutt (1999), *India's Foreign Policy*, New Delhi: Vikas Publishing House, Reprint, p. 435. Also, Atish Sinha and Madhup Mohta (2007), *Indian Foreign Policy: Challenges and Opportunities*, New Delhi: Academic Publishers.
2. Harsh V. Pant (2016), *Indian Foreign Policy: An Overview*, New Delhi: Orient BlackSwan,
3. V.P. Dutt (1999), *India's Foreign Policy*, *op. cit.*
4. *Ibid.*
5. See the news item, "Mother of all battles", *Frontline* (2014), Chennai: July 25.
6. Samir Pradhan (2016), "Gulf's Role in India's Energy Security", in Dadwal and Sinha (ed.) *Non-Traditional Security Challenges in Asia: Approaches and Responses*, New Delhi: Routledge.
7. See in this connection, *The Statesman* (2017), New Delhi: Oct. 2.
8. Al-Buluwi, as quoted by Ozden Zeynep Oktav (2019), "Turkey-Saudi Rivalry: Conflicting Visions for a Future Middle East", *Politics Today*, August 27; on line source: https://politicstoday.

org/turkey-saudi-rivalry-conflicting-visions-for-a-future-middle-east/, accessed on 15 December 2020.

9. Tamer Fakahany (2018), "Turkey's military action to put an end to YPG's control in Afrin", Toronto Star, April 21; on line source: www.thestar.com/news/world, accessed on 15 December 2020.
10. *Ibid.*
11. Oktav, *op. cit.*
12. As quoted in Oktav, *op. cit.*
13. Aditi Bhaduri (2019), "A new security paradigm in the Gulf region", *International Affairs Review*, 31 August; on line source: http://internationalaffairsreview.com, accessed on 16 December 2020.
14. *Ibid.*
15. *Ibid.*
16. *Ibid.*
17. *Ibid.*
18. *Ibid.*
19. As quoted by Mohammed Darghmeh (2018), "Abbas tells India PM he seeks multi-country peace mediation", Associated Press, February 10; on line source: https://apnews.com/article/5af68016e5ca4bc88ae50afdc64fe894, accessed on 16 December 2020.
20. Samir Pradhan (2016), *op. cit.*
21. *The Hindu* (2020), "No dilution in India's support to Palestinian cause: UN committee on Palestine", 04 March; on line source: No dilution in India's support to Palestinian cause: UN committee on Palestine, accessed from https://www.thehindu.com/news/, accessed on 16 December 2020.
22. Muhsin Puthan Purayil (2020), "Twitter Diplomacy and Iran-India Relations", South Asian Voices, August 27; on line source: https://southasianvoices.org/twitter-diplomacy-and-iran-india-relations, accessed on 16 December 2020.
23. Anchal Vohra (2017), "Syria hesitant about India's role in reconstruction after Modi's Israel visit", *Hindustan Times*, August 17; on line source: http://www.hindustantimes.com, accessed on 16 December 2020.
24. Samuel Rajiv (2018), "Imparting New Dynamism to India's Engagements with West Asia", SPMRF, March 20; on line source: http://www.spmrf.org, accessed on 16 December 2020.
25. Embassy of India, Muscat, Oman (2018), "Visit of Prime Minister of India to Oman, 2018"; on line source: https://www.indemb-oman.

gov.in/page/visit-of-prime-minister-of-india-to-oman-2018/, accessed on 17 December 2020.

26. C. Raja Mohan (2018), "As India looks west", *The Indian Express*, Feb 10; on line source: https://indianexpress.com/article/opinion/columns/as-india-looks-west-5057824/, accessed on 17 December 2020.
27. David Malone (2017), *Does the Elephant Dance? Contemporary Indian Foreign Policy*, New Delhi: Oxford University Press, Eighth impression.
28. *Ibid.*
29. Manish Chand (2017), "New Spark in India-Israel Bonding", *India and World*, New Delhi: TG II September.
30. *The Hindustan Times* (2018), "World loves Bollywood, Israel loves Bollywood, I love Bollywood: PM Netanyahu meets celebrities", January 19; on line source: https://www.hindustantimes.com/india-news/world-loves-bollywood-israel-loves-bollywood-i-love-bollywood-pm-netanyahu-meets-celebrities/story-r0lNqaQpU, accessed on 17 December 2020.
31. Malone (2017), *op. cit.*
32. I.P. Khosla (2007), "India and Afghanistan" in Atish Sinha and Madhup Mohta (ed.), *Indian Foreign Policy: Challenges and Opportunities*, New Delhi: Academic Foundation, p. 548.
33. *Ibid.*
34. *Ibid.*
35. Manvendra Singh (2020), "India has invested too much in Afghanistan to let Taliban hold sway again with US blessings"; *ThePrint*, March 03; on line source: https://the print.in, accessed on 17 December 2020.
36. Khurshid Mahmud Kasuri (2015), *Neither a Hawk nor a Dove*, New Delhi: Penguin Viking, p. 545.
37. Rudra Chaudhuri and Shreyas Shende, "Dealing with Taliban: India's Strategy in Afghanistan After US Withdrawal", https://carnegieindia.org/2020/06/02/dealing-with-taliban-india-s-strategy-in-afghanistan-after-u.s.-withdrawal-pub-81951dated, accessed on 7 June 2020.
38. *Ibid.*
39. Ranjit Gupta (2017), "West Asia", *IPCS Special Report: 3 Years of Modi Government*, 17 August.

11

Recent Developments in Global Politics: QUAD; AUKUS; Return of the Talibans in Afghanistan

Sohini Nayak

Introduction

The ever-changing trends of global order in the past two decades have always been in response to myriad geopolitical demands of substantial competitions; with a view to harnessing the best potential of a region. Perpetually, there is a constant renewal of theoretical perspectives, aimed at widening the diplomatic pursuit of countries as they negotiate and interact with each other. Here comes the diversification and multi-polarization of international relations,[1] intertwining the interests of the global community at large, consequently leading to multilateral co-operations.[2] This aspect of global diplomacy has been often levied as an instrumental structure through power distribution and cooperative strategies, in turn enhancing global governance and the apparent absence of any hierarchy,[3] motivated to transform an area of contention to one of cooperation and peace. The concept of multilateralism has been often regarded as a 'an architectural form'—a principle of organizing through three basic cornerstones—"indivisibility, generalized principles of conduct and diffused reciprocity".[4] As an 'ensemble' it targets the best possible utilization of a group through a generalized outlook and principles of conduct for the best purpose of the locale they are based in.[5] Premised on this perspective, this chapter primarily aims at discussing three vital cohesive developments of the recent past—the formation of the Quadrilateral Security Dialogue (QUAD), the evolution of the Australia-United Kingdom and United States (AUKUS) trilateral security pact and the striking world alliance with regard to the resurrection of the Taliban in Afghanistan—that have brought together multilateral narratives for peaceful resolutions, finally attempting to address the growth and development of the domain as well as the people therein. Synonymously, the paper shall also refer to these developments through the lens of a complicated network of associations, resulting in resistance, thereby calling for a more flexible outlook for international stability, beyond just blatant national interest.[6]

Understanding the QUAD

The Quadrilateral Security Dialogue, officially addressed as the QUAD, finds its roots in the 2004 natural disaster—the Indian Ocean Tsunami—as a form of response and quick resilience for recovery.[7] Eventually, a 'Tsunami Core Team' comprising four major world powers—the United States of America, Australia, Japan, and India came to be formed that would facilitate and cooperate with each other for the immediate relief activities through a multilateral framework and was never meant to be permanent.[8] Nonetheless, with the initiative of Japan's 'value-oriented diplomacy', the quadrilateral setup reached one notch higher, to create an 'arc of freedom and prosperity' in the Indian Ocean region, in turn rediscovering the group's further purpose in 2006.[9] This was the same year when former Prime Minister of India, Dr. Manmohan Singh, while in Tokyo, reiterated the formation of a dialogue along with Japan and other "like-minded countries in the Asia-Pacific region."[10] Taking up the thread from here, in 2007, during his address in the Indian Parliament, former Japanese Prime Minister Shinzo Abe, put forward the notion of a 'free and open Indo-Pacific region' through the "Confluence of the Two Seas" and a theme of broader Asian re-imagination that furthermore strengthened the basis of the formation of the QUAD as a systematic approach.[11] Through this initiative, the vitality of the Indo-Pacific region, often regarded as the 'maritime underbelly of Asia' and a major fulcrum of competition and convergent security interests for being world's economic 'centre of gravity' came to be highlighted as well. Consequently, there was a high probability for the zone to grow as a theatre of power struggle because of the presence of major central global powers, inevitably requiring a strategic framework for discussion and deliberation.[12]

Ultimately, the physical manifestation of QUAD evolved on the side-lines of the 2007 Association of South East Asian Nations (ASEAN) and the ASEAN Regional Forum's (ARF) summit in Manila, Philippines, where the four nations met and actualized their further plan of action. The same year, QUAD also participated in a naval exercise with Singapore in the Bay of Bengal, under the aegis of the 'Exercise Malabar' in order to solidify its commitment to regional security.[13] From 2006-08, this setup was basically projected as an ad-hoc consultative arrangement with the key motive of maintaining maritime security.[14] It must be mentioned here that this development attracted sharp criticism from China, perceiving the design as anti-Chinese and an attempt to contain the increasing geopolitical footsteps of the country in the Indo-Pacific with a partnership of an "axis of democracies". However, there were also several counter-arguments that claiming that this association was far from being a 'quadripartite security alliance' and just a 'natural partnership' between countries that did not have coherently defined values.[15] This is primarily because even though all the four nations claimed that the naval interactions were not on the lines of defence with 'no security implication', the Malabar is undoubtedly a multilevel war-gaming naval exercise that also includes combat manoeuvres apart from simple Humanitarian Assistance and Disaster Relief (HADR) programmes and anti-terrorism mechanisms.[16] The most recent participation was 25th edition of the Malabar Exercise that began off the Guam Coast in the Pacific Ocean on 26 August 2021 and was completed by end of the month. This anti-QUAD Chinese sentiment was in fact one of the reasons why QUAD 1.0 had failed right at the very outset along with a few other assumptions that followed.

By 2008, Australia had already decided to withdraw from any further dialogue of this stature because it would disrupt the Sino-Australian relationship and the role that China was playing in becoming the largest buyer of Australian exports, replacing Japan.[17] Similarly, India too was apprehensive to directly involve itself in any sort of foreign policy approach that held within itself the potential of creating a rift in the already volatile region.[18] In order to be safeguarded against any argument of India being opposed to its very own Non-Aligned principle, the then Manmohan Singh Government had clarified that this movement of India was predominantly to solidify its relationship with all the "major partners". Moreover, the country's relationship with Canberra was also not very cordial at this time, often blamed at the former's nuclear ambitions and the refusal of Australia to sell uranium to India.[19] This was the time when India had signed the nuclear deal with USA (2007), garnering a lot of global attention as well suspicion.[20] Similarly, there were also limitations that came from Japan regarding its participation in the QUAD as Article 9 of its Constitution and the pacifist public sentiments bounded its defence partnerships. Also, Prime Minister Abe—one of the main spokespersons of the initiative had stepped down from power, resulting in reduced efforts. With this, the QUAD had gone into a hiatus, if not totally obsolete from national diplomacy with reduced fervour until, as recent as 2017 when it started gathering solid momentum yet again.

The resurrection of QUAD 2.0 began sometime in 2012 when China's 'aggressive assertiveness' and a coercive demeanour with increased military competence in the region was being widely acknowledged along with the Chinese Belt and Road Initiative (BRI) that could have strategic implications.[21] Around this time, Prime Minister Abe, after assuming office for the second time, elaborately supported a new concept of the 'democratic security diamond'—to "safeguard the maritime commons stretching from the Indian Ocean region to the western Pacific" often regarded as a QUAD remake. The USA, India and Australia would form, along with Japan, each point of the diamond and be vocal about Chinese coercion in both the South and East China Seas, that had the chance of becoming 'Lake Beijing' from which aircraft carriers and "nuclear attack submarines, capable of launching missiles with nuclear warheads" could be launched with the sole purpose of unnerving the region.[22] By 2016, all the partner countries had outlined their own formal objectives for the Indo-Pacific. An institutional space was created across all the QUAD countries. "A 2016 Defence White Paper identified geopolitical shifts in the Indo-Pacific as central to Australia's security, the US renamed its Pacific Command to Indo Pacific Command (USINDOPACOM), Japan identified challenges and opportunities in the Free and Open Indo Pacific (FOIP), and India set up a dedicated Indo-Pacific desk at its foreign ministry."[23] So primarily, the concept and maintenance of a 'rules-based order' with mutual commitment, preserving the freedom of navigation, democratic values, rationality and openness came forward—converging the interests of all the nations.[24] At this juncture it must be noted that apart from this conglomerate, USA, Japan, and Australia had also been engaging trilaterally since 2006, making them far more comfortable with each other. In 2014, they held their first trilateral summit which culminated into a 2018 announcement for trilateral partnership in infrastructure projects in the Indo-Pacific. Again, in 2015, Australia, India and Japan organized their first trilateral dialogue and in 2018, USA, India, and Japan held their first trilateral summit.[25]

Since 2017, the QUAD countries have met regularly at the working and ministerial levels. All the four stakeholders met again in Manila, Philippines on the side-lines of the East Asia Summit where the discussion was mainly on "issues of common interest in the Indo-Pacific region".[26] This initiative was mainly based on the decision of then US Secretary of State Rex Tillerson and then Japanese Foreign Minister Taro Kono, who decided to give this grouping a second chance. Since then, bimonthly meetings have taken place between senior foreign ministry officers and annual meetings between the foreign ministers of the four countries. The third QUAD Ministerial meeting took place in February 2021.[27] There were also discussions of "QUAD Plus" mechanism with the inclusion of the ASEAN countries for a more overarching periphery of functioning and making an impression that there is "strength in numbers".[28] The present QUAD 2.0 has been moving on the lines of success because of the regularity of the bilateral exercises and consensus generation regarding the conclusion of several agreements. Apart from this, all the four countries are willing to upgrade their cooperation and build trust among their militaries, build greater interoperability and bring about renewed and stronger political ties amongst each other.[29] The reflection of this new resolution came through during the Quad Leader's Summit on 24 September 2021, hosted by the newly elected American President Joe Bident at the White House, with invitations to Australian Prime Minister Scott Morrison, Indian Prime Minister Narendra Modi and Japanese Prime Minister Yoshide Suga. This was in fact the first ever in-person QUAD leader's summit.[30]

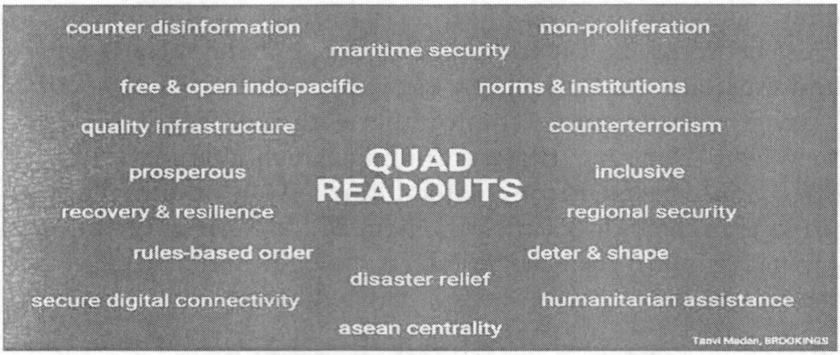

Figure 11.1: Quad's potential areas of cooperation

Source: Tanvi Madan, "What you need to know about the 'Quad'", *Brookings*, October 5, 2020, https://www.brookings.edu/blog/order-from-chaos/2020/10/05/what-you-need-to-know-about-the-quad-in-charts/

In this summit, a multifaceted arrangement has been undertaken that talks about "shared security and prosperity"; "shared values" and "shared futures", apparently on the same lines as Chinese campaign of "building a community with a shared future for mankind". The agenda includes issues like "vaccine diplomacy, infrastructure development, North Korean denuclearization and Afghanistan" and has no overt mention of China whatsoever.[31] The precursor to this event was a video conference of March 2020 among the senior leaders of the QUAD countries, initiated by the USA, to discuss the ongoing COVID-19 pandemic, to be continued on a weekly basis. The meeting had also included New Zealand, South Korea, and Vietnam—also three vital Indo-Pacific countries.[32] It was clearly mentioned that these seven countries would come together to oversee the global economy in these trying times, share technology and also facilitate people to people interactions. Many analysists have referred to this development as the basis of the aforementioned "QUAD Plus".[33] However, what is very interesting to note is the absence of Indonesia from this grouping, given its great strategic significance in the region. Geopolitically, this particularly country is located right at the epicentre of the Indo and the Pacific subregions. "Indonesia is adjacent both to the region's most complex maritime territorial dispute and to its major shipping routes. It is also democratic, a rising power, and has an uncertain relationship with China."[34] This absence has been often critiqued reinforcing the underdeveloped outlook of the QUAD and the fact that this is still an idea that requires further evolution. The QUAD is also often called a "divisive and exclusivist" concept of the Western powers concept by Moscow, along with being addressed as the 'Asian NATO' by China. In 2018, China's Foreign Minister, Wang Yi, had called the organization as "foam in the ocean, destined to dissipate soon". However, no one can deny the anxiety that China has been having in the recent past.[35] In conclusion, how and what the four partners decide to move ahead, only time can say.

Towards a Novel Australia-United Kingdom-United States Trilateral Partnership

On September 15, 2021, the world keenly witnessed the rise of a new partnership in the form of AUKUS—an acronym for the Australia-United Kingdom-United States "enhanced trilateral security partnership". Prime Minister Boris Johnson of UK, US President Joe Biden, and Australian Prime Minister Scott Morrison issued a joint statement premised upon beginning consultations to help Australia acquire at least eight nuclear powered (not armed) submarines for the Royal Australian Navy that will in turn maintain peace and stability in the Indo-Pacific region.[36] Taking the idea of rules-based order forward, joint capabilities, and interoperability would be enhanced under the

Box 11.1: The QUAD Timeline

2004: The Tsunami Core Team is formed between USA Japan, Australia and India.

May 2007: Working level meeting of QUAD in Manila, Philippines.

August 2007: QUAD conducted naval exercises with Singapore.

2008: Soon after the Malabar Exercise, Australia left the alliance.

2011: After the Great East Japan Earthquake, the country received support from Australia, USA, and India.

2012: Shinzo Abe comes back to power with the democratic security diamond.

2013: The QUAD countries acknowledged their mutual threat of Chinese aggression.

2017: Japan made an announcement to propose a top-level dialogue with USA, India, and Australia to counter Chinese aggression.

2017: Australia began its re-negotiation with the QUAD partners, formally. "Senior officials met on the side-lines of the ASEAN summit in Manila. Biannual meetings continued at the senior official level. Also happening this year, a Japan-India civil nuclear cooperation agreement."

2019: First Ministerial level meeting of QUAD 2.0.

2020: All the four navies participated in a joint naval exercise.

2021: In March 2020, a virtual QUAD meeting was hosted by US President Joe Biden with Australian Prime Minister Scott Morrison, Indian Prime Minister Narendra Modi, and Japanese Prime Minister Yoshihide Suga. They formed working groups on Covid-19 vaccines, climate change, and technological innovation and supply-chain resilience.

2021: The first in-person summit was conducted on 24th September at the White House, which solidified and reiterated commitments.

Source: Nikhil Natarajan, "From 2004 Tsunami to COVID-19: A Timeline of QUAD elevation," *Prokerala News*, September 23, 2021, https://www.prokerala.com/news/articles/a1200158.html, Accessed on 05 November 2021.

umbrella of AUKUS, just like the QUAD, with initial efforts focussed on multidimensional aspects like cyber capabilities, artificial intelligence, quantum technologies, and additional undersea capabilities.[37] Interestingly, this initiative has been extended as a sub-security agreement of the QUAD that will reveal its intentions and structured objectives in the near future with intra-regional alliances and beyond.[38]

All the partner countries clearly mentioned that at least eighteen months would be required to chart out the specificities of the deal and the submarine designs to be provided to Australia are the US Virginia-class attack submarines and the UK Astute-class submarine, fuelled with US weapons-grade uranium that have been in production since 1999 and 2001. Additionally, they have life-of-ship cores which entails no refuelling during their design lives of approximately three decades.[39] This deal replaces the one that Australia reached with France in 2016 and the former had received 12 French Suffren-class submarines equipped with conventional propulsion and not the nuclear propulsion used by France. However, Australia was not ready to develop the infrastructure of supplying the required fuel. Now, with the new deal and life-of-ship cores, it can avoid the production of its nuclear fuel, refuelling of the submarine reactors or even disposal of the spent fuel. They could just buy it easily from USA or UK and then give it back for disposal after the decommissioning of the submarines, making the process much easier in nature.[40]

Strategically speaking, France has been side-lined from the Indo-Pacific theatre—the first member of the European member to become a part of the region in 2018—as a direct implication of the AUKUS. French Prime Minister Emmanuel Macron and Foreign Minister Jean-Yves Le Drian and armed forces minister Florence Parly clearly expressed their disappointment when Australia cancelled the purchase of France's Attack-class submarines that would entail heavy penalty worth thousands of millions of Euros.[41] In consequence, French ambassadors have been recalled back from Canberra and Washington with the cancellation of the Franco-British Defence Ministers' Summit and the delaying of the EU-Australia trade agreement negotiations, the former supporting France citing breach of trust by its transatlantic and Indo-Pacific allies.[42] This is how the bilateral relationship has clearly suffered a loss with analysts arguing that this gap in trust can now be only filled through focus on non-defence issues like trade and economy, between EU and Australia as a whole.[43]

In general, there was a lukewarm international response to this new partnership as a defensive posture of one group can often be apprehended as an offensive posture of another group in the region. While one section believed that this development would be beneficial in treating the military imbalance against China, the other apprehended an escalated arms race or heightened conflict in the region. A nuclear weapon state selling nuclear submarines to a non-nuclear weapon state has been noted widely as the presence of enriched uranium fuel can be detrimental for non-proliferation perspectives. Uranium can be easily weaponised into building a simple gun-type nuclear weapon like the Hiroshima bomb and also encourage terrorist attacks.[44]

According to Articles I, II, and III of the Non-proliferation Treaty (NPT), Nuclear Weapon States (NWS) are not supposed to transfer nuclear weapons technology to any recipient, let alone inspire, accommodate or induce any NWS to manufacture or acquire them.[45] The Asia Pacific region is already a volatile zone of contention with the presence of nuclear abled rivals like India and Pakistan and such a step will only heighten the tension. Countries like Australia can use a loophole that allows it to remove the nuclear material from the inspection system of the International Atomic Energy Agency (IAEA), setting a negative example to future proliferators to use naval reactor programs without any backlash.[46] Since the probability of inspection and declarations known as safeguards—the basic idea of deterrence—will not be present, such transfer in the name of extended deterrence will undoubtedly instigate others to remain on the nuclear guard as well.[47] Even though it is very clear that the trilateral partnership intends to contain China, the latter labelling it as "extremely irresponsible," the implications of AUKUS for the region can bear a heavy cost in the future. Nonetheless, AUKUS has been trying its best to forward that the submarine deal will only revolve around naval nuclear propulsion. It will not transfer any nuclear weapons to Australia for that matter. Also, the pact will not contravene the Nuclear Non-Proliferation Treaty or the South Pacific Nuclear Free Zone Treaty.[48]

It is quite evident that Australia was increasingly concerned about its backyard—the Pacific Island states—being invested with Chinese infrastructural investments along with Chinese trade sanctions against it after Australia decided to probe the investigation regarding the origins of the COVID-19 virus.[49] It has been debated that Australia has come across as a natural partner for USA, given its strategic location and shared world view, for an anti-Chinese pact. Furthermore, it is already being viewed as an offensive stance for the ASEAN countries as well, although AUKUS talks about "Southeast Asia, ASEAN Centrality, and ASEAN-led architecture."[50] The secrecy that was surrounded around its formation says otherwise and has also led to a divided front among the Southeast Asian nations. On the one hand, countries like Malaysia and Indonesia have portrayed their objections to AUKUS and on the other hand Singapore and Philippines offered their supportwith Vietnam that has also been covertly supporting the pact. Furthermore, beyond ASEAN, Russia has also expressed concern over AUKUS, along with New Zealand, that has denied the presence of any Australian nuclear submarines in its territorial waters. The main argument that has been presented revolves around the probability of other nuclear weapon countries like India joining this program to deter Pakistan and China. In response, Beijing will definitely come up with a new pact of defence, further worsening the situation.[51] The most lethal outcome may be through a Sino-Russian partnership, redoubling down on their own naval cooperation. Strategists have held on to possibilities like Russian Navy operating with the Chinese—made aircraft carriers and the development of lethal drones and vertical launch fighters.[52] Thus, this pact has the tendency of bringing about the notion of a 'new cold war' in the region, of which most of the stakeholders are sceptical.

The Resurgence of the Taliban in Afghanistan

The seizure of Kabul, Afghanistan by the military group Taliban, in August 2021, was one of the landmark events in international relations, calling out for global coalition against war on terror. After two decades of being ousted by the United

States led forces in 2001, the Taliban resurrected again with the collapse of the government of Afghanistan under President Ashraf Ghani while the world kept looking at distraught citizens desperate to get out, as spectators.[53]

The war torn South Central Asian country of Afghanistan was ruled by the extremist Islamic group from 1996 to 2001, with their own version of strict Shariya law or Islamist law.[54] The Taliban or "students" in Pashto language had primarily emerged in northern Pakistan with the withdrawal of the Soviet troops from Afghanistan, sometime in 1994. The roots of this group lie in the Pashtun movement that is often believed to be funded by religious seminaries of Saudi Arabia that preached the hard-line version of Sunni Islam. Even though their primary aim had been to restore peace and security with their own version of the Sharia, what came next was a brutal domination and abuse of human rights.[55] With time, the influence of the Taliban kept widening. In 1995, they captured the province of Herat, bordering Iran and after a year, in 1996, they captured Kabul, overthrowing the Government of President Burhanuddin Rabbani—one of the founding fathers of the Afghan Mujahideen that had fought against Soviet occupation. By 1998, the Taliban had come to control around 90 percent of Afghanistan.[56] During these years, the rule in the country has been often described as tyrannical, with a harsh amalgamation of the theocratic intolerance, ethnocentrism and anarchic brutality, remaining committed to protracted war.[57] This was in complete contrast to what the Afghans had thought the scenario would be, as they were extremely weary of the infighting of the Soviets and made the Taliban popular so that they could ward away corruption or curb lawlessness. At this juncture, the Pakistani Inter-Service Intelligence (ISI) had also lent support to this movement which inevitably led to their association with the terrorist organization, Al Qaeda along with participation in conducting terrorist tactics.[58]

The main focus on the Taliban came on 11 September 2001, after the attacks on the World Trade Centre in New York, USA, that had shaken the world to the core. The Taliban was blamed for hosting the main accused of this attack—Osama Bin Laden within its geographical territory. In aftermath, the USA launched a military coalition attack in Afghanistan on 7 October 2001 and ensured the collapse of the Taliban regime. Many leaders of the Taliban, like Mullah Mohammad Omar and Bin Laden had supposedly fled to the Pakistani city of Quetta.[59] Since this period, Afghanistan had been going through a series of developments that tried to ensure stability in the nation but were moving towards failure. The Taliban had also carried out an attack in 2012 on the base camp of the NATO (North Atlantic Treaty Organization—a 28 country military and political alliance that had its base) with no negotiated peace. Around this phase, in 2015, the Taliban gained control of a provincial capital of Kunduz that hinted at its growing power.[60]

In February 2020, the Taliban signed a peace deal with the United States of America that initiated direct talks after decades. As put froward by analysts, during this phase, the Taliban were shifting their tactics from complex attacks in cities to military outposts to do away with killing hundreds of Afghan civilians. Nonetheless, the attacks on journalists, judges, peace activities, and women in positions of power continued, reiterating the fact that the Taliban had not changed at all.[61] The very next year, President Joe Biden announced in April 2021 that the American forces would leave Afghanistan by September 11, for good, after around two decades of being there and what seems to be the "longest war".[62] In this scenario, the USA deployed troops to remove thousands of people who were either in its troops or were civilians in favour of the mission. There was desperation witnessed in the airport of Kabul as the people wanted to flee the country as a result of their memories of the Taliban brutality. Many people also raised questions about Biden's decision as the country committed to the restoration and preservation of human rights around the world had made the contrary choice in Afghanistan.[63]

In the geopolitical forefront, many strategists have created the narrative of this Afghan theatre being used by USA and China for pursuing its great power competition. The Chinese have been very proactive in their negotiations with the Taliban so as to keep its border areas in the Wakhan corridor free from the Islamist support for the separatist Uighur Muslims who are time and again revolting in the Xinjiang province. In exchange, the Chinese are also prepared to give recognition to the "new Taliban" along with economic aid to Afghanistan.[64] This is mainly a very "cautious alliance" between the two countries as the Taliban has declared China to be its "main partner". This is more because China has found a new source of liaison for its Belt and Road Initiative with investment opportunities in the vulnerable Afghanistan. There are also Afghan refugees living in China over the years. However, this will not be possible if Afghanistan remains politically unstable.[65]

Additionally, the Troika Plus comprising China, Pakistan, Russia and the USA have also had their discussions as a multilateral forum to decide whether or not the new Taliban Government can be given recognition. While Russia wants to wait and see "how the regime will behave", Pakistan has already welcomed the Taliban by stating that it has rightfully ended the US "slavery" in Afghanistan.[66] Arguments have been forwarded for India to adopt a proactive stance towards the Taliban as the latter shares a good bond with Pakistan. In fact, India's Foreign Minister S. Jaishankar's visit to Iran in 2021 for a bilateral exchange had coincided with the visit of the Taliban delegation. Iran had also spoken in favour of an India-Iran partnership in "ensuring security in the region, especially Afghanistan, and Tehran welcoming New Delhi's role in establishment of security in Afghanistan."[67] Synonymously, Iran is also close to Beijing, which makes it important for India to remain within this nexus so that it can become an important partner in the process. India also convened a regional security dialogue on Afghanistan on 10 November 2021 in New Delhi. The Security Dialogue was attended by representatives from India, Iran, Russia, Kazakhstan, Kyrgyzstan, Tajikistan, Turkmenistan, and Uzbekistan. China and Pakistan did not join the dialogue. The convening of the dialogue showed India's willingness to play a proactive role as far as Afghanistan was concerned. What is now required is the establishment of trust between the partners vis-à-vis Afghanistan along with addressing the weak pre-existing social ties that can actually help the country with the acknowledgement in international forums like the United Nations, as it wants.

Conclusion

All the three cases in this chapter have been having serious debates and discussions in global politics despite the complexities that are still prevailing and all-pervasive in nature. From the Indo-Pacific to Central Asia, these developments have been revolving around the same major powers or actors who want to create their own niche and dominance. However, the problem lies in the lack of any unanimity in opinion that has been juxtaposed with the memories of the past failures in regional integration through multilateral forums. Such forums can only function if the partners are like minded. If not, then the situations will keep on treading the path of further complication, finally leading to the region failing in all its aspects—economically, politically as well as with regard to the people who make the region.

Endnotes

1. Ministry of Foreign Affairs (MOFA), Public Information Bureau, Govt. of Japan (1975), "Diplomatic Blue Book for 1975," December 1976, https://www.mofa.go.jp/policy/other/bluebook/1975/1975-1-1.htm. Accessed on 01 October 2021.
2. *Ibid.*
3. Hanns W. Maull, "Multilateralism: Variants, Potential, Constraints and Conditions for Success," *SWP Comment*, German Institute for International and Security Affairs, 9, (2), March 2020, https://www.swp-berlin.org/publications/products/comments/2020C09_multilateralism.pdf. Accessed on 01 October 2021.
4. James A. Caporaso, "International Relations Theory and multilateralism: the search for foundations," http://www.rochelleterman.com/ir/sites/default/files/Caporaso%201992.pdf. Accessed on 01 October 2021.
5. *Ibid.*
6. Ministry of Foreign Affairs (MOFA), Public Information Bureau, Govt. of Japan (1975), "Diplomatic Blue Book for 1975," *op. cit.*
7. H.D.P. Envall, "The Quadrilateral Security Dialogue: Towards an Indo-Pacific order?" Policy Report, S. Rajaratnam School of International Studies, Nanyang Technological University,

Singapore, September 2019, https://www.rsis.edu.sg/wp-content/uploads/2019/09/PR190909_The-Quadrilateral-Security-Dialogue.pdf. Accessed on 01 October 2021.

8. *Ibid.*
9. Ministry of Foreign Affairs of Japan, Government of Japan (2006), Seminar "Arc of Freedom and Prosperity: Japan's Expanding Diplomatic Horizons,"Speech by Mr. Taro Aso, Minister for Foreign Affairson the Occasion of the Japan Institute of International Affairs, November 30, 2006, https://www.mofa.go.jp/announce/fm/aso/speech0611.html. Accessed on 01 October 2021.
10. Ministry of Foreign Affairs, Government of Japan, "Visit to Japan of His Excellency Dr. Manmohan Singh, Prime Minister of India (Summary)," Regional Affairs (MOFA), December 15, 2006, https://www.mofa.go.jp/region/asia-paci/india/pmv0612.html. Accessed on 01 October 2021.
11. Ministry of Foreign Affairs of Japan, Government of Japan, "Confluence of the Two Seas," Speech by H.E Mr. Shinzo Abe, Prime Minister of Japan, at the Parliament of the Republic of India, August 22, 2007, https://www.mofa.go.jp/region/asia-paci/pmv0708/speech-2.html. Accessed on 01 October 2021.
12. Sohini Nayak, "Maritime Opportunities Await the India-Japan-France Trilateral," Special Report (133), Observer Research Foundation, March 31, 2021, https://www.orfonline.org/research/maritime-opportunities-await-the-india-japan-france-trilateral/#:~:text=The%20Indo-Pacific%2C%20often%20regarded%20as%20the%20%E2%80%98maritime%20underbelly%E2%80%99,keen%20attention%20of%20global%20powers%20in%20recent%20years. Accessed on 01 October 2021.
13. Shishir Gupta, "QUAD to reject 2007 Chinese veto on its foreign policies," *Hindustan Times*, March 11, 2021, https://www.hindustantimes.com/india-news/quad-to-reject-the-2007-chinese-veto-on-its-foreign-policies-101615438862807.html. Accessed on 01 October 2021.
14. Girish Luthra, "The Indo-Pacific Quest for the Quad's Spirit," Issue Brief No. 473, Observer Research Foundation, July 2021, https://www.orfonline.org/research/the-indo-pacific-quest-for-the-quads-spirit/. Accessed on 01 October 2021.
15. Jyotsna Mehra, "The Australia-India-Japan-US Quadrilateral: Dissecting the China factor," ORF Occasional Paper (264), Observer Research Foundation, August 2020, https://orfonline.org/wp-content/uploads/2020/08/ORF_OccasionalPaper_264_Quad.pdf. Accessed on 01 October 2020.

16. Krishna Kaushik, "The Malabar Exercise of QUAD nations, and why it matters to India," *The Indian Express*, August 31, 2021, https://indianexpress.com/article/explained/malabar-exercise-of-quad-nations-why-it-matters-to-india-7472058/. Accessed on 01 October 2021.
17. Jyotsna Mehra, "The Australia-India-Japan-US Quadrilateral: Dissecting the China factor," *op. cit.*
18. Jayshree Bajoria and Esther Pan, "The US-India Nuclear Deal," *Council on Foreign Relations*, November 5, 2010, https://www.cfr.org/backgrounder/us-india-nuclear-deal. Accessed on 01 October 2021.
19. Jyotsna Mehra, "The Australia-India-Japan-US Quadrilateral: Dissecting the China factor," *op. cit.*
20. *Ibid.*
21. Lalit K. Jha, "China has adopted a more aggressive policy towards the Indo-Pacific region—US Pentagon," *ThePrint*, March 20, 2021, https://theprint.in/world/china-has-adopted-a-more-aggressive-approach-to-the-indo-pacific-region-us-pentagon/625140/. Accessed on 02 October 2021.
22. Lavina Lee, "Abe's Democratic Security Diamond and New Quadrilateral Initiative: An Australian Perspective," *The Journal of Southeast Asian Affairs*, 30(1), https://www.researchgate.net/publication/319979427_ABE%27S_DEMOCRATIC_SECURITY_DIAMOND_AND_NEW_QUADRILATERAL_INITIATIVE_AN_AUSTRALIAN_PERSPECTIVE. Accessed on 02 October 2021.
23. Jyotsna Mehra, "The Australia-India-Japan-US Quadrilateral: Dissecting the China factor," *op. cit.*, 9.
24. *Ibid.*
25. "The Quad: An emerging multilateral security framework of democracies in the Indo-Pacific region," European Parliament, European Union, 2021, https://www.europarl.europa.eu/RegData/etudes/BRIE/2021/690513/EPRS_BRI(2021)690513_EN.pdf. Accessed on 02 October 2021.
26. Premesha Saha, "The Quad in the Indo-Pacific: Why ASEAN remains cautious," Issue Brief No. 229, Observer Research Foundation, February 2018, https://www.orfonline.org/wp-content/uploads/2018/02/ORF_IssueBrief_229_QuadASEAN.pdf. Accessed on 02 October 2021.
27. The Quad: An emerging multilateral security framework of democracies in the Indo-Pacific region," *op. cit.*

28. Renato C. De Castro, "The Revival of the Quad and the Emergence of the Indo-Pacific as the 21st Century Geopolitical Region," Albert Del Rosario Institute for Strategic International Studies, 2018, https://www.academia.edu/36652548/The_Revival_of_the_QUAD_and_the_Emergence_of_the_Indo_Pacific_as_the_21st_Century_Geopolitical_Region. Accessed on 02 October 2021.
29. *Ibid.*
30. Carla Freeman, Mirna Galic, Brian Harding, Daniel Markey and Vikram J. Singh, "What the Quad Leaders' Summit Means for the Indo-Pacific Amid Rising Tensions with China," Analysis and Commentary, United States Institute of Peace, September 28, 2021, https://www.usip.org/publications/2021/09/what-quad-leaders-summit-means-indo-pacific-amid-rising-tensions-china. Accessed on 04 October 2021.
31. *Ibid.*
32. "The Quad: An emerging multilateral security framework of democracies in the Indo-Pacific region," European Parliament, European Union, 2021, *op. cit.*
33. *Ibid.*
34. H.D.P. Envall, "The Quadrilateral Security Dialogue: Towards an Indo-Pacific order?" *op. cit.*
35. "The Quad: An emerging multilateral security framework of democracies in the Indo-Pacific region," European Parliament, European Union, 2021, *op. cit.*
36. Clair Mill, John Curtis and Louisa Brook Holland, "The AUKUS Agreement," *House of Commons Library*, United Kingdom Parliament, October 11, 2021, https://commonslibrary.parliament.uk/research-briefings/cbp-9335/. Accessed on 05 October 2021.
37. "Joint Leaders Statement on AUKUS," Briefing Room, The White House, September 15, 2021, https://www.whitehouse.gov/briefing-room/statements-releases/2021/09/15/joint-leaders-statement-on-aukus/. Accessed on 05 October 2021.
38. Sheraz Wahid, "AUKUS: A Pact of Global Security or a Threat to Global Peace?" *Eurasia Review*, October 15, 2015, https://www.eurasiareview.com/15102021-aukus-a-pact-of-global-security-or-a-threat-to-global-peace-oped/#:~:text=The%20AUKUS%2C%20which%20has%20raised%20serious%20concerns-%20of,fundamentally%20a%20great%20step%20forward%20for%20global%20security. Accessed on 06 October 2021.
39. Frank N. Von Hippel, "The Australia-UK-US Submarine Deal: Mitigating Proliferation Concerns," *Arms Control Today*, 51 (9), 10

November 2021, https://sgs.princeton.edu/sites/default/files/2021-11/vonhippel-2021-aukus.pdf. Accessed on 05 November 2021.

40. *Ibid*.
41. Premesha Saha and Rahul Kamath, "AUKUS: An Asian and European perspective," *Expert Speak*, Observer Research Foundation, September 30, 2021, https://www.orfonline.org/expert-speak/aukus-an-asian-and-european-perspective/. Accessed on 05 October 2021.
42. *Ibid*.
43. *Ibid*.
44. Frank N. Von Hippel, "The Australia-UK-US Submarine Deal: Mitigating Proliferation Concerns," *op. cit.*
45. "2005 Review Conference of the Parties to the Treaty on the Treaty of the Non-Proliferation of Nuclear Weapons (NPT)," Department of Disarmament Affairs, United Nations, May 2-25, 2005, https://www.n.org/en/conf/npt/2005/npttreaty.html. Accessed on 06 October 2021.
46. James A. Acton, "Why the AUKUS Submarine Deal is bad for Nonproliferation—And what to do about it," Commentary, Carnegie Endowment for International Peace, September 21, 2021, https://carnegieendowment.org/2021/09/21/why-aukus-submarine-deal-is-bad-for-nonproliferation-and-what-to-do-about-it-pub-85399. Accessed on 06 October 2021.
47. *Ibid*.
48. Clair Mill, John Curtis and Louisa Brook Holland, "The AUKUS Agreement," *op. cit.*
49. Premesha Saha and Rahul Kamath, "AUKUS: An Asian and European perspective," *op. cit.*
50. Un Kheang, "AUKUS and the Need for ASEAN Unity," *Opinion* (3), 13, Cambodia Development Center, October 12, 2021, https://cd-center.org/wp-content/uploads/2021/10/P124_20211011_V3IS13_EN.pdf. Accessed on 13 October 2021.
51. Sheraz Wahid, "AUKUS: A Pact of Global Security or a Threat to Global Peace?" *op. cit.*
52. Anabelle Custodio, "The unintended consequences of the AUKUS deal have been uncovered by the US government, with the resultant negative consequences for the UK," List, October 30, 2021, https://list23.com/299393-the-unintended-consequences-of-the-aukus-deal-have-been-uncovered-by-the-us-government-with-the-res/. Accessed on 01 November 2021.

53. Sohini Nayak, "The Nepalese plight in Afghanistan," *Expert Speak*, Observer Research Foundation, August 19, 2021, https://www.orfonline.org/expert-speak/the-nepalese-plight-in-afghanistan/. Accessed on 01 November 2021.
54. "Who are the Taliban and what's happening in Afghanistan?" *BBC United Kingdom*, August 17, 2021, https://www.bbc.co.uk/newsround/58221225. Accessed on 01 November 2021.
55. "Who are the Taliban?" BBC, August 18, 2021, https://www.bbc.com/news/world-south-asia-11451718. Accessed on 01 November 2021.
56. *Ibid.*
57. "The Taliban," Program for Culture and Conflict Studies, https://nps.edu/documents/105988371/107571254/The+Taliban.pdf/81b62278-cfc1-407a-a495-4a1c7dae9552. Accessed on 04 November 2021.
58. *Ibid.*
59. "Who are the Taliban?" BBC, *op. cit.*
60. *Ibid.*
61. *Ibid.*
62. Rakesh Sood, "The Taliban," Commentary, Observer Research Foundation, July 16, 2021, https://www.orfonline.org/research/the-return-of-the-taliban/. Accesses on 04 November 2021.
63. Maya Mirchandani, "The realignment of geopolitics after the Taliban takeover and what it means for India," *Expert Speak*, observer Research Foundation, August 18, 2021, https://www.orfonline.org/expert-speak/the-realignment-of-geopolitics-after-the-taliban-takeover-and-what-it-means-for-india/. Accessed on 05 November 2021.
64. *Ibid.*
65. Magnus Marsden, "China, Afghanistan, and the Belt and Road Initiative: Diplomacy and Reality," *The Diplomat*, September 15, 2021, https://thediplomat.com/2021/09/china-afghanistan-and-the-belt-and-road-initiative-diplomacy-and-reality/. Accessed on 05 November 2021.
66. "Troika Plus to discuss Afghan crisis," July 31, 2021, https://www.msn.com/en-in/news/world/troika-plus-to-discuss-afghan-crisis/ar-AAMMoYP, accessed on 05 November 2021.
67. Tridivesh Singh Maini, "Taliban Takeover of Afghanistan: Implications for India," The Geopolitics, August 19, 2021, https://thegeopolitics.com/taliban-takeover-of-afghanistan-implications-for-india/. Accessed on 05 November 2021.

12

Vision of a New World Order and India's Role in It

Aneek Chatterjee

Two decades of the twenty-first century are over. We have entered the third decade. During this time, China has emerged as a serious competitor to the United States (US) for the top power tag in global politics and economy. China has already overtaken the US as the number one economy in the world. With a strong military; significant voice in multilateral forums like the UNO, WTO, NSG, G-20 and others; presence in markets all over the world, China has arrived as a challenger to American power calculations during the first two decades of the twenty-first century. The former President of the US Donald Trump waged a trade war with China, as he considered China as a rival to American superiority. There are projections about a new Cold War in global politics between the US and China. Will the world emerge as a bipolar one in the future? Currently, the world is unipolar with America as the only superpower in global politics. But at the same time, international politics shows tendencies of a multipolar world with China, Russia, Germany, European Union, India, Brazil, Indonesia and other noteworthy powers having potentials to transform the current unipolar nature of the world. But the spectacular rise of China fuels the probability of a bipolar world order by the middle of the twenty-first century. Despite the unprecedented crisis the world faced due to the Covid-19 pandemic, China's economic growth was not affected significantly, like many other countries. As a consequence, China's rise in international politics continued unabated fuelling speculations of a bipolar world order. However, at this juncture, when we are stepping into the third decade of the twenty-first century, a multipolar world order appears to be more feasible with the rise of a few powers noted above. Where do we place India in this changing international order? India has power ambitions, but will the country be able to find an important place in the global power matrix? In the following sections of this chapter, India's position and role in a new world order in the twenty-first century will be analysed.

India's growth story was more visible after 1991, when the country launched its economic reforms. Since then India achieved an average annual real GDP growth rate of 6.6 percent during the last three decades (1991-2020), which is substantial, if compared to 1.5 to 3.5 percent average annual real GDP growth from 1947 to 1990. There is little doubt that this economic growth made the country noticeable in international politics. But it would be rather naïve to assume that India made its mark in global politics only after its economic liberalization in 1991. Since its independence in the year 1947, India played a significant role in the decolonization process of nations in Asia, Africa, and Latin America. The country was one of the founding members of the United Nations as well as the Non-Aligned Movement (NAM). For a long time during the Cold War period, India played a prominent role in the NAM, which made the country a noteworthy actor in global politics. From the very beginning of its journey as an independent country, India participated in the peace-keeping process of the UN and other humanitarian activities of this world organization. However, despite ideological success of the NAM, India's foreign policy choices were circumscribed by Cold War politics, which was dominated by the two superpowers. The end of the Cold War and India's economic liberalization were almost simultaneous, giving the country expanded opportunities to rethink its foreign policy. India utilized these opportunities well. With the disintegration of the Soviet Union, India began to come closer to the remaining superpower in world politics, the US. Economic liberalization opened up India's big market to the world and the industrialized West began to grow interest in India due to its business and investment potentials. As a consequence Foreign Direct Investment (FDI) in India increased substantially during the first two decades of the 21st century. India's two-way trade with major powers of the world and multilateral blocs also grew during this time. The Indian growth story caught the attention of the world with leading economic institutions like the International Monetary Fund (IMF), the World Bank, PricewaterhouseCoopers, Morgan Stanley, et al. projecting India among the top three economies in the world after China and USA by 2030.

But everything is not hunky dory about the Indian growth story. There are challenges, and these challenges are stupendous. At the beginning of the third decade of the 21st century, many hindrances are affecting Indian economy. Per capita income in India is low; it is a primary producing economy, which refers to dependence on agriculture. Around 52 percent of Indians are engaged in agriculture, but agriculture's contribution to national income hovers around a meager 14 percent. Capital formation in India is also low. With a high growth rate of population, there is severe pressure on social infrastructure. Unemployment and poverty levels are high in the country. Conditions of health and hygiene, literacy, roads, availability of water and electricity are not satisfactory and not at par with developed countries of the world. Indian industry has a growing service sector, but insufficient manufacturing initiatives, making generation of employment difficult. One route to a strong manufacturing sector is to have sufficient linkages to global value chains. India may go for the use of foreign intermediate goods to boost its exports. Therefore, India's journey to become a leading power of the world would not be very easy. The country must overcome all challenges noted above to become a strong global power. As students of International Relations know, national power is dependent on several factors like a country's geography, economy, military capability, leadership, and efficacy of the population, political stability and a few other issues; it is impossible to go for a study of National Power (NP) calculations without taking into account these factors. And among these factors, economy of a nation is one of the most crucial phenomena in any power projection. India is a nuclear power with a strong military, and by all calculations done by leading economic institutions, Indian economy is growing fast. If India can manage its social institutions and infrastructure, the country may emerge stronger. It is beyond doubt that Covid-19 pandemic has adversely affected Indian economy, and it will take some time for the Indian economy to recover from the slowdown created by Covid-19. But this is true about all economies in every part of the globe. Therefore, from a comparative point of view, economic slowdown has not been confined to India; it has been a global phenomenon. India needs to adopt proper corrective measures to bring back the economy on track. Side by side, India must also concentrate on developing its social infrastructure in order to emerge as a strong contender for a leading power tag in world politics.

From the perspective of foreign policy, how will India play an active role in global politics? A strong economy with resultant development in social infrastructure may act as the backup force for an engaging foreign policy in the future. India must try to engage all nations and multilateral forums in future for an effective foreign policy. Side by side bilateral engagements must also be given due priority. The term 'engagement' here refers to a comprehensive engagement with all important nations of the world. But never forget the less important actors as well. In an era of economic diplomacy, all nations, important or less important, must be engaged. India must also work for a rule-based world order to encourage a shared community of nations. India is world's largest democracy. India must also try to reap democratic dividends more aggressively, like the US, Britain, and France. Since independence in 1947, India remained a steadfast democracy. But till date Indian foreign policy has not been very active in reaping the democratic dividends from the global community. In simple words, India must try to promote democracy as the base for a rule-based world order. Such a world order is less prone to conflicts and produces a convenient milieu for effective economic diplomacy.

In the year before the pandemic (2018), India's share of global trade hovered around a meager 2 percent. India accounted for only 1.7 percent of total global exports, and 2.6 percent of total global imports.[1] In comparison, China's share of total global trade was 10.86 percent and US share was 10.27 percent.[2] Therefore, trade figures before the pandemic revealed that India required to strengthen its economic diplomacy to a great extent. The following table shows percent share of total global trade by countries in the year before the pandemic (2018).

Table 12.1: Per Cent Share of Global Trade in the Year Before the Pandemic (2018)

Name of Country	Per Cent Share of Global Trade
China	10.86
USA	10.27
Germany	7.66
Japan	3.75
France	3.62
UK	3.58
Netherlands	3.15
South Korea	2.93
Hong Kong	2.79
Singapore	2.71

Source: The Global Economy.Com (2019), "Per Cent of World Exports: Country Rankings"; on line source: https://www.theglobaleconomy.com/rankings/share_world_exports/. Accessed on 06 December 2020.

Table 12.1 shows that India was not among the top ten countries with substantial share of global trade in the year before the pandemic (2018). India actually ranked thirteen in that year, as far as percent share of global trade was concerned. A country with major power aspirations must climb up the ladder. India should make concrete plans to augment its share of global trade. In the year 2020, during the pandemic, India's total exports dipped further and India slipped to 19th position in total exports among countries.[3] With decreasing volume of imports also in the same year, India's total trade volume suffered too. Table 12.2 shows export, import and total trade volumes of thirteen leading countries of the world in respective areas (i.e. export, import, total trade volume). India did not figure in this list of thirteen leading countries in global trade:

Table 12.2: Leading Countries in World Trade in the Year 2020

Name of Country	Exports (in bn.US $)	Imports (in bn.US $)	Total Trade Volume (in bn.US $)
China	2591.12	2055.75	4646.87
USA	1431.64	2407.55	3839.19
Germany	1380	1170.79	2550.79
Netherlands	674.48	596.75	1271.23
Japan	641.38	634.51	1275.89
Hong Kong	548.77	569.77	1118.54
South Korea	512.50	467.63	980.13
Italy	496.11	422.88	918.99
France	488.35	582.35	1070.7
Belgium	419.34	394.64	813.98
Mexico	417.67	393.25	810.92
UK	403.32	634.71	1038.03
Canada	390.67	413.71	804.38

Source: Statista.com, "Leading export countries worldwide in 2020", on line source: https://www.statista.com/statistics/264623/leading-export-countries-worldwide/; also, 'Leading import countries worldwide in 2020", https://www.statista.com/statistics/268184/leading-import-countries-worldwide/. Accessed on 30 Sept. 2021.

As evident from Table 12.2, India lagged behind many countries in the year 2020 in global exports, imports and total trade volume. India's total export to the world was US$ 276.23 billion. With a total import of US$ 371.92 billion, India's trade volume stood at US$ 648.15 billion in 2020.[4] Therefore, India must put more vigour in augmenting its share in world trade. The initial target should be to reach 5 percent of total global trade in a span of 7-8 years, and then move further. Of these, merchandise exports from India to the world should go up substantially. Indian foreign policy must give priority on expanding economic diplomacy in the near future.

Closely linked to export growth, is manufacturing. It is an area Indian economy must put more emphasis on. Currently, Indian economy is reliant more on the service sector. Indian Service sector contributed more than 55 percent of GVA (Gross Value Added) to the economy, whereas the manufacturing sector contributed only 29 percent of GVA in 2019-20.[5] There is nothing wrong in the development and growth of the service sector; but the contribution of manufacturing sector to the overall growth of Indian economy is equally important. The success of Indian service sector is noteworthy: India has become one of the largest exporters of information, computer and telecommunications services; and these services have been crucial for productivity growth. India now needs to realize its potential in manufacturing. It has a good climate, abundance of raw materials and labor force. But manufacturing sector in India is presently constrained by the small scale of production, low productivity, trade restrictions, and infrastructure gaps. These bottlenecks need to be cleared for India to emerge as a manufacturing power. The country must also aim to become a global hub for manufacturing like China became earlier and Vietnam has emerged in the recent past. But so far, India is lagging behind ASEAN countries in this respect. For example, a recent Nomura Securities study of 56 companies that had relocated bases from China found that 26 companies moved their factories to Vietnam; but only three to India.[6] The country must also pay serious attention to this issue.

An area which is crucially important for India's global power tag is its maritime security. Safeguarding and securing the sea routes for enhanced trade and for countering adversaries are of immense importance. Maritime security is also important for combating terrorism. In this context, it is important to recall that the perpetrators who masterminded the 26/11 attacks on the Indian commercial city of Mumbai came through sea routes. Therefore, India must develop a strategic vision of maritime security. This strategic vision will focus more on the Indian Ocean, an important sea route for global trade. Currently, India defines its maritime security as extending from the Gulf of Hormuz in West Asia to the Straits of Malacca in South-

East Asia, as outlined in the Indian Ministry of Defence's Annual Report.[7] This large maritime zone provides some of the world's busiest sea routes for merchandise trade. Control of this maritime zone by any single power may prove to be detrimental for India's national interests; as this maritime zone is critical to India's economic growth and prosperity. Needless to say here that India's strategic vision of maritime security must include developing a world class navy to safeguard country's interests in the Indian Ocean region. The need of the hour is to modernize Indian navy with sophisticated equipments and ammunitions, and bring it at par with world's advanced naval forces. It must be quick to respond to any crisis in any part of sea waters around the globe, including, certainly, the Indian Ocean region. As pointed out, this region is crucial not only for India's economic progress, but also for peaceful global trade and business.

It is time that Indian foreign policy look up to South American countries with renewed zeal. South America which comes under the label 'Latin America and the Caribbean' (LAC) in trade-related statistics, remained an overlooked zone in Indian foreign policy. There have been limited political, security, and economic engagements between India and South America. One criterion of measurement of this limited engagement may be drawn from trade statistics. In the year 2020, India's total trade with LAC nations was US$ 27 billion (*source*: Exim Bank, India). In the same year India's total trade with Africa was US$ 56 billion, with the European Union, nearly US$ 100 billion, and with the whole of Asia, nearly US$ 500 billion (*source*: *Ibid.*). These figures show that India could not make much progress in its economic diplomacy with South America. In comparison, China's total trade with LAC countries in 2020 was US$ 315 billion (*source*: Congressional Research Service), eleven times more than India's trade volume with LAC nations. Therefore, India must relook its LAC policy, and engage the region more through strengthening of political, economic, and security relations. The region has big emerging markets in Brazil, Mexico, Argentina, and Chile and India must try to tap the potentials. India must also engage smaller nations in the region.

Likewise, India's economic engagements with Africa and two developed nations of the South, Australia and New Zealand need to be bolstered. As noted above, India-Africa trade in the year 2020 was to the tune of US$ 56 billion. In the same year China's trade with African nations reached US$ 185 billion, way ahead of India. Despite the 'Quad' rhetoric, where Australia, India, Japan, and the US are strategic partners, India's economic relations with Australia, an advanced nation, require more attention. The total volume of India-Australia trade in the year 2020 was a meager US$ 24 billion. In the same year China-Australia two-way trade reached a volume of US$ 169 billion. India-New Zealand (NZ) trade was only US$ 2.0 billion in 2020. In the same year China-NZ trade reached US$ 32 billion, and China became the largest trading partner of NZ. Table 12.3 offers a quick comparison between India and China as far as trade relations with some regions and countries are concerned in the year 2020.

Table 12.3: India's and China's Trade Volumes with Some Regions and Countries in 2020

Name of Region/ Country	India's Total Trade (in US$ billion)	China's Total Trade (in US$ billion)
Latin America & the Caribbean (LAC)	27	315
Africa	56	185
Australia	24	169
New Zealand	2.0	32

Source: Compiled by the author from different Govt. sources like the Exim Bank Data, Ministry of Commerce, Govt. of India; Australian Parliament; Ministry of Foreign Affairs (MOFA), China; Congressional Research Service, USA; New Zealand Foreign Affairs and Trade

Central Asia is a region India wants to connect, but it has not engaged the region much. New Delhi has been pursuing the 'Connect Central Asia' policy since 2012, but India's presence in the region requires further boost. The first meeting of the 'India-Central Asia Dialogue' was held in Samarkand, Uzbekistan on 13 January 2019. The second meeting was held in the digital video conferencing mode on 28 October 2020. All five nations of the Central Asian region, namely Kazakhstan, Kyrgyz Republic, Tajikistan, Turkmenistan, and Uzbekistan participated in the second dialogue meeting. Afghanistan attended the meeting as a special invitee. The meeting discussed close cooperation between India and Central Asian countries in political, security, economic and commercial, development partnership, humanitarian, and cultural spheres. An India-Central Asia Business Council was also launched in February 2020 to further trade and commercial engagements between India and Central Asian countries. While these are welcome initiatives, India is still lagging behind many other countries in harnessing the potentials of the region. India's bilateral trade with countries of the region in 2020 was US$ 2.0 billion which is less than 0.5 percent of India's overall trade volume. In contrast China's trade with Central Asian countries stood at US$ 100 billion in the same year. Clearly, more thrust is required on the part of Indian diplomacy to engage Central Asian countries in meaningful ways. Out of India's total trade with the region in 2020, Kazakhstan accounted for 55 percent; Uzbekistan 20 per cent; Turkmenistan 10 percent; Kyrgyzstan 9 percent and Tajikistan 6 percent. These figures reveal that India has huge scope to expand trade with Uzbekistan, Tajikistan, Turkmenistan, and Kyrgyzstan. India must concentrate on individual nations for expansion of trade volumes which will, in turn make trade and commercial relations with the region healthy.

India has some constraints in engaging Central Asia for robust trade and commercial relations. India does not have direct road links to the region. It has to depend on the political will of Afghanistan and Pakistan to forge commercial links with Central Asia through the land route. While Pakistan is an enigma for Indian diplomacy, frequent political instability in Afghanistan also hinders India's plans in the region. In contrast, China has direct land borders with three countries of the region (Kazakhstan, Tajikistan, and Kyrgyzstan). Therefore, it is easier for China to establish close trade links with Central Asia through land routes. Having acknowledged these constraints, it must also be recognized that India was late vis-à-vis China to discover the huge potential of the region. Moreover, a country aspiring the big power tag, must also overcome such constraints. India must tap the hitherto unexplored areas in trade and commercial relations, like information and technology; construction; pharmaceuticals; tea; jute and spices. Besides energy security, India's overall trade relations with countries of Central Asia must give more emphasis on these areas in the near future.

India must also make deeper connections with Eastern, Central and South European countries. Many of these nations, especially in East and Central Europe, were former Soviet bloc countries with whom India enjoyed warm relations for decades. While India enjoyed political proximity with many countries in these regions, India must seek to establish strong economic engagements with these nations now and in the future. Hungary, Czech Republic, Slovenia, Bulgaria, Cyprus, Serbia, Turkey, Lithuania, Latvia and other nations in these regions may offer immense trade and commercial opportunities for Indian business, at both government and non-government levels. China has already made inroads into the markets of these nations. India, although late compared to China, must now resuscitate its trade relations with countries of these regions. While India's trade with the European Union as a whole is noteworthy, India certainly overlooked countries of these areas of Europe for increased trade engagements. India has the potential to penetrate emerging and flourishing markets of these regions. India can participate in infrastructural development, cyber security, matters related to information technology, and merchandise trade in goods in countries noted above. Currently, Central and Eastern Europe account for a negligible portion of India's global trade. The need of the hour is to engage these regions more, and to expand trade significantly. A minimum of seven to eight percent of India's total trade must be with countries of these regions by 2026. This is a realistic projection, achievable by India if proper actions are taken in the near future. As a nation with big power ambitions, India must deviate from selective engagements with nations, and concentrate more on engagements, bilateral and multilateral, with a global outlook.

However, global engagements in foreign affairs need adequate foreign policy establishments back home. Any country, on the road to a big power status, must strengthen its foreign affairs departments, side by side with its internal affairs mechanisms. In India, manpower in foreign policy establishments is still inadequate, believes this author. According to a Ministry of External Affairs (MEA, Govt. of India) report, "The present cadre strength of the service stands at approximately 850 officers manning around 193 Indian missions and posts abroad and the various posts in the Ministry at home." This cadre strength is insufficient for a country with an emerging power tag. It must be doubled in the next five years. According to this report, intake into the Indian Foreign Service has averaged between 30-35 persons annually. This intake capacity must also be doubled in the next five years, and proper fiscal allocation made in this regard. Foreign policy issues are of crucial importance for a country pursuing the road to a big power status. Indian foreign policy establishments must be strengthened, if we want to be on this road.

So far this analysis has projected India's tasks at hand, at the domestic and foreign policy segments, if the country wishes to be labeled as a big power. A succinct summary of these tasks are presented in Box 12.1 below for a quick and better understanding:

Box 12.1: India's Tasks at Hand on the Road to a Big Power Tag

India's Tasks at Hand—Domestic Issues

1. Improvement of social infrastructure in health and hygiene; literacy; roads; availability of water and electricity
2. More reduction of poverty and unemployment
3. Lesser dependence on agriculture. Move away from primary producing economy
4. More capital formation
5. Balanced contribution of service and manufacturing sectors to the economy
6. To emerge as a global value chain and manufacturing hub

Foreign Policy Issues

1. Put more emphasis on economic diplomacy
2. Increased share of global trade
3. Emphasis on maritime security
4. Move away from selective engagements to global engagements in bilateral and multilateral relations
5. Increased presence in global forums
6. Strengthen foreign policy establishments

After highlighting India's tasks, it's time to locate India in the global power matrix in the third decade of the 21st century (2020-30) and thereafter. In simple words, where do we see India in the global power structure now and in the future? But before locating the place of India in the global power hierarchy, it is important to look at different regions of the world, albeit briefly, and find out important powers from these regions. The analysis of different regions begins with the Euro area. Europe was hit hard during WW II and as a consequence, European economy suffered heavily after the War. This factor, coupled with the emergence of two nuclear weapon superpowers, led to the decline of European political fortunes. In erstwhile colonies of many European nations like Britain, France, Spain, the Netherlands, Portugal freedom movements gathered momentum, thereby blocking important sources of raw materials and money to support these fledging economies. Although both superpowers presented economic and military packages (like Marshal Plan, Warsaw Pact, etc.) to their respective blocs in Europe, these were not enough to establish the lost glory of Europe from political and economic points of view.

After the War, European countries, dominant in global politics for more than two centuries (from industrial revolution to WW II), declined in power. In simple words, they lost their glory to the newly emerged superpowers after the War. However, due to their strong industrial bases, Western European countries could follow roads of development and growth during 1948 to 1973. But the 1973-75 economic recession dealt a severe blow to these nations' development growth. In a significant book titled *The European Economy Since 1945*, Barry Eichengreen observed that the GDP growth rate per capita of western European countries fell by more than half from 1950 to 1973 and from 1973 to the year 2000.[8] Hence, for a period of 50 years after WW II (1950 to 2000), GDP per capita of Western Europe was low. The picture in East Europe was bleaker. With centralized socialist economy, and excessive dependence on Soviet Union, East Europe fell back further from an economic point of view. Eichengreen believes that Europe's economic deceleration happened due to factors beyond its control. One major factor was obviously the Cold War between the two superpowers where Europe was used as a major venue of rivalry. Economies in West and East Europe were programmed according to the plans of the superpowers.[9] Cold War affected Europe more than it helped. Europe tried to comeback. The European Union (EU) was formed for economic integration and revival after the end of the Cold War, although EU's roots could be traced back to the year 1950. But due to political heterogeneity among members, the EU never became an epicenter of power in global politics. Brexit happened and Russia never joined the EU. Therefore, EU remained as an important economic actor, but a mere political spectator.

Britain and France, two nuclear weapon states and permanent members of the UN Security Council, no longer enjoy strong political influence in world politics, as they used to earlier. But due to their strong industrial and technological bases, these two countries will be in the reckoning in global power calculations in the foreseeable future. However, two other countries in the region, Germany and Russia have the potential to bounce back. Germany, with its strong industrial, technological and agricultural bases, currently enjoys a better position among European nations. Germany is big (in terms of territory) by European standards, a sizeable military, and a stable economy. Therefore, it may join global power race in the near future. On the other hand, Russian economy is not very strong at this moment. But Russia is a great military power to reckon with. It has inherited more than 90 per cent of nuclear arsenals from the erstwhile Soviet Union. Geographically, Russia is the world's biggest nation, with a strong agricultural base. If Russia can manage its economy well, it is going to be a formidable actor in global politics in the future. Turkey is also coming up as an emerging economy. Hence, Turkey remains in the reckoning from this region. Therefore, from Europe, Germany and Russia, besides EU, Britain, France, and Turkey will be important actors in international power equations.

In the vast Asia and Asia Pacific regions, there are many economic powerhouses. China, Japan, South Korea, Singapore, Brunei, Australia, India, New Zealand, Indonesia are either strong or strong emerging economies. But not all of them are considered in global power equations, due to several factors. Some of these nations are either geographically small; or without potent military; having inadequate and ageing population; and also, reluctant to join the global power race. Japan is industrially and technologically well advanced, but it had adopted provisions in the constitution after WW II not to develop any military. Hence, Japan, despite its economic achievements, had never been in the global power game since WW II. But on the basis of its economic, industrial, and technological strengths, Japan is always considered important. Two neighbors in Asia, China and India, have the capability and willingness to be in the race for a global power status. Both China and India are among the five largest economies in the world in 2020 in terms of nominal GDP. Their growth projections are bright, and it is expected that by 2030, these two countries will rank as top two largest economies in the world. These two neighbors will continue to grow till 2050, and remain in the top two positions. A PricewaterhouseCoopers (PWC) report published in 2017 put China at number one, and India at number two in terms of GDP growth at Purchasing Power Parity (PPP)[10] till 2050. When we are talking about Asian countries, Indonesia and Vietnam must also be referred to as growing economies. Indonesia will feature among the top five largest economies by 2050 and Vietnam among the top twenty by that year.[11] But both nations have institutional and infrastructural inadequacies, without sufficiently strong militaries. As a consequence, Indonesia and Vietnam may have to be contended with middle power or above tags in the near future.

From other regions such as Latin America and Africa, a few countries are emerging, in terms of economic development, but not so much in terms of social institutions and infrastructures. Countries like Brazil, Mexico, South Africa, and Nigeria are projected to have higher economic growth in the next 30 years, till 2050. Currently, Brazil is the tenth largest economy in the world and the largest in Latin America in terms of GDP at PPP. Brazil will move into the top five largest economies in the world by 2050.[12] The services sector accounts for 63 percent to total GDP. Brazil must also think in terms of developing manufacturing sectors within its economy, in order to remain among the top. Currently, Mexico does not figure in the top ten, but it will move into the top seven largest economies in the world in 2050 in terms of GDP at PPP. In that year Mexico will be at the seventh position among the top ten largest economies of the world.[13] Mexico is the second largest economy in Latin America with a better prospect of growth. Mexican economy is export oriented, and the contribution of service sector accounts for 62 percent to total GDP. Like the recommendation for Brazil, Mexico must also think in terms of developing manufacturing sectors to sustain growth. These two countries will also enjoy middle power or above status in the world over the next few decades.

South Africa is the most developed country in the African continent. It was the largest economy in Africa till 2014, when it was overtaken by Nigeria. In the South African economy service sector accounts for 73 percent to country's total GDP. Manufacturing accounts for 13.9 percent, and agriculture only 2.6 percent. Therefore, contribution of manufacturing and agricultural sectors to national economy is minimal in South Africa. This may result in uneven economic growth in the future. Annual real GDP growth rate in Nigeria was 3.80 percent from 1982 to 2019, which may be considered satisfactory, if not substantial. Currently, Nigeria is one of the most developed nations in Africa, with a potential for further growth. Service sector accounts for 50 percent of the total GDP of the nation. Nigeria currently ranks at 22 among top economies in terms of GDP at PPP. It will move to the 14th position in 2050.[14]

Therefore, from the vast African continent, South Africa and Nigeria remain the top picks in the global power game. However, due to several other social constraints, they will be tipped as middle powers.

Finally, this analysis moves on to the US, currently the richest and most powerful nation in the world, in terms of political and economic influences. It is ranked in 2020 as the largest economy in the world in terms of nominal GDP, and second largest in terms of GDP at PPP. It will remain among the top three economies in the world till 2050.[15] It has strong industrial, technological and agricultural bases, sufficient and productive human resource and a large foreign exchange reserve. Since WW II, the US has enjoyed the status of a superpower having tremendous impact on global politics and economy. Needless to say that it was the first nuclear state in the world with a sufficiently strong military and defence production system. In short, the US is considered as the number one power in international politics since the end of the Cold War after the disintegration of Soviet Union. The US will continue to be a top power in the coming years.

India and the Global Power Matrix in the Future

From the preceding analysis, it became possible to figure out some important powers in global politics at this point of time or in the near future. These are: America, China, Britain, Germany, Russia, Japan, the EU, France, India, Brazil, South Africa, Indonesia, Nigeria, Vietnam, South Korea, Turkey, et al. Among these nations, the US and China may be identified as top powers now and in the next three decades, till 2050. Others are either major powers or potential major powers. Some are middle powers also. Therefore, during the third decade of the current century (2020-30), global power projections would be like this: **Top Powers:** USA, China; **Major Powers:** Britain, Japan, Russia, France, EU; **Potential Major Powers:** India, Germany, Brazil, Indonesia; **Middle Powers:** South Africa, Mexico, Nigeria, Vietnam, South Korea, Turkey.

Currently, the US and China remain at the top in power calculations. As discussed earlier, they are strong economies and potent military powers. A recent report put the US as number one military power in the world, and China as number three this year.[16] These two nations are technologically advanced with solid agricultural bases. They will continue to be 'Top Powers' in the world till 2030. Britain, Japan, Russia, France and the EU are included as 'Major Powers' on the basis of their economic strength, military potentials, and levels of industrial and technological advancement. They will be in this position till 2030. The 'Potential Major Powers' are close in the race, but they are a little behind in economic progress, industrial and technological advancement, military strength, and strong social infrastructures. The 'Middle Powers' are rising up the ladder as far as important attributes of National Power (NP) are concerned. All nations included in this category have found places in the PricewaterhouseCoopers (PWC) and Global Fire Power (GFP) Reports cited in this article. But there will be a few changes in global power calculations from 2030 to 2050. Countries with strong NP credentials will remain in the list; but there will be a few surprises during the next two decades. Therefore, future power projections of nations during 2030-50 would be like this: **Top Powers:** China, USA; **Major Powers:** Britain, India, Japan, Russia, EU; **Potential Major Powers:** Germany, Brazil, Indonesia; **Middle Powers:** South Africa, Mexico, Nigeria, Vietnam, South Korea, Turkey.

As evident from the projection stated above, France is absent from the list of 'Major Powers'. In the PWC projection of strong economies in 2050, France is not within the top ten in the world. In fact, France remained a dilemma while preparing the table. France, a nuclear state and a permanent member of the UN Security Council, has fallen back in global power game at this point of time. It may rise again or it may go down further, because no power projection is fully absolute. This proposition applies to all countries mentioned in the two projections (2020-30 and 2030-50) above. However, from their economic growth rates, and on the basis of different variables of NP discussed earlier, these projections have been prepared, with a view to have some idea about important actors in global politics in the near future. Coming back to France, this author would like to place the country in between 'Major Powers' and 'Potential Major Powers' from 2030 to 2050, with a tilt toward the former. There are seventeen countries in the projection from 2030-50; and with the addition of France the number goes up to eighteen. In all possibility, these eighteen states will be important in global power equations in the future.

Conclusion: Whither International Order?

Therefore as far as 'Top Powers' in international politics are concerned, there will be no significant change in the near future. Status quo will be maintained, because both the US and China identified in the table as top powers enjoy these tags now. India will enjoy the status of a 'Major Power' from 2030 to 2050 on the basis of its growing economic strength and strong military. India is projected to develop technologically with equivalent development in its social institutions and infrastructure. France may not be in this category after 2030. In 'Potential Major Powers' and 'Middle Powers' segments, there will be a few surprises, as Table 12.2 illustrates. Nations from developing areas of Asia, Africa, and Latin America will feature more in these segments pushing out developed regions of Europe. Brazil's and Indonesia's labels as potential major powers and middle power tags for South Africa, Mexico, Nigeria, Vietnam, and South Korea indicate a shift in global power equations. These nations are also mentioned in the PWC Report and in the GFP Report cited earlier. This shift in power equations may be termed (loosely of course) as a shift from Global North to Global South, as far as these segments of power position in world politics are concerned.

As observed in the preceding analysis, the US and China will enjoy dominant positions in global politics for the next three decades (2020-50). Will there be a new Cold War between these two nations? In my view, this possibility is remote, if we take into account a few factors. During the four and half decades long Cold War between the US and Soviet Union, these two nations had negligible trade relations and investment in the markets of both countries. In simple words, economic diplomacy was absent in America-Soviet Relations during the Cold War.

As a consequence, politics dominated over economic issues in superpower relations during the Cold War. On the contrary, economics play a major role in Sino-American relations today. American investment in Chinese market and China's investment in American soil are substantial. They are also strong trading partners, unlike Cold War superpower relations. Sino-American economic interests will rule over political differences in the future also. Moreover, 'soft power' issues will also impact bilateral relations. As I have argued elsewhere, Chinese Americans will play an important role in determining American policies toward China and American private business will put pressure on all American governments to be less harsh on China.[17] Chinese students currently provide a good amount of revenue and talent to American universities. Higher education in the US will not risk losing these Chinese students and accompanying revenues. Taking into account these factors, a Cold War like scenario is ruled out in Sino-American relations in the future. On the contrary, a new 'Balance of Power' politics may emerge in international relations in the future, say around 2040-50. In this new 'Balance of Power' countries in the 'Top', 'Major Power', and 'Potential Major Power' categories, as identified in Table 12.2, may play important roles. However, like any Balance of Power system, this one will remain fragile, with ups and downs.

Endnotes

1. Press Information Bureau (PIB), Government of India (2019), "Indian Global Trade Share", posted on 27 November; on line source: https://pib.gov.in/PressReleasePage.aspx?PRID=1593704. Accessed on 06 December 2020.
2. *Source*: The Global Economy.Com (2019), "Per Cent of World Exports: Country Rankings"; on line source: https://www.theglobaleconomy.com/rankings/share_world_exports/. Accessed on 06 December 2020.
3. *Source*: Index Mundi (2021), "Country Comparisons—Exports: top 100", on line source: https://www.indexmundi.com/g/r.aspx?v=85&t=100. Accessed on 30 Sept. 2021.
4. Aaron O'Neill, "Export of goods from India 2020", Statista.com; on line source: https://www.statista.com/statistics/263662/export-of-goods-from-india/. Accessed on 30 Sept. 2021. For India's import figures, Aaron O'Neill, "Import of goods to India 2020", Statista.

com; on line source: https://www.statista.com/statistics/263647/import-of-goods-to-india/. Accessed on 30 Sept. 2021.

5. Ministry of Finance, Govt. of India, "Economic Survey, 2019-20"; on line source: https://www.prsindia.org/report-summaries/economic-survey-2019-20. Accessed on 24 Dec. 2020.
6. Lee Kah Whye, "Why Manufacturers are not Rushing into India", *Mint*, 27 Oct. 2019; on line source: https://www.livemint.com/industry/manufacturing/why-manufacturers-are-not-rushing-into-india-11570429217983.html. Accessed on 24 December 2020.
7. Ministry of Defence, Govt. of India (2019), "Annual Report: 2018-2019", p. 5.
8. Barry Eichengreen (2006), *The European Economy Since 1945*, Princeton University Press.
9. *Ibid.*
10. PricewaterhouseCoopers (2017), "The World in 2050"; on line source: https://www.pwc.com/gx/en/research-insights/economy/the-world-in-2050.html. Accessed on 26 December 2020.
11. *Ibid.*
12. *Ibid.*
13. *Ibid.*
14. *Ibid.*
15. *Ibid.*
16. Global Fire Power (2020) "2020 Military Strength Ranking"; on line source: https://www.globalfirepower.com/countries-listing.asp. Accessed on 30 Dec. 2020.
17. Aneek Chatterjee (2020), "China After Covid 19: Projections and Reality", New Delhi: *Diplomatist*, 24 April; on line source: http://diplomatist.com/2020/04/24/china-after-covid-19-projections-and-reality/. Accessed on 31 December 2020.

Index